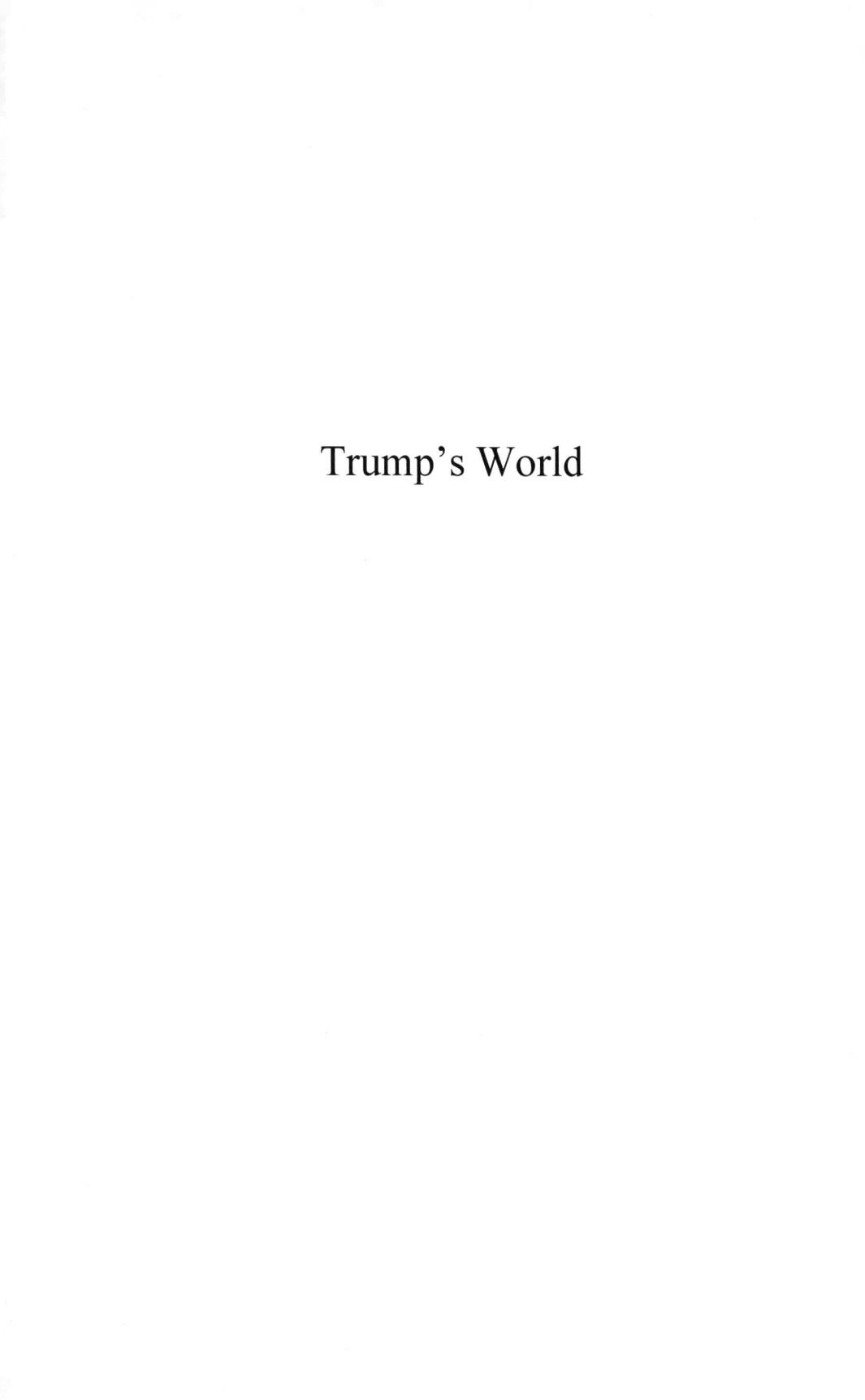

Trump's World

Trump's World

*Peril and Opportunity in
US Foreign Policy after Obama*

John Davis

LEXINGTON BOOKS
Lanham • Boulder • New York • London

Published by Lexington Books
An imprint of The Rowman & Littlefield Publishing Group, Inc.
4501 Forbes Boulevard, Suite 200, Lanham, Maryland 20706
www.rowman.com

6 Tinworth Street, London SE11 5AL

Copyright © 2019 by The Rowman & Littlefield Publishing Group, Inc.

All rights reserved. No part of this book may be reproduced in any form or by any electronic or mechanical means, including information storage and retrieval systems, without written permission from the publisher, except by a reviewer who may quote passages in a review.

British Library Cataloguing in Publication Information Available

Library of Congress Cataloging-in-Publication Data

ISBN 9781498589741 (cloth : alk. paper)
ISBN 9781498589758 (electronic)

∞™ The paper used in this publication meets the minimum requirements of American National Standard for Information Sciences Permanence of Paper for Printed Library Materials, ANSI/NISO Z39.48-1992.

Contents

Preface		vii
Acknowledgments		xiii
Introduction		1
1	The Unknown: Trump, America First, and the Future of Multilateralism?	15
2	The Opportunity: Trump and Foreign Economic Policy	33
3	The Revision: Trump and the War on Terrorism	55
4	The Challenge: Trump and the Rebuilding of the US Military	93
5	The Nightmare and Potential for a New Reality: Trump and North Korea	117
6	Confronting Chaos: Trump and the Middle East	147
7	The Reckoning: Trump, Russia, and China	183
Conclusion		217
Bibliography		251
Index		273
About the Author		281

Preface

Long before the conclusion of the 2016 presidential election, I made the decision to write an outline for two book proposals, one for President Hillary Rodham Clinton and another for President Donald J. Trump.

With the outcome of the election settled and Donald Trump declared the 45th President of United States, I quickly modified the outline and created a proposal that developed into a comprehensive analysis of what would become the details for *Trump's World: Peril and Opportunity in US Foreign Policy after Obama*.

In designing the parameters of this project, I was struck by the level of partisanship that had been directed against candidate Trump. The partisan offensive against Trump reached a new level during the post-election period. At that time, I reworked the proposal once again to include not just the usual partisanship that incoming presidents confront, but additionally I elected to embrace and expound upon the hyper partisanship that would define Trump's stewardship of US foreign policy.

At the time, I thought it important to address an important query: what is behind the hyper partisanship? In time, there was a recognition that groups within the body-politic of the United States were behind much of the hyper partisanship. These groups are likely to play a major role in US foreign policy throughout the Trump presidency. To place the hyper partisanship in context, discussion about the biased atmosphere became the subject of discourse in the media, among scholars, and most certainly among former members of the foreign policy establishment that dutifully served in the administrations of President George W. Bush and President Barack Obama. In an example of the latter, Dennis Blair, the former director of national intelligence during the Barack Obama administration warned action is required to prevent "Washington's toxic partisanship" from "infecting foreign policy."[1]

Blair's warning is certainly justified. Some however questioned if the warning came too late.

I contend the situation is far worse than described by Blair. For starters, this is not just a Washington problem but a national issue. Second, this is not just an infection but rather a nascent cancer that if not addressed could further damage our national interests and ultimately the Republic itself.

Below is a brief sketch of divergent groups and their attitudes toward the current occupant of the White House. This examination assists in unraveling some of the critical players in the hyper partisan atmosphere that is undermining American foreign policy and is critical to understanding the biased nature of numerous commentators that offer evaluations of Trump's stewardship of various components of the implementation of US external relations with the world.

The first group is a combination of Democrats, "the never Trumpers"—Republicans who refuse to support the former business mogul's policies around the world, and an unreceptive media which unleashed a litany of negative appraisals of President Trump's foreign policy agenda. The lucid critiques surfaced during the presidential campaign (and continue) in the wake of Trump's incessant divisive statements and numerous foreign policy pronouncements that this group contends is inconsistent with traditional bipartisan approaches.

At another level, elements of the foreign policy establishment (the second group) is equally concerned about the president's statements and the new unchartered direction. In an illustration of the condemnation and concern expressed by the foreign policy elite, Thomas Wright, an expert at the Brookings Institution, angrily stated, "Diplomats are more alarmed than ever. For the first time since the second world war, the fundamental principles of US foreign policy—alliances, the open global economy and America's leadership—are endangered."[2]

Many senior members of the Republican foreign policy establishment refused to consider serving in the Trump foreign policy bureaucracy. At the other end of the political spectrum, nearly three-hundred Democrats resigned their positions *en masse* at the State Department, refusing to participate in the implementation of President Trump's agenda, one they viewed diluted long-established foreign policy principles of the United States. There is another reason for the protests and the exodus from Foggy Bottom: many of the mid-level and senior members of the department recognized that Trump is hell-bent on implementing an agenda designed to destroy "all-things Obama."

Despite the detractors, President Trump constructed a sustainable support network (this represents the third group) which included Republicans from "Red States" and a coalition of supporters (Democrats, Republicans, and Independents in the "flyover states" and aspects of the military to name a few) that welcomed Trump's "fresh foreign policy approach." This group asserts the era of "kicking the can down the road is over." This coalition anticipated that President Trump would defeat the Islamic State, end the North Korea problem, challenge Russia and China, and confront, if not contain, Iran's regional influence.

Collectively, these groups ushered in one of the most divisive periods in the history of the Republic. In this examination of the unprecedented polarized period in American history, the author provides numerous quotes from these groups, often without response to capture the hyper partisanship.

In addition to the hyper partisanship, there are several unique variables that assist in comprehending Trump's foreign policy. Those perspectives include President Trump's messaging and foreign policy agenda which in many ways fueled the hyper partisanship. This includes significant campaign statements, tweets, and major foreign policy pronouncements.

A subsequent set of variables are critical to understanding the Trump agenda. Those variables consist of the description of the perils and opportunities that will govern the Trump administration's foreign policy. There is a useful third variable that represents a vital component to expound upon the difficulties that would confront the 45th President of the United States—how would Trump manage a series of challenges that are connected to issues bequeathed to him by President Barack Obama? Among the unfinished issues leftover from the Obama era include the threats posed by China, Russia, North Korea, Iran, the chaos in the Middle East, and the Islamic State. In the conclusion, the author utilizes these variables as a framework to provide a comprehensive assessment of President Trump's stewardship of US foreign policy.

The book opens with an Introduction. The introduction explores three disparate issues concerning President Trump and US foreign policy. The first issue examined is Trump's campaign foreign policy statements and how they inform us about the president's priorities. The second issue examined are the debates surrounding Trump's worldview. The third issue explored in the introduction are the perils and opportunities associated with Trump in the realm of foreign policy and how the president's response to a myriad of challenges could cause anxiety at home and abroad or, if handled adroitly, they may set the stage for Trump's successful stewardship of US foreign policy.

Chapter 1, "The Unknown: Trump, America First, and the Future of Multilateralism," addresses Trump's relentless message of economic nationalism. Second, this chapter addresses an apparent contradiction—America First or the president's acceptance of traditional US multilateral arrangements—and how the Trump administration's poor messaging and the multiple iterations of America First created uneasiness among our allies and anger among enemies of the United States. Third, the chapter explores the implementation of America First and then evaluates how the signature pillar of

President Trump's foreign policy may create "counter-US hysteria" that could unleash a new wave of anti-Americanism around the world.

The second chapter—"The Opportunity: Trump and Foreign Economic Policy"—examines the president's efforts to redefine American trade priorities, his efforts to challenge the trade practices of China, The European Union, Japan, South Korea, and the problematic North Atlantic Free Trade Agreement (NAFTA), to name a few. In addition, the chapter examines whether, as maintained by the president and his advisors, the administration's foreign economic strategy could unleash a sustained economic renaissance which Trumpites believe could fuel economic growth rates that exceed four percent. The chapter addresses a series of significant questions: What are the components of Trump's bold economic initiative? What are the prospects for success? Will Trump's foreign economic policy unleash a trade war(s)?

Chapter 3 ("The Revision: Trump and the War on Terrorism") examines Trump's campaign statements and how he stated he would "quickly defeat" the Islamic State. The chapter then explores the administration's strategy and tactics against the Islamic State. The chapter then addresses several queries. For example, after destroying the caliphate, how is the administration dealing with the evolving Islamic State insurgency? Additional issues to be examine include, how does Trump propose to deal with Al Qaeda Central and its affiliates? How will President Trump alter President Obama's strategy in Afghanistan? The answers to these questions are critical if we are to comprehend and assess President Trump's quest to revise the war on terrorism.

In Chapter 4, "The Challenge: Trump and the Rebuilding of the US Military," the author explores Trump's penchant for using executive orders to institute change in the direction of the government of the United States. The executive order titled "Rebuilding the US Armed Forces" is central to understanding the president's attempt to reequip and redefine the mission of the American military. The order represents the first step in the fulfillment of one of Trump's campaign promises: to fix "the depleted military." Critics argued there are a series of questions regarding President Trump's restoration of the military and how those changes could impact American foreign policy. Those questions include the following: How will Trump accomplish the restoration of the military? What are the likely areas of change? What strategy or doctrine will govern this change? Will the "new military" meet the security requirements of the current and future threats to US interests?

Chapter 5 is a fascinating examination of "The Nightmare and Potential for a New Reality: Trump and North Korea." As is known, officials in President Obama's State Department warned then President-Elect Donald Trump that North Korea would be his top priority. A series of provocative North Korean missile tests validated the statement made by the officials in the Obama administration. This chapter addresses a series of questions, how will Trump confront the North Korean threat? Is the president prepared to institute a policy that redefines the US-North Korea relationship? Additionally, this chapter addresses Trump's hardline approach and evaluates the administration's quest to create "new cooperative efforts" to force the rogue regime in North Korea to end their destabilizing policies. A question begs, what are the consequences if Trump's approach fails?

"Confronting Chaos: Trump and the Middle East" (Chapter 6) explores why the Middle East remains the most volatile region in the world. Following a brief look at Trump's campaign statements, the chapter examines the continuing fallout from the Arab Spring and the emergence of the Islamic State, Iran's attempt to expand their regional power, instability in Iraq and Syria, the Russian presence in Syria, the proxy war in Yemen, the fallout from the Jamal Kashoggi affair and its impact on US-Saudi relations, and the ongoing impasse in the Israeli-Palestinian negotiations represent some of the divisive issues that are addressed in the region.

There is the prevailing interpretation that Trump's unwavering campaign statements in support of Israel, and his threat (and now decision) to move the US embassy to Jerusalem, and presidential support for Israeli sovereignty over the Golan Heights, along with an Executive Order that restricted the movement of citizens from several states in the region (Iran, Libya, Somalia, Sudan, Syria, and Yemen) "could become a dividing line in the Middle East."[3] These are just a sample of the numerous issues that await President Trump. This chapter addresses how Trump will deal with these issues. There is another issue addressed in the chapter. Given administration efforts to redefine US security interests in the region, will President Trump's policies advance stability in the region or lead to greater instability and unleash a new wave of anti-Americanism?

Chapter 7 ("The Reckoning: Trump, Russia, and China") explores how the president plans to manage two of the most significant bilateral relationships, each of which if mismanaged could undermine his foreign policy agenda. During the campaign, Trump repeatedly spoke of Russia in glowing terms. Why? Trump argued he had hoped for a productive relationship with Russian President Vladimir Putin. Once in office, President Trump clarified his position toward Russia arguing that while good relations represented the goal, he understood that such a relationship is not likely given Russian meddling in the 2016 presidential election. In contrast to the president, several of Trump's senior foreign policy officials, former Secretary of Defense James Mattis, former Secretary of State Rex Tillerson, and later his replacement, Mike Pompeo, publicly expressed a hardline position toward Russia. At issue, how will the Trump administration deal with Russia? Additionally, given Russia's intervention in Ukraine and in Syria, the support of Iran, and the ongoing controversial Mueller investigations surrounding alleged collusion with Russia, on what basis can the president pursue a productive relationship? Is it possible that Trump can negotiate a grand bargain that may lead to a more productive relationship with Moscow?

In the case of China, Trump criticized the Asian power over currency manipulation, Beijing's destabilizing actions in the South China Sea, failure to rein in North Korea, and warned that he would end the US trade deficit with China. Critics warned the president is setting the stage for a possible showdown with China. Are the critics correct? Put another way, how will Trump manage this important bilateral relationship?

This chapter addresses what is emerging as "The Reckoning: Trump, Russia, and China." The chapter examines in exhaustive detail how President Trump's policies with Russia and China could assist in creating a stable world or advance the path to instability in two key US bilateral relationships. This chapter lays out "the potential rules" that could govern US-Russia and US-China relationships in the future.

The pages that follow provide a window into the unprecedented hyper partisanship that engulfed American foreign policy and ultimately threatens the interests of the United States. In addition, the author details President Trump's comprehensive statements, tweets, agenda, and if taken individually or collectively illustrate an abandonment of traditional bipartisan features of American foreign policy. The author addresses a profound query: is the president correct—Is it time to create or alter current post-World War II frameworks to restore US primacy in international system? There is another dimension. If the president is incorrect how will his expansive agenda impact US relationships with its core allies, impact the American economy and international trade, American leadership, and interests?

NOTES

1. Blair, Dennis, "Don't Let Washington's Toxic Partisanship Infect Foreign Policy, Too," *The Hill*, April 18, 2018. Accessed on January 21, 2019.

2. Crowley, Michael, "Trump Fails to Impress Foreign Policy Experts," *Politico*, April 27, 2016. http://www.politico.com/story/2016/04/donald-trump-foreign-policy-speech-reaction-222544. Accessed on January 21, 2019.

3. Malsin, Jared, "How Trump's Presidency Could Become a Dividing Line in the Middle East," Timeinc.net, https://time.com/4658762/donald-trump-middle-east-saudi-arabia-egypt/.

Acknowledgments

This project emerged out of the turbulent 2016 presidential campaign. Throughout the campaign, foreign policy took its place among the plethora of issues for voters, scholars, and the media. In addition, this project is a by-product of multiple consultations with a host of individuals. I owe a debt of gratitude to these individuals that provided a wealth of assistance in the development of this project. Specifically, I would like to thank many colleagues (those within academia and those within the think tank community inside and outside Washington, DC) for acting as a sounding board as the project moved from the idea to proposal stage.

There is special group of individuals that provided a wealth of background information and those that agreed to be quoted in this study. I cannot thank them enough for the source material that appears in this study. There is a secondary group of individuals that I spoke to that assisted in ensuring that I had complete understanding of the hyper partisanship that engulfed the Trump presidency, most notably in the area of US foreign policy. In addition, it became apparent why this variable (the hyper partisanship), particularly if it continues to pervade this and subsequent presidential administrations, could ultimately impact the future of the Republic.

The classroom represented a proving ground for many ideas contained in the book. Thus, I would also like to give thanks to my students in a host of classes where I used a segment of the course—Impact of President Donald Trump on World Order—to test many ideas contained in the book. The reaction of the students to these ideas had a profound role in the development of the book. And last, but certainly not least, many thanks to my editor and her assistant, and others that participated in the production of this book for their incredible efforts.

Introduction

A host of individuals from the media, pundits, and members of the foreign policy elite have lambasted Donald Trump as dangerous and unpredictable. A few examples are instructive. Max Fisher, a reporter from the *New York Times*, argued, "Perhaps owing to his years in the competitive world of New York real estate development, Mr. Trump seems to approach foreign policy as a series of deals, each divided between a winner and a loser."[1]

In a far more unflattering appraisal, Doug Bandow, a foreign policy scholar at the Libertarian Cato Institute, made the following statement after observing a Trump speech, "He called for a new foreign policy strategy, but you don't really get the sense he gave one."[2] In a comprehensive analysis, Thomas Wright, a scholar at the Brookings Institution articulated that Trump "consistently expresses 'opposition to America's alliance relationships; opposition to free trade; and support for authoritarianism.'"[3]

Trump's World: Peril and Opportunity in US Foreign Policy after Obama moves beyond the partisan criticism that dominated the appraisals of the president's stewardship of US interests around the world. The introduction explores three disparate issues concerning President Donald Trump and US foreign policy. The first issue examines Trump's campaign foreign policy statements and major speeches and how they inform us about the president's priorities. The second issue examines the debates surrounding Trump's worldview. The third issue explores the pitfalls and opportunities afforded to Trump in the realm of foreign policy and how the president's responses to those issues could cause anxiety at home and abroad or, if handled adroitly, he may set the stage for the successful stewardship of US foreign policy.

Understanding the three core issues as discussed in the introduction are critical to set the stage for the examination of larger questions that are addressed in the remaining chapters. Those questions are as follows: What are the consequences if President Trump instituted the policies he espoused during the campaign? Under what circumstances will President Trump use force? The answer to this query will provide details on the components of "The Trump Doctrine" and whether the president's misapplication of force could lead to an unnecessary war? Finally, how does Trump avoid an expansive set of foreign policy issues and the potential for conflict associated with issues (among them, ISIS, China, Russia, North Korea, Iran, and chaos in the Middle East) that have been bequeathed to him by President Barack Obama which could undermine his efforts to grow the economy and upend his foreign policy agenda? Taken collectively, the answers to these queries will determine the extent to which Trump's stewardship of a hyper partisan American foreign policy will lead to peril or opportunities. In addition, Trump's stewardship of US foreign policy will assist in determining the extent to which American external relations are reshaped by the president's agenda.

THE CAMPAIGN AND TRUMP'S FOREIGN POLICY STATEMENTS AND SPEECHES

Presidential campaigns provide an important window into a candidates' viewpoints on major issues in US foreign policy. When the candidate is not a politician and lacks experience in foreign policy, the campaign statements assume greater prominence. The media and the foreign policy establishment, many of which did not want Trump in the White House, scrutinized each foreign policy statement or major foreign policy address. Despite the partisan scrutiny, it is important to ask how did Trump's statements and addresses help to inform us about his foreign policy priorities?

During a *CNN* Town Hall in Milwaukee, Wisconsin on March 29, 2016, Trump made the following explosive statement: "You have so many countries already—China, Pakistan, you have so many countries, Russia . . . now that have them. Now, wouldn't you rather, in a certain sense, have Japan have nuclear weapons when North Korea has nuclear weapons?"[4] Leaders in Japan and South Korea dismissed Trump's idea. Trump's statements set off alarm bells among allies around the world, in the media, and within the American foreign policy elite.

Within days of Trump's comments, President Barack Obama, without mentioning the New York billionaire by name, criticized the candidates' controversial statement. In a statement made during a press conference at a Nuclear Security Summit, President Obama argued, "The comments tell us [about] the person who made the statements doesn't know much about foreign policy, or nuclear policy, or the Korean Peninsula or the world generally."[5] Additionally, Obama made this telling observation: "I said before that people pay attention to American elections. What we do is really important to the rest of the world. Even in those countries that are used to a carnival atmosphere in their own politics want sobriety and clarity when it comes to US elections."[6]

Not only did a sitting president criticize Trump over his problematic statement that Japan and South Korea should seek a nuclear deterrent in response to North Korea's quest to expand their arsenal, there is another point associated with Obama's criticism: Trump's statement proved to be remarkably naive, dangerous, and it "would reverse decades of bipartisan US foreign policy and would increase nuclear proliferation."[7]

In what was advertised as a major address, on April 27, 2016, Trump stated that "Our foreign policy is a complete and total disaster. No vision, no purpose, no direction, no strategy. Today, I want to identify five main weaknesses in our foreign policy."[8] The initial problem with US foreign policy, according to Trump, is that "Our Resources Are Overextended."[9] In a clarification of the point, Trump observed, "President Obama has weakened our military by weakening our economy. He's crippled us with wasteful spending, massive debt, low growth, a huge trade deficit and open borders."[10] Trump argued if elected he would work to improve American jobs and initiate a spending increase that would restore US armed forces[11] to a level of unquestioned prominence.

The second problem with US foreign policy, according to Trump, is "our allies are not paying their fair share."[12] This criticism is directed at members of the long-standing North Atlantic Treaty Organization (NATO). It is time, said Trump, for "Our allies [to] . . . contribute toward the financial, political and human costs of our tremendous security burden."[13] On how he would handle this issue, the candidate argued, "The whole world will be safer if our allies do their part to support our common defense and security."[14]

On the third weakness, Trump asserted, is that "our friends are beginning to think they can't depend on us."[15] At the center of the problem, the candidate articulated, is that President Obama simply "disliked" select allies of the United States and supported "our enemies."[16] For Trump he questioned why Obama consistently undermined traditional allies, most notably Israel, and "negotiated a disastrous deal with Iran."[17]

Fourth, according to Trump, "our rivals no longer respect us."[18] There are two issues according to Trump that should trouble all Americans. Trump argues enemies no longer respect the United States.[19] Second, the candidate believed no one "takes us seriously anymore."[20] Viewed collectively, Trump argued Obama's policies emboldened "rivals and challengers" and increased instability around the world.

On the final problem with the American approach to external relations, Trump argued the United States failed to articulate any discernable foreign policy objectives in post-Cold War world. Trump promised that once elected he would implement a coherent foreign policy based "on shared interests" with US allies abroad.[21] The candidate subsequently issued a statement in this critical portion of the speech that alarmed multilateralists which they argued undermined a critical component of bipartisan US foreign policy. Trump stated that he promised to get "out of the nation-building business."[22] This statement pleased the candidates' supporters, but the left, never-Trumper's, and elements of the foreign policy elite (from the both sides of the political divide) asserted the statements confirmed their suspicions of Trump's foreign policy agenda.

On September 6, 2016, Trump endeavored to use a foreign policy address to link Hillary Clinton to a series of failed and "endless wars and conflicts" that unfolded during the Obama presidency. In the words of Trump, "For years, we have been caught up in endless wars and conflicts under the leadership of failed politicians and a failed foreign policy establishment in Washington DC. The same people who made every wrong decision in Iraq, Afghanistan, Libya, Syria, Egypt, China and Russia are the same people who are advising Hillary Clinton."[23]

There is another objective associated with Trump's speech: to draw a salient distinction between himself and Clinton. A confident Trump asserted, "I am proud instead to have the support of our war fighting generals, active duty military officers, and top military experts who know how to win—and know how to keep us out of endless war. Today, 88 retired US generals and admirals signed a letter of endorsement."[24] Then the president shifted his statements to what he referred to as "one of the biggest differences between me and Hillary Clinton."[25] On those differences, Trump stated, "She favors what has been called military adventurism—rushing to invade countries, displacing millions of families, then inviting the refugees into our country—creating power vacuums filled by terrorist groups like ISIS. I believe in a foreign policy based on our national interests that focuses on American security and regional stability—instead of using our military to create Democracies in countries with no Democratic history."[26]

Some of the most revealing and at times controversial statements made by the candidate occurred during a series of interviews between Trump and David Sanger of the *New York Times*. Sanger set out to address Trump's position on the need to support Kurdish fighters, which operated in Syria as a "local ally" in the struggle to defeat the Islamic State. As to the candidates' position, Trump made the following comment: "I'm a fan of the Kurds."[27]

Trump's statement is contrary to the position held by Recep Tayyip Erdoğan, the leader of Turkey, who argued Kurdish fighters are nothing more than terrorists and a threat to the security of his country. In a clarification of his position, Trump asserted, "Well, it would be ideal if we could get them all together. And that would be a possibility. But I'm a big fan of the Kurdish forces. At the same time, I think we have a . . . very successful relationship with Turkey. And it would be really wonderful if we could put them somehow both together."[28] Trump then stated the relationship with Erdoğan, should he be elected president, would be a productive one following a series of diplomatic meetings.[29]

Sanger's interview with Trump pivoted to the problematic US relationship with Mexico. The exchange addressed the candidates' position on immigration, the border wall, and trade (the North American Free Trade Agreement (NAFTA)). In a long and not always articulate rejoinder, Trump declared, "I think we'll have a very good relationship with Mexico, and it will be a fair relationship. Right now, Mexico is a massive loss for us. But I think it will be a very, very fair relationship and a very good relationship but right now, Mexico, we are losing on the border and we are losing on trade. We have billions of dollars of trade deficits with Mexico. Drugs are pouring in across the border. And they are beating us both on the border and with trade. I think we'll have a better relationship than we do now."[30]

On the controversial topic of NAFTA, Trump argued, "I would pull out of NAFTA in a split second. NAFTA is signed by Bill Clinton. . . . It's the worst trade deal ever signed in the history of this country and one of the worst trade deals ever signed anywhere in the world. NAFTA is a disaster."[31]

How did Trump's statements and addresses assist in informing us about his foreign policy priorities? When examining Trump's campaign statements, particularly those during interviews or those that are in response to queries during Town Hall meetings or Presidential Debates, the candidates' answers are devoid of a serious understanding of the details of specific foreign policy issues and the full appreciation of the need to explicate how he would protect US interests.

That said, Trump's foreign policy speeches endeavored to identify what the candidate and key foreign policy advisers attempted to represent the major flaws in President Obama's policies whether in the case of the ineffectual anti-ISIS strategy, the problematic bilateral relations with Russia and China, the failure to curtail or end North Korea's nuclear weapons program, and he pointed out the dilemmas associated with the nuclear deal with Iran (the Joint Comprehensive Plan of Action [JCPOA]).

At another level, Trump used campaign pronouncements to assert that because of President Obama's problematic stewardship of US foreign policy, he opined that American allies questioned our reliability and leadership. Additionally, Trump's foreign policy addresses identified how state and non-state actors were emboldened to fill power vacuums around the world in the absence of American leadership.

There are however a host of problems connected to Trump's campaign statements and addresses. Trump repeatedly provided comments that induced uneasiness among our allies and the candidate incessantly issued statements that undermined bipartisan aspects of "shared concerns" among Democrat and Republican presidents. These comments represented a "gift" to his Republican primary opponents and to Hillary Clinton who used them against Trump during presidential debates and in campaign advertisements during the general election. In each case, Clinton zeroed in on Trump's rhetoric to demonstrate that he "is dangerous"[32] and "too divisive and lacks the temperament"[33] to protect US interests around the world.

There is another far more revealing critique of Trump's statements and foreign policy addresses. On several occasions, Trump spoke of a new direction, but he never presented a coherent alternative to the Obama or Clinton approaches to US foreign policy. Lastly, throughout the presidential one can assert that in the absence of a framework and guiding principles, it is difficult to discern Trump's foreign policy agenda or his priorities.

TRUMP'S WORLDVIEW

A candidates' worldview—a collection of guiding frameworks that assist in determining presidential actions or in its simplest form, the way one looks at the world—was a subject of great speculation within the media during the 2016 presidential election. In time, Trump's worldview quickly developed into a subject of intrigue and partisan rancor. There are however a host of individuals that endeavored to provide a serious examination of Trump's worldview.

WHAT IS TRUMP'S WORLDVIEW?

During the campaign and well into his presidency, many commentators concluded Trump either lacked a worldview or his worldview is incoherent. For example, John Feffer, the co-director of Foreign Policy in Focus at the Institute for Policy Studies, commented, "The nonsense written about Trump's global views has been truly staggering."[34] Feffer then stated, "It's not easy to get a bead on Trump's worldview. His comments on foreign policy have frequently been incoherent, inconsistent, and just plain ignorant. He hasn't exactly rolled out a detailed blueprint of what he would do to the world if elected. Trump is clearly winging it in interviews with journalists . . . ."[35] The scholar then made this statement: "Trump has said enough to pull together a pretty good picture of what he'd do if suddenly in a position of nearly unchecked power (thanks to the expansion of executive authority under both Bush and Obama)."[36] Additionally, Feffer argued that "President Trump would offer an updated version of Teddy Roosevelt's old dictum: speak loudly and carry the biggest stick possible. It's not an alternative to US empire—just a cruder rendition of it."[37]

There are those that describe Trump's worldview through the prism of the candidates' rhetoric and campaign speeches. In an illustration of this characterization of Trump's conception of the world, consider this perspective: "Beneath his specific proposals—or pronouncements—there does appear to be a guiding worldview. Mr. Trump seems to see the world as chaotic and threatening and inhospitable to traditional American objectives like democracy promotion or international institutions. In this world, the United States must pursue its interests narrowly, unilaterally and with unapologetic force."[38]

There are several observers that evaluate Trump's worldview through the prism of Steve Bannon, one of the candidates' senior campaign advisers and later his chief political advisor inside the White House. For example, Michael Auslin, is the Williams-Griffis fellow in Contemporary Asia at the Hoover Institution, concluded, "If Trump has a worldview based largely on instinct (as many want to believe), Bannon animates that instinct into policy. The 'logic,' therefore of Trump's foreign policy appears to be largely mediated through Bannon. If so, then either Bannon also supports the status quo in affairs purely foreign, or there is a tension at the center of the White House that will have to resolve itself."[39] He added this supplemental statement: "When a foreign policy is really about the home front, in Trump's view, then his more radical instincts are pursued (such as on free trade); conversely, on issues that are purely foreign in their impact, such as alliances or US security policy, Trump is far more willing to follow the status quo, at least for now."[40]

Colin Kahl, former national security advisor to Vice President Joe Biden, and Hal Brands, distinguished professor of Global Affairs at Johns Hopkins University School of Advanced International Studies, provided an interesting perspective of Trump's worldview. According to Kahl and Brands, "Beneath all the rants, tweets, and noise there is actually a discernible pattern of thought—a Trumpian view of the world that goes back decades. Trump has put forward a clear vision to guide his administration's foreign policy—albeit a dark and highly troubling one, riddled with tensions and vexing dilemmas."[41]

Kahl and Brands conclude there are "three dangers"[42] that are at the center of the president's worldview: radical Islam, "unfair trade deals and the trade practices," and illegal immigration.[43] In the mind and rhetoric of Trump, these threats are as follows:

> The first is the threat from "radical Islam"—which, for the president and many of his closest advisors, poses an existential and "civilizational" threat to the United States that must be "eradicated" from the face of the Earth. . . . Second, Trump portrays unfair trade deals and the trade practices of key competitors as grave threats to the US economy and therefore a national security priority. In

> Trump's view, "disastrous trade deals" like NAFTA have gutted American manufacturing and depressed wages for millions of American workers. Third, and finally, Trump has consistently railed against illegal immigration. . . . He has also consistently framed immigration as an issue of personal and national security, arguing that illegal immigration is associated with crime, drugs, and terrorism. . . . And, tying the issue back to his diagnosis of the terrorist threat, Trump has consistently portrayed Muslim refugees, immigrants, and the children of immigrants as a "Trojan horse" for the spread of radical Islam in the United States.[44]

In the view of Kahl and Brands, President Trump created an "America First" grand strategy to confront these three threats.[45] This point is clarified by a statement made by Trump during the inaugural address: "From this day forward, it's going to be . . . America First. Every decision on trade, on taxes, on immigration, on foreign affairs will be made to benefit American workers and American families."[46] The grand strategy, the authors conclude, is not without dilemmas. As argued by Kahl and Brands, "Trump's "America First" grand strategy diverges significantly from—and intentionally subverts—the bipartisan consensus underpinning US foreign policy since World War II."[47] Equally troubling, "the period in which the ideas upon which one campaigns are translated into the day-to-day initiatives by which one governs—is likely to be far messier than is normally the case."[48]

Not discussed by many pundits is that presidential worldviews evolve as the office holder obtains more experience in understanding the threat environment and in response to crises that develop over the course of an administration. Thus, the presidential election and the numerous questions about a candidates' and president's worldview represent a small sample of the numerous issues of an evolving process.

Some two-plus years into his presidency, Trump continues to refine his worldview. Thus far, after a review of the available evidence, the author contends Trump's worldview includes the following components. It is one that places a high-degree of importance on America First. Second, President Trump insinuated that historical international frameworks are outmoded and have placed a heavy burden on the United States and they undermine the US position of leadership and interests around the world. The president called for "a different approach" one that recognizes that post-World War II frameworks must be adjusted to the current era and one that works to regain American dominance and leadership in the world. Third, the president implies that he intends to dramatically reduce the use of force and American intervention around the world. Fourth, during the campaign and during his presidency, Trump demonstrated an aversion against nation-building. Fifth, the president publicly and privately articulated that the United States must be prepared to confront "challenger states"—such as Russia, China, Iran, and North Korea. These states offer dissimilar challenges to American and allied interests. Sixth, the author concurs somewhat with Kahl and Brands regarding the "three dangers." However, the author believes there appears to be a reset within the administration. The prevailing evidence indicates only one of the three threats is currently at the "center of the president's worldview." It is the threat of "unfair trade deals and the trade practices." Threats posed by radical Islam and illegal immigration are now viewed as corollary threats (second tier issues not at the level of the dangers posed by Russia, China, Iran, or North Korea) by the president and most of his senior advisors.[49]

PITFALLS AND OPPORTUNITIES FOR TRUMP IN THE AREA OF FOREIGN POLICY

The Trump presidency unfolds during a unique and dangerous period in the history of the United States. During this period, President Trump will be forced to confront a series of pivotal foreign policy challenges. The challenges exist in three areas: state actors, violent non-state actors, and trade. There are a host of pitfalls and opportunities associated with these three areas that are likely to develop into major challenges for President Trump.

On confronting state actors and their threats to American interests, China, Russia, Iran, Syria, or North Korea, taken individually or collectively, could produce a period of extended tumult and anxiety for President Trump and his senior foreign policy advisors. A discussion of the potential pitfalls with China and Iran are instructive.[50]

In the case of China, during the presidential campaign Trump accused Beijing of currency manipulation and for the instability in the South China Sea. Additionally, China's ongoing military build-up is perceived as a threat across the region, and the Trump administration made no secret that it is unhappy with Beijing's continuing failure to rein in North Korea's nuclear ambitions. The critical question is this: will Trump seek to contain China or rollback their gains in the region?

The prevailing perception is that "Donald Trump appears determined to curb China's growing power. . . . When it comes to dealing with China, Trump has two points in his favor—his air of menacing unpredictability and his commitment to raise defense spending—although both come with major asterisks attached."[51] Additionally, there are a host of "commentators have suggested that Trump will seek to emulate Nixon's 'madman' act in order to pressure China and other adversaries into making concessions."[52] If you add the ever-widening trade war with China, Sino-American relations are entering a dangerous period. In the end, if Trump push's too hard and misconstrues China's intentions, though highly unlikely, a Sino-US war may unfold. Such a conflict could be catastrophic for both countries and increase already spiraling regional instability. Iran's ever-expanding regional power remains one of the major pitfalls for President Trump. During the campaign, Trump described Iran as "the world's number one terrorist state."[53] He threatened to reinsert American sanctions against Tehran, and Trump threatened to 'rip up' the 2015 Iran nuclear deal."[54]

As president, Trump quickly learned that walking away from the Iran nuclear agreement could "risk alienating the European Union, the United Kingdom, France, Germany, China and Russia, which would make enforcing any new sanctions more difficult."[55] There are other perils associated with the president's increasingly hardline approach with Iran.

The Trump administration is serious about reducing Iran's influence in Iraq. A critical point of contention is that in the wake of the coalition defeat of Islamic State forces in Mosul and in areas in Western Iraq, the president envisages a daunting task to rollback Iran's influence in the country. Second, the Trump administration is actively weighing more direct support to Saudi Arabia in the conflict with Iran's Shiite Houthi ally in Yemen.[56] In the awake of the Jamal Kashoogi Affair, the Trump administration is weighing their options. There are "other flashpoints." Potential areas of contention include "Iranian ballistic missile tests, more unilateral US sanctions, [and] stand-offs between the Iranian and US navies in the Gulf"[57] represent a few areas of disagreement that could unleash hostilities.

Confronting violent non-state actors, most significantly, the Islamic State, Al Qaeda Central, some of their affiliates to include Al Qaeda in the Arabian Peninsula (AQAP) and Al-Nusra Front (Jabhat Fateh al-Sham), represent just a few of the pitfalls that await President Trump.

During a debate in 2015 in Las Vegas, Trump referred to the Islamic State as "thugs."[58] Trump then stated "These are terrible people in ISIS, not masterminds. And we have to change it from every standpoint."[59] One thing is certain, following the collapse of the twin pillars, Mosul and Raqqa, President Trump reaped all the benefits from ending the Islamic States' caliphate.

Unfortunately, in the wake of the collapse of the Islamic States' caliphate there are several pitfalls that await the president. Among them, the president must confront the Islamic States' in a host of sanctuaries, to include but not limited to Afghanistan, Algeria, Egypt, Indonesia, Lebanon, Libya, Pakistan, Philippines, Somalia, and Yemen. The point is that Islamic State will not be defeated quickly. The conflict will be one of long duration and costly. And there is this reality, after morphing into an insurgency there is evidence the Islamic State reconstituted itself into a threat in Iraq and Syria.[60]

President Trump recognized that dealing with Al Qaeda will prove equally problematic. If Trump is engaged in long term and costly operations with this transnational network, a critical query remains: how will the president's confrontation with radical Islamists impact Trump's domestic agenda?

Dealing with a plethora of violent non-state actors will provide a host of opportunities for the Trump administration. First among them, President

Trump campaigned on moving away from President Obama's approach. Second, there are opportunities that arise in dealing with AQAP and other affiliates around the world. For example, the American military launched nearly 100 airstrikes against AQAP in the opening year of the administration. Is the president seeking to contain or defeat AQAP? That answer is not yet known. As Trump redefines the war on terror, a major opportunity is on the horizon: the president can increase the global response, and if a successful strategy is erected, Trump can substantially assert he played a consequential role in the decline of transnational terrorism.

For President Trump trade could be an area of trepidation or an opportunity that could significantly benefit his domestic agenda and foreign policy legacy. Throughout the campaign, Trump used trade as a weapon to demonstrate the failures of President Obama's policies. Additionally, during speeches and presidential debates, Trump employed trade to his advantage against establishment politicians. In a statement that validates this point, during a speech before supporters in Monessen, Pennsylvania on June 28, 2016, Trump argued, "Our politicians have aggressively pursued a policy of globalization—moving our jobs, our wealth and our factories to Mexico and overseas."[61] In a subsequent example, Trump promised that when elected, he planned "to make good on campaign promises to rip up or renegotiate free trade deals within his first 100 days in office."[62]

There are however several significant pitfalls that could have serious domestic and international trade implications. Critics charge "Trump will find it difficult to roll back a trade agreement that has been in place so long and includes protections against unilateral withdrawal."[63] NAFTA fits into this category. As will be pointed out later, President Trump successfully renegotiated an updated version (The United States-Mexico-Canada Agreement or USMCA) of the trade agreement.

A second dilemma concerns the fallout of President Trump's executive order to withdraw from the Trans-Pacific Partnership (TPP) Agreement. Opponents of the decision "worry that China will move to fill the economic vacuum as America looks inward and will expand its sway over Asia and beyond."[64] If China succeeds, US trade influence in the region will decline and markets for American goods could suffer as well. Third, economics around the world argue that President Trump's "America First mantra" could unleash trade wars which could also impact international trade. Put another way, America First, in the view of many could unleash a new wave of anti-Americanism around the world. On April 12, 2018 President Trump issued a statement via Twitter that indicated his administration appeared ready to consider rejoining the TTP. In the tweet, President Trump stated, his administration would consider rejoining the TTP "if the deal were substantially better than the deal offered to President Obama."[65] There were subsequent no changes to TTP. The president has made no additional statement about rejoining the multilateral accord.

Despite opposition to Trump's trade agenda, the president intends to use this issue to create a foreign economic policy that he believes expands US markets abroad and creates new jobs for the American worker. A critical component of President Trump's new approach will come from a course correction that reduces if not eliminates China's trade surplus with the United States. These issues collectively illustrate some of the opportunities afforded to the president in international trade.

NOTES

1. Fisher, Max, "What Is Donald Trump's Foreign Policy?" *New York Times*, November 11, 2016. https://www.nytimes.com/2016/11/12/world/what-is-donald-trumps-foreign-policy.html. Accessed on July 8, 2017.
2. Crowley, Michael, "Trump Fails to Impress Foreign Policy Experts," *Politico*, April 27, 2016. http://www.politico.com/story/2016/04/donald-trump-foreign-policy-speech-reaction-222544. Accessed on July 8, 2017.
3. Ibid.
4. Full Rush Transcript: Donald Trump, *CNN* Milwaukee Republican Presidential Town Hall. *CNN* March 29, 2016. http://cnnpressroom.blogs.cnn.com/2016/03/29/full-rush-transcript-donald-trump-cnn-milwaukee-republican-presidential-town-hall/. Accessed on July 8, 2017.
5. Rafferty, Andrew, "Obama: Trump Doesn't Know Much About Nuclear Weapons, Or the World," *NBC News*, April 1, 2016. http://www.nbcnews.com/politics/2016-election/obama-trump-doesn-t-know-much-about-nuclear-weapons-or-n549476. Accessed on July 9, 2017.
6. Ibid.
7. Donald Trump on Foreign Policy—On The Issues. www.ontheissues.org/2016/Donald_Trump_Foreign_Policy.htm. Accessed on July 9, 2017.
8. Donald J. Trump Foreign Policy Speech. DonaldJtrump.com. April 27, 2016. http://www.donaldjtrump.com/press-releases/donald-j.-trump-foreign-policy-speech. Accessed on July 9, 2017.
9. Ibid.
10. Ibid.
11. Ibid.
12. Ibid.
13. Ibid.
14. Ibid.
15. Ibid.
16. Ibid.
17. Ibid.
18. Ibid.
19. Ibid.
20. Ibid.
21. Ibid.
22. Ibid.
23. Trump Speech: Clinton Email Corruption Disqualifies Her from Seeking Presidency, September 6, 2016. North Carolina. https://www.donaldjtrump.com/press-releases/trump-speech-clinton-email-corruption-disqualifies-her-from-seeking-presidency. Accessed on July 9, 2017.
24. Ibid.
25. Ibid.

26. Ibid.
27. Transcript: Donald Trump on NATO, Turkey's Coup Attempt and the World. *New York Times*, July 22, 2017. https://www.nytimes.com/2016/07/22/us/politics/donald-trump-foreign-policy-interview.html. Accessed on July 24, 2017.
28. Ibid.
29. Ibid.
30. Ibid.
31. Ibid.
32. [No Author] "Hillary Clinton Hammers 'Dangerous' Donald Trump After Vladimir Putin Praise," *Agence France-Presse*, September 9, 2016. http://www.ndtv.com/world-news/hillary-clinton-hammers-dangerous-donald-trump-after-vladimir-putin-praise-1456436. Accessed on July 24, 2017.
33. Press Trust of India (PTI), "Clinton Campaign Attacks Trump, Says He is 'Too Divisive,' Lacks Presidential Temperament," Indian Express.com, May 4, 2016. http://indianexpress.com/article/world/world-news/clinton-campaign-attacks-trump-says-he-is-too-divisive-lacks-presidential-temperament-2783586/. Accessed on July 24, 2017.
34. Feffer, John, "The Myth of Trump's Alternative Worldview," *Foreign Policy in Focus (FPIS)*, August 3, 2016. http://fpif.org/myth-trumps-alternative-worldview/. Accessed on July 24, 2017.
35. Ibid.
36. Ibid.
37. Ibid.
38. Fisher, "What Is Donald Trump's Foreign Policy?"
39. Auslin, Michael, "Logic, But No Guarantees for Trump's Foreign Policy," *National Review*, February 21, 2017. http://www.nationalreview.com/corner/445100/donald-trump-foreign-policy-logic-worldview. Accessed on July 24, 2017.
40. Ibid.
41. Kahl, Colin and Brands, Hal, "Trump's Grand Strategic Train Wreck," *Foreign Policy*, January 31, 2017. https://foreignpolicy.com/2017/01/31/trumps-grand-strategic-train-wreck/. Accessed on July 29, 2017.
42. Ibid.
43. Ibid.
44. Ibid.
45. Ibid.
46. Ibid.
47. Ibid.
48. Ibid.
49. There are those that argue the "caravans" of migrant individuals from Central America and the president's response indicate that immigration remains a central issue. I am not yet convinced, especially given the list of issues outline as tier issues in the Trump administration's initial National Security Strategy document, that immigration is considered a top-tier threat.
50. The pitfalls governing relations with Russia, North, Korea, Syria, and the problematic relationship with Saudi Arabia in the wake of the murder of Jamal Kashoogi are discussed in subsequent chapters, the conclusion and the afterword.
51. Boot, Max, "Donald Trump's Pivot Through Asia," *ForeignPolicy.com*, December 27, 2016. http://foreignpolicy.com/2016/12/27/the-pivot-to-asia-obama-trump/. Accessed on July 29, 2017.
52. Ibid.
53. Fattahi, Kambiz, "The Rising Risk of Showdown Between Trump and Iran," *BBC*, February 21, 2017. http://www.bbc.com/news/world-middle-east-38961027. Accessed on July 29, 2017.
54. Ibid.
55. Ibid.
56. DeYoung, Karen and Ryan, Missy, "Trump Administration Weighs Deeper Involvement in Yemen War," *Washington Post*, March 17, 2017. https://www.washingtonpost.com/world/national-security/trump-administration-weighs-deeper-involvement-in-yemen-war/2017/

03/26/b81eecd8-0e49-11e7-9d5a-a83e627dc120_story.html?utmterm=.151d14b3dc55. Accessed on July 29, 2017.

57. Fattahi, "The Rising Risk of Showdown Between Trump and Iran."

58. Palletta, Damian, "Clinton vs. Trump, Where They Stand on Foreign Policy Issues," *Wall Street Journal* [No Date]. http://graphics.wsj.com/elections/2016/donald-trump-hillary-clinton-on-foreign-policy/. Accessed on July 29, 2017.

59. Ibid.

60. The author will address the Islamic States' resurrection in Iraq, Syria, and elsewhere around the world in Chapter 3 The Revision: Trump and the War on Terrorism.

61. Donald J. Trump Address: Declaring American Economic Independence. Monessen, Pennsylvania, June 28, 2016. https://www.donaldjtrump.com/press-releases/donald-j.-trump-addresses-re-declaring-our-american-independence. Accessed on July 29, 2017.

62. [No Author, *NPR* Staff] "5 Big Foreign Policy Challenges for President-Elect Trump." *NPR*, November 12, 2016. http://www.npr.org/sections/parallels/2016/11/12/501145459/5-big-foreign-policy-challenges-for-president-elect-trump. Accessed on July 29, 2017.

63. See, "5 Big Foreign Policy Challenges for President-Elect Trump."

64. Baker, Peter, "Trump Abandons Trans-Pacific Partnership, Obama's Signature Trade Deal," *New York Times*, January 23, 2017. https://www.nytimes.com/2017/01/23/us/politics/tpp-trump-trade-nafta.html?_r=0. Accessed on July 30, 2017.

65. As quoted in, Liptak, Kevin and Diamond, Jeremy, "Senators: Trump is Reconsidering his Stance on TTP Trade Deal," *CNN*, April 12, 2018. https://www.cnn.com/2018/01/12/politics/trump-tpp-reconsidering/index.html. Accessed on January 23, 2019.

Chapter One

The Unknown

Trump, America First, and the Future of Multilateralism?

There is the unfortunate and common misperception that during and after the conclusion of the 2016 presidential election campaign that Donald Trump's electoral victory signaled "the end of multilateralism." A statement in the inaugural address confirmed the suspicions of the president's critics: "We will seek friendship and goodwill with the nations of the world. But we do so with the understanding that it is the right of all nations to put their own interests first."[1] The words "in their own interests" is all the alarmists required to assert Trump is prepared to gut world order, end the American era of primacy, and upend bipartisan traditions" that existed since World War II. There is something else that developed in the wake of the statement: many foreign policy experts asserted the statement exemplified Trump's "economic unilateralist impulse."

From another perspective, there is another dimension of "Trumpism" that indicates the president is more likely to adopt multilateralism when it advances American interests. In another passage of the inaugural address, Trump acknowledged, "Our foreign policy calls for a direct, robust and meaningful engagement with the world."[2] Proponents of the president's position argued this statement may be the most promising indication of the direction of the Trump administration's foreign policy. There are those however that are wary of the president's statement.

An administration source provided another justification for disagreement and alarm with the administration's policy. In an interview with an administration official, the individual noted, "multilateralism may serve our interests, but we will dictate when and where we employ it, not our allies and certainly not our enemies. For now, . . . [administration utilization of] multilateralism remains an unknown quantity."[3]

This chapter addresses a contradiction—America First or the president's acceptance of traditional US multilateral arrangements. The chapter then addresses how the president's policy is creating uneasiness among our allies and anger among enemies of the United States. Second, the chapter details how Trump's "America First policy" may create "counter-US hysteria" that could produce a new wave of anti-Americanism around the world.

GENESIS: UNDERSTANDING THE EVOLUTION OF AMERICA FIRST

The origin of the phrase "America First" predates the candidacy and presidency of Donald Trump. For example, in his bid for reelection, President Woodrow Wilson used the campaign slogan, "He Kept Us Out of War, America First,"[4] to defeat former Supreme Court Justice Charles Evans Hughes.

In a subsequent example, a "three pronged nationalistic America First policy of limited intervention in the world coupled with limited immigration and high tariffs on foreign imports at home"[5] represented the ideological foundations of the Republican Party during the 1920s.

In a third example, to reorient US foreign policy after the end of the Cold War, then presidential candidate, Pat Buchanan, in a speech in 1991 titled, "A Crossroads in Our Country's History," forcefully argued, "We call for a new patriotism, where Americans begin to put the needs of Americans First, for a new nationalism where in every negotiation, be it arms control or trade, the American side seeks advantage and victory for the United States."[6] Buchanan, further defined America First, with this statement: "The people of this country need to recapture our capital city from an occupying army of lobbyists, and registered agents of foreign powers hired to look out for everybody and everything except the national interest of the United States."[7]

A day after President Trump's inaugural address, the media was awash with stories that addressed the subject of America First. In a telling example, *NPR*'s Ron Elving argued that "assuming he is aware of at least some of that history, Trump is demonstrating his confidence that his adoption of a phrase can supersede its past."[8] Additionally, "The president may say he wants 'America First' to mean 'we will not be ripped off anymore,' but shaking off the phrase's ugly past, especially after an inauguration speech that offered little outreach to the millions of Americans who fear what his presidency may bring, could prove difficult."[9]

The open warfare on Trump's America First approach overlooked several critical components: the president's evolving statements on the subject and its implementation. As a private citizen and throughout the presidential campaign, Trump made a host of statements that outlined the path of the development of his America First slogan.

The foundations of the candidates' version of America First may be found in one of Trump's books, *Time to Get Tough: Make America Great Again!* In this book, Trump mused about policy matters and what needed to change if the country is to reverse decades of decline. In an excerpt from the book, Trump wrote:

> I love America. And when you love something, you protect it passionately—fiercely, even. We are the greatest country the world has ever known. I make no apologies for this country, my pride in it, or my desire to see us become strong and rich again. After all, wealth funds our freedom. But for too long we've been pushed around, used by other countries, and ill-served by politicians in Washington who measure their success by how rapidly they can expand the federal debt, and your tax burden, with their favorite government programs. America can do better. I think we deserve the best. That's why I decided to write this book. The decisions we face are too monumental, too consequential, to just let slide. I have answers for the problems that confront us. I know how to make American rich again.[10]

The passage provided a window into the issues and nascent thinking of Trump's love of country, those external factors that were behind the decline of the United States, and the inability of Washington politicians to enact policies that restored the promise of the country. Instead, Trump asserted the country was "ill-served by politicians."[11] Equally important, many issues—federal debt, taxes, absence of respect for America, and many others—that were addressed in the book which mirrored in many ways some of the issues that were used during a populist campaign that set the stage for his electoral victory over Hillary Clinton.

The essential characteristics of Trump's America First were unveiled during a speech at the Mayflower Hotel in Washington, DC on April 27, 2017. Candidate Trump used the address to offer more specifics about America First and his priorities in foreign policy. In the words of Trump, "My foreign policy will always put the interests of the American people, and American security, above all else."[12] Trump added this critical supplemental point: "America is going to be reliable again."[13]

The speech identified other features that would assist in comprehending Trump's views on foreign policy. Most notably, Trump addressed five central issues the candidate promised to reverse once he assumed the presidency. Those issues include (1) reversing the weak economy and overextension of our military; (2) ensuring that US allies are "paying their fair share" of the burden in dealing with threats to security; (3) guarantee that "our allies can depend on us"; (4) make sure the enemies of United States respect us; and (5) "since the end of the Cold War," the United States has "lacked a coherent foreign policy," one which "the American people can understand and embrace."[14] Central to reversing the decline and disrespect of the United States, Trump used these words to not only return to the America First mantra, but to provide a window into the most rudimentary objective of how he would conduct the external relations of the country. The candidate informed the world his foreign policy would be based on rudimentary tenets of national security interests.[15]

In July candidate Trump provided supplemental details about America First. The following exchange between Trump and several *New York Times* reporters helps to explain why the candidates' use of the slogan is different from how others have used the concept in the past.

Sanger: This is an America First day you are having out there.

Trump: Yeah.

Sanger: We talked about that a little bit at the last conversation. Does America First take on a different meaning for you now? Think about its historical roots.

Trump: To me, America First is a brand-new modern term. I never related it to the past.

Sanger: So, it's not what Lindbergh had in mind?

Trump: It's just, no. In fact, when I said America First, people said, "Oh, wait a minute, isn't that a historical term?" And when they told me, I said: "Look, it's America First."

Sanger: You were familiar with the history of the phrase.

Trump: I was familiar, but it wasn't used for that reason. It was used as a brand-new, very modern term.

Haberman: What does it mean to you?

Trump: Meaning we are going to take care of this country first before we worry about everybody else in the world.[16]

Once in office, President Trump and senior administration officials worked to flesh out a definitive set of guidelines that are designed to refute negative appraisals of America First. An additional objective associated with the guidelines appeared to guarantee that the Trump administration had complete control over the narrative and the debates surrounding the president's America First approach. As displayed on the White House website, the essential guidelines of the "America First Foreign Policy" include the following:

> The Trump administration is committed to a foreign policy focused on American interests and American national security. Peace through strength will be at the center of that foreign policy.... Defeating ISIS and other radical Islamic terror groups will be our highest priority.... Next, we will rebuild the American military.... Finally, ... we will embrace diplomacy.[17]

These guidelines have been used to assist in identifying some of the foreign policy priorities of the Trump administration.

As is always the case in nearly every incoming administration, bureaucratic turf wars assume center stage. For senior advisors within the Trump administration, several priority issues—the Islamic State, Iran, Afghanistan, Libya, and Somalia—created divisions both on the interpretation of America First and how it would be implemented. These debates exposed a dilemma that haunted and undermined a coherent set of approaches as to how to deal with these issues during the early months of the Trump presidency. Internal debates on the topics listed previously, and a plethora of debates concerning the struggle for power among President Trump's senior White House advisors, undermined administration efforts to control the narrative. The media used these debates, many of which were leaked to the press, to undermine President Trump's leadership and created a cloud of doubt.

In an example of an early turf war among key advisors, Greg Haffe, a reporter for the *Washington Post* argued, "The big question going forward is how much intervention an 'America First' foreign policy can accommodate."[18] Subsequently, Haffe stated, "The debate about 'intervention an America First' is one where there are already divisions developing within the administration over how to deal with Iran,[19] with emphasis on Tehran's support for their Houthi allies in Yemen." On this point Haffe asserted, "Already some of the battle lines are being drawn on Iran, where Mattis has championed a relatively modest approach that focuses on working with Saudi and UAE forces to roll back Iranian influence in Yemen."[20]

On the divisions about how to confront Iran's influence in Iraq and Syria, "some Iran hawks in the White House have warned that such a strategy is insufficient to counter growing Iranian influence in Syria and Iraq."[21] There are administration officials scattered throughout the national security bureaucracy that assert an effort must be made to confront Iran in both countries. These "officials have pressed for a major campaign to confront Iran in the two countries even as the United States and its allies battle the Islamic State. At issue, what is the extent of Iranian influence inside Iraq? The hawks have maintained that without a sizable US push in the coming year, Iran will come to dominate Iraq."[22] This view is not share by Trump's senior advisors in "the Pentagon and the State Department" that "do not such see the situation in such dire terms."[23]

There are other critical issues, most notably, involving the Islamic State, Afghanistan, Libya, and Somalia, where bureaucratic discord will again come to the fore. The most interesting of these debates concerns how the administration ultimately deals with the continuing threat posed by the Islamic State. Thus far, the battle against the Islamic State continues. This is the perspective expressed by Secretary of Defense James Mattis and former national security adviser H. R. McMaster.[24] Still others inside the administration viewed this "formulation is too broad."[25]

In most of these policy debates concerning the implementation of the America First approach, the role of multilateralism often assumed permeated the internal debates. On dealing with the Islamic State, the issue is settled: "The Trump Administration will work with international partners."[26] In this regard, President Trump continued to rely upon the anti-ISIS diplomatic coalition, but privately the administration continued to seek more reliable military partners.

CRITICISM OF TRUMP'S AMERICA FIRST FOREIGN POLICY APPROACH

Throughout the general election and well into the Trump presidency, critics attacked the America First slogan. After the president's inaugural address, the attacks were unrelenting. Critics disparaged the president's slogan because it undercut traditional bipartisan foreign policy multilateral frameworks and potentially surrendered American leadership. In short, critics charged to be successful the president's slogan had to sacrifice long-held multilateral traditions.

Nicholas Burns, a well-known senior diplomat that served Republican and Democratic presidents, made the following observation of President Trump's inaugural address, "An extremely disappointing speech. I fear this speech spells retreat from American openness to the world and inspired and hopeful American leadership around the world."[27]

Lawrence J. Haas, a senior fellow at the American Foreign Policy Council, provided a memorable critique of President Trump's America First approach. Haas observed the president's foreign policy is problematic. That is, it focused attention on the threat posed by the Islamic State. However, Haas noted, "terrorism surely isn't more threatening to US security than Russia's resurgence in its region and beyond, China's aggression in the Pacific or Iran's hegemonic activities"[28] are threats that the president seemed to undervalue. Instead, said Haas, "That Trump mentioned none of those challenges reinforces fears that he cares little about longstanding US responsibilities to lead the liberal order or that he doesn't understand why we fulfill them in the first place."[29] There is another issue, the president must not dismiss traditional tenets of American foreign policy. On this point, Haas observed, in "the true path to pursuing 'America First . . . is not to turn away from the world but, instead, to turn toward it with renewed gusto, to restore our traditional role of defending freedom and promoting democracy.'"[30]

In another analysis, Terence Szuplat, one of President Barack Obama's former speechwriter's, offered this critical assessment of Trump's America First-led approach to US foreign policy. He noted that Trump shifted away from how previous American presidents defined our relationship with the rest of the world.[31] In addition, Szuplat noted the America First slogan "is a world view that quickly collapses under its own contradictions."[32] America is not respected around the world anymore," he claimed during the campaign, and yet the first days of his Presidency demonstrate that an 'America First' agenda risks alienating the United States from much of the world."[33]

Writing for the *Huffington Post*, Daniel Wagner, asserted, one of the central dangers of Trumpism is that "His election as president of the US implies an assault on a great many things, but none of them has as much potential negative global impact as the coming assault on multilateralism."[34] Wagner further explained that in "the postwar era, the world has been clearly transformed for the better by the ever-freer flow of information, people, money, trade and investment."[35] Trump he argued threatened that well-established positive history which he argued was buttressed as a result of US-created multilateral institutions.[36]

Wagner subsequently offered an observation on the implications of the president's approach: "If Mr. Trump's dystopian view of the world comes to pass," many of the post-World War II pillars of the international liberal order are "at risk."[37] Postwar allies are at risk and trade wars would become commonplace. He argued that "these are some of the potential outcomes of a collapse of multilateralism. . . . Better buckle up."[38]

Stewart M. Patrick, a fellow with the Council on Foreign Relations, asserted that "Trump's ambitions portend a rupture with more than seven decades of US global engagement dating from the end of World War II—as well as a break with older American values."[39] In a further explanation of the consequences of America First, Patrick argued "Trump's election as US president could have seismic consequences for international cooperation. . . . Taken at face value, Trump's ambitions . . . signal a new US global role that is more insular, transactional, and narrowly interest-driven."[40] Patrick also noted that "Gone is any mention of US global leadership, the promotion of universal values, or the defense of a 'free world.'"[41]

In another illustration of the impact of America First on international trade, John Cassidy of *The New Yorker* asserted, that after withdrawing from "the [Trans Pacific Partnership] T.P.P., the Trump administration has effectively disowned the US-led model of globalization and free trade that both of the country's major parties have subscribed to for decades."[42] This decision according to Cassidy, "created more uncertainty about the world's most important bilateral relationship: the one between the United States and China."[43] Additionally, Cassidy articulated, "Trump's 'America First' vision is . . . is parochial, overtly nationalist, and focused on obtaining immediate benefits for his alienated supporters. If he isn't careful, it could turn out to be a recipe for a New World Disorder."[44]

Writing for *The Nation*, author William J. Astore offered this disapproving assessment of Trump's approach. Astore's evaluation commences with what he believes is a rudimentary question: "What does an 'America-First' foreign policy look like under President Donald Trump?"[45] Thereafter, Astore endeavors to answer the question. In his analysis, he observes: "Forget the ancient label of isolationism. . . . Welcome to Trump's new era of winning. It's not really about ending wars, but exerting 'global reach/global power' while selling loads of weaponry. It promises to spread or prolong chaos in Iraq, Yemen, and possibly Iran, among other countries."[46]

Astore's analysis represents one of the most interesting evaluations of America First but it received little traction in the media and within foreign policy circles inside and outside the Beltway. Why? The reason behind the fact this analysis received so little coverage is that it focused attention on the military implications of America First. The bulk of the criticism of America First concentrated on multilateralism with emphasis on trade and post-World War II frameworks that established the liberal international order.

AMERICA FIRST: IMPACT ON MULTILATERALISM

The previous critiques provided a window into the opposition and concern about the consequences of America First. Additionally, many of those that opposed the president's approach are critical of its impact on what is nearly a century-old effort of American-created multilateral frameworks.

Given the multiple appraisals associated with America First, irrespective of the administration's attempts to clarify the slogan's meaning and purpose, the Trump White House believed their efforts have been "lost in translation." From the perspective of the administration critics have a launched a multipronged attack on a key pillar of the president's foreign policy. America First is viewed as isolationist by some, unilateralist by others, and a still larger segment argued it is a threat to multilateralism. Not to be overlooked, there are those that view America First through the prism of partisan politics.

To illustrate what the administration construed as a continuing misconception of the president's approach, there are those that argued that America

First is an instrument of unilateralism. In an illustration of the perception that America First will lead to increased unilateral actions, Julie Pace, a reporter with the *Associated Press*, made this statement: "America First agenda might well mean an America more willing to act alone."[47]

There are those that proclaimed President Trump improperly blames the American decline on multilateralism. In a confirmation of this perspective, George Friedman, the chairman of Geopolitical Futures, observed, "Trump's core strategic argument is that the United States is overextended. The . . . reason for this overextension is that the United States has substituted a system of multilateral relationships for a careful analysis of the national interest."[48] Friedman made this additional comment: "In this reading, Washington is entangled in complex relationships that place risks and burdens on the United States to come to the aid of some countries."[49]

The point of Friedman's assessments is that President Trump is opposed to select multilateral frameworks where the evidence indicated such frameworks hamper US national security interests and where too many partners fail to meet their obligations, leaving the United States to fit the bill.

President Trump argued on multiple occasions our North Atlantic Treaty Organization (NATO) partners have failed to meet their financial obligations, leaving the United States to repeatedly pick up the bill for multiple military operations. Trump also asserts the alliance failed to adequately adjust to the threat posed by transnational terrorism. Because of the failure of alliance partners to make this adjustment, the United States on too many occasions, asserted President Trump has been forced to carry the burden of confronting terrorism alone without the direct participation of most of the NATO members.

During the third leg of his initial foreign trip, President Trump once again reminded NATO members during a speech in Brussels, Belgium that 5 out of 28 allied states have met the burden of appropriating 2.5 percent of their GDP toward funding defense. Representing one of the states that has not met its burden, an upset with the president's statement that "German's are very bad for trade,"[50] German Chancellor Angela Merkel bristled at President Trump's statement. In addition to the statement, Merkel argued there is increasing distance between President Trump's position on Russia and Climate Change treaty and many NATO members. In a populist response delivered on the campaign trail, Merkel forcefully articulated that events during the NATO meeting and the G-7 gathering indicated, "The times in which we could rely fully on others—they are somewhat over. We have to know that we must fight for our future on our own, for our destiny as Europeans."[51]

This statement is not just aimed at the United States but also the United Kingdom. Merkel's message is viewed as a counterweight to Trump's America First. In this context, Merkel may be pushing for a "Europe First" or an "EU First." These slogans are representative of the fallout from what observers view as a G-7 meeting that proved to be highly contentious.[52] Time will tell if Trump, Merkel, and Prime Minister Theresa May of Britain are able to mend fences. Viewed another way, Merkel, during her reelection bid, used the alliance discord for domestic political purposes.

There are other treaties, such as the North American Free Trade Agreement (NAFTA) which Trump articulated during the presidential campaign represented "a total disaster for the US and has emptied our states of manufacturing and our jobs. Never again,"[53] argued the president.

The Obama administration negotiated the Trans Pacific Partnership (TPP) and viewed the agreement as a major tool to expand international trade and open markets for American exports. However, prior to the criticism unleashed by the New York real estate mogul during the presidential election there is evidence that many scholars illustrated why the TPP is a flawed agreement. For example, *New Yorker* columnist Adam Davidson argued, "the pro-TPP Peterson Institute for International Economics estimated that, by 2030, the agreement would have raised American [Gross Domestic Product] G.D.P. by just half a percentage point."[54] Davidson makes this additional critical point: "The United States already engages in extensive commerce with most of the pact's signatories, and many trade barriers have already been removed."[55]

While embracing the use of problematic verbiage, in his own way President Trump is arguing the multilateral frameworks created in the post-World War II order are antiquated and have negatively affected American interests, and thus require major adjustments to meet the threats of the current era.

Friedman offered a similar point: Trump argued that "the key is to recognize that the post-World War II period of multilateralism is over, and that continuing to act otherwise is harming the United States' interests."[56]

On the problems associated with "Trumpism" and how they have been misinterpreted, Friedman observed, "Trump has actually said most of these things in a rather disjointed way. But if we ignore rhetorical flaws and look at the substance of what he has said, he has a coherent and radical foreign policy."[57] On how Trump is attempting to reorder American priorities, Friedman acknowledged that he is "proposing a redefinition of US foreign policies based on current realities, not those of 40 years ago."[58] Moreover, he noted that Trump is proposing "a foreign policy in which American strength is maximized in order to achieve American ends. . . . US policy has been reflexively committed to arrangements that are three-quarters of a century old. The world has changed, but the shape of US policy has not."[59]

In the final analysis, there are those that have simply overreacted to Trump's campaign rhetoric. There is another issue: many partisan critics have attacked America First without a clear understanding of its regional and global implications. This argument does not assert America First is not without its problems. For example, the Trump administration has yet to calm the anxieties of allies around the world that fear the implementation of America First may undermine long-established multilateral frameworks. Many US allies have expressed fears not only about the administration's commitment to cooperation but the direction of American leadership. American allies are rightfully concerned about whether the Trump administration is shifting to isolation. If the administration is shifting towards isolationism there is the perception, especially after a litany of Trump campaign statements, whether in confronting Russia, dealing with a rising China, or with confronting Iran and North Korea's nuclear ambitions, some allies are worried if they could count on President Trump's leadership.

To calm fears of the president's critics inside and outside the United States, the Trump administration continued to use the White House website as an instrument to clarify the purpose of America First. The major dilemma is that as articulated during the presidential campaign and from statements by the administration since President Trump assumed office, collectively the administration's "messaging" has proven to be problematic.

To address the misperceptions surrounding America First, the Trump White House decided to utilize the State Department to correct false interpretations surrounding the administration's new approach to foreign policy.[60] The decision to rely on former Secretary of State Rex Tillerson to communicate the significance of America First and its role in redefining US foreign policy signaled two critical changes. In the early months of the administration, critics charged that Tillerson was sidelined and played no major role in decision making. Second, given the proposed cuts to the State Department's budget many incorrectly assumed that the "foggy bottom" would not have a major role in policy debates. Tillerson's address on America First represented an attempt to disprove the misperceptions concerning his influence in the administration and the clout of the State Department.

In an address to State Department employees in the Dean Acheson Auditorium in Washington, DC on May 3, 2017, Secretary Tillerson offered these details on the meaning and purpose of America First. In the words of Tillerson:

> I want to share my perspective as to how . . . this administration's policies of "America First" fit into our foreign policy. . . . So, let's talk first about my view of how you translate "America First" into our foreign policy. And I think I approach it really that it's America First for national security and economic prosperity, and that doesn't mean it comes at the expense of others. Our partnerships and our alliances are critical to our success in both of those areas. But as we have progressed over the last 20 years—and some of you could tie it back to the post-Cold War era as the world has changed, some of you can tie it back to the evolution of China since the post-Nixon era and China's rise as an economic power, and now as a growing military power—that as we participated in those changes, we were promoting relations, we were promoting eco-

nomic activity, we were promoting trade with a lot of these emerging economies, and we just kind of lost track of how we were doing. And as a result, things got a little bit out of balance. . . . These are really important relationships to us and they're really important alliances, but we've got to bring them back into balance.[61]

To provide clarification on the implementation of America First, Tillerson observed when it comes to "asking . . . NATO members to really meet their obligations" or "[how] we deal with our trading partners . . . we've got to bring that back into balance because it's not serving the interests of the American people well."[62] In the end, Tillerson stated America First "doesn't have to come at the expense of others, but it does have to come at an engagement with others. So . . . we're building our policies around those notions. . . . But at the end of it, it is strengthening our national security and promoting economic prosperity for the American people."[63] Tillerson argued that America First does not mean an abandonment of bedrock principles. He noted, "our foreign policy actions are our fundamental values: our values around freedom, human dignity, the way people are treated."[64] But Tillerson asserted that American values remain at the core of the Trump administration's foreign policy. He argued that states change, non-state actors are the march, and therefore the United States must adapt to a rapidly evolving security environment.[65]

Tillerson's remarks articulated why the administration asserts America First is needed and how it promoted rather than undercut the utilization of multilateralism as an instrument to implement US foreign policy. There are still unknown aspects of the approach that remain unanswered. If there needs to be a new era of "balancing" as stated by Tillerson, how does America First achieve this objective? Second, based on statements by candidate Trump and others by Tillerson, there is an increasing perception the administration has taken the position that several multilateral frameworks are antiquated and require adjustments (and perhaps done away with entirely). However, the president, Tillerson, and the current Secretary of State, Mike Pompeo, have yet to articulate how America First seeks to deal with current threats and protect old and transitory national interests. Until President Trump and the Mike Pompeo-led State Department end the confusion surrounding these issues and concerns about the administration's use of multilateralism to implement critical areas of US foreign policy, the anxiety at home and abroad about the impact of America First will continue.

In the wake of the conclusion of President Trump's initial first foreign trip, not yet convinced there is a full appreciation of America First, National Security Advisor, McMaster and White House Director of the National Economic Council, Gary D. Cohn (former administration officials), used a *Wall Street Journal* opinion piece to validate the significance of the America First approach. McMaster and Cohn argued the president's America First approach is about "ensuring security and prosperity for our nation. America will not lead from behind. This administration will restore confidence in American leadership as we serve the American people."[66] McMaster and Cohn offered this supplemental statement: "America First does not mean America alone. It is a commitment to protecting and advancing our vital interests while also fostering cooperation and strengthening relationships with our allies and partners."[67]

As articulated by McMaster and Cohn, America First had two additional purposes. On the first point, America First is about the restoration of American leadership and a return to US traditional roles. McMaster and Cohn argued President Trump's, "historic trip represented a strategic shift for the United States."[68] Both individuals believed "America First signals the restoration of American leadership and our government's traditional role overseas—to use the diplomatic, economic and military resources of the US to enhance American security, promote American prosperity, and extend American influence around the world."[69]

McMaster and Cohn further asserted America First also served as a warning to the adversaries of the United States. That is, it informs our "adversaries . . . that we will not only take their measure, deter conflict through strength, and defend our interests and values."[70] For those adversaries "that choose to challenge our interests [they] will encounter the firmest resolve."[71]

The analysis unveiled by McMaster and Cohn quieted critics of America First for an extended period. Additionally, the *Wall Street Journal* piece presented a framework that provided relief for many foreign policy experts that previously were skeptical of the implementation of America First. Still, there are critics that remain unconvinced of the purpose and implementation of the administration's slogan.

President Trump introduced yet another iteration of America First. However, President Trump's address at the United Nations on September 19, 2017 reignited the controversy. The following except touched off a new round of discourse on the purpose of America First:

> As President of the United States, I will always put America first, just like you, as the leaders of your countries will always . . . put your countries first. All responsible leaders have an obligation to serve their own citizens, and the nation-state remains the best vehicle for elevating the human condition. But making a better life for our people also requires us to work together in close harmony and unity to create a more safe and peaceful future for all people. The United States will forever be a great friend to the world, and especially to its allies. But we can no longer be taken advantage of or enter into a one-sided deal where the United States gets nothing in return. As long as I hold this office, I will defend America's interests above all else.[72]

The excerpt is replete with examples of what the Trump administration would not do and rather than ways in which the United States is prepared to lead. The audience assembled in the General Assembly auditorium is used to listening to American leaders provide leadership on what the international community should do to work together to resolve a specific set of problems or to act collectively to respond to a threat whether in the form of Al Qaeda or the Islamic State or to respond to one initiated by a state such as in the form of Iraq's Saddam Hussein's invasion of Kuwait. Trump lectured and spoke incessantly of America First, a topic that was intended to inform rather than inspire.

Washington Post columnist E. J. Dionne argued, "Trump Shows 'America First' is Utterly Incoherent."[73] Dionne further asserted, "the most alarming part of an address that was supposed to be a serious formulation of the president's grand strategy in the world was the utter incoherence of Trump's 'America First' doctrine. The speech tried to rationalize 'America First' as a great principle."[74] Dionne noted that on "Every effort Trump made to build an intellectual structure to support it only underscored that his favored phrase was either a trivial applause line or an argument that, if followed logically, was inimical to the United States' interests and values."[75]

In a subsequent assessment of the address, two *LA Times* reporters, Noah Bierman and David Lauter, argued, "The speech offered the most fleshed-out definition yet of the Trump doctrine, a style of big-power nationalism that the president and his advisors have also labeled 'principled realism' and 'America First.'"[76] In addition, Bierman and Lauter assert America First "brushed aside decades of American policy in favor of an approach that was dominant in the 1940s and 1950s."[77] As part of the analysis, this statement appeared: "You really are seeing 'America First' campaign rhetoric being turned into a global strategy."[78]

In the final analysis, the criticism this time is that America First is now viewed through multiple prism. For some, America First still remains "incoherent." Others argue America First had a multi-prong quality. This is a reference to the America First serving in the capacity of a campaign slogan and a global strategy. It remains to be seen how the administration's approach will make use of the old multilateral frameworks. Well into the Trump presidency, this remains "the unknown" quality of America First. Time and future crises represent the twin variables that will assist in resolving this crucial debate.

NOTES

1. Remarks of President Donald J. Trump—As Prepared for Delivery in the Inaugural Address. January 20, 2017, Washington, DC. The White House, Donald J. Trump. https://www.whitehouse.gov/inaugural-address. Accessed on March 12, 2018.

2. "President Trump Addresses a Joint Session of Congress: A Call for 'Direct, Robust, and Meaningful Engagement with the World.'" DipNote Bloggers, February 28, 2017. https://blogs.state.gov/stories/2017/02/28/en/president-trump-addresses-joint-session-congress-call-direct-robust-and. Accessed on March 12, 2018.

3. Author interview with Trump administration official.

4. Rubino, Rich, "Trump Was Not First to Use the 'America First' Slogan," *Huffington Post*, April 17, 2017. http://www.huffingtonpost.com/entry/the-etymology-of-america-first_us_5889767de4b0628ad613de3f. Accessed on March 15, 2018.

5. Ibid.

6. A Crossroads in Our Country's History, New Hampshire State Legislative Office Building. December 10, 1991. Buchanan for President. http://www.4president.org/speeches/buchanan1992announcement.htm. Accessed on March 15, 2018.

7. Ibid.

8. As quoted in, Calamur, Krishnadev, "A Short History of 'America First,'" *The Atlantic*, January 21, 2017. https://www.theatlantic.com/politics/archive/2017/01/trump-america-first/514037/. Accessed on March 15, 2018.

9. Ibid.

10. Donald Trump, *Time to Get Tough: Make America Great Again!* (Washington, DC: Regnery, 2011), p. 7.

11. Donald Trump on Foreign Policy, HugeDomains.com. http://www.ontheissues.org/2012/DonaldTrumpForeignPolicy.htm. Accessed on March 15, 2018.

12. "Donald J. Trump Foreign Policy Speech." DonaldJTrump.com. April 27, 2016. https://www.donaldjtrump.com/press-releases/donald-j.-trump-foreign-policy-speech. Accessed on March 15, 2018.

13. Ibid.

14. Ibid.

15. Ibid.

16. Transcript: Donald Trump on NATO, Turkey's Coup Attempt and the World. *New York Times*, July 22, 2017. https://www.nytimes.com/2016/07/22/us/politics/donald-trump-foreign-policy-interview.html. Accessed on March 29, 2018.

17. As quoted in "America First Foreign Policy. President Donald J. Trump, The White House. January 20, 2017. https://www.whitehouse.gov/america-first-foreign-policy. Accessed on July 29, 2017.

18. Haffe, Greg, "The Battle to Define An 'America First' Foreign Policy Divides the Trump White House," *Washington Post*, March 18, 2017. https://www.washingtonpost.com/world/national-security/the-battle-to-define-an-america-first-foreign-policy-divides-the-trump-white-house/2017/03/18/d436acf2-09b3-11e7-93dc-0f9bdd74ed1story.html?utm_term=a76c8fe58ee1. Accessed on March 29, 2018.

19. Ibid.

20. Ibid.

21. Ibid.

22. Ibid.

23. Ibid.

24. Ibid.

25. Ibid.

26. See, "America First Foreign Policy."

27. Crowley, Michael, "Foreign Policy Experts Fret Over Trump's America First Approach," *Politico*, January 20, 2017. http://www.politico.com/story/2017/01/2017-trump-inauguration-foreign-policy-reaction-233924. Accessed on April 3, 2018.

28. Haas, Lawrence J., "Trump's Troubling Retreat," *US News & World Report*, January 24, 2017. https://www.usnews.com/opinion/world-report/articles/2017-01-24/trumps-america-first-foreign-policy-will-hurt-real-americans. Accessed on April 3, 2018.

29. Ibid.

30. Ibid.

31. Szuplat, Terence, "Why Trump's 'America First' Policy Is Doomed to Fail," *The New Yorker*, February 3, 2017. http://www.newyorker.com/news/news-desk/why-trumps-america-first-policy-is-doomed-to-fail. Accessed on April 3, 2018.
32. Ibid.
33. Ibid.
34. Wagner, Daniel, "Trump and the Coming Death of Multilateralism," *The Huffington Post* [No Date] http://www.huffingtonpost.com/daniel-wagner/trump-and-the-coming-deat_b_12915974.html. Accessed on April 3, 2018.
35. Ibid.
36. Ibid.
37. Ibid.
38. Ibid.
39. Patrick, Stewart M., "Donald Trump's Global Agenda: What Have You Got to Lose?" *Council on Foreign Relations*, November 15, 2016. http://blogs.cfr.org/patrick/2016/11/15/donald-trumps-global-agenda-what-have-you-got-to-lose/. Accessed on April 3, 2018.
40. Ibid.
41. Ibid.
42. Ibid.
43. Cassidy, John, "Donald Trump's New World Disorder," *The New Yorker*, January 24, 2017. http://www.newyorker.com/news/john-cassidy/donald-trumps-new-world-disorder. Accessed on April 3, 2018.
44. Ibid.
45. Astore, William J., "What Does an 'America-First' Foreign Policy Actually Mean?" *The Nation*, April 13, 2017. https://www.thenation.com/article/what-does-an-america-first-foreign-policy-actually-mean/. Accessed on April 3, 2018.
46. Ibid.
47. Pace, Julie, "Trump Raises Prospect of America More Willing to Act Alone on Global Stage," www.pbs.org. December 27, 2016. http://www.pbs.org/newshour/rundown/trump-signals-shift-obamas-focus-multilateralism/. Accessed on April 3, 2018.
48. Friedman, George, "Donald Trump Has a Coherent, Radical Foreign Policy Doctrine," *Realclearworld.com*, January 20, 2017. http://www.realclearworld.com/articles/2017/01/20/donald_trump_has_a_coherent_radical_foreign_policy_doctrine_112180.html. Accessed on April 3, 2018.
49. Ibid.
50. Faiola, Anthony, "'The Germans Are Bad, Very Bad': Trump's Alleged Slight Generates Confusion, Backlash," *Washington Post*, May 26, 2017. https://www.washingtonpost.com/world/trumps-alleged-slight-against-germans-generates-confusion-backlash/2017/05/26/0325255a-4219-11e7-b29f-f40ffced2ddbstory.html?utm_term=39c574e03a14. Accessed on April 3, 2018.
51. Smale, Alison and Erlanger, Steven, "Merkel, After Discordant G-7 Meeting, Is Looking Past Trump," *New York Times*, May 28, 2017. https://www.nytimes.com/2017/05/28/world/europe/angela-merkel-trump-alliances-g7-leaders.html?r=0. Accessed on April 3, 2018.
52. Henley, John, "Angela Merkel: EU Cannot Completely Rely on US and Britain Anymore," *The Guardian*, May 28, 2017. https://www.theguardian.com/world/2017/may/28/merkel-says-eu-cannot-completely-rely-on-us-and-britain-any-more-g7-talks. Accessed on April 3, 2018.
53. "Donald J. Trump Foreign Policy Speech."
54. Davidson, Adam, "What the Death of the T.P.P. Means for America," New Yorker.com, January 23, 2017. https://www.newyorker.com/business/adam-davidson/what-the-death-of-the-t-p-p-means-for-america. Accessed on April 3, 2018.
55. Ibid.
56. George, "Donald Trump Has a Coherent, Radical Foreign Policy Doctrine."
57. Ibid.
58. Ibid.
59. Ibid.

60. Bendix, Aria, "Rex Tillerson Spells Out US Foreign Policy," *The Atlantic*, May 3, 2017. https://www.theatlantic.com/news/archive/2017/05/rex-tillerson-america-first-foreign-policy/525309/. Accessed on April 3, 2018.
61. Secretary of State Rex Tillerson. Remarks to US Department of State Employees, Dean Acheson Auditorium, Washington, DC, May 3, 2017. https://www.state.gov/secretary/remarks/2017/05/270620.htm. Accessed on April 3, 2018.
62. Ibid.
63. Ibid.
64. Ibid.
65. Ibid.
66. McMaster, H. R. and Cohn, Gary D., "America First Doesn't Mean America Alone," *Wall Street Journal*, May 30, 2017. https://www.wsj.com/articles/america-first-doesnt-mean-america-alone-1496187426. Accessed on April 3, 2018.
67. Ibid.
68. Ibid.
69. Ibid.
70. Ibid.
71. Ibid.
72. Remarks by President Trump to the 72nd Session of the United Nations General Assembly. The White House, Office of the Press Secretary. The United Nations, New York. September 19, 2017. https://www.whitehouse.gov/the-press-office/2017/09/19/remarks-president-trump-72nd-session-united-nations-general-assembly. Accessed on April 3, 2018.
73. Dionne, E. J., "Trump Shows 'America First' is Utterly Incoherent," *Washington Post*, September 20, 2017. https://www.washingtonpost.com/opinions/trump-shows-america-first-is-utterly-incoherent/2017/09/20/05462002-9e42-11e7-8ea1-ed975285475e_story.html. Accessed on April 3, 2018.
74. Ibid.
75. Ibid.
76. Bierman, Noah and Lauter, David, "In UN Speech, Trump Defines his Foreign Policy Doctrine as Sovereignty for Major Powers," *LA Times*, http://www.latimes.com/politics/la-na-pol-trump-un-analysis-20170919-story.html. Accessed on April 3, 2018.
77. Ibid.
78. Ibid.

Chapter Two

The Opportunity

Trump and Foreign Economic Policy

The American foreign policy agenda is dominated by war, transnational terrorism from the Islamic State and Al Qaeda, threats from Russia, China, North Korea, and Iran, just to name a few. By contrast, economic concerns have "often been relegated to the back burner." Known for *The Art of the Deal*,[1] during the 2016 president campaign, candidate Trump indicated foreign economic policy would be an integral component of his foreign policy. Armed with a cabinet that represents some of the brightest minds from cooperate America, President Trump argued his administration is poised to create "new markets" for US goods and create new trade agreements that will benefit the American worker and the US economy.[2]

Consistent with the key words in the title of the book, foreign economic policy represents a double-edged sword for the Trump presidency. That is, foreign economic policy could lead to "peril" and it holds an "opportunity" to assist the president with his objective of obtaining GDP rates of three to four percent. At issue, will the president's foreign economic policy lead to discord in the international trade order or assist in achieving the GDP rates' growth Trump boasted about during the 2016 presidential campaign and during the early months of his presidency?

UNDERSTANDING FOREIGN ECONOMIC POLICY

A question begs, what is foreign economic policy? Historically, "foreign economic policy"[3] is derived "from their national interests [of a state] which attach a high priority to the success of its own economy. These interests include the creation of stable well-paying jobs . . . and the achievement of maximum economic growth."[4]

The best response both on what is and what it represents is contained in the statement made by historian Daniel J. Sargent. Sargent provides this detailed description: "Foreign economic policy involves the mediation and management of economic flows across borders. Over two-and-a-half centuries, the context for US foreign economic policy has undergone dramatic change."[5] In addition, Sargent asserts, "The United States now leads a system in which it formally played no dominant part. It is no longer on the periphery but maintains the world's largest economy, and beginning in the post-World War II period, the United States," through the creation of frameworks, established the rules that governed the international liberal trade order.[6]

During this incredible period of transition, US foreign economic policy "has involved delicate tradeoffs between diverse interests—political and material, foreign and domestic, sectional and sectoral."[7] Another critical feature of US foreign economic policy is that it combines "ideas and beliefs" that developed during the "Enlightenment-era" convictions in the "pacifying effects of international commerce to late 20th-century convictions about the efficacy of free markets."[8] Beginning in the post-WWII period, "US foreign economic policy . . . expanded in scope and reach as the United States" increased its "managerial responsibility for the world economy."[9]

It is important to briefly examine some of the foreign economic policies of select American presidents. Some of the administrations include President Warren G. Harding and President Calvin Coolidge, President Ronald Reagan, President Bill Clinton, George W. Bush, and President Barack Obama. The policies of these administrations provide a foundation for the peril and opportunity that exists during the Trump administration's attempt to "refashion" American foreign economic policy.

Foreign economic policy is by no means a new concept. It emerged as a critical component of the American government in the 1920s in wake of the short-lived depression. In what became known as the first phase of Americanization,[10] the foreign economic policies of President Warren G. Harding and President Calvin Coolidge, covering "the period 1922–1929 represented a period of significant economic activity in the United States."[11]

John Hendrickson, who is a research analyst with the think tank Public Interest Institute, argues, "The economic policies of Presidents Harding and President Coolidge did much to ameliorate the 1920–1922 depression."[12] In an address at the Gettysburg battlefield, Coolidge said that there were three things that contributed to the economic recovery: dramatic decrease "in debt, taxes, and spending."[13]

At this point, a booming national economy was underway. According to Hendrickson, covering the period 1920 to 1929, United States produced much of the world's coal, steel, petroleum, and natural gas.[14] At this point, US foreign economic policy was second to none.

In the aftermath of World War I, the United States emerged as the unquestioned leader of the international order and could have created a new international economic order. However, "despite grandiose Wilsonian plans, the United States quickly lapsed into relative disregard for events abroad."[15] Upon his return to the United States after negotiating the Treaty of Versailles, President Woodrow Wilson quickly understood the political winds shifted dramatically. The Senate refuse to ratify the treaty, refused American entry into "the League of Nations, disavowed responsibility for European reconstruction."[16] At the time, the Isolationists prevented the United States from seizing the reigns of global leadership and creating an international economic order that would be administered and dominated by America.

Foreign economic policy remained a critical component of US foreign policy during the 1930s and most notably during the 1940s. During the post-World War II period, American foreign economic policy played a role in underwriting the restoration of war torn Western Europe. This repayment effort represented the initial American effort to construct "the global monetary and financial system," a system which the United States ultimately led.[17]

Foreign economic policy underwent a dramatic change during the presidency of Ronald Reagan. Much of the shift is a result of Reagan's pursuit of a new Cold War with the Soviet Union and the reality the president had to confront a debilitating economic recession. As part of the president's approach to confronting the Soviet Union, Reagan increased the stringent rhetoric and implemented a five-year plan to rebuild the American military.[18] As part of his domestic plan, President Reagan recognized that improving the international trade environment would prove critical to the American recovery which endured an extended recession. Thus, despite being overshadowed by more traditional foreign policy issues, the president understood the importance of foreign economic policy to the US economy.

On the importance of Reagan's foreign economic policy, Robert Zoellick, currently a senior fellow with the Belfer Center for Science and International Affairs and former head of the World Bank Group, delivered this statement during the keynote address to the FPRI Annual Dinner on November 9, 2015: The president "believed that international institutions should boost growth, opportunity, and human rights."[19] Zoellick also noted that during a period of "economic flux, the international economic system needed to adapt."[20] According to Zoellick, "Reagan did not want international rules to constrict domestic economic revival, and he stirred controversy by rejecting counterproductive international schemes."[21]

In the second term, Reagan "steered the International Monetary Fund to a new role in the Latin American debt crisis. It led a major recapitalization of the World Bank to support developing countries' economic reforms and debt rescheduling—until banks could write down losses."[22] By 1985, President Reagan instructed "Treasury Secretary James Baker launched a process of international economic coordination in the G-7. The United States pushed to expand global trade through the launch of the Uruguay Round of trade talks."[23] And in 1986, despite the decline in US-Soviet relations, Reagan permitted the Russians "to purchase four million tons" of American wheat[24] a deal that significantly benefited the US economy.

American foreign economic policy entered a period of adjustment as the bipolar ideological competition between the United States and Soviet Union concluded. International Relations scholars, Chris Dolan and Jerel Rosati write, "The end of the Cold War led to the emergence of a global economic realignment that limited America's ability to implement its strategy of becoming the unquestioned arbiter of the globalizing world economy."[25]

The adjustment included modifications from the economic threats posed by the European Union (EU), China's accelerating economic rise, and India's nascent economic revival represented some of the significant changes that President Bill Clinton and subsequent US presidential administrations would have to contend with.

Taking advantage of good fortune, the Clinton administration made use of the "peace dividend" to reduce defense spending. This decision proved critical in assisting President Clinton in meeting his mandate to fix the ailing American economy. Of equal importance, foreign economic policy played an important role. Foreign economic policy assisted in the establishment of "new markets" for US goods and as a by-product created jobs for the American worker.

President Clinton had several achievements in the foreign economic realm. The president "successfully" renegotiated the North American Free Trade Agreement (NAFTA), ensuring what Clinton believed would include tangible benefits for American workers and US businesses.[26] The administration implemented a "get tough" approach "with Japan for its past use of so-called managed trade tactics against US products."[27]

In the second term, a critical objective of the Clinton administration's foreign economic policy agenda centered on China. Clinton pushed for and achieved "engagement" with China.[28] Another objective of the administration called for China's admission into the World Trade Organization (WTO). The administration believed that when forced to adhere to WTO rules, the export of American goods to China would lead to the reduction of the US trade deficit with Beijing.[29] Though US businesses did have access to China's markets, the American trade imbalance expanded in favor of Beijing. President Trump's special trade representative Robert Ligthizers asserted one of momentous mistakes was the decision to allow China entry into the WTO. It used the organization as a cover noting that many of the unfair trade practices taken by China are not "necessarily viewed" as violations by the

WTO.[30] In the final analysis, President Clinton did have one of the more productive records in foreign economic policy, but his mishandling of China"[31] impacted Sino-American trade relations for decades.

The foreign economic policy record of the administration of George W. Bush is mixed. In the opening two years of the Bush administration, there were some notable achievements. Those achievements include the following: "The passage of fast-track negotiating authority and the launch of the Doha Round of WTO negotiations."[32] In addition, the Bush administration "pursued a coherent strategy of 'competitive liberalization' in which multilateral, regional, and bilateral agreements reinforce and catalyze one another."[33]

At the other end of the spectrum, over an extended period, foreign economic policy did not play a significant role in US foreign policy during the Bush administration. The central issue behind the decline of foreign economic policy is often linked to the inaction of Congress. C. Fred Bergsten, an economist, author, and former assistant secretary for international affairs at the Treasury Department during the Carter administration offered this analysis:

> US foreign economy policy has been mired in stalemate. For eight years, Congress refused to authorize the president to negotiate new trade agreements. When it finally did so in 2002, it was thanks only to a series of protectionist concessions on the part of the Bush administration. Legislation to replenish the International Monetary Fund (IMF), meanwhile, languished for more than a year at the height of the Asian financial crisis. It was rescued only by the intervention of a farm bloc seeking new funding for sales to major overseas markets.[34]

The Bush administration's quest for "competitive liberalization"[35] met with minimal success. In the end, foreign economic policy took a back seat to the war on terrorism and the polarizing Iraq War. During the close of the administration "the shift back to Afghanistan" also worked to undermine a coherent foreign economic policy.

President Obama "did not begin his presidency with a strong focus on foreign economic policy"[36] during the opening year of the administration. While the president did not declare a formal trade policy, he did make a very significant statement: "I think it would be a mistake . . . at a time when worldwide trade is declining for us to start sending a message that somehow we're just looking after ourselves and [are] not concerned about world trade."[37] Beyond this statement, the Obama administration focused on the economic stimulus and healthcare legislation.

President Obama's foreign economic vision during the second term encompassed an approach that included the following components. The Obama administration "doubled down on tough enforcement of our trade agreements. Over the course of the Obama Administration, [they] . . . brought 24 trade enforcement cases to date to the World Trade Organization (WTO)–including 15 cases against China."[38] Second, the Obama administration "spurred sustainable and inclusive growth, both at home and abroad."[39] The Obama administration made substantial use of the WTO. For example, "at the WTO, [the administration] updated the multilateral trading system to the realities of the 21st century, tackling emerging issues important to developed and developing economies."[40] Third, the administration in regional and bilateral relationships designed to "unlock opportunity for American workers and industry."[41] And fourth, in a major achievement, the administration "negotiated and concluded high-standard trade agreements like the Trans-Pacific Partnership (TPP) to expand the export of 'Made-in-America' goods and help make the US economy the world's production platform of choice."[42] These four components set the stage for the creation of a trade policy that contributed to minimal economic growth in the wake of the global financial crisis.

For many, the Obama administration's foreign economic policies were deemed problematic. Craig VanGrasstek, a distinguished professor at Harvard's Kennedy School of Government, offered this critique: the president "has shown that it will take action to avoid being labeled protectionist, but it has yet to demonstrate any eagerness to make trade liberalization an important part of its economic recovery program."[43] There was considerable rhetoric about the significance of foreign economic policy, however, other than TTP, the Obama administration did not have any significant accomplishments.

With so much discord in the world, and questions abound about the status of American leadership, confronting a plethora of "unfinished foreign policy issues" left over from the Obama era, and given that an unpredictable president now occupies the White House, it is believed that a dramatic dose of foreign economic policy is just what is needed in Washington.

On the cure associated with foreign economic policy, Bergsten made this incredible statement: "Most important, foreign economic policy could rescue overall US foreign policy."[44] In a critique of the foreign policy of President George W. Bush, Bergsten stated, "The United States' biggest problem in the international arena is its tendency to act unilaterally on a range of issues. Such unilateralism is demonstrably ineffective and thus thankfully rare in the economic domain."[45]

TRUMP AND THE PERILS AND OPPORTUNITIES OF FOREIGN ECONOMIC POLICY

Thus far, President Trump has not made a formal declaration of what would constitute his administration's foreign economic policy. Much of the inability of the "Trump administration . . . to settle on a coherent [foreign economic] policy on everything from NAFTA to steel imports is a result of the continuing tug of war between the administration's 'America First' advisers and advocates [at the State and Treasury Departments that assert what is] . . . needed is a more global approach that pays heed to US allies."[46]

Long after the intense bureaucratic struggle over the administration strategy, there are five components that form the framework of the administration's foreign economic policy. Those components include (1) the roots of the president's foreign economic policy, (2) campaign statements, (3) the America First mantra, (4) Trump's statements condemning globalization, and (5) the renegotiation of trade agreements.

THE ROOTS OF TRUMP'S FOREIGN ECONOMIC POLICY

The foundations of Trump's foreign economic policy are "rooted" in Republican and conservative economic traditions. President Trump, during an economic policy speech in Michigan, the candidate argued for the need to resurrect American manufacturing. To revive American manufacturing, Trump called for a "new economic model—the American model."[47] In many of his many campaign and presidential speeches, "Trump often recalls the economic nationalism of previous presidents."[48] In one speech, Trump noted, "Our great Presidents, from Washington to Jefferson to Jackson to Lincoln, all understood that a great nation must protect its manufacturing, must protect itself from the outside. . . ."[49]

As Hendrickson points out, "President Trump's American model . . . is not necessarily new, but rather, a rediscovering of the older Republican tradition."[50] Hendrickson argued it is important to recall a quote from Patrick J. Buchanan, who previously wrote, "in leading Republicans away from globalism to economic nationalism, Trump is not writing a new gospel. He is leading a lost party away from a modernist heresy—back to the Old-Time Religion. . . ."[51] Buchanan continued: "The economic nationalism and protectionism of Hamilton, Madison, Jackson, and Henry Clay, and the Party of Lincoln, McKinley, Teddy Roosevelt, and Coolidge, of all four presidents on Mount Rushmore, made America the greatest and most self-sufficient republic in history."[52]

Hendrickson asserts that "Republican presidential administrations, especially before World War II, followed an economic approach" that contains ideas very much consistent with those "that President Trump is advocating."[53] Hendrickson further asserts that Charles Kesler, a senior fellow at Claremont Institute, the foundations of the president's approach to foreign economic policy is indeed linked to "early 20th-Century" Republican presidents. Hendrickson quotes Kesler: "Mr. Trump's policies suggest that what he calls his 'common sense' conservatism harks back to the principles and agenda of the old Republican Party, which reached its peak before the New Deal."[54] Another significant point relates to the president's business skills. Those skills will be in a high demand as the administration embarks on a host of renegotiations of several trade agreements.[55]

In another point that supplements the understanding of the evolution of Trump's foreign economic policy, is that "some of the policies of the pre-World War II Republicans that are similar to President Trump's policy preferences." In the end, the economic nationalism embraced by Trump is rooted in the president's reconceptualization of foreign economic policy from previous Republican presidents.

Campaign Statements and the Development of Foreign Economic Policy

One may look to the campaign to comprehend the emergence of Trump's approach to foreign economic policy. Some of Trump's signature issues that appeared in campaign rallies and speeches called for protecting Americas declining manufacturing base, renegotiating NAFTA, and China's threat to the international trade order.

The issue of decline in US manufacturing jobs represented a central theme for Trump on the campaign trail. Trump was effective in linking Hillary Clinton to the decline in manufacturing jobs. For example, during a campaign address Trump stated:

> It was also Clinton, [then] the secretary of state, who shoved us into a job-killing deal with South Korea. . . . This deal doubled our trade deficit with South Korea and destroyed nearly 100,000 American jobs. As Bernie Sanders said, Hillary Clinton voted for virtually every trade agreement that has cost the workers of this country . . . millions of jobs. Trade reform and the negotiation of great trade deals is the quickest way to bring our jobs back to our country.[56]

It is statements such as these that assisted Trump in reaching disaffected workers in the Rust Belt and beyond. Oddly, a message concerning workers in America is usually one that you anticipate from a Democratic presidential candidate rather than one which is a Republican.

Gerald P. O' Driscoll Jr., a senior fellow at the Cato Institute and previously served as vice president and director of policy analysis with Citibank, and Dr. Tyrus W. Cobb, who previously served as special assistant to President Ronald Reagan for National Security Affairs and as a director of Soviet, European, and Canadian Affairs from 1983–1989, offered an important assessment of Trump's foreign economic policy. Driscoll and Cobb assert, "On the economic front, Trump lamented the decline of American manufacturing and the exodus of jobs overseas. He vowed that 'there would be consequences.'"[57] The evaluation then shifted to Trump and China: "He has said that China is 'killing' us on trade. . . ."[58] What is the Trump doctrine for China and our Transpacific alliances? The final critical piece of the assessment addressed Trump as an agent of change: "Successive US Administrations have not rethought American foreign policy since the end of the Cold War. Regardless of his electability, Trump may have initiated a much-needed foreign policy rethink."[59]

During the campaign Trump not only railed against Obama's failed trade policies, but he used the addresses and stump speeches to recapture a forgotten past, a period of American glory. For example, during a campaign event, Trump issued this statement: "It's time for the American people to take back their future. . . . Very sadly, we lost our way when we stopped believing in our country. America became the world's dominant economy by becoming the world's dominant producer."[60] Trump asserted, "We can't continue to do that. It can be corrected, and we can correct it fast when we have people with the right thinking."[61] Statements like these reinforced Trump's new economic vision of the country. It is this vision that shaped his path to the White House.

AMERICA FIRST AND FOREIGN ECONOMIC POLICY

The Trump administration's foreign economic policy is linked to the "America First" and statements about the slogan that were delivered during the campaign and by commentators that attempted to clarify the president's trade agenda.

Colin Kahl, senior fellow at the Freeman Spogli Institute for International Studies' Center for International Security and Cooperation, and Hal Brands, distinguished professor of global affairs at Johns Hopkins University, asserted that America First represents a critical feature of trade policy. They assert that "Trump has signaled a willingness to embrace a protectionist and mercantilist foreign policy more familiar to the 19th and early 20th centuries than to the 21st."[62]

As to evidence, Kahl and Brands used the following excerpt from President Trump's inaugural address to validate their analysis: "From this day forward, it's going to be only America first. Every decision on trade, on taxes, on immigration, on foreign affairs will be made to benefit American workers and American families."[63] President Trump spoke of the need to "protect our borders from . . .other countries [that are] . . . stealing our companies and destroying our jobs."[64]

As part of the internal deliberations within the administration, there are discussions about "a pending Commerce Department report into whether to restrict steel imports to protect national security."[65] The Trump administration "is quietly preparing sweeping new trade policies to defend the US steel industry, a move that could reverberate across global economies and incite other countries to retaliate."[66] While there is concern in the European Union and Canada, about the pending restrictions on steel, the measure is meant to send a signal to China, which is notorious for dumping cheap steel in the United States. The pending report represents for those inside and outside the United States that America First is set to play a pivotal role in foreign economic policy.

In a subsequent example, in an op-ed piece titled, "America First Doesn't Mean America Alone," which appeared in the *Wall Street Journal* on May 30, 2017, two previous administration officials, H. R. McMaster, the National Security Advisor, and Gary Cohn, the Director of the National Economic Council, delivered this statement following the conclusion of President Trump's initial foreign trip:

> Ensuring American economic prosperity is also critical to our national interests. In Saudi Arabia, President Trump helped facilitate $110 billion in defense investments that will strengthen regional and American security and create American jobs. He also announced nearly $270 billion in agreements with private-sector enterprises from the US, spanning the financial-services, energy, technology, mining and manufacturing industries. These efforts will enhance job creation and investment in America.[67]

The *Wall Street Journal* piece clarified administration foreign economic policy objectives in that Saudi Arabia represented a vital piece in the cementing of a trade a strategic partnership that could be used to pursue future mega bilateral trade initiatives inside and outside the Middle East. The critical feature of the article is the focus on job creation, important in that is a major component of the president's agenda.

During a speech on July 16, 2017, President Trump "kicked off his 'Made in America' week at the White House . . . by showcasing products made in all 50 states and promoting an 'America First' approach to manufacturing and trade."[68] In the speech, President Trump stated, "We want to build, create and grow more products in our country using American labor, American goods and American grit. American workers, farmers and innovators are really the best in the world."[69] In addition, the president explained, the restoration of the manufacturing base "will not only restore our wealth, it will restore our pride in ourselves, it will revitalize our independence. We will protect our workers, promote our industry and be proud of our history because we will put America First."[70]

President Trump's bold and controversial decision to withdraw from the Paris Accord is very much consistent with the principles of America First. Former press secretary, Sean Spicer made the case for the administration's decision to withdraw from the Climate Change agreement: "The president's number one priority is to get the best deal for the American people. The president has made it very clear that he is committed to making the best deal for the America, American workers and American manufactures."[71]

As anticipated, President Trump's decision unleashed wide-spread condemnation at home and abroad. John Kerry, secretary of state during the Obama administration, asserted, "This step does not make America first, it makes America last."[72] In another example, Martin Wolfe, a reporter, argued, "We live in a world the US made. Now it is unmaking it. You cannot ignore that reality."[73]

TRUMP, GLOBALIZATION, AND FOREIGN ECONOMIC POLICY

Trump railed against globalization during the campaign. In an illustration of his contempt for globalization, in a speech at Alumisource in Monessen, Pennsylvania on June 27, 2016, Trump made this comment: "Our politicians have aggressively pursued a policy of globalization—moving our jobs, our wealth and our factories to Mexico and overseas. Globalization has made the financial elite who donate to politicians very . . . wealthy."[74]

In another portion of the speech, Trump associated his trade policies to protectionism and against what the candidate referred to as "globalism." In the words of the candidate, "It is the consequence of a leadership class that worships globalism over Americanism. This is a direct affront to our founding fathers, who . . . wanted this country to be strong. They wanted [it] to be independent and they wanted it to be free."[75] Trump then stated, "our founding fathers understood" the importance of trade, much specifically in manufacturing.[76] In case of George Washington, according to Trump he promoted "domestic manufacturing will be among the first consequences to flow from an energetic government."[77] The candidate then pivoted to Abraham Lincoln, who warned, "the abandonment of the protective policy by the American government will produce want and ruin among our people."[78]

There are some truths to President Trump's criticisms of globalization. In short, there is little doubt that globalization impacts the American economy. However, there is something the president and other detractors of globalization have failed to recognize: Globalization impacts the economies of all states around the world in one form or another. Second, the United States owes their rise to the position of leadership of the global order, in part, to tangible benefits amassed from globalization.

Prior to the emergence of President Trump, "US foreign policy [has been] . . . dominated by war, terrorism, and weapons of mass destruction, [and] economic concerns [were]. . . relegated to the back burner."[79] Thus far, President Trump endeavored to balance security and trade policy. However, critics argued that the president spent too much time on bashing globalization. At some point these same critics argued that globalization represented a vehicle for US economic expansion and its dominance of international trade. In addition, Hendrickson makes this significant argument: Stopping the advance of globalization would be very dangerous to US foreign policy because globalization—more than terrorism or the end of the Cold War—has been the dominant force for change in international affairs in the past 50 years.[80] Trump and those that subscribed to this view should recognize that, "rightly or wrongly," globalization "is equated with Americanization in much of the world."[81]

During a period of disparagement of globalization within the United States, there is another scapegoat afoot for the cause of the ills for the American economy and the loss of jobs for its workers: competitors. China is the most significant competitor, not only because they threaten the American preeminent role as the dominant economy, but because of the omnipresent trade surplus it maintains with the United States. Because of the competition emanating from China, during the campaign and well into his presidency, Trump launched a host of statements that essentially argued that Beijing is undermining the American economy and threatening jobs in the United States (A similar argument was made by Reagan and later George H. W. Bush against Japan during the 1980s through 1992).

In addressing this issue, Bergsten made the following comment concerning China and other potential competitors. He noted that new competitors provide "attractive markets for US exports and investment. . . ."[82]

Irrespective of the dilemmas of the globalization, the United States under Trump (and future American leaders) must adjust for the sake of the American economy and for the US position and its standing in the international economic order. Though President Trump continues to display his contempt for globalization, it is here to stay.

As the President of the United States and the leader of the global economic order, "The case for globalization will have to be made persuasively, forcefully, and repeatedly. . . . The economy would suffer from trade restrictions."[83] If not, the president could jeopardize American leadership and standing if the administration shifts away from "constructive cooperation with other nations on issues at the top of their agendas."[84] A question begs, well into the implementation of the Trump administration's foreign economic policy, how will it impact the American and global economy?

THE RENEGOTIATION OF TRADE AGREEMENTS AND FOREIGN ECONOMIC POLICY

President Trump campaigned on negotiating, and where appropriate, the need to renegotiate trade deals that could benefit the American worker and the US economy. The Trump White House continued to refine that message. In an instructive example, on the White House website, which read, "Trade Deals That Work For All Americans," the administration made it clear that it is determined to negotiate better trade deals. To clarify the point, the White House argued: "With tough and fair agreements, international trade can be used to grow our economy, return millions of jobs to America's shores, and revitalize our nation's suffering communities."[85]

In implementing its strategy, the administration restated their intention to withdraw from the Trans-Pacific Partnership (TTP) and renegotiate NAFTA. On NAFTA, the White House issued this warning: "If our partners refuse a renegotiation that gives American workers a fair deal, then the President will give notice of the United States' intent to withdraw from NAFTA."[86]

President Trump directed Commerce Secretary Wilbur Ross "to identify all trade violations and to use every tool at the federal government's disposal to end these abuses."[87] In addition to the commerce secretary, the secretary of Treasury Mnuchin and the special trade representative Lighthizer are also responsible for searching and ending the abuses.

In addition to the previous the statement, the White House issued a subsequent statement. The statement detailed the administration's "free trade agenda."[88] Some of the details included the following. Through trade negotiations the president seeks to "put America First."[89] Second, the president intends to renegotiate NAFTA.[90] A third objective called for the renegotiation of the United States-Korea Free Trade Agreement.[91] The fourth objective President Trump intended to "roll back the Obama Administration's bad deal on Cuba that benefitted the Cuban regime at the expense of the Cuban people."[92] The fifth and final component, called for productive trade negotiations that curtailed if not eliminated China's trade surplus.[93] There is corollary component associated with China which called for eliminating the "unfair trade practices" that Beijing implemented to undercut US exports. It is this corollary component that set the stage for the trade war.

With high profile cabinet officers that previously worked on Wall Street, and a president skilled in the art of negotiation, the Trump administration informed the world that it is determined to pursue a comprehensive trade agenda aimed at restoring balance with major US trading partners and renegotiate "bad trade deals" that were concluded under the Clinton and Obama administrations.

The Trump administration agenda has been remarkable successful thus far. The United States and South Korea agreed to a free trade agreement

(Korean Free Trade Agreement (KORUS)) in 2012. It is this agreement that President Trump targeted to refashion the trade imbalance that exists with several major players.

Trump's threat to cancel KORUS is one of many subjects discussed in distinguished author Bob Woodward's book, *Fear: Trump in the White House*. In the book, with respect to KORUS, the author makes the case that several senior administration officials refused to implement the president's Oval Office order "We are getting out of KORUS."[94]

This statement, according to Woodward, was made in the presence of senior officials. At the conclusion of the meeting, President Trump ordered a creation of a draft of a letter that would be sent to the leader of South Korea which would formally terminate the trade agreement in favor of negotiating a new deal, one more favorable to US trade interests and the American worker. The initial letter was never delivered to the president. Woodward makes the case that Gary Cohn, the president's chief economic advisor, and Rob Porter, the White House staff secretary and organizer of documents for the president, engaged "in subterfuge." That is, Cohn and Porter worked to ensure the president never saw the formal letter. In fact, the draft letter was removed from the president's desk.[95] The action by the Cohn and Porter, according to Woodward, is based on the desire by both to "work together to derail what they believed were Trump's most impulsive and dangerous orders."[96] The decision by Cohn and Porter in the words of the Woodward "was no less than an administrative coup d'etat, an undermining of the will of the president of the United States and his constitutional authority."[97]

During numerous interviews to promote the book Woodward incessantly mentioned the above incident. The incident certainly assisted in selling the book. There is a major problem, however, with the story. In spite of the intrigue in "the administrative coup d'etat" and efforts to undermine the president's agenda, Trump still implemented the policy which culminated in an amended trade deal.

During a meeting with South Korean President Moon Jae-in on June 30, 2017, President Trump stated, "For many, many years the United States has suffered through many trade deficits."[98] The president then opined, "We want something that is going to be good for the American worker."[99] The Trump administration promised to end the annual trade deficits with South Korea.

Commerce Secretary Wilbur Ross noted, "there are a lot of very specific problems"[100] with the agreement. Most notably the South Korean government engaged in unfair trade practices in two sectors, the automobile industry and steel industries. The administration argued that because the United States has annually run trade deficits with South Korea, they have announced their intention to renegotiate KORUS.

After months of negotiations, and during the height of tensions with North Korea over the regimes threat to launch a long-range missile targeting Guam, President Trump threatened to withdraw from KORUS. After subsequent deliberations with key administration trade officials and facing domestic pressure from the business community over the potential loss of markets and American jobs, President Trump resumed negotiations with South Korea. The negotiations entered a pivotal phase.

Following multiple high-level meetings, the United States and South Korea reached agreement on modifying key components of KORUS. The agreement "modified tariffs and automotive quotas."[101] In implementing this approach and therefore "declining to invoke US trade law," President Trump avoided the need for congressional approval. On the significance of the trade agreement, an upbeat and triumphant President Trump stated, "We are now going to start sending products to South Korea. These outcomes give the finest American-made automobiles, innovative medicines and agricultural crops much better access to Korean markets."[102]

The Trump administration's objective to renegotiate the NAFTA trade deal will prove far more difficult than KORUS. The central issue concerns if Trump is unable to push Canada and Mexico into agreeing to his terms, is the president prepared to withdraw from the agreement?

The Trump administration informed the parties—Canada and Mexico—about the details of the US government's objectives. Under the auspices of the Office of United States Trade Representative, Lighthizer issued the administration's objectives for the renegotiation of NAFTA. The administration objectives include a thorough renegotiation of the agreement. In addition, the Trump administration sought a new agreement that reduced "the US trade deficit and is fair for all Americans by improving market access in Canada and Mexico for US manufacturing, agriculture, and services."[103]

The second objective called for "adding a digital economy chapter and incorporating and strengthening labor and environment obligations that are currently in NAFTA side agreements."[104] A third objective argues "the administration will work to eliminate unfair subsidies, market-distorting practices by state owned enterprises, and burdensome restrictions on intellectual property."[105]

The administration faced additional hurdles in the renegotiation of NAFTA. For starters, there are three parties to the treaty (unlike KORUS which was a bilateral agreement). Second, NAFTA is a far more comprehensive treaty that the bilateral trade agreement negotiated between the United States and South Korea. Third, relations between the United States and Mexico and the United States and Canada (if one adds the negative interpersonal enmity between President Trump and the Prime Minister Trudeau, this relationship increased the likelihood of trade deal) collectively increased the likelihood the US leader could walk away (something Trump repeated threatened) from the deal. Finally, the Mexican presidential campaign, and the eventual defeat of Enrique Pena Nieto by Andres Manuel Lopez Obrador, increased the pressure to produce a deal in advance of the Mexican succession.

Earlier, the United States expressed the multiple concerns it had with NAFTA. Mexico and Canada had their own concerns about renegotiating the treaty. In an assessment of the Mexican position, Hugo Perezcano Diaz, a former Mexican trade official, warned if the US president is willing to walk away from the agreement without recognizing his government's positions then "we have to call Trump's bluff and if he wants to walk away from NAFTA, well, so be it."[106]

From the beginning, the government of Canada took a hardline approach. Providing a sense of Canada's position, Dan Ciuriak, a senior fellow at the Centre for International Governance Innovation and former chief economist at Canada's department of Foreign Affairs, commented, "The general principle is that there should be no compromise."[107]

The issue of consequence for Canada is centered on Chapter 19 which is a "dispute mechanism" based on American law whereby all parties of the agreement turn to as a mechanism to resolve any perceived violations of the accord. The Trump administration expressed "a desire to abolish the dispute-resolution panel"[108] of six experts, two representatives from each of the three countries. In the early negotiations, Canada refused to agree to any changes on Chapter 19.

With significant media hype, the opening round of negotiations, which took place in Washington, DC, occurred with few significant accomplishments. After each party expressed their positions, it was clear that no breakthrough would occur over the course of the frantic discussions. After the unveiling of the participant positions, the media and pundits expressed that it appeared highly likely the Trump administration may walk away from NAFTA.

The second phase of negotiations commenced in Mexico City. The government of Mexico reiterated their earlier position. The Canadian position appeared to harden. Prime Minister Trudeau publicly expressed his disapproval of President Trump's threats to abrogate US participation in the treaty as nothing but a "bullying tactic." Despite the repeated threats by the president, the Mexican government privately did not believe Trump was prepared to withdraw from NAFTA. After five tense days of negotiations, no agreement appeared on the horizon. Amid the negotiations, President Trump issued a tweet where he threatened to withdraw from the treaty if the resistance from Mexico and Canada did not end. The parties did release a joint statement, "Important progress was achieved in many disciplines and the Parties expect more"[109] which attempted to reduce the tensions, but the diplomatic note could not paper over the obvious disagreements.

A third round of negotiations convened in Ottawa, Canada. Pressure mounted for an agreement. Domestic politics within each of the countries whether from the political parties, the business class, and workers from each country, openly expressed their positions on the potential for an economic crisis impacting each of three participants if NAFTA collapsed. The pressures and potential political consequence to amend the treaty failed. For President Trump politically he was positioned to walk away from the agreement. Such a decision (compared the leaders of Canada and Mexico) would have had limited ramifications because he would have fulfilled a campaign promise "to walk away" from a bad deal that did not benefit the American people. The collapse of NAFTA could produce the loss of millions of American jobs and markets and profits for American businesses, but the Americans would blame Mexico and Canada for failing to compromise.

The relations between Canada and the United States continued to decline as both Trudeau and Trump launched verbal attacks at the NATO meetings. In recognition that Canada appeared unlikely to soften their positions on NAFTA, a shrewd President Trump conducted bilateral discussions with Mexico on amending the treaty without Trudeau's participation. In September of 2018, the negotiation tactic produced an agreement between the United States and Mexico on a series of issues that substantially altered NAFTA.

Internal and external pressure mounted on Trudeau to agree to changes in the agreement. If the leader of Canada failed to reach an agreement with the other two parties, the United States and Mexico would have concluded a separate bilateral deal that would have scrapped NAFTA and left out Canada. The domestic political realities forced Trudeau to reach an agreement which meant accepting much of what had been agreed to by the United States and Mexico.

After an extended period "of rancorous talks that raised doubts about whether any accord was possible,"[110] the United States, Mexico, and Canada reached accord on a new agreement (USMCA) that nullified NAFTA. A jubilant President Trump during the signing ceremony between the parties, stated, "We worked hard on this agreement. It's been long and hard. We've taken a lot of barbs and a little abuse, and we got there. It's great for all of our countries."[111] The ratification of the new accord by the all parties is all that remains before it is implemented.

The Sino-US trade dispute evolved into a trade war that many observers expressed could impact the international economy. Over the course of 2018, both parties have engaged in several rounds of negotiations aimed at ending the long simmering and expanding trade war. Most recently, the parties agreed to "a pause" where each party agreed not to implement any new measures (tariffs) that would affect the economy of the other. The United States however joined twelve other allies in a condemnation of China's decade-plus "campaign to steal technology and corporate secrets" aimed at advancing their position on a global scale.[112] The Trump administration's response, implemented by Treasury Secretary Mnuchin, represented another anti-China initiative designed to force Beijing to end their negative trade practices. Canada's seizure of Huawei executive Meng Wanzhou, claiming her company violated American sanctions on trade with Iran, resulted in China's detainment of several Canadian business officials. This tit-for-tat set of actions is unlikely to change the bargaining position of the United States or China. The United States is however in a far more advantageous position than China. There is another significant reason why the United States is in more advantageous position to withstand the tariffs administered by China. With trade agreements with South Korea, Mexico, and Canada, and a short-term trade agreement with the European Union, the Trump administration essentially cleared its agenda of trade disputes and is now poised to work with the EU, Asian, and other countries around the world to create a coalition effort to force China to agree to substantial behavioral changes in their trade practices.

Foreign economic policy is poised to play a pivotal role during the Trump presidency. For the detractors, the criticism is obvious. There are a host of skeptics that remain concerned about the protectionist rhetoric that emanated from the campaign and was unveiled in presidential speeches.[113]

There of course is the concern about America First, the bashing of globalization, and the outcome of the Sino-US trade dispute. Around the world "concern" is the operative word. That concern is about how the president's trade policy could induce dramatic change that may undermine international trade and long-standing international frameworks. At home, these critics believe an already sputtering economy could spiral downward. Thus, the left asserts Trump's foreign economic policy is poised, in the words of Richard Wolfe, "To Make America Weak Again"[114] and cause harm to international economic order.

From the inception of the Trump presidency, the administration's trade policy revolved around two objectives. On the first, a central goal is "to boost US economic growth."[115] The second objective is the requirement to increase "the rate of GDP growth to three to four percent, doubling the rate achieved over the last decade."[116] Treasury Secretary Mnuchin repeats these twin objectives whenever the opportunity presents itself.

President Trump could use foreign economic policy as an important instrument in securing new markets and as a by-product to create millions of American jobs in the emerging markets and within the markets of major competitors of the United States. There is a political consequence that those on left fear: abundant jobs and a strong economy could lead to the reelection of Donald Trump. One thing is certain, foreign economic policy exemplifies the peril and opportunities that could dominate the Trump presidency.

NOTES

1. Trump, Donald, *Trump: The Art of Deal* (Ballantine Books, 2015).
2. Ahmed, Salman and Bick, Alexander, "Trump's National Security Strategy: A New Brand of Mercantilism?" *Carnegie Endowment for International Peace*, August 17, 2017. http://carnegieendowment.org/2017/08/17/trump-s-national-security-strategy-new-brand-of-mercantilism-pub-72816. Accessed on October 4, 2018.
3. Bergsten, C. Fred, Chapter 1, "A New Foreign Economic Policy of the United States," Peterson Institute for Economics. https://piie.com/publications/chapterspreview/3802/1iie 3802.pdf. Accessed on October 4, 2018.
4. Ibid.
5. American Foreign Economic Policy. American History Oxford Research Encyclopedia. http://americanhistory.oxfordre.com/view/101093/acrefore/9780199329175001.0001/acrefore-9780199329175-e-52. Accessed on October 4, 2018.
6. Ibid.
7. Ibid.
8. Ibid.
9. Ibid.
10. For more on the "three waves of Americanization," see Thommesen, Kjartan, "From Excitement to Burnout in 80 Years the Americanization of Europe (1919–1999)," Master's Thesis, 2008. https://www.duo.uio.no/bitstream/handle/10852/26255/FromxExcitementxtox-Burnoutxinx80xYears.pdf?sequence=1. Accessed on October 4, 2018.
11. Hendrickson, John, "The Roots of Trump's Economic Policy," *American Conservative*, May 31, 2017. http://www.theamericanconservative.com/articles/the-roots-of-trumps-economic-policy/. Accessed on October 4, 2018.
12. Hendrickson, John, "President Coolidge's Economics Lesson," Coolidgefoundation.org, August 8, 2014. https://coolidgefoundation.org/blog/president-coolidges-economics-lesson/. Accessed on October 5, 2018.
13. Ibid.
14. Ibid.
15. Freidan, Jeff, "Sectoral Conflict and Foreign Economic Policy, 1914–1940," *International Organization*, No. 42.1 (Winter 1988). http://pages.ucsd.edu/~jlbroz/Courses/POLI142B/syllabus/friedensector.pdf. Accessed on October 5, 2018.
16. Ibid.
17. Ibid.
18. Schneider, Greg and Merle, Renae, "Reagan's Defense Buildup Bridged Military Eras," *Washington Post*, June 8, 2004. http://www.washingtonpost.com/wp-dyn/articles/A26273-2004Jun8.html and Thompson, Loren, "Why Trump Needs a Five-Year Defense Plan on Day One," *Forbes*, December 22, 2016. https://www.forbes.com/sites/lorenthompson/2016/12/22/why-president-trump-needs-a-five-year-defense-plan-on-day-one/2/#781079a93e95. Accessed on October 5, 2018.
19. Zoellick, Robert, "The Currency of Power: Economics & Security in US Foreign Policy," *FPRI*, January 2016. https://www.fpri.org/wp-content/uploads/2016/01/zoellick-dinner-transcript.pdf. Accessed on October 5, 2018.
20. Ibid.
21. Ibid.
22. Ibid.
23. Ibid.
24. Cohen, Stephen D., *The Making of United States International Economic Policy Principles, Problems, and Proposals for Reform, 5th Edition* (New York: Praeger, 2000), p. 14.
25. Dolan, Chris and Rosati, Jerel, "US Foreign Economic Policy and the Significance of the National Economic Council," *International Studies Perspectives* (2006) 7, pp. 102–123. http://people.cas.sc.edu/rosati/documents/dolanrosati.NEC.pdf. Accessed on October 6, 2018.
26. Ibid.
27. Ibid.
28. Ibid.

29. Ibid.
30. Setser, Brad W., "US-China Trade War: How We Got Here," *Council on Foreign Relations*, July 9, 2018. https://www.cfr.org/blog/us-china-trade-war-how-we-got-here. Accessed on October 6, 2018.
31. Ibid.
32. Bergsten, C. Fred, "Foreign Economic Policy for the Next President," *Foreign Affairs*, March/April 2004. http://www.mafhoum.com/press7/185E19.htm. Accessed on October 6, 2018.
33. Ibid.
34. Ibid.
35. More details on the concept, see Bergsten, C. Fred, "Competitive Liberalization and Global Free Trade: A Vision for the Early 21st Century," Peterson Institute for International Economics (PIIE) Working Paper 96-15. January 1996. https://piie.com/publications/working-papers/competitive-liberalization-and-global-free-trade-vision-early-21st. Accessed on October 7, 2018.
36. Destler, I. M., Chapter 11 "First, Do No Harm" Foreign Economic Policy Making Under Barack Obama," School of Public Policy, Center for International and Security Studies (CISS) at Maryland, 2011. http://cissmdev.devcloud.acquia-ites.com/sites/default/files/papers/first_do_no_harm_destler.pdf. Accessed on October 7, 2018.
37. Ibid.
38. Froman, Ambassador Michael, "Trade, Growth, and Jobs: US Trade Policy in the Obama Administration," Washington International Trade Associate (WITA), February 28, 2017. http://americastradepolicy.com/trade-growth-and-jobs-u-s-trade-policy-in-the-obama-administration/#.WZjMmIWcHIU. Accessed on October 7, 2018.
39. Ibid.
40. Ibid.
41. Ibid.
42. Ibid.
43. Barfield, Claude and Levy, Philip I., "In Search of an Obama Trade Policy," American Enterprise Institute (AEI) August 5, 2009. https://www.aei.org/publication/in-search-of-an-obama-trade-policy/. Accessed on October 7, 2018.
44. Bergsten, "Foreign Economic Policy for the Next President."
45. Ibid.
46. Restussia, Andrew and Cook, Nancy, "Trump's Trade Plan Sets Up Global Clash Over 'America First' Strategy," *Politico*, June 30, 2017. http://www.politico.com/story/2017/06/30/trump-america-first-trade-plan-clash-240123. Accessed on October 7, 2018.
47. Hendrickson, "The Roots of Trump's Economic Policy."
48. Ibid.
49. Ibid.
50. Ibid.
51. Ibid.
52. Ibid.
53. Ibid.
54. Ibid.
55. Ibid.
56. Read Donald Trump's Speech on Trade, *Time*, June 28, 2016. http://time.com/4386335/donald-trump-trade-speech-transcript/. Accessed on October 8, 2018.
57. O'Driscoll Jr., Gerald P. and Cobb, Tyrus W., "Trump on US Foreign and Economic Policy," *CATO Institute*, May 1, 2016. https://www.cato.org/publications/commentary/trump-us-foreign-economic-policy. Accessed on October 8, 2018.
58. Ibid.
59. Ibid.
60. Donald Trump's Speech on Trade, *Time*, June 28, 2016.
61. Ibid.
62. Kahl and Brands, "Trump's Grand Strategic Train Wreck."
63. Ibid.

64. Ibid.
65. Restussia and Cook, "Trump's Trade Plan Sets Up Global Clash Over 'America First' Strategy."
66. Ibid.
67. McMaster, H. R. and Cohn, Gary D., "America First Doesn't Mean America Alone," *Wall Street Journal*, May 30, 2017. https://www.wsj.com/articles/america-first-doesnt-mean-america-alone-1496187426. Accessed on October 8, 2018.
68. Haynes, Danielle, "Trump Puts 'America First' in Manufacturing, Trade Speech," UPI.com, July 17, 2017. https://www.upi.com/Trump-puts-America-first-in-manufacturing-trade-speech/2081500317847/. Accessed on October 8, 2018.
69. Ibid.
70. Ibid.
71. Wilkinson, Tracy, "Trump's 'America First' Policy Changes US Role on World Stage," *LA Times*, June 2, 2017. http://www.latimes.com/nation/la-fg-trump-assess-20170602-story.html. Accessed on October 8, 2018.
72. Ibid.
73. Ibid.
74. Diamond, Jeremy, "Trump Slams Globalization, Promises to Upend Economic Status Quo," *CNN*, June 28, 2016. http://www.cnn.com/2016/06/28/politics/donald-trump-speech-pennsylvania-economy/index.html. Accessed on October 8, 2018.
75. Donald Trump's Speech on Trade, *Time*, June 28, 2016.
76. Ibid.
77. Ibid.
78. Ibid.
79. Bergsten, "Foreign Economic Policy for the Next President."
80. Ibid.
81. Ibid.
82. Ibid.
83. Ibid.
84. Ibid.
85. Trade Deals That Work for All Americans. The White House, Donald J. Trump. https://www.whitehouse.gov/trade-deals-working-all-americans. Accessed on October 9, 2018.
86. Ibid.
87. Ibid.
88. President Donald J. Trump's Six Months of America First. White House, Office of the Press Secretary. July 17, 2017. https://www.whitehouse.gov/the-press-office/2017/07/20/president-donald-j-trumps-six-months-america-first. Accessed on October 9, 2018.
89. Ibid.
90. Ibid.
91. Ibid.
92. Ibid.
93. Ibid.
94. Woodward, Bob, *Fear: Trump in the White House* (New York: Simon and Schuster, 2018), p. *xx*.
95. Ibid.
96. Ibid., *xix*.
97. Ibid.
98. Gillespie, Patrick, "Trump Administration Seeks to Renegotiate South Korean Trade Deal," *CNN Money*, July 13, 2017. http://money.cnn.com/2017/07/12/news/economy/trump-renegotiate-trade-deal-south-korea/index.html. Accessed on October 9, 2018.
99. Brunstrum, David and Lambert, Lisa, "Trump Renegotiating 'Rough' US Trade Deal with South Korea," *Fox Business*, June 30, 2017. http://www.foxbusiness.com/politics/2017/06/30/trump-renegotiating-rough-us-trade-deal-with-south-korea.html. Accessed on October 9, 2018.
100. Gillespie, "Trump Administration Seeks to Renegotiate South Korean Trade Deal."

101. Lee, Youkyung, Tweed, David and Leonard, Jenny, "Trump Clinches His First Trade Deal With Revamped South Korea Pact," *Bloomberg News*, September 24, 2018. https://www.bloomberg.com/news/articles/2018-09-24/trump-clinches-his-first-trade-deal-in-revamped-south-korea-pact. Accessed on October 9, 2018.

102. Ibid.

103. USTR Releases NAFTA Negotiation Objectives. Office of the US Special Trade Representative Executive Office of the President. Washington, DC. July 2017. https://ustr.gov/about-us/policy-offices/press-office/press-releases/2017/july/ustr-releases-nafta-negotiating. Accessed on October 9, 2018.

104. Ibid.

105. Ibid.

106. Chase-Lubitz, Jesse, "NAFTA Talks Off to a Rocky Start," *Foreign Policy*, August 16, 2017. http://foreignpolicy.com/2017/08/16/nafta-talks-off-to-a-rocky-start/?utmsource=Sailthru&utmmedium=email&utm_campaign=edpix%208-16&utm_term=%2AEditors%20Picks. Accessed on October 9, 2018.

107. Ibid.

108. Ibid.

109. Higgins, Sean, "US, Mexico and Canada, Conclude 2nd Round of NAFTA Talks," *Washington Examiner*, September 5, 2017. http://www.washingtonexaminer.com/us-mexico-canada-conclude-2nd-round-of-nafta-talks/article/2633462. Accessed on October 9, 2018.

110. Baker, Peter, "Trump Signs New Trade Deal with Canada and Mexico After Bitter Negotiations," *New York Times*, November 30, 2018. https://www.nytimes.com/2018/11/30/world/americas/trump-trudeau-canada-mexico.html. Accessed on October 9, 2018.

111. Ibid.

112. Nakashima, Ellen and Lynch, David, "US Charges Chinese Hackers in Alleged Theft of Vast Trove Confidential Data in 12 Countries," *Washington Post*, December 21, 2018. https://www.washingtonpost.com/world/national-security/us-and-more-than-a-dozen-allies-to-condemn-china-for-economic-espionage/2018/21/20/cdf0338-0455-11e9-b5df-5d387411ac36-story.html. Accessed on October 9, 2018.

113. Ahmed and Bick, "Trump's National Security Strategy: A New Brand of Mercantilism?"

114. Wolfe, Richard, "How Trump's Foreign Policy Threatens to Make America Weak Again," *The Guardian*, July 2, 2017. https://www.theguardian.com/us-news/2017/jul/02/donald-trump-foreign-policy-diplomacy. Accessed on October 9, 2018.

115. Paulson, John, "Trump and the Economy," *Foreign Affairs*, March/April 2017. https://www.foreignaffairs.com/articles/united-states/2017-02-13/trump-and-economy. Accessed on October 9, 2018.

116. Ibid.

Chapter Three

The Revision

Trump and the War on Terrorism

Throughout the presidential campaign Donald Trump made a host of statements that were anathema to Democratic and Republican positions on how to fight terrorism. For example, Trump was critical of President Bush's and President Obama's "protracted and ineffective American engagement in the Middle East."[1] In another major shift from the bipartisan approach to terrorism, Trump asserted, "I would not allow people to come in from terrorist nations. I would do extreme vetting."[2] Trump warned "extreme vetting" would be a high priority in his administration. On Obama's anti-ISIS strategy, Trump viewed the president's approach as ineffectual and disastrous. He was highly critical of President Obama's fondness of announcing US military options to the enemy. On this point, Trump warned, "If I win, I don't want to broadcast to the enemy exactly what my plan is."[3]

As president, Trump increased US combat fire power in Iraq and Syria to confront the Islamic State. The objective, said Trump, is to "soundly and quickly defeating ISIS."[4] In Yemen, President Trump approved a highly controversial SEAL Team-led raid and ordered over 30 airstrikes against Al Qaeda in the Arabian Peninsula (AQAP) within the opening months of the administration. At issue, what is President Trump's strategy to defeat ISIS? How does Trump propose to deal with Al Qaeda Central and their affiliates? How would Trump confront the Taliban in Afghanistan? The answer to these questions is critical if we are to comprehend and assess President Trump's quest to revise the war on terrorism.

TRUMP'S CAMPAIGN STATEMENTS ON TERRORISM

Throughout the 2016 presidential campaign, candidate Trump provided a host of campaign statements on terrorism. Speaking about ISIS and the internet, during the fifth Republican debate on December 15, 2015, Trump offered this comment: "ISIS is using the Internet better than we are using the Internet. What I wanted to do is . . . get our brilliant people from Silicon Valley and other places and figure out a way that ISIS cannot do what they're doing."[5]

In a controversial statement, Trump then expressed why the Islamic States' use of cyberspace had to be halted. According to Trump, "I don't want them using our Internet to take our young, impressionable youth and watching the media talking about how they're masterminds—these are masterminds."[6] In typical Trumpian rhetoric, the candidate boasted about using the cyberspace instrument to locate the terror network: "We should be able to penetrate the Internet and find out exactly where ISIS is and everything about ISIS. And we can do that if we use our good people."[7] In what was advertised as a major foreign policy address, speaking to an audience on April 27, 2016 in Washington, DC, Trump's speech highlighted the candidates' position on a range of issues from America First, the need to rebuild the US military, American relations with Russia and China, and global trade. The centerpiece of the address focused on the Islamic State.

On the Islamic State, Trump made it clear the transnational terror group would become a high priority in his administration. On dealing with the Islamic State, Trump was prepared to work with those states that have been previously threatened by ISIS.[8] There is an important caveat associated with Trump's view of the anti-ISIS coalition. All states participating in the coalition must increase their share of involvement.[9] Thus, previous states (and additional states) that participated in coalition must be prepared to shoulder their load of responsibility. Trump's statement to coalition members is consistent in many ways with NATO's requirement to do more against Islamic terrorism.

The address shifted to radical Islam and immigration. In perhaps the most forceful aspect of the address, Trump reminded allies in the Middle East and North Africa that transnational terrorism is occurring within their regions and they must work a deal with the threat of radical Islam within their borders.[10] The candidate warned every effort must be made to increase border security to end the threat. The candidate made it clear that if elected he was prepared to prevent extremism through the introduction of tough immigration policies. Trump recognized that his rhetoric did have an ultimate objective: to prevent "the next San Bernardino," or perhaps another September 11, 2001. Put another way, the United States had to be more vigilant in the protection of the homeland.[11]

On how he would deal with the threat posed by ISIS, Trump asserted, "Their days are numbered."[12] Trump promised that he would be vigilant and unpredictable, traits he believed President Obama lacked. The former president exposed "everything" said Trump. In the view of the candidate Obama even held a press conference to announce troop movements. He then returned to a familiar theme: Trump promised ISIS's tenure would end abruptly.[13]

In a statement delivered on August 2, 2016 that reiterated Trump's promise to defeat the Islamic State in Libya, and one which simultaneously criticized his Democratic opponent Hillary Clinton, the candidate forcefully argued, "We have no choice but to bomb them. They [ISIS] have taken over Libya. That was another one of Hillary Clinton's duties—they have taken over Libya. . . . We have to bomb them. . . . I would do what you have to do to get rid of ISIS."[14]

Later in the month, in a subsequent address on August 15, 2016, Trump delivered one of his most detailed assessments of the threat posed by the Islamic State. In the speech, the candidate stated:

> Overseas, ISIS has carried out one unthinkable atrocity after another. Children slaughtered, girls sold into slavery, men and women burned alive. Crucifixions, beheadings and drownings. Ethnic minorities [are] targeted for mass execution. Holy sites desecrated. Christians driven from their homes and hunted for extermination. ISIS rounding-up what it calls the "nation of the cross" in a campaign of genocide. We cannot let this evil continue. Nor can we let the hateful ideology of Radical Islam . . . reside or spread within our own countries. We will defeat Radical Islamic Terrorism, just as we have defeated every threat we have faced in every age before. But we will not defeat it with closed eyes, or silenced voices.[15]

Trump incessantly focused on the need to target the ideology of the Islamic State. There is a major problem with the campaign rhetoric. Trump repeatedly talked about defeating the terror group by targeting their caliphate. During his presidency, Trump would learn that ending the caliphate does not equate to defeating the ideology of the Islamic State.

In addition, the speech criticized President Obama's anti-ISIS approach and that of Clinton's. As articulated by Trump, "Anyone who cannot name our enemy, is not fit to lead this country. Anyone who cannot condemn the hatred, oppression and violence of Radical Islam lacks the moral clarity to serve as our President. . . . What have the decisions of Obama-Clinton produced?"[16] The result of these decisions said Trump is chaos, loss of American lives, and the expansion of the Islamic State. In Libya, the US ambassador and three other Americans perished in an assault on our consulate and CIA base. In time, Trump and his foreign policy advisors surmised ISIS was able to establish a base in that country to conduct operations. The Obama administration's failure to confront ISIS during its infancy permitted the terror group to establish control over large areas of territory in Syria. Over time, the Islamic State established sanctuaries in over thirty countries. In Trump's view, the collective impact of Obama-Clinton decision making produced chaos in the region. The Obama-Clinton foreign policy set the stage for ISIS and their subsequent expansion in the region and around the world. Second, the Obama-Clinton polices unleashed instability in an already unstable region, and the administration's policies increased the regional influence of Iran.[17]

The speech additionally contained statements about how Trump would address the threat should he become president. According to Trump, "If I become President, the era of nation-building will be ended. Our new approach, which must be shared by both parties in America, by our allies overseas, and by our friends in the Middle East, must be to halt the spread of Radical Islam."[18] Trump then issued this statement, one that in hindsight would become a pivotal component of his strategy:

> As President, I will call for an international conference focused on this goal. We will work side-by-side with our friends in the Middle East. . . . We will partner with King Abdullah of Jordan, and President Sisi of Egypt, and all others who recognize this ideology of death that must be extinguished. We will also work closely with NATO on this new mission. I also believe that we could find common ground with Russia in the fight against ISIS. My Administration will aggressively pursue joint and coalition military operations to crush and destroy ISIS, international cooperation to cutoff their funding, expanded intelligence sharing, and cyberwarfare to disrupt and disable their propaganda and recruiting.[19]

During the inaugural *NBC News* Commander-in-Chief Forum on September 7, 2016, Clinton and Trump were invited to address questions on military issues, national security, and veteran's affairs. In a response to a question on the threat posed by the Islamic State, Trump issued this response:

> I mean, part of the problem that we've had is we go in, we defeat somebody, and then we don't know what we're doing after that. We lose it, . . . you look at Iraq, what happened, how badly that was handled. And then when President Obama took over it . . . was actually somewhat stable. . . . He said when we go out [that is when] . . . ISIS was formed. This was a terrible decision. Then the candidate issued this problematic response: I've always said, [we] shouldn't be there, but if we're going to get out, take the oil. If we would have taken the oil, you wouldn't have ISIS, because ISIS formed with the power and the wealth of that oil.[20]

Once again, the candidate addressed a question about his plan to defeat the Islamic State. Trump responded to a query by Matt Lauer, the moderator of the forum, with this statement: "I have a plan. . . . If I win, I don't want to broadcast to the enemy exactly what my plan is. . . . And let me tell you, if I like maybe a combination of my plan and the generals' plan, or the generals' plan, if I like their plan"[21] it would be implemented.

Later that same day, during a speech at the Union League of Philadelphia, the candidate stated, "In a Trump administration, our actions in the Middle East will be tempered by realism. The current strategy of toppling regimes, with no plan for what to do the day after, only produces power vacuums that are filled by terrorists."[22] Trump then stated his "guiding objectives" in the region would be based on "Gradual reform" and "not sudden and radical change."[23] Trump then promised in his administration to "work with any country that shares our goal of destroying ISIS and defeating radical Islamic terrorism, and form new friendships and partnerships based on this mission."[24]

The key portion of the speech addressed when Trump planned to unveil his plan. In the words of Trump: "Immediately after taking office, I will ask my generals to present to me a plan within 30 days to defeat and destroy ISIS. This will require military warfare, but also cyber warfare, financial warfare, and ideological warfare—as I laid out in my speech on defeating Radical Islamic terrorism several weeks ago."[25]

One of the major problems associated with Trump's campaign pronouncements on terrorism is that he spent too little time addressing Al Qaeda and their affiliates. In addition, Trump never revealed a detailed plan about how he would deal with the renowned and still dangerous transnational terror organization. This issue is something the media did not address in the questioning of the candidates, Republican or Democrat, during the party debates and later during the general election.

TRUMP DISCARDS OBAMA'S COUNTERTERRORISM APPROACH

Throughout the 2016 presidential campaign, the issue of importance for the campaign concerned Donald Trump's plan to defeat the Islamic State. Another issue that was equally significant but escaped media scrutiny is how Trump or Clinton would respond to transnational terrorism after Obama? Within the US foreign policy establishment, it was understood about the need to debate how the candidates would address the threat posed by the Islamic State, but there was a larger issue that awaited Clinton and Trump. The foreign policy establishment recognized the next president must be prepared to deal with a resurgent Al Qaeda Central, a still formidable Al Qaeda in the Arabian Peninsula (AQAP), Al Nusra Front (Al Qaeda in Syria), Boko Haram, Al Shabaab, and other affiliates of the late Osama bin Laden's transnational empire. In short, neither candidate, Trump or Clinton were forced to address this substantial issue. These issues, however, represent something President Trump is now confronting.

In the wake of presidential campaigns, incoming US presidential administrations—George W. Bush through President Barack Obama—were often given advice from Think-Tanks on how to manage a problem in US foreign policy. It is this advice, often unsolicited, that is provided to assist an incoming administration. Across Washington, DC, if these places of advanced learning recognized the creation of a counterterrorism strategy for dealing with the Islamic State, Al Qaeda, other like-minded radical terrorist groups would emerge as one of the new administration's most important instruments of foreign policy.

Months into the Trump administration, the International Crisis Group (ICG) is one of several organizations that offered advice to the president. The ICG released a report that endeavored an "executive summary" which detailed the evolving terrorist threat and the inherited problems that remained after the Obama era concluded.

> In pledging to destroy the Islamic State (ISIS), US President Donald J. Trump looks set to make counterterrorism a centerpiece of his foreign policy. His administration's determination against groups that plot to kill Americans is understandable, but it should be careful when fighting jihadists not to play into their hands. . . . Most importantly, aggressive counterterrorism operations should not inadvertently fuel other conflicts and deepen the disorder that both ISIS and al Qaeda exploit. The new US administration has inherited military campaigns that are eating deep into ISIS's self-proclaimed caliphate. . . . ISIS is in retreat, its brand diminished. For many adherents, its allure was its territorial expansion; with that gone, its leaders are struggling to redefine success. Al Qaeda could prove harder to suppress. Its affiliates fight across numerous war zones in coalitions with other armed groups, its operatives are embedded in local militias, and it shows more pragmatic adaptability to local conditions.[26]

Having provided the issues in the realm of terrorism that would impact the Trump administration, the ICG provided recommendations (in the form of things to avoid) in dealing with radical Islamic terrorism. As stated in their report, "So long as wars continue and chaos persists, jihadism will thrive, whatever ISIS's immediate fate. . . . The new administration should avoid"[27] the following: (1) "angering communities, (2) aggravating other fronts, and (3) defining the enemy too broadly."[28]

The ICG concluded that "angering communities" is a reference to the possibility of increased civilian casualties following the anticipated Trump administration's stepped-up tempo of operations against the Islamic State. In a war "for the hearts and minds" of the local population, the Trump administration must avoid unnecessary collateral damage. This advice is essential in the objective to retake Raqqa or in Yemen. Thus, "Loosening rules and oversight designed to protect civilians, as has been suggested, would be a mistake."[29]

The "aggravation of other fronts" argues that as the Trump administration's use of local forces (the Kurdish fighters) to retake territory from the Islamic State in Syria, this support will increase the likelihood of a response by the government of Turkey against what they view as a terrorist threat. Additionally, Syrian government forces, with support from Russia or from Iran (or their Hezbollah allies) could also target US-backed Kurdish fighters. There is another important scenario: "support for Gulf allies should not mean a blank check for the Saudi-led Yemen campaign, which—if wrongly prosecuted—would play further into al Qaeda's hands."[30]

If the Trump administration "defines the threat" of the Islamic State too broadly it could lead to too much attention on this terror group and not enough focus on other groups, whether in the form of Boko Haram, Al Shabab, or AQAP. There is another danger: too much focus on ending the Islamic States' caliphate could mean less focus on the terror groups' sanctuaries elsewhere around the world. These recommendations are significant, but the absence of a counterterrorism strategy is far more problematic. This begs a question, what is President Trump's approach to terrorism?

Over the course of the first year-plus of the administration, President Trump did not implement a counterterrorism strategy. Though there is no formal presidential address or a speech by the secretary of defense or any other official for that matter, there is evidence of components that provide a sense of President Trump's approach. Those components include the following: (1) the administration will pursue ideology as an instrument to defeat radical Islamic terrorism; (2) make use of an international conference to enlist Muslim states to work to distinguish radical Islamic ideology and increase the participation of these countries to actively engage in an alliance to defeat the Islamic State and other transnational terrorist groups; (3) changes in US immigration policy to assist in the defeat of terrorism in the homeland; (4) a reliance (and perhaps and expansion) on the counterterrorism infrastructure developed during the administration of George W. Bush; (5) the decision to target the Islamic State and to include Al Qaeda and their affiliates in the administration's approach; (6) create a new strategy in Afghanistan; and (7) following the review of "the Pentagon's findings" that resulted in two significant presidential changes, the Pentagon used the modifications to assist in the implementation of President Trump's approach to defeat radical Islamic terrorism. Those decisions include (a) "delegated authority to the right level to aggressively in a timely manner move against enemy vulnerabilities"[31] and (b) "directed a tactical shift from shoving ISIS out of safe locations in an attrition fight to surrounding the enemy in their strongholds so we can annihilate ISIS (The impact of these decisions will be discussed later in the chapter.)."[32]

An early indication of Trump's approach on how he would deal with terrorism is found in his August 15, 2016 address. In that address Trump spoke of "how to Make America Safe Again."[33] In the opening portion of the address, and consistent with the candidates' anti-establishment foreign policy, Trump used the speech to indicate that if he assumed the White House he was prepared to shift away from his predecessors' approach. As stated in the address, Trump argued, "In the 20th Century, the United States defeated Fascism, Nazism, and Communism. Now, a different threat challenges our world: Radical Islamic Terrorism."[34] Thus, Trump is prepared to add ideology as a central feature of his war with Radical Islamic Terrorism.

On this point, Masood Farivar, a former journalist and former chief of the Afghanistan Service at the Voice of America (VOA) in Washington, DC, provided clarity of Trump's new path: "In its emphasis on ideology," the president's war on terrorism "puts him at odds with his two immediate predecessors."[35] The previous two presidents, Bush and Obama, "avoided casting the war on terror in ideological terms for fear of alienating Muslim allies."[36] Trump has boldly "stressed . . . the need to counter [the Islamic State] ideologically."[37]

To validate the significance of ideology in defeating terrorism, Trump made this statement: "Containing the spread of radical Islam must be a major foreign policy goal of the United States. Events may require the use of military force. But it's also a philosophical struggle, like our long struggle in the Cold War."[38]

Blaise Misztal, the Director of the Bipartisan Policy Center in Washington, argued, "I think by seeing the threat as an ideological one, President Trump will see the problem as not just stopping attacks but stopping the spread of that ideology and stopping the potential for further radicalization."[39] Trump's address provided validation of this point: "We will defeat Radical Islamic Terrorism, just as we have defeated every threat we have faced in every age before. . . . To defeat Islamic terrorism, we must also speak out forcefully against a hateful ideology that provides the breeding ground for violence and terrorism to grow."[40] This statement is consistent with what Trump referred to as "a new approach."[41]

To further advance the new approach, Trump argued, once in office he would implement a new strategy that would require increased cooperation and shared responsibilities between the United States and its allies in MENA and beyond to stop the spread of radical Islam.[42] Nation-building is something President Bush engaged in Afghanistan and Iraq. In the case of President Obama, he continued nation-building in Afghanistan, but in the second term he shifted toward a policy of containing the Taliban. Trump stressed the need to avoid nation-building.

Next Trump informed the world about the second component of his approach. In the words of Trump, "As President, I will call for an international conference focused on" confronting the Islamic State and radical Islam. He spoke of partnering with Saudi Arabia, Egypt, and "others who recognize this ideology of death that must be extinguished."[43] President Trump implemented this component during his first foreign trip to Saudi Arabia where the US leader spoke before an audience of 55 Muslim countries in May of 2017.

A corollary aspect called for an increased role for NATO to further act as instrument of counterterrorism to defeat ISIS. In the address, Trump stated, "We will also work closely with NATO on this new mission."[44] This is an important statement because previously Trump claimed "NATO was obsolete" due to the failure to "adequately" confront terrorism.[45] He subsequently changed course, announcing, "since my comments they have changed their policy and now have a new division focused on terror threats."[46] President Trump implemented this aspect of his campaign plan during the third phase of the foreign trip which included a stopover trip to NATO headquarters in Brussels. It is during this trip that NATO members agreed to formally join the anti-Islamic State coalition.[47]

Trump eluded to another corollary component of the approach when he argued, it may be possible to partner with Russia to defeat the Islamic State.[48] Given Russia's behavior in the Ukraine, the support for the regime of Bashar al-Assad in Syria, the continuing political fallout over Russian efforts to meddle in the 2016 presidential campaign, the investigations into the allegations that Trump campaign officials colluded with Russian intelligence have collectively delayed any efforts to include Moscow as a coalition partner in the war on terrorism.

The speech represented an effort by Trump to clarify that he intended to create a more robust coalition where member states are prepared to take a more decisive role to defeat the Islamic State.[49] Trump argued throughout the campaign and the opening year of his administration that changes in US immigration policy is essential in defeating radical Islamic terrorist efforts to foment unrest and to launch terrorist attacks inside the homeland. In the address, Trump provided details of this component of the plan. Trump warned his administration was prepared to implement strict guidelines that would only "admit into this country those who share our values and respect our people."[50]

Later in the address, Trump stated, "To put these new procedures in place, we will have to temporarily suspend immigration from some of the most dangerous and volatile regions of the world that have a history of exporting terrorism."[51] Despite the campaign rhetoric, and the implementation of two executive orders within the opening months of the Trump presidency, this component of the plan suffered several defeats in the lower courts. Ultimately, the president's executive order was upheld by the Supreme Court in a 5-4 decision on June 26, 2018.

Based on a review of the Pentagon's early counterterrorism operations, it is clear that there are components of Trump's approach that will rely heavily on the counterterrorism infrastructure that assumed prominence during the post-9/11 period under President Bush.[52] For example, while President Obama relied on Central Command (CENTCOM) and Special Operations Command (SOCOM), among current and retired senior military leaders, there is the view that if the United States is to make substantial progress against radical Islamic terrorism, then the tempo of operations and the spread of those operations must target ISIS, Al Qaeda, and other transnational terrorist sanctuaries around the world.

In a speech delivered before an audience of senior military officials at MacDill Air Force Base in Tampa, Florida on February 6, 2017, President Trump observed, "Central Command and . . . [Special] Operations Command are at the very center of our fight against radical Islamic terrorism."[53] Trump stressed the service and commitment of the forces associated with commands, and the speech identified that the forces participating in these organizations will be called upon to expand their operations to meet the current threats.

Trump made the Islamic State the central focus of his plans to alter how the country should deal with terrorism during the campaign, and he promised that if he were elected president, he would address this threat. Once in office, while there is significant attention on ISIS, after huddling with senior foreign policy advisors, President Trump made a prudent decision to include Al Qaeda and their affiliates as a major focus of his plan to revamp the American approach to dealing with radical Islamic terrorism.

To understand the significance of the decision to include Al Qaeda and the affiliates in the plan, it is important to note that President Obama stated that they are "on the run,"[54] "decimated,"[55] and "on their heels."[56] The reality is that Al Qaeda is back and is poised to reclaim leadership of the global jihadist movement.

To underscore the threat, Thomas Joscelyn, a terrorist expert employed at the Foundation for Defense of Democracies, in testimony before the Senate Foreign Committee, noted "One of the common [themes] that was repeated was that ISIS was concerned with controlling territory, whereas al Qaeda is not."[57] Joscelyn made this important additional statement: "This is false. Al Qaeda has a different strategy. . . . They are building Islamic emirates [in this context territory ruled by the terrorist group] . . . in several countries, including Yemen."[58]

In a comparison to the threat posed by ISIS and Al Qaeda, in testimony before the House Homeland Security subcommittee, terrorism expert Geoff Porter asserted, "While the Islamic State is burning very brightly, it's also burning very quickly. . . . And Al Qaeda has employed a more conservative, longer-term strategy and is likely to be more enduring of an organization than the Islamic State will be."[59]

Equally troubling, AQAP in Yemen and Al Shabaab in Somalia, Al Qaeda in the Islamic Maghreb (AQIM) and Ansar al Shariah in North Africa, and other resurgent groups are causing significant instability. To confront these threats, the Pentagon made it clear it intends to address these threats. The Obama administration haphazardly launched drone strikes or infrequent special operation raids aimed at eliminating high value targets. The Trump administration will employ drone strikes and special operations raids, but the objective is to invest in a more sustained strategy which targets Al Qaeda and their affiliates with the objective of eliminating the leadership, the support structures, and overtime, the sanctuary itself. This represents a new component and will require time to implement and assess. The sustained air strikes against (over one hundred) AQAP and the "targeting [of] a cluster of buildings in central Marib province that were thought to be used as a base of operations and to plan attacks abroad"[60] that are under the control of Al Qaeda Central in Yemen demonstrate the Trump administration's seriousness in rolling back a period of terrorist expansion and extended terrorist-related violence in the country.

TRUMP'S PLAN FOR ISIS

President Trump's anti-Islamic State strategy is shrouded in secrecy. For many, this is hardly a new revelation. Throughout the presidential campaign, Trump railed against President Obama for consistently broadcasting his decisions, actions, and military moves against ISIS. In typical Trumpian fashion, he overstated the former president's actions. That said, the Obama administration's advertisement of the initial plans to retake Mosul in 2015 and the incessant announcement of the dispatch of US troops to Iraq proved unnerving to Trump. The candidate, as did many senior military leaders in the Pentagon, believed such declarations allowed ISIS an opportunity to adjust to US and coalition tactics. Trump promised that he would not follow the Obama pattern. This explains the secrecy surrounding Trump's anti-ISIS plan. Well into his presidency, there are indications the anti-ISIS plan is being implemented. Thus far, Trump succeeded in implementing his campaign rhetoric which up to this point emerged as a critical feature of the administration's plan to confront the Islamic State. With the secrecy surrounding Trump's plan, is there any available evidence to indicate the existence of the president's strategy?

During the transition period, a crucial decision was made. At the time, senior foreign policy advisors thought it prudent to forego a review of President Obama's anti-ISIS strategy. Oddly, there was a similar sentiment within the Pentagon. Thus, the Trump administration made the decision to jettison President Obama's ISIS strategy. There was a salient problem: the secretary of defense designated James Mattis had not yet been confirmed by the Senate. Still, President Trump and Mattis were in accord that it was important to quickly move on from the Obama-era way of fighting the war against ISIS. A source in the Pentagon informed the author that long before his confirmation Mattis had "sketched" a preliminary plan of action.[61] It is unclear if he had shared that plan of action with Chairman of Joint Chiefs of Staff General James Dunford. Given that Dunford and Mattis are both from the same military service (they are both Marines) it is likely that there were discussions between the two about the viability of the secretary's plan.

Following Mattis's Senate confirmation on January 20, 2017, and following a series of conversations over several days with the senior military officials within the Pentagon, discussions with Joseph L. Votel, the commanding general of Central Command, and Lieutenant General Sean MacFarland, the commander of the Combined Joint Task Force-Operation Inherent Resolve (OIR), the secretary of defense moved swiftly to finalize the details of the long-awaited Pentagon-mandated plan of action to defeat the Islamic State. After meeting the approval of senior military leaders, Secretary of Defense Mattis formally delivered the plan to the White House.

On January 28, 2017, President Trump issued a presidential memorandum titled "Plan to Defeat the Islamic State of Iraq and Syria."[62] The memorandum directed the Secretary of Defense and other senior Pentagon officials "to develop and subsequently implement a strategy for defeating ISIS."[63] The memorandum is divided into multiple sections. These sections comprise what the administration believed constituted a comprehensive plan of action. The components of the plan include the following. Section 1 of the National Security Memorandum 3, which details that the "Policy" articulates that "It is the policy of the United States that ISIS be defeated."[64] "Policy Coordination" which is found in Section 2 observes that "policy coordination, guidance, dispute resolution, and periodic in-progress reviews . . . be provided through the interagency process."[65] The other major component or Section 3 (better known as "Plan to Defeat ISIS") requires Secretary Mattis to immediately develop "a new plan to defeat ISIS."[66] The secretary must submit a preliminary draft to the president within 30 days.

The final plan consisted of several components: "(a) a new more 'comprehensive strategy' to defeat ISIS; (b) changes to rules of engagement on the 'use of force against ISIS'; (c) the inclusion of the utilization of public diplomacy and cyberspace 'to isolate and delegitimize ISIS and their ideology'; (d) identify new coalition partners in the fight against ISIS; (e) creation of means to restrict financial support to ISIS; and (f) a provide an internal administration approach to 'robustly fund the [anti-ISIS] Plan.'"[67] The memorandum received high praise, particularly because it represented a clear indication that President Trump was prepared to dramatically depart from President Obama's anti-ISIS strategy.

In most cases, there were those that did not necessarily endorse the plan but understood the need to shift away from President Obama's strategy and the "political consequences." In one example, in the words of Andrew Exum, a former Obama administration official that served in the Pentagon, stated, "Donald Trump is going to defeat the Islamic State, and Americans need to be fine with that. . . . But the fall of the Islamic State is going to happen, and . . . Trump will take credit for the Islamic State's defeat."[68]

That said, the initial Trump plan is not without its critics. There are those that argued the plan is too vague. Other critics of the plan are far more detailed in their criticism. For example, Anthony H. Cordesman, a leading defense expert from the Center for Strategic and International Studies, offered this negative evaluation: "The key problem is that the Memorandum is poorly worded, sets the wrong goals, and does so out of context. ISIS is only one part of the threat posed by Islamic extremism, and only one of many threats and problems that affect US interests in the Middle East."[69]

Irrespective of the criticism, Secretary Mattis pressed forward and delivered the classified plan to President Trump in late February of 2017. As anticipated, neither the Pentagon nor the White House provided any specific details of the plan. However, in a carefully orchestrated set of statements, the Pentagon did release what some believe are "nondescript aspects" of the plan.

On the plan, Pentagon spokesman, Navy Captain Jeff Davis, stated, "It is a plan to rapidly defeat ISIS."[70] Davis also added "This is really a framework for broader discussion."[71] Davis intimated the plan is still evolving. Specifically, Davis noted, "It's not a 'check-the-block, pick A or B or C' kind of a plan. This is a broad plan. It is global. It is not just military. It is not just Iraq/Syria."[72] In the words of Robert Burns and Lolita C. Baldor, writers for the Military.com, "the "emerging strategy will target not just Islamic State militants but also Al Qaeda and other extremist organizations, whose goal is to attack the United States."[73]

The plan contained other significant features. For example, "Along with the potential realignment of alliances, for the first time an option [existed] to deploy a significant number of US ground forces into Syria. While US military officials are apparently split on the decision, one of the DoD's options details engaging US forces 'around Raqqa to help push ISIS fighters out.'"[74] According to Hal Brands, a senior fellow at the Center for Strategic and Budgetary Assessments, such a plan might involve the deployment of "4,000 to 5,000 US troops . . . to help accelerate operations around Raqqa."[75]

Decision making on how to respond to the threat posed by the Islamic State is another area of change. During the Obama presidency the military had less access to the president, and during much of the conflict with the

Islamic State, beyond the secretary of defense, many of the decisions were dominated by officials from the national security council.

Senior military leaders enjoyed greater involvement in the decision-making process. From the beginning of the administration, the Pentagon offered President Trump a wealth of military options.[76] In addition, "DoD's planning cycle broke new ground" and the Pentagon's proposals to confront ISIS were often developed "in close coordination with interagency partners" which included officials from State, Treasury, and the intelligence community.[77]

During a Pentagon Press conference on May 19, 2017, Defense Secretary Mattis stated that President Trump "delegated authority to the right level to aggressively and in a timely manner move against enemy vulnerabilities."[78] Mattis acknowledged the plan "directed a tactical shift from shoving ISIS out of safe locations in an attrition fight to surrounding the enemy in their strongholds so we can annihilate ISIS."[79] There is another important component of the strategy, according to Mattis: "The intent of the strategy is to prevent the return home of escaped foreign fighters. . . . We don't simply transplant this problem from one place to another. . . . This threat is a long-term threat."[80]

Amazingly, there are some individuals that assert the anti-ISIS strategy remains the same. As stated by Kevin Bacon and Marcus Weisgerber, national security reporters for *Defense One*, "What's new isn't the strategy—the US is still executing the Obama-era 'by, with, through' approach in which direct assaults are conducted by local partner forces."[81] Mattis quickly dismissed this criticism by acknowledging, "The operational and tactical difference has been clear."[82]

There is another major difference between Obama and Trump approaches. That contrast is identified in the decline in the restrictions on the battlefield. On this point Mattis and Chairman of Joint Chiefs of Staff, General Joseph Dunford, "characterized ISIS as a shadow of its former self and doomed to lose all of its territory. They credited looser restrictions on generals and a shift to surround-and-annihilate tactics."[83]

On the decline in restrictions and decision making, Mattis noted "He [President Trump] made the decision. We took the decision and executed it for an accelerated campaign. . . . No longer will we have slow decision cycles because Washington, DC, has to authorize tactical movements on the ground."[84] Mattis made this additional statement, "Two significant changes resulted from President Trump's review of our findings. First, he delegated authority to the right level to aggressively and in a timely manner move against enemy vulnerabilities. Secondly, he 'directed a tactical shift' [emphasis added]: surround ISIS fighters, instead of just pushing them out of a given territory."[85] In the final analysis, Trump's strategy permitted coalition forces "to annihilate" ISIS fighters on the battlefield.

A cottage industry quickly developed from the "resistance" and never-Trumpers which continued to argued Trump's anti-ISIS plan provided no major difference from Obama's approach. Critics point to the continuing use of "by, with, and through" as an indication the Obama strategy is still in existence. This point is correct. However, there are a host of indicators that validate that there have been substantial changes in the strategy. On the battlefield, under Trump, SOF units operating in Syria and Iraq are closer to front lines, often leading the charge against ISIS. In addition, there is glaring difference in the tempo of operations. The Pentagon's "encirclement tactic" against the Islamic State is another significant contrast between the Trump and Obama approaches.

Pentagon Spokesman, Captain Jeff Davis asserted, there are other differences: "Diplomacy is a key part of the plan."[86] In addition, Davis inserted another statement that he believed would be critical to understanding the Trump administration's strategy to defeat ISIS: the plan would incorporate all components of national power which would be accompanied by a "trans-regional approach"[87] that would rollback transnational terrorism. This plan appeared aimed at attacking ISIS in its strong-holds in sanctuaries around the world as well as destroying the caliphate.

TRUMP, COUNTERTERRORISM, ALLIANCE DIPLOMACY, AND ISIS

The Trump administration's diplomacy and the trans-regional approach were on display during the opening leg of the president's nine-day foreign policy trip. Normally, the initial trips by US presidents are short and frequently involve excursions to close neighbors such as Canada or Mexico.

President Trump's initial destination was in Saudi Arabia. Speaking to fifty-five majority Muslim countries in Riyadh, the capital of Saudi Arabia, on May 21, 2017, in a speech advertised as an opportunity to reset damaged US relations with the Muslim World, and designed to enlist the participants in real and consequential struggle against Islamic extremism,[88] President Trump delivered a memorable address.

In a formal attempt to construct a genuine coalition against Islamism, President Trump warned, "If we do not stand in uniform condemnation of this killing—then not only will we be judged by our people, not only will we be judged by history, but we will be judged by God."[89]

To further engage the participants, the president warned, "This is not a battle between different faiths, different sects, or different civilizations. This is a battle between Good and Evil."[90] President Trump delivered this statement to solicit the support of the participants: "If everyone in this room does their fair share and fulfills their part of the burden [the threat can be defeated]. Terrorism has spread across the world. But the path to peace begins right here, on this ancient soil, in this sacred land."[91]

Throughout the speech, Trump informed the participants that "America is prepared to stand with you."[92] The president again shifted to the need of burden sharing. In the words of the president, "The nations of the Middle East cannot wait for American power to crush this enemy for them. The nations of the Middle East will have to decide what kind of future they want . . . for their countries. . . . It is a choice between two futures—and it is a choice America cannot make for you."[93]

To continue to push for the need for diplomacy during the war on terrorism,[94] Trump stated, "We must seek partners . . . to make allies of all who share our goals. Above all, America seeks peace—not war. Muslim nations must be willing to take on the burden, if we are going to defeat terrorism and send its wicked ideology into oblivion."[95]

In the joint effort, all states in the region must work to deny sanctuary to ISIS. Trump acknowledged that cooperation is well under way. Examples of the existing cooperation could be found in the multi-state cooperation against the struggle with the Taliban in Afghanistan, the states working with Central Command in the struggle with the Islamic State, and a new area cooperation that followed the signature of the participations on the document that created the Terrorist Financing Targeting Center, which "is-chaired by the United States and Saudi Arabia, and joined by every member of the Gulf Cooperation Council."[96] President Trump warned "there is still much work to do. I ask you to join me . . . to work together, and to fight together—because united, we will not fail."[97]

President Trump's address to leaders of the Muslim World drew high praise. Saudi Arabia's King Salman offered this significant opinion: the speech represented, "a turning point in relations between the two countries."[98] On the address and its impact on accelerating Muslim participation "in a real" coalition against radical Islamic terrorism, King Salman made this statement: Trump called for Muslim leaders to "take firm measures to target the financing of terrorism."[99] The Foreign Minister of the United Arab Emirates, Anwar Garash, used Twitter to express his assessment: "Bravo President Trump. Effective and historic speech defining approach towards extremism and terrorism with candid respect and friendship."[100]

President Trump's address to NATO members in Brussels, Belgium represented another opportunity by the American leader to ensure that members of the Western alliance are onboard in counterterrorism efforts to confront and defeat the Islamic State. On the need for NATO to increase their counterterrorism capacity, President Trump asserted, "Terrorism must be stopped in its tracks, or the horror you saw in Manchester and so many other places will continue forever."[101] Trump shifted to the issue of immigration: "You have thousands and thousands of people pouring into our various countries and spreading throughout, and in many cases, we have no idea who they are. We must be tough and we must be vigilant. The NATO of the future must include a great focus on terrorism and immigration."[102]

A critical portion of the presidential address return to a campaign theme: NATO members must meet their share of the burden. In the address, President Trump articulated, "Two percent is the bare minimum for confronting today's very real . . . threats. If NATO countries made their full and complete contributions, then NATO would be even stronger than it is today, especially from the threat of terrorism."[103]

In an address delivered to American forces at the Naval Air Base in Sigonella, Italy, on May 27, 2017, President Trump once again returned to the theme of terrorism. In his message, President Trump stated, "To every service member from Italy, from a NATO country, we want to thank you for your friendship, and for partnering with us in the fight to defeat terrorism and protect civilization. Better believe it. Terrorism is a threat . . . to all of humanity—and together, we will overcome this threat. We will win."[104]

To many observers, despite the problematic verbiage unleashed during the campaign, President Trump quietly revised the anti-ISIS coalition. Equally important, coalition members openly respected President Trump's leadership and his overt, if not boastful, attitude of destroying the Islamic State. In the final analysis, the international community appeared serious and committed to confronting ISIS.

A NEW APPROACH IN AFGHANISTAN

Then candidate Barack Obama viewed Afghanistan as "the right war"[105] and "the war we have to win."[106] Once in office, President Obama's administration could not settle on a coherent strategy. A few examples are instructive. President Obama correctly stated, "the future of Afghanistan is inextricably linked to the future of its neighbor, Pakistan."[107] This strategy was subsequently dubbed AF-PAK. The strategy represented the Obama administration's attempt to confront terrorism in South Asia. In Afghanistan, the Obama administration conducted all too numerous reviews of their Afghanistan strategy. The administration could not settle on appropriate troop levels to sustain the administration's rhetoric which called for the "defeat" of the Taliban.[108] In the wake of the decision to shift to "the counterterrorism plus strategy," faced with the reality of the costs of nation building, President Obama withdrew 33,000 American troops from the country. Critics charged the decision is indicative of a policy that is in "serious trouble."[109]

In Pakistan, the Obama administration pursued a policy of "coercion and confrontation."[110] In the words of Vali Nasr, a former senior Obama administration official in the State Department, who assisted in its implementation, asserted "the policy failed."[111] The pressure and the confrontation only increased the divisions between the United States and Pakistan. In the end, both parties contributed to the policies failure.

Pakistan's failure to reign in a litany of terrorist groups that created sanctuaries within the country undermined the relationship with the United States. The inability of the government of Pakistan to confront the Haqqani Network, the Pakistani Taliban (Terhrik-I-Taliban Pakistan TTP), and arrest members of the Quetta Shura (Afghan Taliban leaders operating in Pakistan) further undermined the US-Pakistani relationship. The US Drone strikes, and most certainly the attendant civilian casualties, the Special Forces raid in Abbottabad, which concluded in the death of Osama bin Laden, collectively represented the events that ultimately ruptured the relationship. The South Asian component of the Obama administration's counterterrorism was a disaster.

What is Trump's past and present statements on counterterrorism in Afghanistan? Long before announcing his candidacy, Trump released the following tweet on November 21, 2013, "Do not allow our very stupid leaders to sign a deal that keeps us in Afghanistan through 2024-with all costs by USA MAKE AMERICA GREAT!"[112]

After declaring his candidacy, on several occasions Trump was asked to clarify his previous statements on Afghanistan. For example, during a *CNN* interview in October of 2015, Trump was queried on whether US troops should remain in Afghanistan. Trump responded this way: "We made a terrible mistake getting involved there in the first place. Are they [US troops] going to be there for the next 200 years?"[113] Trump then issued this comment: "I would leave the troops there, begrudgingly. You probably have to because that thing will collapse about two seconds after they leave."[114]

During an interview with former *Fox News* host Bill O'Reilly on April 28, 2016, Trump was asked "What exactly will you do about Afghanistan?"[115] The candidate issued the following response: "I would stay in Afghanistan. It's probably the one place we should have gone in the Middle East because it's adjacent and right next to Pakistan which has nuclear weapons."[116]

Trump's statements during two interviews, one in October 2015 and the other in April 2016, indicated the candidate "deviated" from his November of 2013 tweet. Would the candidates' inconsistencies on his views about Afghanistan impact his presidency?

In the opening month of his presidency, President Trump quietly authorized the military to provide a proposal for a new strategy in Afghanistan. Over the course of the internal military debate about a proposal for a shift in US strategy in Afghanistan, several media narratives developed: will the president request additional troops in Afghanistan? If the president agreed to additional troop increases, does this violate Trump's campaign pledge of

"America First"? These issues would resurface in wake of the president's August 21, 2017 address.

In response to the twin narratives, former press secretary Sean Spicer informed the media that President Trump desires details about an overall strategy.[117] The administration's focus, according to Spicer, has moved beyond a rudimentary request for additional troops. Spicer issued this supplemental statement: "One of the things he has asked his national security team to do is to actually rethink the strategy. What are we doing to achieve the goals you are asking about? How. . . . do we win, how do we eliminate the threat?"[118] The issue of America First was not addressed by Spicer.

In the wake of the review and the subsequent delivery of the proposal for a new strategy, President Trump was now ready to speak to the American people "on the way forward" in Afghanistan and South Asia. Speaking to military personnel at Fort Myer in Arlington, Virginia, President Trump opened his address with the following statement: "I am here tonight to lay out our path forward in Afghanistan and South Asia."[119] In a recognition of the political fallout and negative statements from the media, President Trump issued the following statement to address what White House officials recognized would be part of the post-speech commentary: "My original instinct was to pull out. But all my life I've heard that decisions are much different when you sit behind the desk in the Oval Office. . . . I studied Afghanistan in great detail. After many meetings . . . I arrived at three fundamental conclusions about America's core interests in Afghanistan."[120]

The "three fundamental conclusions about America's core interests in Afghanistan" include the following.[121] First, the administration is seeking "an honorable and enduring outcome worthy of the tremendous sacrifices that have been made."[122] Second, the president reminded everyone of the "consequences of a rapid exit are both predictable and unacceptable."[123] Those consequence could mean a potential 9/11-style attack and certainly would permit ISIS to fill a power vacuum left in the absence of American forces. Third, the threat in Afghanistan and "in the broader region are immense."[124] When one adds the threat posed by "20 US-designated foreign terrorist organizations are active in Afghanistan and Pakistan"[125] with potential conflict between two countries (Pakistan and India), the president was prepared to implement a strategy that could potentially deal with threats to US regional interests.

The Trump administration understood that its interests in Afghanistan and Pakistan were obvious: stop the resurgence of safe havens that could permit terrorists to target the United States, and "we must prevent nuclear weapons and materials from coming into the hands of terrorists and being used against us, or anywhere in the world for that matter."[126]

Then President Trump unveiled the administration's "four-pillar" counterterrorism strategy for Afghanistan and South Asia. The first pillar of the administration's strategy required a shift from "a time-based approach to one based on conditions." The second pillar called for the synergy of diplomatic, economic, military, and political power to ensure the defeat of the Taliban. The third pillar relied on the cooperation of Pakistan. This component to a certain extent is consistent with Obama's strategy; however, President Trump promised to pressure the long-time ally to confront the numerous terrorist groups that have taken root in the country. The president's South Asia strategy included a partnership with India to assist in providing financial and political support to the government of Afghanistan. In the fourth pillar the president called for the removal of restrictions that precluded victory and the president promised to provide US armed forces personnel with the means to pursue victory.[127]

The president then asserted that he anticipated that coalition partners must provide support in struggle against the Taliban: "We will ask our NATO allies and global partners to support our new strategy with additional troops and funding increases in line with our own. We are confident they will."[128]

The address contained an important set of words directed specifically for American troops: "Our troops will fight to win. . . . From now on, victory will have a clear definition: attacking our enemies, obliterating ISIS, crushing al Qaeda, preventing the Taliban from taking over Afghanistan, and stopping mass terror attacks against America before they emerge."[129]

President Trump's address was well received. In a salient example, Afghan President Ashraf Ghan welcomed President Trump's commitment to the security of the country: "I am grateful to President Trump and the American people for this affirmation of support for our efforts to achieve self-reliance and for our joint struggle to rid the region from the threat of terrorism. The Afghan government welcomes renewed US emphasis on seeing security in Afghanistan as part of a wider regional package."[130]

In another praise-worthy statement, Hamdullah Mohib, the Afghan ambassador to the United States, offered this assessment of the address: "President Trump has embraced a strategy that gives Afghanistan what it needs, a shift away from talking about timetables and numbers to letting conditions on the ground determine military strategy."[131]

Jack Keene, CEO of the Institute for the Study of War, stated that he was "impressed" by Trump's address. Keene then offered this detailed analysis: "Because we finally got a commander-in-chief who speaks honestly, not just to the troops in front them . . . but he spoke so honestly to the American people. And we've had this political deception for such a long time dealing with Afghanistan and you put your finger on it."[132]

Senator John McCain and Senator Lindsey Graham, both frequent critics of Trump, were solidly behind the president. Senator McCain made this analysis of the address: "I commend President Trump for taking a big step in the right direction with the new strategy for Afghanistan. I believe the President is now moving us well beyond the prior administration's failed strategy of merely postponing defeat."[133] Senator Graham provided a similar assessment: "I assure you a lot of people in Congress will be behind the president. The game has changed with Pakistan; the gloves are off in Afghanistan. I am very pleased with this plan and I am very proud of our president."[134]

A frequent critic of the president, retired Air Force General Michael Hayden, the former head of the CIA and National Security Agency during the Obama administration, praised Trump's decision making that created the strategy shift in Afghanistan. According to Hayden, President Trump followed "the traditional deliberative process of the American national security establishment."[135] From the point of view of Hayden, this meant "the departments and agencies weigh-in with their views, options were developed, debated and held up against the available intelligence."[136] Then Trump provided guidance and eventually implemented a policy to increase US forces in Afghanistan and install a strategy to regain territory under the control of the Taliban.

Critics of the address argued the president did not provide details on the number of troops that would be dispatched to Afghanistan. In addition, critics asserted the president did not explain what constitutes the conditions for withdrawal or victory. Much of the criticism came from a familiar source. That is, the "resistance movement" was again on display. This time Democratic Congressional leaders targeted President Trump's Afghan strategy address. House Minority Leader Nancy Pelosi provided this analysis: "The President said he knew what he was getting into and had a plan to go forward. Clearly, he did not. The President's announcement is low on details [and] ... he is declaring an open-ended commitment of American lives with no accountability to the American people."[137]

Senator Sherrod Brown (D-Ohio) stated, President Trump is requiring more of American forces "without a plan to transfer power to the Afghan government or a plan to leave the country. A commitment to 'win' is not a clear strategy, and our troops on the ground in Afghanistan deserve more. Let me be clear—we cannot commit more troops and taxpayer dollars to this war until we have a clear exit strategy."[138]

No matter the perspective, left, right, independent, foreign, or domestic, Afghanistan is now "Trump's War." His strategy is now in the crosshairs of counterterrorism experts the world-over. There will be several things to watch. Will Trump adjust the strategy by augmenting the number of US military personnel in Afghanistan? Will Trump succeed in obtaining support from India, Pakistan, and NATO? If the Taliban expands their territorial control in Afghanistan, will Trump withdraw American armed forces from the country? These and other questions are the central components of future assessments of Trump's war on terrorism.

TRUMP'S COUNTERTERRORISM STRATEGY, RESURGENT ISLAMIC STATE, AND THE DECISION IN SYRIA

President Trump previewed his administration's counterterrorism approach during the unveiling of the December 2017 National Security Strategy (NSS) document. The document provides this statement which indicates why the jihadist threat is a major priority for the Trump administration: "jihadist terrorist organizations represent the most dangerous threat" to the United States.[139]

To confront this threat, the NSS called for implementing six "priority actions." The administration believes "the disruption of terrorist plots" is critical to defeating terrorists.[140] The Trump administration, like the previous two administrations, spoke about the need for increased cooperation, at home and abroad, between law enforcement, the intelligence community, and the treasury department.[141] Second, the administration calls upon "the military and operating agencies" to "take direct action" against those terrorist organizations that threaten the United States.[142] Third, the United States would work with partner states to "eliminate terrorist sanctuaries."[143] Fourth, the Trump administration pledged to "sever sources of strength" which is a reference to "financial, material, and personnel supply chains terrorist organizations.[144] This action also calls for the disruption of the ability terrorist organizations to "message and recruit."[145] Fifth, another critical action called for "sharing the responsibilities" in defeating the threat. For the Trump administration, they viewed coalition activities and responsibilities critical to confronting any regional and international terrorist threat.[146] Sixth, the Trump administration enlisted law enforcement, the Department of Homeland Security, and American intelligence to "deny violent ideologies the space" to take root in communities within the States.[147]

The Trump administration's NSS document, collectively viewed the "six priority actions" as an initial policy to counter the threat and to "stay on the offensive against violent non-state groups that target the United States and our allies."[148] The Trump administration further noted that the United States is prepared to "pursue threats to their source."[149]

The NSS document devoted less than two pages to the administration's response to terrorism. Thus, it is succinct and covers significant ground in fleshing-out how the administration will deal with jihadists. From another perspective brevity is odd since Trump spent significant time during the presidential campaign and the opening year-plus talking about the radical Islamic terrorism. Overall, this section served as a precursor to the National Counterterrorism Strategy which was released at the close of the second year of the Trump presidency.

Criticism of President Trump's initial NSS is very much consistent with the hyper partisanship which has engulfed every aspect of the administration's foreign policy. Distinguished national security analyst, Elliott Abrams, noted, "the criticisms of the NSS came from predictable quarters" and more often than not, the evaluations of the document "merely reflect the writer's attitude toward the President rather than a fair assessment of the document."[150]

NATIONAL COUNTERTERRORISM STRATEGY

The release of President Trump's National Counterterrorism Strategy (NCS) was highly anticipated. During the roll-out of the document, President Trump confidently stated: "When it comes to terrorism, we will do whatever is necessary to protect our nation."[151]

Most interesting, the NSC consisted of several of the same instruments that were contained in the NSS. There are however some notable differences. What is contained in the NSS represented a precursor of things to come. Put another way, the sections of NSS devoted to counterterrorism represented an outline, a draft of what would be later released in the NCS. There is another critical departure in the NCS. The NSS is composed of six priority actions. Whereas the NCS contains six components that "places America First" in seeking to protect the homeland and US interests around the world. Contained within each of the components are six corollary actions that assist in the implementation of each component of the Trump administration's counterterrorism strategy.

The six components of the Trump administration's counterterrorism strategy include the following: (1) "Pursuing terrorists to their source," (2) "isolate terrorists from their sources of support," (3) "modernize and integrate US counterterrorism tools," (4) "protect American infrastructure and enhance resilience," (5) "counter terrorist radicalization and recruitment," and (6) "strengthen the counterterrorism capabilities of American partners around the world."[152]

The absence of space prevents a comprehensive examination of each component of the president's counterterrorism strategy. Instead, the evaluation explores critical features of some aspects of the strategy. Scholars assert that while the strategy differs significantly from previous counterterrorism approaches, one feature proved to be conspicuous: continuity.

President Trump's foreign policy agenda challenged previous bipartisan approaches to national security. That approach was tempered in the counterterrorism strategy in that there is less of an effort to criticize previous approaches and more of an attempt to express "a new path" to responding to the threat of terrorism.

With respect to continuity, Trump's counterterrorism continues, even expands upon, cooperation with regional and NATO allies. Whether in the case of Iraq, Afghanistan, and the Kurdish fighters in Syria, the document continues an approach that relies on partners to defeat terrorism. In short, consistent with previous administrations, Trump's document "prioritizes partnerships around the world" to produce "sustainable counterterrorism."[153]

The Trump administration asserts the United States must pursue terrorists to their source. This aspect of the strategy argues that it is important to disrupt terrorist plots, kill high-value leaders, but the administration believes it is important to destroy sanctuaries and insurgent forces to prevent the reemergence of the threat. To assist in this effort the Trump administration states that it is prepared to work "by, with and through partners"[154] to prevent terrorists from threating American interests. This is one aspect of Trumpian rhetoric that appears in the document. In another illustration, the document repeats a previous statement made by a host of officials: "America First, does not mean America alone."[155] In this context "cooperation is only loosely cloaked in Trumpian terms."[156]

The US government relies on several multiple corollary actions that consist of "targeting key terrorists and terrorist groups"; "enhance reach into denied areas overseas"; effectively use "the law of armed conflict (LOAC) detention as counterterrorism tool"; expand cooperation of federal, state, and local counterterrorism information sharing, and "amplify the impact of counterterrorism operations with strategic communication."[157] These actions are designed as compliments to the pursuit of terrorists around the world.[158]

The second component of the administration's counterterrorism strategy requires the ability to "isolate terrorists from their sources of support." This component is a continuation of the strategy initiated under President Bush and subsequently used by President Obama. However, the Trump administration argues that actions by previous presidents to disrupt terrorists developed after the terrorist entity is often at the zenith of its power. For example, the Obama administration waited a year-plus before instituting a credible response to disrupt the Islamic States' multiple sources of financing. The extended delay permitted ISIS to sustain the financing of their caliphate, create sanctuaries around the world, recruit foot soldiers, and launch a wave of terrorist attacks in the Middle East and beyond.

Every component is critical to understanding an administration's approach to counterterrorism. This is true of the previous administrations that have claimed to fight "a war on terrorism." The Trump administration's bold strategy is a salient departure from previous administrations. In an illustration of the point, the third component of the strategy calls for the modernization and integration of American counterterrorism instruments. The document calls for "advancing detection capabilities and capacity" and sharing that information with American partners to disrupt terrorist plots or potentially destroy a terrorist sanctuary.[159]

The strategy requires "harnessing technologies" to improve counterterrorism responses to terrorist groups that continually adapt to US and coalition tactics on the battlefield. In addition, this component calls for continually "updating counterterrorism policies," enhance the "collection, discovery, and exploitation of identity information" that supports the Trump administration's long-term mission to defeat radical Islamic terrorism.[160] There are several objectives associated with the component. Constructing a "holistic picture of terrorists' identities," exploit technology to enhance the capture and removal of terrorists from the battlefield, expand the sharing of information between executive agencies and departments and between the federal, state, and local officials.[161] Finally, with the enhancement in technology and improvement in cooperation, the Trump administration hopes to improve counterterrorism capabilities to "preempt emerging threats."[162]

Taken collectively, the administration asserted the strategy "builds on lessons learned" from "previous counterterrorism experiences"[163] and the approach provides a "new path toward strengthening the security"[164] of the United States. The strategy continues the focus on "diplomatic engagement, development assistance, and security assistance" that assists American partners in confronting local terrorist threats.[165] The document calls for the apprehension and detention of terrorists. This requires a place to detain them; this translates into retaining, not closing, the detention facility in Guantanamo, Cuba. The ultimate objective of the counterterrorism strategy is to "internationalize counterterrorism efforts" and reduce "reliance on the United States."[166] There is one caveat: The Trump administration however retains the right "to have independence of action."[167]

The strategy is an improvement over the Obama administration's 2011 counterterrorism document. That said, the document does have its shortcomings. As is the case with previous national counterterrorism strategy documents, the Trump administration's iteration is "short on specifics."[168] Another problem, the document calls for counter radicalization and recruitment, but it is not clear how the administration intends to accomplish this vital objective. One of the concerns of many in the counterterrorism community, is that many professionals expressed concern that President Trump and any number of senior advisors could undermine "their own counterterrorism strategy."[169] As discussed below, President Trump's initial statement on the withdrawal of US forces in Syria is very much consistent with this view.

SYRIA AND THE ISLAMIC STATE: THE TRANSITION IN THE WAR ON TERRORISM

Destroying the caliphate of the Islamic State represented the centerpiece of the counterterrorism strategies of President Obama and President Trump.

Reclaiming territory captured by the Islamic State in Iraq represented an easier task for the US-led anti-ISIS coalition. Though the Islamic State controlled Mosul, the second largest city in Iraq, and created and sustained sanctuaries across Sunni-dominated areas of the country, the counterterrorism landscape remained favorable to coalition forces.

The ever-increasing number of US-trained Iraqi security forces, the presence of Iranian intelligence in the country, and Shiite paramilitary forces (also referred to as Popular Mobilization Forces or PMF), combined with 5,000-plus American forces, with support from US-led coalition air superiority, the outcome of the struggle with the Islamic State was preordained. Few counterterrorism professionals, once the Obama administration committed to changes in their original counterterrorism strategy, which included increases in US troops, better use of special forces, and increased tempo of operations, believed the Islamic State could sustain control over territory in Iraq for an extended period.

With the increased tempo of operations and the implementation of the Trump administration's "annihilation strategy," the countdown to the dissipation of the Iraqi component of the Islamic States' caliphate quickened. After the recapture of Mosul, and territory in the Western areas near the Iraq-Syrian border, on behalf of the US-led coalition President Trump proclaimed victory over the Islamic State.

The counterterrorism landscape in Syria proved far more complex for the United States. A civil war raged unabated. Genocide and civilian displacement and human rights abuses continued. There are other significant issues. For starters, Syrian government forces, backed by Russian air and ground units, Iranian Quds forces, Hezbollah fighters, are engaged in conflict with anti-government forces. That not being enough, Al Qaeda in Syria controlled territory in the country. Often overlooked, the government of Israel engaged in intermittent clashes with Syrian government units and forces from Hezbollah and Iran.

Turkey too is engaged in Syria. Turkey's involvement in Syria further complicated the counterterrorism landscape. Turkish forces entered Syria out of national security concerns. The central issue for the Turkish government is the size and potential of American-backed Kurdish fighters which they viewed as a terrorist entity and linked to anti-government Kurdish forces within Turkey (The Kurdistan Workers Party or PKK). In Syria, the Kurdish fighters captured territory previously controlled by the Islamic State. In response to the presence of the US-backed Kurdish fighters near the Syrian-Turkish border, the government of Turkey deployed forces into Syria to provide a buffer and Erdogan repeatedly pledged to destroy the US ally.

The Obama administration, followed by the Trump administration, warned Turkey about any military offensive against US-backed Kurdish fighters. The counterterrorism landscape consisted of other complications.

For example, US Special Forces not only trained their Kurdish allies, but they engaged in operations with their ally against fighters of the Islamic State. In the skies above Syria, US and Russian pilots conducted intelligence and offensive air strikes against perceived threats on the ground.

US-backed Syrian Democratic Forces, which were in the final phase of operations against the Islamic State in their last remaining strong-hold in Hajin, in the wake of a telephone conversation with President of Erdogan of Turkey, President Trump declared victory over the Islamic State via Twitter on December 19, 2018. The key statement contained in the tweet involved the following words: "We have won against ISIS" and it's time "our . . . young men and women—they're all coming back [home]."[170] The statement gave the impression that US forces would be withdrawn from Syria immediately.

The immediate consequence of the decision produced several resignations from senior administration officials. Secretary of Defense Mattis resigned after failing to convince the president of the consequences of the decision. Mattis's letter of resignation demonstrated his displeasure with Trump's decision in Syria, the withdrawal of 7,000 troops in Afghanistan, and the president's mistreatment of the NATO allies. Within days of Mattis's resignation, Brett McGurk, the envoy in charge of the anti-ISIS coalition, submitted his resignation.

President Trump previously caused a controversy following an earlier statement that US forces would be withdrawn from Syria. In the wake of an extended period of consultation, senior advisors informed the president of the consequences of leaving Syria too soon. That is, the conditions on the ground—that ISIS was not yet defeated, Iran would expand its influence in the country, and Turkey would likely target US-backed Kurdish fighters—were not met. The Trump White House subsequently took back the decision to withdraw from Syria.

In the wake of the president's most recent impulsive decision, one which blind-sided the Pentagon and senior commanders and diplomats in the region, critics unleashed a storm of criticism. In an instructive illustration, veteran *New York Times* foreign affairs reporter Helene Cooper argued the president discarded "17 years of American military policy."[171] She also argued, "Mr. Trump overturned the post-9/11 national security consensus, the reverberations" from the decision "spanned the globe."[172]

In another assessment, Kevin Bacon, the executive editor of *Defense One*, issued this statement. Prior to the inauguration of Donald Trump, "I reported that US elite troops and commanders were worried that the incoming commander in chief lacked the patience" to complete the mission in Syria.[173] In the wake of the president's stunning decision, Bacon concluded, "Now we know the answer: No."[174]

Congressional leaders from both sides of the political divide expressed their outrage over the president's impetuous decision. After meetings with senior officials and a subsequent one-on-one meeting with the president, Lindsey Graham, a Trump loyalist, the Republican Senator, announced the president was not abandoning the Kurds and felt more reassured about the impact of Trump's decision. In addition, Graham stated, during the private conversation with the president he "talked about Syria" and provided details the Senator concluded made him feel "better about where we are headed."[175]

The decision to withdraw US forces from Syria by itself is problematic. There are a several additional factors that further support this argument. The decision itself was based on a telephone conversation between President Trump and President Erdogan of Turkey. That meant the decision occurred outside of the interagency process which would have permitted senior foreign policy officials to air their views.

There is a second equally troubling aspect of the decision: potentially outsourcing US counterterrorism in Syria to an individual, Erdogan, well-known for his human rights abuses and his threats to annihilate US-backed Kurdish fighters whom the government of Turkey considers nothing more than terrorists could lead to a disastrous outcome.

Third, the evidence suggests the Turkish army may be unable to retain control over territory currently possessed by Kurdish fighters. In addition, it is argued that Turkey's military is ill-equipped to sustain counterinsurgency operations against a resurgent Islamic State in Syria. There is another significant issue: one within the Turkish military. Two senior and highly respected military officers, General Ismail Metin Temel, "the commander who runs the Iraq and Syria fronts and built a reputation for his leadership skills during the Euphrates Shield and Olive Branch operations in Syria,"[176] and Brigadier General Mustafa Barut, well-known and respected officer in charge of the fourth commando brigade, were stripped of the titles and "transferred to desk jobs."[177] The reason for Erdogan's decision to demote both generals is that they openly opposed military operations against the Kurdish fighters.[178] Additionally, the other reason that forced the decision by the leader of Turkey is that Temel and Barut expressed concern about the costs (political and financial) of an open-ended commitment to confront the Islamic State in Syria.[179]

Fourth, President Trump's impulsive decision undermined US credibility with their coalition allies in and outside the region. There is something else: the decision undermined a critical statement made by President Trump. The president stated previously, "Our Friends will never question our support, and our enemies will never doubt our determination"[180] The reality is President Trump's decision to withdraw US forces from Syria did unleash criticism from American allies around the world. The concern is over the potential abandonment of an ally—the SDF—and allowing Iran to expand their influence in the country.

In a response to the decision to withdraw from Syria, during a cabinet meeting covered by reporters, President Trump addressed the criticism. Trump stated, "We're getting out and we're getting out smart."[181] Additionally, the president stated, "I never said I'm getting out tomorrow."[182]

From another perspective, senior administration officials succeeded in their effort to acquire several pivotal clarifications which include a four-month withdrawal timetable, one that is conditions-based, reassurances that Turkey would not attack the US-backed SDF, and "once US troops leave Syria and was assuring the NATO ally that it would have a buffer zone in the region to help protect its own interests."[183]

The Trump administration made another decision to reduce the clamor of the impending withdrawal of US forces in Syria. Two months after the original decision to withdraw all American forces, the White House announced that 200 peacekeeping forces would remain in Syria. General Dunsford, the chairman of the joint chiefs of staff, characterized the decision this way: "This is about campaign continuity." General Dunsford made this additional statement: "We . . . always had planned to transition into a stabilization phase, where we train local forces to provide security to prevent the regeneration of ISIS."[184] The description of US forces as peacekeepers by the White House is not a term viewed as acceptable to the Pentagon. The view from the Department of Defense is that US forces will engage in training and intelligence gathering.[185] The Pentagon will not comment on whether US forces will engage in military activities.

The period following the exit of American forces will determine if the decision to withdraw from Syria represented a smart strategy or an unforced and costly political and strategic error by President Trump. In other words, the outcome of the decision highlights the pitfalls and opportunities that exist in US foreign policy in the Trump era.

Despite the controversy surrounding President Trump's decision to withdraw US forces from Syria, there is little doubt the war on terrorism from a strategy and tactical perspective has most certainly been revised. President Trump's NSS and NCS documents represent continuity with respect to the need and support of local forces to engage terrorists around the world. The documents call upon the continued use of coalitions. However, much like with NATO, the Trump administration calls for increased participation or sharing of the burden by participants in the anti-ISIS coalition or in regional partnerships such as the Combined Joint Task Force in the Horn of Africa. There is another area of continuity, intelligence sharing but with a change. The Trump administration has called for increased intelligence sharing among executive department and agencies within the US government and among critical allies. It is unknown if there will be enhanced "reciprocal intelligence sharing" with US regional allies. Finally, disruption of financial support for terrorist organizations is another area of continuity. But once again, there is a revision. The Trump administration wants to continue to disrupt funding sources of transnational terror entities, but it wants to ensure that financial resources of future "start-up" terrorist organizations are targeted from the beginning rather than waiting until that entity reaches its zenith of power before acting to curtail the finances of the next ISIS or Al Qaeda.

The revision is demonstrated in the comprehensive national counterterrorism strategy. Each of the components of the strategy illustrate the wide-ranging counterterrorism approach of the Trump administration. Then consider this point: after the introduction of each of the components, the document then provides "multiple priority of actions" that support and enhance each aspect of the overall strategy.

Another conspicuous aspect of the Trump administration strategy is its uniqueness. For example, the Obama administration unveiled a separate counter radicalization (extremism) document. The Trump administration includes counter radicalization as a component of its overall strategy. The approach, as a source in the administration contends, is to ensure "a linkage or synergy between all aspects of the strategy."[186]

There are additional areas of divergence from previous administrations. The Trump administration announced that it intends "to pursue terrorist threats to their source," to constantly "modernize and integrate new terrorist tools," and that counterterrorism would have to serve another role—to "protect the critical infrastructure networks" of the United States.[187] These are features that demonstrate the administration's desire to shift away from previous approaches to waging the war on terrorism. In addition, the Trump administration states that it will only pursue those terrorist networks that "are threats to the United States."[188] This is a major shift from President Bush who promised to destroy all "terrorist groups of global reach."[189] The Trump administration's approach provides a dose of reality which asserts all terrorist groups are not threats to the United States. This translates into preserving valuable resources to target "actual and potential threats" to American interests.

It is important to discuss other features of the revision of the war on terrorism. Previously, the US government offered an off-ramp to terrorists on the battlefield. This is a reference to allowing an "exit point" that would permit terrorists to leave a specific area. The Trump administration implemented an "annihilation strategy" which required the destruction of a terrorist entity on the battlefield. This approach was conducted by the US-backed SDF in the battle of Raqqa and Deir al-Zior. In each battle ISIS fighters were surrounded, and the bulk were engaged and slaughtered by the SDF. Where required US air assets were requested to target ISIS fighters fleeing both zones of battle.

The counterterrorism approach is not without its flaws. For starters, the reliance on local forces (whether in Iraq or Syria) has not led to "the complete defeat" of the Islamic State. The caliphate of the Islamic State is eliminated, but the transnational network has morphed into an insurgency with an estimated 20,000–30,000 combined fighters in Iraq and Syria. The resurrection of the Islamic State is the next frontier for the Trump administration's war on terrorism. That frontier includes Iraq, Syria, Libya, Afghanistan, and beyond where there is a resurgence of the Islamic State in these and other areas.[190]

Trump's decision to withdraw US forces in Syria remains murky. Critics questioned if "Trump ever read his strategy."[191] The very impulsive decision undermines a well-crafted strategy, one that was well-received by most counterterrorism professionalism. The decision to withdraw US forces from Syria undermined many of Trump's campaign statements, most notably those concerning abandoning allies and faith the United States is committed to completing the mission—this one in Syria. The other issue is whether allies trust the government of Turkey to confront the Islamic State in Syria.

In fairness, the president does have a credible fallback strategy—5,000-plus American troops reside in Iraq and massive air power at Trump's disposal to launch attacks to protect US-backed Kurdish allies or to prevent Iran from seizing territory in Syria. The president dispatched Secretary Pompeo and National Security Advisor Bolton to reassure regional allies the Trump administration is not abandoning its strategy, their allies, and the commitment to defeat the Islamic State.

There is one additional conspicuous problem with NCS document—it lacks a regional response. When one reads the document it is bold, however, without mentioning the central regions (e.g., MENA and East and West Africa) by name and how the strategy would be implemented to deal with a plethora of threats in those areas, the approach is open to criticism. One would hope the administration is preparing subsequent counterterrorism documents to deal with this glaring weakness.

In the end, President Trump achieved his objective—radically altering the war on terrorism and the US government's strategy to confront a wealth of transnational threats. The remaining years of the Trump presidency will determine the degree to which the president continues to modify the US participation in "the long-war," if the president takes steps to reduce American commitments in the multiple fronts on the war on terrorism, or if he scores victories over other transnational terrorist groups around the world.

NOTES

1. Smith, Julianne, Rizzo, Rachel, and Twardowski, Adam, "US Election Note: Defense Policy After 2016," Chatham House, US and the Americas Program, August 2016. https://

www.chathamhouse.org/sites/default/files/publications/research/2016-08-16-us-election-note-defence-smith-rizzo-twardowski.pdf. Accessed on December 3, 2018.

2. Hartmann, Margaret, "I Would Not Allow People to Come in From Terrorist Nations. I would Do Extreme Vetting," *New York Magazine*, July 15, 2016. http://nymag.com/daily/intelligencer/2016/07/trump-nice.html. Accessed on December 3, 2018.

3. French, David, "Trump and Clinton—Unfit to be Commander-in-Chief," *National Review*, September 6, 2016. http://www.nationalreview.com/article/439848/foreign-policy-donald-trump-hillary-clinton-unfit-be-commander-chief. Accessed on December 3, 2018.

4. Greenberg, Jon, "Trump Touts Plan to Defeat ISIS," *Politifact*, February 28, 2017. http://www.politifact.com/truth-o-meter/promises/trumpometer/promise/1375/develop-plan-defeat-isis-30-days/. Accessed on December 3, 2018.

5. By Team Fix, "5th Republican Debate Transcript, Annotated: Who Said What and What it Meant," *Washington Post*, December 15, 2015. https://www.washingtonpost.com/news/the-fix/wp/2015/12/15/who-said-what-and-what-it-meant-the-fifth-gop-debate-annotated/?utm_term=341106972edf. Accessed on December 3, 2018.

6. Ibid.

7. Ibid.

8. "Donald J. Trump Foreign Policy Speech." DonaldJTrump.com. April 27, 2016. https://www.donaldjtrump.com/press-releases/donald-j.-trump-foreign-policy-speech. Accessed on December 3, 2018.

9. Ibid.

10. Ibid.

11. Ibid.

12. Ibid.

13. Ibid.

14. Vladimirov, Nikita, "Trump: US Has 'No Choice but to Bomb' ISIS in Libya," *The Hill*, August 2, 2016. http://thehill.com/blogs/ballot-box/presidential-races/290115-trump-us-has-no-choice-but-to-bomb-isis-in-libya. Accessed on December 3, 2018.

15. Full Text: Donald Trump's Speech on Fighting Terrorism. *Politico*, August 15, 2016. http://www.politico.com/story/2016/08/donald-trump-terrorism-speech-227025. Accessed on December 3, 2018.

16. Ibid.

17. Ibid.

18. Ibid.

19. Ibid.

20. Beckwith, Ryan Teague, "Read Hillary Clinton's and Donald Trump's Remarks at A Military Forum." *Time*, September 7, 2016. http://time.com/4483655/commander-chief-forum-clinton-trump-intrepid/. Accessed on December 8, 2018.

21. Ibid.

22. Transcript of Donald Trump's Speech on National Security in Philadelphia. *The Hill*, September 7, 2016. http://thehill.com/blogs/pundits-blog/campaign/294817-transcript-of-donald-trumps-speech -on-national-security-in. Accessed on December 8, 2018.

23. Ibid.

24. Ibid.

25. Ibid.

26. "Counterterrorism Pitfalls: What the US Fight Against ISIS and Al Qaeda Should Avoid," International Crisis Group, Special Report Number 3, Middle East and North Africa March 22, 2017. https://www.crisisgroup.org/middle-east-north-africa/gulf-and-arabian-peninsula/iraq/003-counter-terrorism-pitfalls-what-us-fight-against-isis-and-al-qaeda-should-avoid. Accessed on December 10, 2018.

27. Ibid.

28. Ibid.

29. Ibid.

30. Ibid.

31. Department of Defense Press Briefing by Secretary Mattis, General Dunford and Special Envoy McGurk on the Campaign to Defeat ISIS in the Pentagon Press Briefing Room, News

Transcript. US Department of Defense. May 19, 2017. https://www.defense.gov/News/Transcripts/Transcript-View/Article/1188225/department-of-defense-press-briefing-by-secretary-mattis-general-dunford-and-sp/. Accessed on December 11, 2018.
  32. Ibid.
  33. Full Text: Donald Trump's Speech on Fighting Terrorism, *Politico*, August 16, 2016. www.politico.com/story/2016/08/donald-trump-terrorism-speech-227025. Accessed on December 11, 2018.
  34. Ibid.
  35. Farivar, Masood, "Trump Pledges War on Radical Islam," *Small Wars Journal* (Voice of America), January 18, 2017. http://smallwarsjournal.com/blog/trump-pledges-war-on-radical-islamic-terrorism.
  36. Ibid.
  37. Ibid.
  38. Ibid.
  39. Ibid.
  40. Donald Trump's Speech on Fighting Terrorism.
  41. Ibid.
  42. Ibid.
  43. Ibid.
  44. Ibid.
  45. Ibid.
  46. Ibid.
  47. Cook, Lorne, "NATO Chief Says Allies to Join Anti-ISIS Coalition," Military.com, May 25, 2017. http://www.military.com/daily-news/2017/05/25/nato-chief-says-allies-join-anti-isis-coalition.html. Accessed on December 12, 2018.
  48. Ibid.
  49. Ibid.
  50. Ibid.
  51. Ibid.
  52. For more on this point, see Davis, John, "Obama, Trump, and Bush's Counterterrorism Infrastructure," January 23, 2017. http://www.editor-in-chieftheglobalwaronterrorism.com/blog/obama-trump-bushs-counterterrorism-infrastructure/. Accessed on December 12, 2018.
  53. Remarks by President Trump to Coalition Representatives and Senior US Commanders. The White House, Office of the Press Secretary. MacDill Air Force Base, Tampa, Florida, February 6, 2017. https://www.whitehouse.gov/the-press-office/2017/02/06/remarks-president-trump-coalition-representatives-and-senior-us. Accessed on December 13, 2018.
  54. See Lucas, Fred, "Obama Has Touted Al Qaeda's Demise 32 Times Since Benghazi Attack," CNSNews.com, November 1, 2012. http://www.cnsnews.com/news/article/obama-touts-al-qaeda-s-demise-32-times-benghazi-attack-0. Accessed on December 13, 2018.
  55. Ibid.
  56. Ibid.
  57. Scarborough, Rowan, "With ISIS in Crosshairs, Al Qaeda Makes Comeback," *Washington Times*, April 2, 2017. http://www.washingtontimes.com/news/2017/apr/2/al-qaeda-come-back-widens-terror-war-for-donald-tru/. Accessed on December 13, 2018.
  58. Ibid.
  59. Ibid.
  60. Finch, Asa and Kesling, Ben, "US Forces Attack Al Qaeda in Yemen," *Wall Street Journal*, May 23, 2017. https://www.wsj.com/articles/u-s-forces-attack-al-qaeda-in-yemen-1495531409. Accessed on December 13, 2018.
  61. Based on author background interview with a military official.
  62. "Presidential Memorandum Plan to Defeat the Islamic State of Iraq and Syria." The White House Office of the Press Secretary, January 28, 2017. https://www.whitehouse.gov/the-press-office/2017/01/28/plan-defeat-islamic-state-iraq. Accessed on December 13, 2018.
  63. Ibid.
  64. Ibid.
  65. Ibid.

66. Ibid.
67. Ibid.
68. Exum, Andrew, "Donald Trump Will Defeat ISIS," *The Atlantic*, February 17, 2017. https://www.theatlantic.com/international/archive/2017/02/donald-trump-will-defeat-isis/517062/. Accessed on December 13, 2018.
69. Cordesman, Anthony H., "The Wrong Presidential Memorandum on Defeating ISIS and an Uncertain Memorandum on Rebuilding the US Military," The Center for Strategic and International Studies (CSIS), February 2, 2017. https://www.csis.org/analysis/wrong-presidential-memorandum-defeating-isis-and-uncertain-memorandum-rebuilding-us. Accessed on December 14, 2018.
70. Sisk, Richard, "Mattis Gives White House Tentative Plan for Rapid Defeat of ISIS," Military.com, February 28, 2017. http://www.military.com/daily-news/2017/02/28/mattis-gives-white-house-tentative-plan-rapid-defeat-isis.html. Accessed on December 14, 2018.
71. Ibid.
72. Burns, Robert, and Baldor, Lolita C., "Pentagon Presenting Counter-ISIS Plan to White House," *Military Times*, February 27, 2017. http://www.militarytimes.com/articles/new-anti-isis-strategy-may-mean-deeper-us-involvement-in-syria. Accessed on December 14, 2018.
73. Ibid.
74. Swick, Andrew, "The DoD's "New" Plans for ISIS," *Georgetown Security Studies Review* (GSSR), March 6, 2017. http://georgetownsecuritystudiesreview.org/2017/03/06/the-dods-new-plans-for-isis/. Accessed on December 14, 2018.
75. Ibid.
76. Ibid.
77. Ibid.
78. As quoted in Pawlyk, Oriana, "Mattis: Trump Empowered Commanders to 'Annihilate ISIS,'" Military.com, May 19, 2017. http://www.military.com/daily-news/2017/05/19/mattis-trump-empowered-commanders-annihilate-isis.html. Accessed on December 14, 2018.
79. Ibid.
80. Ibid.
81. Bacon, Kevin and Weisgerber, Marcus, "New Tactics, Quicker Decisions Are Helping to 'Annihilate' ISIS, Pentagon Says," DefenseOne.com, May 19, 2017. http://www.defenseone.com/threats/2017/05/new-tactics-quicker-decisions-are-helping-annihilate-isis-pentagonsays/138 024/. Accessed on December 14, 2018.
82. Ibid.
83. Ibid.
84. Ibid.
85. Ibid.
86. Burns and Baldor, "Pentagon Presenting Counter-ISIS Plan to White House."
87. Ibid.
88. Gardner, Frank, "Trump Urges Muslim Leaders to Lead Fight Against Radicalization," BBC.com, March 22, 2017. http://www.bbc.com/news/world-us-canada-39989548. Accessed on December 15, 2018.
89. President Trump's Speech to the Arab Islamic American Summit. The White House, Office of the Press Secretary. May 21, 2017. https://www.whitehouse.gov/the-press-office/2017/05/21/president-trumps-speech-arab-islamic-american-summit. Accessed on December 15, 2018.
90. Ibid.
91. Ibid.
92. Ibid.
93. Ibid.
94. For more on the role of diplomacy and partnerships in the war on terrorism, see the following, Davis, John, "Diplomacy and the War on Terrorism," May 15, 2017. http://www.editor-in-chieftheglobalwaronterrorism.com/diplomacy-war-terrorism/ and Davis, John, "Partnerships and the War on Terrorism," February 28, 2017. http://www.editor-in-chieftheglobalwaronterrorism.com/partnerships-war-terrorism/. Accessed on December 15, 2018.
95. Ibid.

96. President Trump's Speech to the Arab Islamic American Summit.
97. Ibid.
98. Hensch, Mark, "Saudi King: Trump Visit a 'Turning Point,'" *The Hill*, May 22, 2017. http://thehill.com/homenews/administration/334615-saudi-king-trump-visit-a-turning-point. Accessed on December 15, 2018.
99. Ibid.
100. Boulos, Nabih, "Trump's Speech Draws Mixed Reaction, Including Plenty of Anger, In the Muslim World," *LA Times*, May 22, 2017. http://www.latimes.com/world/la-fg-trump-muslim-react-20170521-story.html. Accessed on December 15, 2018.
101. Remarks by President Trump at NATO Unveiling of the Article 5 and Berlin Wall Memorials—NATO Headquarters. Brussels, Belgium. The White House, Office of the Press Secretary, May 25, 2017. https://www.whitehouse.gov/the-press-office/2017/05/25/remarks-president-trump-nato-unveiling-article-5-and-berlin-wall. Accessed on December 15, 2018.
102. Ibid.
103. Ibid.
104. Remarks by President Trump and First Lady Melania Trump to Troops and Families. Naval Air Base Sigonella, Italy. The White House, Office of the Press Secretary. May 27, 2017. https://www.whitehouse.gov/the-press-office/2017/05/27/remarks-president-trump-and-first-lady-melania-trump-troops-and-families. Accessed on December 15, 2018.
105. Dreyfuss, Richard, "Obama's Afghan Dilemma," *The Nation*, December 2, 2008. https://www.thenation.com/article/obamas-afghan-dilemma/. Accessed on December 15, 2018.
106. Wilson, Scott, and Cohen, Jon, "Poll: More Americans Disapprove of Obama's Management of Afghanistan War," *Washington Post*, August 25, 2011. https://www.washingtonpost.com/politics/poll-more-americans-disapprove-of-obamas-management-of-afghan-war/2011/04/25/AFBjpnjEstory.html?utm_term=743486f5c42e. Accessed on December 15, 2018.
107. "President Obama's Remarks on New Strategy for Afghanistan and Pakistan," *New York Times*, March 27, 2009. http://www.nytimes.com/2009/03/27/us/politics/27obama-text.html. Accessed on December 15, 2018.
108. The troops levels were explained this way: "Obama ordered the deployment of an additional 21,000 troops. General David McKiernan—who in May was replaced by General Stanley McChrystal as US commander in Afghanistan—had asked for 10,000 more; the White House will decide whether to add those in the fall. By the middle of 2010, the US troop presence will have expanded by nearly one-third, to 78,000. Adding NATO troops, including those slated for deployment through the August Afghan elections, would boost the total coalition troop level to approximately 100,000." For more details, see Simon, Steve, "Can the Right War Be Won?" *Foreign Affairs*, July/August 2009. https://www.foreignaffairs.com/reviews/review-essay/2009-07-01/can-right-war-be-won. Accessed on December 16, 2018.
109. Kalb, Marvin, "Afghan Policy—Suddenly in Serious Trouble," Brookings.edu, February 28, 2012. https://brookings.edu/blog/up-front/2012/28/afghan-policy-suddenly-in-serious-trouble/. Accessed on December 16, 2018.
110. Nasr, Vali, *The Dispensable Nation: American Foreign Policy in Retreat* (New York: Anchor Books, 2013), p. 62.
111. Ibid.
112. Schwarz, Jon and Mackey, Robert, "All the Times Donald Trump Said the US Should Get Out of Afghanistan," *The Intercept*, August 21, 2017. https://theintercept.com/2017/08/21/donald-trump-afghanistan-us-get-out/. Accessed on December 16, 2018.
113. Ibid.
114. Ibid.
115. "Donald Trump on His Foreign Policy Strategy," *Fox News*, April 29, 2016. http://www.foxnews.com/transcript/2016/04/29/donald-trump-on-his-foreign-policy-strategy.html. Accessed on December 16, 2018.
116. Ibid.
117. Bender, Bryan and Johnson, Eliana, "Trump's Campaign Pledges Face Collision in Afghanistan," *Politico*, May 9, 2017. http://www.politico.com/story/2017/05/09/trump-afghanistan-troops-taliban-238179. Accessed on December 16, 2018.

118. Ibid.
119. Remarks by President Trump on the Strategy in Afghanistan and South Asia, Fort Myer, Arlington, Virginia. The White House, Donald J. Trump. Office of the Press Secretary, August 21, 2017. https://www.whitehouse.gov/the-press-office/2017/08/21/remarks-president-trump-strategy-afghanistan-and-south-asia. Accessed on December 16, 2018.
120. Ibid.
121. Ibid.
122. Ibid.
123. Ibid.
124. Ibid.
125. Ibid.
126. Ibid.
127. Hyman, Gerald F., "Trump's New Afghanistan Strategy Isn't Really a Strategy," *National Interest*, November 17, 2017. https://nationalinterest.org/feature/trumps-new-afghanistan-strategy-isnt-really-strategy-23258. Accessed on December 16, 2018.
128. Ibid.
129. Ibid.
130. Bengali, Hashank and Sahi, Aoun, "Pakistan Finds Itself on the Defensive in Trump's Afghan War Strategy," *LA Times*, August 22, 2017. http://www.latimes.com/world/asia/la-fg-afghanistan-trump-reaction-20170822-story.html. Accessed on December 16, 2018.
131. Ibid.
132. Rusty [Name Provided], "Military Leaders, Congress Praise Trump's 'Inspiring' Afghanistan Speech," *The Political Insider*, August 22, 2017. http://thepoliticalinsider.com/trump-afghanistan-speech/. Accessed on December 16, 2018.
133. Ibid.
134. "Trump's Afghanistan Address Generates Wave of Political Reaction," *Fox News*, August 21, 2017. http://www.foxnews.com/politics/2017/08/21/trumps-afghanistan-address-generates-wave-political-reaction.html. Accessed on December 16, 2018.
135. Hayden, Michael V., *The Assault on Intelligence: American National Security in an Age of Lies* (New York: Penguin Press, 2018), pp. 164–165.
136. Ibid.
137. "Trump's Afghanistan Address Generates Wave of Political Reaction."
138. Ibid.
139. National Security Strategy of the United States, White House.gov, December 2017. https://www.whitehouse.gov/wp-content/uploads/2017/12/NSS-Final-12-18-2017-0905-pdf. Accessed on December 16, 2018.
140. Ibid.
141. Ibid.
142. Ibid.
143. Ibid.
144. Ibid.
145. Ibid.
146. Ibid.
147. Ibid.
148. Ibid.
149. Ibid.
150. Abrams, Elliott, "The Trump National Security Strategy," Council on Foreign Relations, Blog Post, December 26, 2017. https://cfr.org/blog/-trump-national-security-strategy. Accessed on December 17, 2018.
151. President Donald J. Trump is Protecting the United States from Terrorism. Whitehouse.gov. October 4, 2018. https://www.whitehouse.gov/briefings-statements/president-donald-j-trump-protecting-america-terrorism. Accessed on December 17, 2018.
152. Ibid.
153. Geltzer, Joshua A., "Trump's Counterterrorism is Relief," *The Atlantic*, October 4, 2018. https://www.theatlantic.com/internationalachive/2018/10/trump-counterterrorism-strategy/572170/. Accessed on December 17, 2018.

154. Ibid.
155. As quoted in Tankel, Stephen, "Has Trump Read His Own Counterterrorism Strategy," *Foreign Policy*, October 12, 2018. https://foreignpolicy.com/2018/1012/has-trump-read-his-own-counterterrorism-strategy/. https://www.whitehouse.gov/wp-content/uploads/2018/10/NSCT.pdf. Accessed on December 17, 2018.
156. Ibid.
157. National Counterterrorism Strategy. The White House, October 2018. Washington, DC. National Counterterrorism Strategy. The White House, October 2018. https://www.whitehouse.gov/wp-content/uploads/2018/10/NSCT.pdf. Accessed on December 17, 2018.
158. Priority actions are linked to each of the six components of the Trump administration's counterterrorism approach. These actions are critical in that they enhance each component and illustrate the creativity and comprehensive aspects of the strategy. Limited space, however, prevents a detailed evaluation of this critical aspect of the strategy.
159. See National Counterterrorism Strategy.
160. Ibid.
161. Ibid.
162. Ibid.
163. See President Donald J. Trump is Protecting the United States from Terrorism.
164. Ibid.
165. Ibid.
166. Ibid.
167. Ibid.
168. Byman, Daniel, "Takeaways from the Trump administration's New Counterterrorism Strategy," Brookings, October 5, 2018. https://www.brookings.edu/blog/order-from-choas/2018/10/05/takaways-from-the-trump-administrations-new-counterterrorism-strategy/. Accessed on December 17, 2018.
169. Ibid.
170. Landler, Mark, Cooper, Helene, and Schmitt, Eric, "Trump Withdraws US Forces," *New York Times*, December 19, 2018. https://www.nytimes.com/2018/12/19/us/politics/trump-syria-turkey-troop-withdrawal.html. Accessed on December 17, 2018.
171. Cooper, Helene, "In a Flash, US Military Policy Turns Inward and Echoes Across the Globe," *New York Times*, December 21, 2018. https://www.nytimes.com/2018/12/21/us/politics/trump-military-syria-mattis-afghanistan.html. Accessed on December 3, 2018.
172. Ibid.
173. Baron, Kevin, "The 'Nightmare Scenario' Has Happened and You're to Blame," *Defense One*, December 21, 2018. https://www.defenseone.com/politics/2018/12/nightmare-scenario-has-happened-and-youre-blame/153748/. Accessed on December 27, 2018.
174. Ibid.
175. Haberman, Maggie, "Trump Mollifies Lindsey Graham on Troop Withdrawal from Syria," *New York Times*, December 30, 2018. https://www.nytimes.com/2018/12/30/us/politics/linsey-graham-syria-trump.html. Accessed on January 7, 2019.
176. Tastekin, Fehim, "Turkish Army Brass at Odds Over Military Operation in Syria," *Al Monitor*, January 4, 2019. https://www.almonitor.com/pulse/originals/2019/01/turkey-syria-some-in-army-oppose-new-operation-against-kurds.html. Accessed on January 7, 2019.
177. Ibid.
178. Ibid.
179. Ibid.
180. See the National Counterterrorism Strategy.
181. Mason, Jeff, "Trump Gives No Timetable for Syria Exit; Wants to Protect Kurds," *Reuters*, January 2, 2019. https://af.reuters.com/article/worldNews/idAFKCN1OW1H1. Accessed on January 9, 2019.
182. Ibid.
183. Ibid.

184. McCann, James, "White House Says 200 Troops Will Remain in Syria," *Stars and Stripes*, February 22, 2019. https://www.stripes.com/news/middle-east/white-house-says-200-troops-will-remain-in-syria. Accessed on February 24, 2019.
185. Ibid.
186. Interview with Trump administration official.
187. See the Trump administration's national counterterrorism strategy document.
188. The National Counterterrorism Strategy.
189. President Bush: "No Nation Can be Neutral in This Conflict." Remarks by the President to the Warsaw Conference on Combatting Terrorism. President George W. Bush, White House, November 6, 2011. Georgewbush-whitehouse.archives.gov. Accessed on January 9, 2019.
190. For more on the Islamic States resurrection, see my blog post, Davis, John, "The Islamic State's Resurrection in Iraq and Syria," editor-in-chieftheglobalwaromnterrorism.com. September 26, 2018. http://www.editor-in-chieftheglobalwaronterrorism.com/the-islamic-states-resurrection-in-iraq-and-syria/. Accessed on January 10, 2019.
191. Tankel, Stephen, "Has Trump Read His Own Counterterrorism Strategy?" *Foreign Policy*, October 12, 2018. https://foreignpolicy.com/2018/10/12/has-trump-read-his-own-counterterrorism-strategy/. Accessed on January 10, 2019.

Chapter Four

The Challenge

Trump and the Rebuilding of the US Military

Critics argued there are several outstanding questions regarding President Trump's restoration of the military and how those changes could impact American foreign policy that must be addressed. In this restoration, President Trump must address a series of questions: How will the administration accomplish the restoration of the military? What are the likely areas of change? What strategy or doctrine will govern this change? Will the "new military" under the Trump administration meet the security requirements for current and future threats to US interests?

TRUMP'S CAMPAIGN STATEMENTS AND THE RESTORATION OF THE MILITARY

During the 2016 presidential election, an "open-letter" was signed by 88 retired senior military officers which demonstrated that rebuilding the military would be a major campaign issue. In expressing their choice, the senior military leaders argued, "The 2016 election affords the American people an urgently needed opportunity to make a long-overdue course correction in our national security posture and policy."[1]

The senior leaders listed several reasons for supporting Trump. They preferred an individual not connected to "the hollowing out of our military" and they wanted an individual committed "to rebuild our military, to secure our borders, to defeat our Islamic supremacist adversaries and restore law and order domestically."[2]

During the campaign Trump incessantly criticized President Barack Obama's misuse of American military power. Additionally, the candidate blamed Obama for the failure to adequately fund the Pentagon and for not improving the readiness of US armed forces. On the campaign trail Trump clarified his positions on these issues.

During the campaign Trump did not commit to a formal strategy to rebuild the American military but he spoke about specific deficiencies within each branch and the need to address those problems. In a statement on September 8, 2016, the candidate expressed deep concern about the decline in defense expenditures. Trump remarked, "History shows that when America is not prepared is when the danger is greatest. We want to deter, avoid and prevent conflict through our unquestioned military dominance."[3] According to a campaign aide, Trump is prepared to seek defense spending at pre-2013 levels.[4]

The month of September provided Trump with an opportunity to repair his relationship with generals in the US armed forces. To understand the genesis of the candidates' troubles, it is important to review a series of self-inflicted wounds that rankled current and retired senior military leaders. During a rally in Ames, Iowa, on November 14, 2015, Trump issued the following statement: "I know more about ISIS (Islamic State) than the generals do."[5]

In late June of 2015, Trump issued the following statement that further undermined his relationship with senior military leaders: "The generals 'don't know much' because they're not winning."[6] It is during a rally in Greenville, NC that Trump attempted to repair the relationship with military leaders. In a statement to the crowd, Trump remarked, "We are going to convey to my top generals and give them a simple instruction. They will have 30 days to submit to the Oval Office a plan for soundly and quickly defeating ISIS."[7]

After belittling generals during the campaign, Trump promised that once in office he would seek their advice in creating an anti-ISIS plan. The stunning reversal did resurrect his relationship with most current and retired senior military leaders. In addition, Trump's change in circumstances was further enhanced because most military leaders refused to support Hillary Clinton.

During a pivotal period during the campaign, on October 6, 2016, Trump continued to shine the spotlight on President Obama's policies which he believed caused the reduction in the size and effectiveness of the US military. In a statement designed to increase the support of members of the armed forces, Trump argued:

> Our forces are depleted. . . . We have the greatest people on Earth, but they're depleted. We have an Army that hasn't been in this position since World War

II, in terms of levels and in terms of readiness and in terms of everything else.... You look at what's happened with our Navy in terms of the number of ships and our armed forces generally ... how they are at almost record-setting. It is very, very unfortunate and very, very dangerous for our country.[8]

Trump argued the dismal state of the military and the American failure to defeat the Islamic State is a result of Obama's leadership and his close civilian advisors which collectively did not listen to the advice of senior military leaders. In a statement with the objective of appealing to the armed forces, Trump stated, "I don't think you've been allowed to fight ISIS . . . the way you wanted. I don't think you've been allowed to fight for Iraq the way you've wanted."[9] The problem from the perspective of Trump is that President Obama and many individuals that worked for the national security council staff simply did "listen to the military people." Trump also argued, "We probably wouldn't be having an ISIS right now" if the White house listened to the military and accepted the early intelligence that existed about the threat.[10] Trump had another problem that is associated with President Obama and decision making regarding the Islamic State: "I think I can say not 'probably.' I think we definitely wouldn't be having an ISIS right now."[11]

On that same day, the candidate was excited to learn that a poll surfaced that indicated members of the armed forces supported his candidacy over his rival Clinton. Brendan McGarry, a reporter for Military.com, asserted that "Many officers and enlisted service members preferred Trump to Clinton. Career-oriented troops favored Trump over Clinton by a 3:1 margin, according to a voluntary online survey conducted by Military.com in October."[12] Perhaps the most revealing data within the poll is that "Across almost every demographic group, from branch of military service to paygrade to gender, Trump was the clear winner in the survey."[13]

During the campaign, Trump had other military-related matters to contend with. When Trump went "off-script" or simply undercut his message (often the absence of statements on how the president would support the increase defense expenditures was enough) to rebuild the military, surrogates were dispatched to clarify the president-elect's positions on defense-related matters. Two individuals, Senator Jeff Sessions and Representative Randy Forbes, were trusted with clarifying Trump's positions.

Senator Sessions argued that "Trump's views are that the United States should advance peace through strength. He believes that the military has been degraded. It needs to be rebuilt. That the sequester has done the damage."[14] In addition, Sessions repeated Trumps quest for an America First-driven foreign policy.[15] Another point often overlooked is the small size of the American Army. Sessions point out the approximate size of the Army is about 480,000, and he suggested that Trump proposed to increase that number to 540,000 troops."[16]

On updating Americas nuclear arsenal, Sessions argued the Obama administration failed to invest in upgrading the nuclear triad. The Senator believed the decline and rapid reduction of the nuclear deterrent could embolden enemies of the United States.[17] Sessions recognized the obvious—Trump would work to revamp the nuclear arsenal of the United States. A modern, more capable deterrent, according to Sessions, would increase the ability of the United States to provide stability and peace.[18]

Representative Randy Forbes addressed the politics of implementing Trump's defense plan. In response to a question, Forbes argued, "The president of the United States can't just implement a plan. The president of the United States has to be able to work with Congress and policy makers to put forth a plan."[19] Forbes argued Trump wanted a dramatic departure from Obama's policies, whereas Clinton would continue to implement the same feckless policies of the former president.[20] Finally, Forbes argued there is another significant difference that a Trump presidency would provide: his defense strategy would be forged inside the Pentagon and not a politicized national security council as was the case under President Obama.[21]

President-Elect Donald Trump tried to strike a different tone in the wake of his electoral victory. In a post-election acceptance speech delivered in the early morning on November 9, Trump issued this statement to calm the fears of those concerned about future US relations with the Republican president: "We will get along with all nations willing to get along with us. We will seek common ground, not hostility; partnership, not conflict."[22]

During the transition period a critical issue assumed center stage: how to move from campaign rhetoric to implementing a policy to rebuild the American military? Leo Shane III and Andrew Tilghman, reporters from the *Military Times*, described the dilemma that confronted the incoming Trump administration. Shane and Tilghman argued, "The common thread between Team Trump's transition discussions and the president-elect's campaign rhetoric is a belief that defense spending has dropped to dangerously low levels, and that the military . . . [for example] needs to add lots of people—more than 160,000 by some estimates—along with investing heavily in new ships and aircraft."[23]

They argued that if the "Trump administration can accomplish even a portion of this, it could reshape how many American troops find themselves assigned to geopolitical hot spots, including the Middle East, Eastern Europe and Southeast Asia."[24] In short, much like Reagan's build-up, Trump's attempt to transform the military could impact the Armed Forces of the United States for decades. To accomplish the transformation of the military, the president must confront an additional hurdle: "Democrats have promised a fight if Trump and his administration insist on increasing defense."[25]

The transition demonstrated the incoming president is ill-prepared to meet the challenge posed by rebuilding the military. Trump nor his small cadre of advisers were more concerned with governing in November and December of 2016; there were no internal debates or policy papers on administration objectives to rebuild the military. The prevailing view is that rebuilding the military would be a by-product of the military and the new secretary of defense designate, a position that was not filled until December 1 by Mattis. Mattis would need substantial time to get up to speed on the needs of the military and develop a national security memorandum to initiate a review of the military preparedness. This largely explains the silence on the issue concerning how the Trump administration planned to rebuild the military.

There were several post-election commentaries that endeavored to express the impact of the decline in defense spending under President Obama. Mike Wynne, a former Air Force secretary, provided this comprehensive analysis of the Obama defense cuts and their impact on the military. Wynne remarked, "After eight years of reckless cuts to national defense, discarded 'red lines,' emboldened competitors, and discouraged allies, the American people are ready for a new direction in Washington."[26] He spoke of the need for a new approach. That approach he said had to be "a fundamental rethinking of what it takes to keep the United States safe and to advance our national interests, in short, to make America great again in the eyes of the world."[27] In addition, Wynne argued, "In all of the military domains—ground, marine, air, space, and cyberspace—we need to restore US leadership."[28]

In contrast to the Obama years, Wynne argues that defense spending under President Trump will be different: "Trump has laid out a comprehensive, detailed, and forward-looking vision for the future of the American military. It is predicated on 'peace through strength' and a sober appraisal of US national interests."[29] Second, expand on the already existing missile defense infrastructure to deal with the threats posed by Iran and North Korea.[30] Third, an accelerated rebuilding of military to include all the services. Trump's vision, according to Wynne identified several additional features.[31] It is a vision that addresses the "crisis our military is facing."[32] This equates to the following as identified in Trump's vision: (1) "building toward a 350-ship Navy, . . . (2) increase the Air Force's [to] 1,200 aircraft, (3) . . . grow the Marine Corps from 27 to 36 battalions, and (4) . . . under the Trump plan, the Army will grow from 490,000 soldiers today to an active end-strength of 540,000."[33]

There is a major problem. Wynne mentioned that Trump 'has laid out a comprehensive, detailed, and forward-looking vision' for the future of the American military. The reality is that during the transition period no such vision existed. Equally important, no vision existed well into the opening months of the Trump administration. The absence of a vision imperiled the incoming president's ability to rebuild the military.

TRUMP AND REBUILDING THE MILITARY

During his initial visit to the Pentagon on January 27, 2017, President Trump used the occasion to focus attention on the administration objective to rebuild the military. A confident President Trump remarked, "I'm signing an executive action to begin a great rebuilding of the armed services of the United States. We're developing a plan for new planes, new ships, new resources, and new tools for our men and women in uniform."[34]

The Presidential Memorandum on Rebuilding the US Armed Forces contained specific information that demonstrates a shift in thinking about how to rearm the military. Some of the key components of the memorandum include:

> By the authority vested in me as President by the Constitution and the laws of the United States, including my authority as Commander in Chief of the Armed Forces of the United States, I hereby direct the following:
>
> Section 1. Policy. To pursue peace through strength, it shall be the policy of the United States to rebuild the US Armed Forces.[35]

The executive order called for improvement in readiness, a new Nuclear Posture Review, a new Ballistic Missile Defense Review, and the president ordered the secretary of defense to produce a National Defense Strategy document that would serve as the blueprint of the defense modernization.[36]

The significance of the executive order validated the United States is shifting away from President Obama's way of thinking and rapidly transitioning to a new approach to accelerate the rebuilding of the military. Appearing on *NPR*'s Morning Edition, retired Army Lieutenant General David Barno, offered this analysis: "The last administration had a strategy that was more of an indirect approach, and it was certainly a long-term approach. I think President Trump might be looking for something with some quicker results and that could put some new options on the table."[37]

President Trump later used the State of Union address to draw attention to his campaign pledge to rebuild the military. During the address, President Trump issued this statement: "To keep America safe, we must provide the men and women of the United States military with the tools they need to prevent war—[and] if they must—they have to fight . . . they only have to win."[38] With respect to the legislative branch, President Trump stated, "I am sending Congress a budget that rebuilds the military, eliminates the defense sequester . . . and calls for one of the largest increases in national defense spending in American history."[39]

The White House provided further clarification of President Trump's efforts to revamp the military. The White House asserted, "Our military needs every asset at its disposal to defend America. We cannot allow other nations to surpass our military capability."[40]

In addition, the White House promised to increase the offensive and defensive capabilities of Cyber Command and to implement a campaign pledge: "do everything it can to make sure our veterans get the care they deserve."[41]

President Trump proposed a $54 billion increase in defense spending for 2018.[42] The request ensured that total defense expenditures rose to $603 billion for fiscal year 2018. On the significance of the increase, during an address at the National Governors Association Meeting, President Trump stated, "This budget will be a public safety and national security budget. . . . And it will include a historic increase in defense spending to rebuild the depleted military of the United States of America at a time we most need it."[43]

The increase in defense spending was criticized as insufficient. In a notable example, Representative Mac Thornberry, the Republican chairman of the House Armed Services Committee, issued this assessment of the president's defense spending request: "It is clear to virtually everyone that we have cut our military too much and that it has suffered enormous damage. Unfortunately, the administration's budget request is not enough to repair that damage and to rebuild the military as the President has discussed."[44] In a subsequent critique, Senator John McCain, the chairman of the Senate Armed Services Committee, remarked, "With a world on fire, America cannot secure peace through strength with just 3 percent more than President Obama's budget. We can and must do better."[45]

Despite the criticism, there are those that argued President Trump's request was sufficient and that there is time for additional increases in subsequent years. Foreign policy analyst Frank Hoffman issued this response: "President Donald Trump has once again confounded his critics. His proposed Defense increase of $54 billion fulfills another of his campaign pledges. . . . The president's announcement is a down payment on that promise. . . . President Trump took the right approach: an incremental first step that demonstrates his commitment.[46]

In late May 2017, President Trump released the administration's proposed 2018 budget. The updated budget clarifies defense priorities across the military. Some of the significant details in defense spending include the following developments: (1) provide resources to "to accelerate the defeat of ISIS";[47] (2) authorize the spending to initiate the reconstruction of the military across the services; (3) increase US cyber capabilities; (4) provide the foundation "for a larger, more capable, and more lethal joint force"; (5) rebuild the US Navy; (6) expand the total number of service personnel in the Army and Marines and accelerate the growth of the Air Force which includes the dramatic production of F-35 next generation fighter.[48]

There are two additional components of the defense budget that is rarely discussed. For example, the budget, "Addresses urgent warfighting readiness needs. Fifteen years of conflict, accompanied in recent years by budget cuts, have stressed the Armed Forces."[49] The budget ensures the United States "remains the best led, best equipped, and most ready force in the world."[50] And second, it "increases DOD's budget authority by $52 billion above the current 2017 level of $587 billion. It is exceeded only by the peak increases of the Reagan Administration. . . . Unlike spending increases for war, which mostly consume resources in combat, the increases in the President's Budget primarily invest in a stronger military."[51]

To draw attention on the need to rebuild the military, one must understand the numerous issues that plagued the armed forces of the United States. Lucas Tomlinson clarified the issues that impacted the armed forces. The reporter used statements by senior officials in the Pentagon to support the claims of a "depleted military":

> "We are outranged and outgunned by many potential adversaries . . . [and] our army in the future risks being too small to secure the nation," McMaster told a Senate Armed Services subcommittee last April. . . . For some, they seek a gradual increase. . . . General Daniel Allyn, vice chief of staff of the Army, said while a third of his 58 brigade combat teams could be ready soon, only three could deploy immediately in the event of sudden conflict. Currently, half of the US Navy F-18 Hornets can't fly, and up to 75 percent of Marine Corps jets are grounded. Roughly half of Air Force B-1 bombers are grounded awaiting spare parts. For many US military jets flown well past their expected life, the shortage of spare parts comes from manufacturers that long stopped making them.[52]

In response to the internal and external issues that defined the American military under the administration of President Obama, during the campaign Trump issued this statement: "Our country will never have had a military like the military we're about to build and rebuild, it won't be depleted for long."[53]

On March 2, 2017, in an address before the "pre-commissioning" of the air craft carrier USS George F. Ford, in Newport News, Virginia, accompanied by Secretary of Defense Mattis, President Trump issued several significant statements. First, the president stated, "In these troubled times, our Navy is the smallest it's been since World War I. In fact, I just spoke with Navy and industry leaders and have discussed my plans to undertake a major expansion of our entire Navy fleet, including having the 12-carrier Navy we need."[54] The president issued this comment: "We will give the men and women of America's armed services the resources you need to keep us safe. . . . We will give our military the tools you need to prevent war and, if required, to fight war and only do one thing: win."[55]

The Challenge 101

The president's address focused on rebuilding the military; however, the speech was directed at rebuilding the Navy, and not about rebuilding all aspects of the armed forces of the United States. In time, the president's focus shifted from conventional forces to those of the irregular forces, the special forces units that would be responsible for confronting "radical Islamic terrorism."

ADDRESSING THE NEED TO INCREASE THE SIZE OF US SPECIAL FORCES

With the rhetoric about increasing the role of the US elite warriors to disrupt terrorist groups, most specifically against the Islamic State and Al Qaeda and their affiliates, a question begs: "Will Trump Break the Special Forces?"[56]

This is very significant question. Inside and outside the Pentagon, a chorus of statements argued there is an overuse (and misuse) of the Special Operations Forces (SOFs) in the United States. Much of the displeasure developed during the Obama administration. With President Obama's aversion to deploy conventional combat forces combined with the decision to extricate American forces from Iraq, the administration expanded the role of Drones and SOFs. The Obama administration's version of the "light footprint strategy"[57] eventually set the stage for the expansion of SOFs and an increase in operational tempo, particularly in Afghanistan and Somalia. The following excerpt underscores the increasing role of the SOFs during the Obama presidency:

> Under Obama, [Special Operations Command] SOCOM . . . added more than 15,000 personnel, and its budget has increased to $10.4 billion from $9.3 billion, according to SOCOM spokesman Ken McGraw. In Iraq and Syria, JSOC is targeting ISIS leaders and external operations, while the 5th Special Forces Group and other US SOF work with Iraqi security forces, Kurds, and Syrian Arab guerrillas. Elsewhere, SOF quietly operate in Libya, maintain a task force in the Horn of Africa and Yemen, and form a significant slice of the 8,400 US troops left in Afghanistan. The number of special operators deployed at any one time is [declined] . . . to 7,500 from a peak of between 12,500 and 13,500 at the height of the wars in Iraq and Afghanistan. Yet as the shrinking US conventional forces largely return to a peacetime training regimen, the operational tempo for SOF has not let up.[58]

There are two critical takeaways. Beginning with John F. Kennedy, who "expanded the Army Special Forces from 2,000 to 10,500 soldiers and founded the Navy SEALs. Under George W. Bush and Barack Obama, special operations forces grew from 38,000 in 2001 to 70,000 in 2016." Military and counterterrorism professionals wonder if President Trump will continue to expand SOFs.[59]

The second takeaway concerns the push-back against the overuse of the SOFs. Andrew Feickert, a military specialist for the Congressional Research Service, argues, "Some have expressed concern that the new Trump Administration could possibly expand USSOCOM's role in defeating terrorism and destroying Islamic State forces, thereby 'breaking' an already heavily committed force."[60] US SOFs "are already stretched thin and on the brink of burn out."[61] Feickert argued there must be a commitment by the administration to not only expand the role of conventional forces but to allow many of those forces to conduct missions currently initiated by special forces.[62]

Inside the Pentagon, senior officials are cognizant of the dilemmas associated with expansion of the missions of US SOFs. In testimony before the House Armed Services Committee on May 2, 2017, Theresa Whelan, the acting assistant Secretary of Defense for Special Operations, warned the deployments have taken a toll on the forces. Whelan then issued several significant statements. The secretary observed, "We've been operating at such a high [operational] tempo for the last decade plus, and with budgets going down, what we've had to do is essentially . . . eat our young, so to speak."[63] Then she issued this warning: "We've mortgaged the future . . . to facilitate current operations."[64]

Retired Lt. General Mark Hertling offered this critique of the Trump administration's objective to expand SOF operations: "You talk about mission creep—this is strategic mission creep all over the world. Special operations just isn't sized to do that."[65] Hertling's criticism, like those of others, is important because given the reality that US SOFs are engaged in over 80 countries around the world. The prevailing view is that unless there is a shift to expand the role of the Army infantry units and US Marines units to deal with ISIS and other transnational networks, the current pace could lead to "the misuse and overuse"[66] of the elite warriors.

Outside the Pentagon, there are those with expectations that President Trump will slowly increase the size and tempo of operations for the SOFs. Mark Moyar, the director of the Center for Military and Diplomatic History, argued that if President Trump continues the path of his predecessors and increases the SOFs, the decision could imperil the elite warriors. Moyar did note there is a positive development: "One virtue of the military veterans in Mr. Trump's national security circle is their ability to reject the unrealistic expectations of military novices, a group that has always been well represented among the White House consiglieri."[67] Additionally, Moyar asserted, "The deployment of Marines to Syria" in May "is an encouraging sign of a willingness to transfer burdens from special units, overutilized by Obama-era greenhorns, to underutilized conventional units."[68]

There is another debate. There is a concern the accelerated deployment of SOFs in the absence of a counterterrorism strategy. Micah Zenko, a senior fellow with the Council of Foreign Relations, argued, President Trump "expanded former President Barack Obama's use of lethal counterterrorism operations in non-battlefield countries—namely Yemen, Pakistan, and Somalia. During the final 193 days of Obama's presidency, there were 21 such operations."[69] Covering "a comparable number of days" President Trump ordered "five times as many operations: at least 92 in Yemen, four in Pakistan, and six in Somalia."[70] There is another "fear about the president's decision making in the use of SOFs," like "his predecessors did, in pursuit of counterterrorism objectives," Trump will turn to the special forces.[71] This issue, according to Zenko, is equally problematic in the absence of an administration counterterrorism strategy.[72]

Increasing the force to defeat the Islamic State, Al Qaeda, and other transnational terrorist threats represents one of the central objectives of the Trump administration. Another subtle objective calls for "Transformation: The Next Evolution of SOF."[73] Transformation is a reference to the preparation of the SOF to confront future threats with new training and fielding more lethal weapons systems.

In testimony before the House Armed Services Committee on May 2, 2017, General Raymond Thomas, the Commander of Special Operations Command, spoke of the need for transformation. General Thomas maintains, the expansion of the SOFs "and ensuring that they are equipped with the necessary resources and authorities to carry out their mission will not take place overnight. What's needed now is a course correction."[74] There is also a need for a counterterrorism strategy.

THE DILEMMA: TRUMP'S FAILURE TO SET DEFENSE PRIORITIES

At some point during the opening month of the Trump administration, the White House posted a link titled "Making Our Military Strong Again." The link reaffirmed that "The Trump administration will pursue the highest level of military readiness. We will provide our military leaders with the means to plan for our future defense needs."[75] The posting read like a campaign statement. The positing however is not a substitute for a speech by President Trump that clarifies the administration's defense priorities.

Despite the incessant comparisons between President Trump and President Ronald Reagan,[76] there is however a significant distinction between the two American presidents: President Reagan entered office with a clear vision on how to rebuild the American military, whereas, President Trump waited well into his second year to unveil his military strategy.

To illustrate President Reagan's plan of action to rebuild the American military, consider the following excerpt: "At the beginning of this year, I submitted to the Congress a defense budget which reflects my . . . long-term plan to make America strong again after too many years of neglect and mistakes."[77]

The speech then shifted to explain the state of the military and the necessity to prepare for future crises. Reagan then offered these words: "When I took office in January 1981, I was appalled by what I found: American planes that couldn't fly and American ships that couldn't sail." And it was obvious that we had to begin a major modernization program to ensure we could deter aggression and preserve the peace in the years ahead."[78]

After several speeches and multiple defense appropriations aimed at increasing spending on the American military, the Reagan defense build-up, with a price tag of nearly a trillion dollars over five years, set in motion one of the essential components of the president's legacy. President Reagan and now President Trump presided over two of four large increases in defense spending in the past 50 years.[79] Historically defense spending comes in waves. The four waves of major increases in defense spending include funding of the Vietnam War during the administration of Lyndon Johnson, President Reagan's build-up during the height of the Cold War, President George W. Bush's military expansion during the Iraq War, and now potentially President Trump.[80]

During the end of the first year of his presidency, Trump finally unveiled his vision to rebuild the military. It is within the White House National Security Strategy (NSS) document that the Trump administration provided details about the plan to rebuild the armed forces of the United States. One of the critical hurdles that President Trump had to overcome is a dilemma that he inherited when he occupied 1600 Pennsylvania Avenue: the inability of the Joint Force to keep pace with "emerging threats and technologies."[81]

In implementing the military reconstruction, the Trump administration recognized "the United States must restore [its] . . . ability to produce innovative capabilities, restore the readiness of our forces for major war, and grow the size of the force so that it is capable of operating at sufficient scale and for ample duration to win across a range of scenarios."[82]

The NSS listed five "priority of actions" that are essential in rebuilding the military. The priority of actions consisted of five interlocking components. Modernization called for the creation of "new capabilities" that resulted in "clear advantages for our military."[83] The second component—improvement in readiness—required the "focus on training, logistics, and maintenance."[84] Without readiness, the military may not be capable of responding to threats to American security interests around the world. Third, acquisition called for the purchase of new more lethal weapons that were affordable and increased the capabilities of the Joint Force. The fourth component concentrated on "capacity." In this context, capacity is a reference to increasing and sustaining the size of the military. With this capacity, the United States, as the Trump vision asserts, intends "to deter conflict and, if deterrence fails, to win in war."[85] In addition, capacity is critical "to defeat enemies, consolidate military gains, and achieve sustainable outcomes that protect the American people and our vital interests."[86] The fifth component called for the ability to "retain a full-spectrum force."[87] In the president's vision "the Joint Force must remain capable of deterring and defeating the full range of threats to the United States."[88] To accomplish this task, the president instructed the Department of Defense to "develop new operational concepts and capabilities to win without assured dominance in air, maritime, land, space, and cyberspace domains."[89] Finally, the NSS focuses attention on another areas that is desperate for attention: the ancient nuclear triad. The triad consists of land based Intercontinental Ballistic Missiles (ICBMs), Submarine Launch Ballistic Missiles (SLMB), and long-range nuclear bombers. This component, the non-conventional build-up, is critical to retain the long-established American nuclear deterrent. A corollary aspect of upgrading the triad calls for "the modernization and sustainment require investing in our aging command and control system."[90]

The NSS document provides the first comprehensive set of details of the president's vision to rebuild the military. In this critical step, Trump's detractors and supporters had something other than rhetoric that emanated from the executive branch. The NSS produced a shift; however, many pundits were surprised that it did contain aspects that were consistent "within the bipartisan mainstream of American foreign policy."[91] The critics of the NSS document, particularly those areas that focused on the refashioning of the military, viewed the military components of the document as supporting "the America First" agenda. A second complaint is that Trump's "initial military budgets" are insufficient to implement the president's vision for a more robust military.

There is another document that provided details of the president's vision to rebuild the military—the National Defense Strategy (NDS). The NDS document provided few details on the types of weapons that would emerged from Trump's vision. Rather, the NDS is a strategy document. The strategy document represents the requirements of "Trump's new military" and details the "strategic environment" that American forces would operate in both regionally and globally. It is a document that "articulates [how the Trump administration's] strategy to compete, deter, and win in [multi-level] . . . environment."[92]

The strategic environment explores state and non-state threats that have undermined US regional and global interests. On the state level, the strategic environment recognizes the US military under the Trump administration must be prepared to confront several great power challenges, one from China and a second from Russia. China's threat is a military challenge in Asia (most notably in the South China Sea) and an ever-evolving global economic and political challenge.

In the case of Russia, the challenge is largely in the military realm. But as Moscow's meddling in the 2016 presidential election and the 2018 midterm election proves, it is one that involves the political realm (and conducted in cyberspace). There are other domains associated with this challenge to include Russia's intervention in the Ukraine and the annexation of Crimea. Equally troubling are the threats to NATO and Moscow's political-military involvement in the Middle East, thanks to the operational bases in Syria.

There are twin regional challenges, one from Iran and the other from North Korea. As the upgrades across the military occur, the Trump administration must be prepared to deal with engaging multiple regional battles that if mishandled can quickly escalate and involve nuclear weapons. In addition, Iran represents a regional threat to US allies. That threat is based on Iran's quest to construct a Shia caliphate. Additionally, in Yemen, Iran is engaged in a proxy war to expand Shia influence in that country.

Engaging these diverse challenges in "this complex strategic environment" requires the Trump administration to "make difficult choices and prioritize what is most important to field a lethal, resilient, and rapidly adapting Joint Force."[93] This combined strategy, the document argues will lead "to victory on the battlefield."

The strategy enlists the support of eleven defense objectives[94] to meet the challenges of the present and the future. Providing appropriate funding to meet those threats will prove difficult in the hyper partisan political divide in Washington, DC. More to the point, Trump will find it increasingly problematic to fund the eleven defense objectives in the Democrat-controlled House of Representatives. Thus, the president will find it difficult to sustain long-term increases in military appropriation to meet Trump's vision.

The Trump vision had to deal with another level of criticism, this time from the Defense Strategy Commission (DSC). The DSC is a bipartisan organization selected by Congress and created to assist and evaluate the Trump administration's defense build-up. The commission endorsed the need to accelerate US defense spending to meet threats posed by China and Russia. The commission did not fully embrace the president's vision. The commission argued that "The United States has lost its military edge to a dangerous degree and could potentially lose a war against China or Russia."[95]

The commission argued the state of readiness of the Army could prove pivotal in the event of extended battle with China or Russia. The commission asserted that the deficiencies in spending over the second half the Obama administration significantly impacted the readiness of the military. Any battle with China and Russia could produce a high-rate of American casualties. In the end, the commission issued this significant statement: "While endorsing the aims [of the Trump administration strategy] . . . , the commission warned that Washington isn't moving fast enough or investing sufficiently to put the vision into practice, risking a further erosion of American military dominance that could become a national security emergency."[96] To assist the Trump administration with the defense build-up, the commission provided 32 recommendations.[97] One of the most critical recommendations called upon the Trump administration to clarify how the government of the United States would defeat China and Russia in a conventional conflict.[98]

There are other sources of discontent associated with the president's attempt to rebuild the military. There is the prevailing view that despite campaign rhetoric, the Trump administration is unlikely to sustain defense budgets in the range of $720-plus billion dollars. As a result, there is the perception that "the proposed military build-up [beyond 2019] isn't happening."[99]

Anthony Cordesman, a senior fellow on defense-related issues for the Center and Strategic and International Studies (CSIS), authored a piquant and comprehensive critique of the failure of President Trump to dramatically increase the defense budget and worse create and implement a clear plan for rebuilding the US military.

Cordesman took issue with what the administration did not discuss. According to Cordesman, "Neither the President nor the White House made any mention of his campaign calls for major increases in Army and Marine Corps manpower, in aircraft for the Air Force, or Ships for the Navy."[100] Cordesman responded to another administration flaw. According to Cordersman, "Aside from touching upon cyberwarfare and missile defense, the President did not announce a single measure to reinforce US national security that would deal with any specific foreign threat, or actual military mission capability."[101] The president did not address the threats or challenges from "China, Russian, North Korea, Iran, or any specific terrorist threat in the speech to the session of Congress."[102]

President Trump and then Secretary of Defense Mattis (and now the acting secretary) have ignored the criticism of the "slow pace of the build-up." The Pentagon privately acknowledged the slow-pace of the defense build-up. John Roth, the Pentagon's Comptroller, did shed light on the administration's underwhelming build-up. Roth stated, "You will not see a growth in force structure. You will not see a growth in the shipbuilding plan. You will not see a robust modernization program."[103]

There are supporters of the president that argue there is a vision to rebuild the military; one that is based on former Secretary Mattis's three-step approach which called for the improvement in "warfighting readiness, to achieve program balance by addressing shortfalls," and to build "a larger, more capable, and more lethal joint force."[104]

There are several problems that are evident with Mattis'sd three-step approach. The obvious issue is that it is not a vision but rather a memorandum for "budget guidance."[105] Second, no one doubts Mattis's brilliance and nearly all are confident that he has set in motion a plan to implement the reconstruction of the armed forces of the United States. In the end, Mattis's efforts (and that of his replacement) is no substitute for a presidential address that unveils President Trump's vision to rebuild the US military. As is the case with previous American leaders, President Trump continues to struggle with the implementation of the rebuilding of American armed forces. Thus far, President Trump's efforts to rebuild the military have sputtered. It will take additional time and massive appropriations to meet the presidents to rebuild the military. There is a major hurdle the president must navigate: "resistance from congressional Democrats." With the Democratic Party in control of the House of Representatives, the president is unlikely to receive the desired funding to meet his vision.

THE EXPANSION OF THE NAVY, THE SPACE FORCE, AND TRUMP'S MISSILE DEFENSE STRATEGY

There are clear signs of rebuilding success. For starters, the size of the US armed forces—across the military services—have increased. The Army and Marines have received advanced weapon systems across the board to compete in an ever-expanding threat environment. The Air Force is receiving advanced aircraft, most notably the F-35. In addition, work proceeds on the replacement to the aging B-2 Bomber. There is something of equal importance that has received too little attention—the improvement of the readiness of the American military.

The Navy is struggling to meet their objectives. Naval ship building expenditures have witnessed only a "modest increase in 2019."[106] That means the objective of 355 ships cannot be obtained until 2023. Defense spending for the Navy has dramatically increased during the Trump presidency. The problem however is that shipbuilding is a slow and laborious process. In the short term, President Trump approved a measure that permits the Navy to increase the total number of vessels in the fleet.

To respond to challenges posed by Russia in the Atlantic Ocean, President Trump agreed to the reactivation of US Navy's 2nd Fleet. According to Admiral John Richardson, the chief of the US Naval Operations, the decision to reactivate the fleet is consistent with the National Defense Strategy.[107] Richardson made this additional point: It "makes clear that we're back in an era of great-power competition as the security environment continues to grow."[108]

The Trump administration hopes that the increased tensions in the Atlantic, which have occurred because of Russia's activities in the Ukraine and in the Baltic Sea, will not lead to "fourth battle of the Atlantic (the others being World War I and II and the Cold War).[109] The Navy "created the 2nd fleet to check Moscow's designs on the Atlantic Rim, especially Europe."[110] Ironically, the 2nd Fleet returns with a similar mission. The decision to activate the 2nd Fleet provides the Navy with greater flexibility and reasserts US presence in the region. Additionally, it permits a genuine pivot to Asia to deal with China's threat to US interests in the region while simultaneously dealing with Russia's challenge in the Atlantic.

The Russian naval threat in the region and in the Arctic should be taken seriously. The US Navy is focusing on the increasingly destabilizing Russian submarine challenge in the region. During an interview in November of 2018, Vice Admiral Andrew "Woody" Lewis warned, "Let's be frank, the Russian undersea threat is real."[111] Lewis also offered this caveat: "There's no question the logical sequence of events with China is they will be there military as well."[112] The point made by the vice admiral is that China (like Russia) is a threat to US interests and naval activity in the Arctic as well.

There is little doubt the expansion of the Navy is a critical component of Trump's effort to revitalize the military. The issue this president must confront, much like previous American leaders, is that due to the technology, the appropriations madness, and the Pentagon bureaucracy, shipbuilding is a long and ever-widening process. The best the president can hope for is a substantial increase in the total number of American warships that assist in meeting mission objectives. In the era of hyper partisan politics and a divided government, a substantial increase in shipbuilding will be viewed as a victory for President Trump given the polemics in Washington.

Another initiative by President Trump—the creation of the Space Force—developed during a speech at the meeting of the National Space Council. The president issued this statement: "I'm here directing the Pentagon to . . . establish a Space Force as the sixth branch of the armed forces."[113] Outer space, once an arena of American dominance is now viewed as an area of weakness. The weakness is that both Russia and China believe that the United States could be defeated in a future great power war if its communication assets are destroyed. Those assets are in outer space. The focus of "the next frontier conflict" is US communication and intelligence satellites. If American communication and intelligence satellites are disabled US command and control of their forces will be significantly impacted.

To protect American vital interests in space, President Trump requested Chairman of Joint Chiefs of Staff General James Dunford to assume responsibility. Within a short period, an intense bureaucratic battle was unleashed inside the Pentagon. If a new service is to be created the existing services expressed concern that funding for current and future projects could be at stake. To reduce the bureaucratic politics within the Pentagon, President Trump shifted responsibility for the management of the new space force to Vice President Mike Pence.

The Trump White House assumed greater control of the future of the Space Force. However, the White House recognized that an internal review of "the way forward" remained in the hands of the Pentagon. After seven-weeks, the Pentagon forwarded the review to the White House. Following several days of analysis, President Trump dispatched Vice President Pence to deliver an address at the Pentagon.

During an August 9, 2018 address the vice president unveiled several points that clarified the future of the Space Force. Pence stated the Pentagon is committed to establishing the US Department of Defense Space Command by 2020. Second, consistent with other services, Pence announced the creation of a new combatant command which ensured the sixth service would be equal to the other services. Third, Pence called for the creation of the Space Development Agency that would assist in the formal creation of the Space Force.[114]

In speaking about the threats to the United States in outer space, Pence asserted, "from Russia and China to North Korea and Iran" each of the countries have "pursued weapons to jam, blind and disable" American "navigation and communications satellites via electronic attacks from the ground."[115] The creation of the Space Force said Pence provides the United States with the ability to respond to these and other threats.

The vice president's speech was well received but the speech failed to address several important issues. Would the space force unify existing space responsibilities of the other services? Would the space command have its own general and budget? These issues were addressed in a subsequent address by the vice president.

Speaking to guests at the Kennedy Space Center in Florida on December 18, 2018, Pence answered the aforementioned questions. The new force, said Pence, "will establish unified control over all our military space operations."[116] In addition, the Space Force would be responsible for developing "space doctrine, tactics, techniques, and procedures that will enable our warfighters" to defend the country.[117] Most notably, the vice president stated the Space Force "will be led by a four-star flag officer."[118]

There are additional hurdles that must be confronted before the Space Force is formally created. The first dilemma is whether the Space Force will become a stand-alone branch, or will it have autonomy within the Air Force? The evidence thus far suggests the Space Force will operate under the umbrella of the Air Force, but it will have substantial operating authority and its own general.[119]

Another dilemma involves the Congress of the United States. Congressional authorization is required before the Space Force can formally become the sixth branch of the armed forces. In the hyper partisan environment, and with Democratic control of the House, it is an open question if the president will be able to obtain bipartisan support. Thus far, Democratic support is strong, but the Space Force is currently not a high priority in Congress. If the congressional authorization for the Space Force is achieved, President Trump will have to spend political capital to make it a reality.

As part of the revitalization of the US military, the Trump administration is determined to upgrade and expand American missile defenses. The most significant statement on missile defense for the administration is located in the 2018 National Defense Strategy document. The statement included the following verbiage: "Investments will focus on layered missile defenses and disruptive capabilities" to contend with "theater missile threats and North Korean ballistic missile threats."[120] It would take a presidential address in January of 2019 before the administration would clarify their policy and its missile defense objectives.

In an address delivered at the Pentagon on January 17, 2019, President Trump unveiled the long-awaited Missile Defense Review (MDR).[121] In the address the president asserted, "All over, foreign adversaries—competitors and rogue regimes—are steadily enhancing their missile threats."[122] In response, President Trump promised to "ensure that we can detect and destroy any missile launched against the United States."[123] Similarly, the president stated, "I will accept nothing less for our nation than the best to meet any threat posed by Russia, China, and Iran."[124]

Overall, the address was praised. Proponents argued the president is investing the political capital necessary to upgrade the missile defense capabilities to confront Russian and Chinese advances in hypersonic technology. In addition, supporters assert the decision to incorporate offensive capabilities now places the onus on competitors. To ensure the administration meets these threats, President Trump promised a major boost in spending to achieve the objectives of the missile defense strategy. Most significantly, the president's embrace of cutting-edge technology is pivotal to restoring US dominance in defense-related matters (in the offensive or in the defensive realms). In an illustration of this point, Thomas Karako, a fellow at the prestigious Center for Strategic and International Studies, made this statement: "The endorsement of [a space sensor layer] . . . and . . . its timely deployment represents the single most significant goal"[125] of the MDR.

Critics warned the MDR will unleash a news arms race.[126] Second, critics charge President Trump is trying to reinvest in Star Wars-type technology that failed to secure the country during the height of the Cold War during the Reagan administration, and is unlikely to provide security in a far more destabilizing security environment that includes Russia, China, Iran, and North Korea. Third, the president's critics assert there is a political reality—Congress. The is a reference to the reality that a divided congress is unlikely to appropriate funding at the level requested by President Trump and senior Pentagon officials.

President Trump's military build-up is well underway. There are several questions that may be used to evaluate if the president is successful in completing his vision. There are major spending increases planned for all services and a subsequent plan to remake the antiquated nuclear triad. Will President Trump receive sufficient funding from a divided Congress? Second, will the president's vision incorporate the recommendations from the Defense Strategy Commission? Finally, how much political capital is President Trump willing to expend to meet his vision of rebuilding the military? The answers to these and other questions will assist in evaluating President Trump's efforts to rebuild the military.

NOTES

1. "Open Letter from Military Leaders." [No Date] https://assets.donaldjtrump.com/MILITARYLETTER.pdf. Accessed on June 10, 2018.
2. Ibid.
3. Diamond, Jeremy, "Trump Calls for Military Spending Increase," *CNN*, September 6, 2016. http://www.cnn.com/2016/09/06/politics/donald-trump-defense-spending-sequester/index.html. Accessed on June 13, 2018.
4. Ibid.
5. Colvin, Jill, "10 Moments from Trumps Iowa," CNSNews.com, November 14, 2015. http://www.cnsnews.com/news/article/10-moments-trumps-iowa-speech. Accessed on June 13, 2018.
6. Grait, Jonathon, "Trump to Ask Generals, Who Know Less Than Trump, for Plan to Defeat ISIS," *New York Magazine*, September 7, 2016. http://nymag.com/daily/intelligencer/2016/09/trump-isis-plan-devised-by-generals-who-dont-know-much.html. Accessed on June 15, 2018.
7. Ibid.
8. Tilghman, Andrew, "Donald Trump Paints a Dismal Picture of Today's Military," *Military Times*, October 3, 2016. http://www.militarytimes.com/articles/trump-paints-dismal-picture-of-todays-military. Accessed on June 15, 2018.
9. Ibid.
10. Ibid.
11. Ibid.
12. Brendan, McGarry, "Trump Surges to Become Next Commander-in-Chief," Military.com, November 9, 2016. http://www.military.com/daily-news/2016/11/09/trump-surges-become-next-commander-chief.html. Accessed on June 16, 2018.
13. Ibid.
14. Cavas, Christopher P. and Gould, Joe, "Top Trump Military Advisers Detail GOP Candidate's Defense Plan," *Defense News*, October 30, 2016. http://www.defensenews.com/articles/trump-defense-plan-detailed. Accessed on June 18, 2018.
15. Ibid.
16. Ibid.
17. Ibid.
18. Ibid.
19. Ibid.
20. Ibid.
21. Ibid.
22. McGarry, "Trump Surges to Become Next Commander-in-Chief," Military.com, November 9, 2016.
23. Shane III, Leo and Tilghman, Andrew, "Trump's Military Will Have More Troops and More Firepower—If He Can Find More Money," *Military Times*, November 20, 2016. http://www.militarytimes.com/articles/donald-trump-military-spending. Accessed on June 23, 2018.
24. Ibid.

25. Ibid.
26. Wynne, Mike, "The Case for Donald Trump on National Defense," Breakingdefense.com, October 31, 2016. http://breakingdefense.com/2016/10/the-case-for-donald-trump-on-national-defense/. Accessed on June 23, 2018.
27. Ibid.
28. Ibid.
29. Ibid.
30. Ibid.
31. Ibid.
32. Ibid.
33. Ibid.
34. "At Pentagon, Trump Declares His Aim of 'Rebuilding' The Military," NPR.org, January 27, 2017. http://www.npr.org/sections/thetwo-way/2017/01/27/511970907/trump-heads-to-the-pentagon-with-an-eye-on-the-war-against-isis. Accessed on June 24, 2018.
35. Presidential Memorandum on Rebuilding the US Armed Forces. The White House Office of the Press Secretary, January 27, 2017. https://www.whitehouse.gov/the-press-office/2017/01/27/presidential-memorandum-rebuilding-us-armed-forces. Accessed on June 25, 2018.
36. Ibid.
37. "At Pentagon, Trump Declares His Aim of 'Rebuilding' The Military."
38. Read the Full Text of Trump's Address to Congress," *PBS NewsHour*, February 28, 2017. http://www.pbs.org/newshour/rundown/read-full-text-trumps-address-congress/. Accessed on June 25, 2018.
39. Ibid.
40. Making Our Military Strong Again, The White House, Donald Trump. https://www.whitehouse.gov/making-our-military-strong-again. Accessed on June 26, 2018.
41. Ibid.
42. Shear, Michael and Steinhauer, Jennifer, "Trump to Seek $54 Billion Increase in Military Spending," *New York Times*, February 27, 2017. https://www.nytimes.com/2017/02/27/us/politics/trump-budget-military.html. Accessed on June 26, 2018.
43. Remarks by President Trump in Meeting with the National Governors Association. State Dining Room. February 27, 2017. https://historymusings.wordpress.com/2017/02/27/full-text-political-transcripts-february-27-2017-president-donald-trumps-speech-at-meeting-with-the-national-governors-association/. Accessed on June 26, 2018.
44. Cohen, Zachary, "Trump Proposes $54 Billion Defense Spending Hike," *CNN*, March 16, 2016. http://www.cnn.com/2017/03/16/politics/donald-trump-defense-budget-blueprint/index.html. Accessed on June 27, 2018.
45. Kheel, Rebecca, "McCain: Trump Defense Budget Not Enough for 'World on Fire,'" *The Hill*, February 27, 2017. http://thehill.com/policy/defense/321374-mccain-trump-defense-budget-not-enough-for-world-on-fire. Accessed on June 27, 2018.
46. Hoffman, Frank, "President Trump's Defense Budget: Just a Down Payment," FPRI.org, March 7, 2017. http://www.css.ethz.ch/content/dam/ethz/special-interest/gess/cis/center-for-securities-studies/resources/docs/FPRI-President%20Trump%27s%20Defense%20Budget%20Just%20a%20Down%20Payment.pdf. Accessed on June 27, 2018.
47. America First-Beginning a New Chapter of American Greatness, Office of Management and Budget. The White House, https://www.whitehouse.gov/sites/whitehouse.gov/files/omb/budget/fy2018/2018_blueprint.pdf. Accessed on June 29, 2018.
48. Ibid.
49. Ibid.
50. Ibid.
51. Ibid.
52. Tomlinson, Lucas, "Military Branches Drafting Expansion Plans as Trump Vows to Rebuild 'Depleted' Force," *Fox News*, February 21, 2017. http://azbizopps.org/wp-content/uploads/2017/02/Military-Branches-drafting-expansion-plans-02-21-2017.pdf. Accessed on June 29, 2018.
53. Ibid.

54. Garamone, Jim, "Trump Calls for 12-Carrier Navy, Promises Rebuilt Military," Defense.gov, March 2, 2017. https://www.defense.gov/News/Article/Article/1100952/trump-calls-for-12-carrier-navy-promises-rebuilt-military/. Accessed on June 29, 2018.
55. Ibid.
56. Naylor, Sean, "Will Trump Break the Special Forces?" *The Atlantic*, December 27, 2016. https://www.theatlantic.com/international/archive/2016/12/trump-special-forces-green-beret-iraq-obama-jsoc/511229/. Accessed on June 29, 2018.
57. For more on this strategy, see Goldsmith, Jack and Waxman, Matthew, "The Legal Legacy of Light Footprint Warfare," *Washington Quarterly*, Summer 2016, pp. 7–21.
58. Naylor, "Will Trump Break the Special Forces?"
59. Moyar, Mark, "America's Dangerous Love for Special Ops," (Opinion Page) *New York Times*, April 24, 2017. https://www.nytimes.com/2017/04/24/opinion/donald-trump-americas-dangerous-love-for-special-forces-ops.html. Accessed on June 30, 2018.
60. Feickert, Andrew, "US Special Operations Forces (SOF): Background and Issues for Congress," *Congressional Research Service* (CRS Report), January 17, 2017. https://fas.org/sgp/crs/natsec/RS21048.pdf. Accessed on June 30, 2018.
61. Ibid.
62. Ibid.
63. Choi, David, "After Multiple Deployments, US Special Forces May Have 'Mortgaged the Future,'" *Business Insider*, May 3, 2017. http://www.businessinsider.com/special-forces-groups-problems-2017-5. Accessed on June 30, 2018.
64. Henniger, W. J., "US Special Operations Forces Face Growing Demands and Increased Risks," *LA Times*, May 26, 2017. http://www.latimes.com/nation/la-na-special-operations-20170525-story.html. Accessed on June 30, 2018.
65. Ibid.
66. Ibid.
67. Moyar, Mark, "America's Dangerous Love for Special Ops."
68. Ibid.
69. Zenko, Micah, "Donald Trump Is Pushing America's Special Forces Past the Breaking Point," *Foreign Policy*, August 1, 2017. http://foreignpolicy.com/2017/08/01/donald-trump-is-pushing-americas-special-forces-past-the-breaking-point-jsoc-navy-seal/. Accessed on June 30, 2018.
70. Ibid.
71. Ibid.
72. Ibid.
73. Thomas, (General) Raymond, The Commander of Special Operations Command in Testimony Before the House Armed Services Committee on Emerging Threats and Capabilities on May 2, 2017. Washington, DC. http://docs.house.gov/meetings/AS/AS26/20170502/105926/HHRG-115-AS26-Wstate-ThomasR-20170502.PDF. Accessed on June 30, 2018.
74. Lohaus, Phillip, "The Uncertain Future of Special Ops," *USNews.com*, June 15, 2017. https://www.usnews.com/opinion/world-report/articles/2017-06-15/trump-needs-to-course-correct-on-obamas-special-operations-forces-policy. Accessed on June 30, 2018.
75. President Donald Trump, "Making Our Military Strong Again." White House, January 27, 2017. https://www.whitehouse.gov/making-our-military-strong-again. Accessed on June 30, 2018.
76. Bruce, Tammy, "The Trump-Reagan Parallels," *Washington Times*, February 22, 2017. http://www.washingtontimes.com/news/2017/feb/22/donald-trump-parallels-with-ronald-reagan-should-b/. Accessed on December 5, 2018.
77. Address to the Nation on Defense and National Security, March 23, 1983. https://reaganlibrary.archives.gov/archives/speeches/1983/32383d.htm. Accessed on December 5, 2018.
78. Ibid.
79. Carson, Joseph G., "National Defense: Is Another Spending Boom on the Horizon?" Allianceberstein.com, February 9, 2017. https://alliancebernstein.com/library/national-defense-is-another-spending-boom-on-the-horizon.htm. Accessed on December 8, 2018.
80. Ibid.

81. National Security Strategy of the United States, White House, December 2017. https://www.whitehouse.gov/wp-content/uploads/2017/12/NSS-Final-12-18-2017-0905.pdf. Accessed on December 8, 2018.
82. Ibid.
83. Ibid.
84. Ibid.
85. Ibid.
86. Ibid.
87. Ibid.
88. Ibid.
89. Ibid.
90. Ibid.
91. Feaver, Peter, "Five Takeaways from Trump's National Security Strategy," *Foreign Policy*, December 18, 2017. https://foreignpolicy.com/2017/12/18/five-takaways-from-trumps-national-security-strategy/. Accessed on December 8, 2018.
92. National Defense Strategy, Washington, DC. 2018. https://dod.defense.gov/Portals/1/Documents/pubs/2018-National-Defense-Strategy-Summary.pdf. Accessed on December 8, 2018.
93. Ibid.
94. The eleven defense objectives include: (1) defending the homeland from attack; (2) sustaining Joint Force military advantages, both globally and in key regions; (3) deterring adversaries from aggression against our vital interests; (4) enabling US interagency counterparts to advance US influence and interests; (5) maintaining favorable regional balances of power in the Indo-Pacific, Europe, the Middle East, and the Western Hemisphere; (6) defending allies from military aggression and bolstering partners against coercion, and fairly sharing responsibilities for common defense; (7) dissuading, preventing, or deterring state adversaries and non-state actors from acquiring, proliferating, or using weapons of mass destruction; (8) preventing terrorists from directing or supporting external operations against the United States homeland and our citizens, allies, and partners overseas; (9) ensuring common domains remain open and free; (10) continuously delivering performance with affordability and speed as we change Departmental mindset, culture, and management systems; and (11) establishing an unmatched twenty-first century National Security Innovation Base that effectively supports Department operations and sustains security and solvency. For more on these points, see the National Defense Strategy document.
95. Sonne, Paul and Harris, Shane, "US Military Edge has Eroded 'to a Dangerous Degree, Study for Congress Finds," *Washington Post*, November 14, 2018. https://www.washingtonpost.com/world/national-security/us-military-edge-has-eroded-to-a-dangerous-degree-study-for-congress-finds/2018/11/13/ea83fd96-e7bc-11e8-bd89-eecf3b178206_story.html?utm_term=ba02ec2e14c55. Accessed on December 14, 2018.
96. Ibid.
97. Ibid.
98. Ibid.
99. Lamothe, Dan, "Critics Say Trump's Proposed Military Buildup Isn't Happening. Wait Until 2019, the Pentagon Says," *Washington Post*, May 23, 2017. https://www.washingtonpost.com/news/checkpoint/wp/2017/05/23/critics-say-trumps-proposed-military-buildup-isnt-happening-wait-until-2019-the-pentagon-says/?utmterm=42371b9803f3. Accessed on December 14, 2018.
100. As quoted in Cordesman, Anthony, "Trump on National Security: Calling for More Spending is Not Enough," Center for Strategic and International Studies (CSIS), March 2, 2017. https://csis-prods3amazonaws.com/s3fs-public/publication/170302_Trump-National-Security-full.pdf?X3z74rLdloZBP_rmDvdX_0h84_lj7Et1. Accessed on December 14, 2018.
101. Ibid.
102. Ibid.
103. Weisgerber, Marcus, "Trump's Military Buildup Won't Begin Until 2019," *Defense One*, May 23, 2017. http://www.defenseone.com/politics/2017/05/trumps-military-buildup-wont-begin-until-2019/138106/. Accessed on December 17, 2018.

104. Garamone, Jim, "Mattis Issues Budget Guidance, Say's 2017 Submission Will Rise," *Defense One*, February 1, 2017. www.army.mil/article/181718/mattis_issues_budget_guidance_says_fiscal_2017_submission_will_rise. Accessed on December 17, 2018.

105. "Document: SECDEF James Mattis' Pentagon Budget Guidance," USNI.org, February 1, 2017. https://news.usni.org/2017/02/01/document-defense-secretary-james-mattis-budget-guidance. Accessed on December 17, 2018.

106. Larter, David, "US Navy to Add 46 Ships in Five Years, but 355 Ships Won't Come for a Long Time," Defensenews.com, February 12, 2018. https://www.defensenews.com/smr/federal-budget/2018/02/13/us-navy-to-add-46-ships-in-five-years-but-355-ships-is-well-over-the-horizon/. Accessed on December 17, 2018.

107. Woody, Christopher, "Here's Why the Navy is Reactivating the 2nd Fleet to Patrol the Atlantic," Taskandpurpose.com, May 7, 2018. https://Taskandpurpose.com/navy-reactiving-2nd-fleet-russia. Accessed on December 18, 2018.

108. Ibid.

109. Ibid.

110. Ibid.

111. Ziezulewicz, Geoff, "Commander of 2nd Fleet Latest to Sound Alarm Over Russia Subs," *NavyTimes.com*, November 28, 2018. https://www.navytimes.com/news/your-navy/2018/commander-of-2nd-fleet-latest-to-sound-alarm-over-russian-subs/. Accessed on December 18, 2018.

112. Ibid.

113. Read Trump's Full Remarks on Immigration, "Space Force" *The Boston Globe*, June 18, 2018. https://www.bostonglobe.com/news/politics/2018/06/read-trump-full-remarks-immigration-space-force/QcLtBX1us0LiL2eW5KrajL/story.html. Accessed on January 4, 2019.

114. Roulo, Claudette, "Space Force to Become Sixth Branch of the Armed Forces," DoDNews.gov, August 9, 2018. https://dod.defense.gov/News/Article/Article/1598071/space-force-to-become-sixth-branch-of-armed-forces/. Accessed on January 4, 2019.

115. Ibid.

116. Remarks by Vice President Pence at Kennedy Space Center, White House.gov, December 18, 2018. https://www.whitehouse.gov/briefings-statements/remarks-vice-president-pence-kennedy-space-center/. Accessed on January 4, 2019.

117. Ibid.

118. Ibid.

119. Insinna, Valeria, "Trump's New Space Force to Reside Under Department of the Air Force," DefenseNews.com, December 20, 2018. https://www.defensenews.com/space/2018/12/20/trumps-new-space-force-to-reside-under-department-of-the-air-force/. Accessed on January 4, 2019.

120. As stated in the "2018 National Defense Strategy."

121. The national missile strategy release was originally scheduled for release in 2017. Due to changes in threats and Pentagon's response to those threats, combined with the decision to incorporate offensive missile defense capabilities, the roll-out was delayed by the Trump administration.

122. Remarks by President Trump and Vice President Pence Announcing the Missile Defense Review. TheWhiteHouse.gov, January 17, 2019. The Pentagon, Arlington, Virginia. https://www.whitehouse.gov/issues/national-security-defense/. Accessed on January 18, 2019.

123. Ibid.

124. Ibid.

125. Seligman, Lara, "Trump's Muscular New Plan to Fend Off Russian and Chinese Missiles," *Foreign Policy*, January 18, 2019. https://foreignpolicy.com/2019/01/17/trumps-muscular-new-plan-to-fend-off-russian-and-chinese-missiles-missile-defense-space/. Accessed on January 20, 2019.

126. Hennigan, W. J., "Donald Trump's Latest Idea Could Lead to an Arms Race," Time.com, January 17, 2019. https://time.com/5506284/donald-trump-nuclear-weapons-missile-defense/. Accessed on January 20, 2019.

Chapter Five

The Nightmare and Potential for a New Reality

Trump and North Korea

An official in the Obama State Department stated, "It was no secret the president was not going to confront North Korea."[1] With engagement and strategic patience with North Korea no longer an option and President Obama unwilling to use force, the prevailing view is that Pyongyang would become a problem for the next president.

As the Obama era closed, senior foreign policy officials within the administration, along with the president, had to accept a painful reality: Donald Trump would become the new occupant of 1600 Pennsylvania Avenue. There would be no smooth transition to Democratic presidential candidate Hillary Clinton. The transition was complicated by the fact the outgoing Obama administration had to prepare the president-elect and his transition officials about the North Korean threat.

Gerald F. Seib, Jay Solomon, and Carol E. Lee, journalists for the *Wall Street Journal*, remarked that in late November of 2016, "The Obama administration considers North Korea" and their nuclear program would emerge as "the top national security priority for the incoming administration, a view it has conveyed to President-elect Donald Trump's transition team."[2] There is something else: "Obama White House officials also handed off detailed options for Trump to address the North Korean crisis, though they are unsure whether top Trump aides—including Matt Pottinger and Alison Hooker, the national security council's top aides for Asia and Korea respectively—have relied on them."[3]

There were demands for a tougher approach to dealing with North Korea. Former chairman of the Joint Chiefs of Staff, Admiral Michael Mullen warned, "If we just sit back and continue to let [Kim Jong Un] evolve, we're going to have someone with that [nuclear] capability, which is unacceptable."[4]

President Trump is now the caretaker of one of the most significant threats that could dominate his administration and one which could easily morph from a crisis to a war. There is a political query often lost in the Trump-North Korea issue: will the president confirm the caricature created by Hillary Clinton and her minions during the 2016 presidential election, or will Trump formally end the long-running North Korean threat? Put another way, will Trump's approach set the United States on a course for peril in the Korean Peninsula or will it create an opportunity for stability in the region?

HERE WE GO AGAIN: A FAMILIAR PATH?

The North Korean threat is by no means a recent phenomenon. North Korea occupied the agendas of four previous American presidents. That is, the administrations of George H. W. Bush, Bill Clinton, George W. Bush, and Barack Obama have each been forced to deal with disparate periods of instability in the Korean Peninsula because of several destabilizing actions by the Democratic People's Republic of Korea (DPRK or North Korea). What were the threats initiated by North Korea, and how did American presidents respond to those threats?

Paul Leventhal, the president of the Nuclear Control Institute and Steven Dolley, the research director of Nuclear Control Institute, asserted, "The North Korean Nuclear Crisis"[5] can be traced back to the 1950s and expands during the decade of the 1960s. Specifically, Leventhal and Dolley argued, "the nuclear research program of the Democratic Peoples' Republic of Korea dates back to the 1950s, when the Korean government entered into nuclear cooperation agreements with the Soviet Union and China. In the mid-1960s, the DPRK received a small research reactor and critical assembly (a research tool used to sustain and study nuclear chain reactions) from the Soviet Union."[6]

The framework of the DPRK nuclear program had its origins during the Cold War. In this context, the starting point occurred under President Dwight D. Eisenhower's "atoms for peace" in 1953. The American leader agreed to share "scientific and technological assistance" with key allies to include Israel, Iran, Iran, South Africa, South Korea, and Taiwan.[7]

In the wake of the American initiative, the Soviet Union in 1954 agreed to cooperate in the "military sphere"[8] with China. Later in that year, the Soviet Union agreed to export a nuclear reactor to China. Two years removed from this cooperation, the Soviet government signed a nuclear agreement with the government of North Korea. After further discussions in "September 1959 the DPRK and the Soviet Union signed a treaty providing Soviet technical assistance for the establishment of a North Korean nuclear research center which created the basis for Soviet assistance in the construction of an experimental reactor in the DPRK."[9] This relationship with Moscow, combined with Pyongyang's inspiration of the nuclear capabilities of China and some of the Soviet's East-bloc allies, identified "the North Korean leadership probably considered this nuclear program quite urgent."[10] The efforts of the North Korean government intensified in the 1960s after DPRK intelligence indicated that South Korea constructed an experimental nuclear reactor in 1962.[11] Within a two-year period, the North Korean government commenced research on their own nuclear reactor.[12] At the time, these actions on the part of the governments of the Soviet Union and China and those of the East-bloc countries did not set off alarm bells in the West or at the United Nations.[13]

For the United States several presidential administrations were forced to come to terms with the ever-expanding North Korean nuclear program. The next section provides a brief examination of the administrations of George H. W. Bush, Bill Clinton, George W. Bush, and Barack Obama and how these presidents responded to the North Korean challenge. The remainder of the chapter examines the North Korean nightmare that President Trump inherited and the potential opportunities that unfolded between the United States and North Korea that changed the course of the relationship between Washington and Pyongyang.

PRESIDENT GEORGE H. W. BUSH

North Korean destabilizing actions in the region did not occur until the administrations of President Ronald Reagan and President George H. W. Bush. The Reagan and Bush administrations worked to ensure the Korean Peninsula remained a nuclear free zone. North Korea's decision to construct a "5 megawatt-electric, gas cooled, graphite moderated nuclear reactor, a clone of Great Britain's first reactor" at Yongbyon infuriated President Reagan. After the discovery of the North Korean reactor, the Reagan administration "pressured the Soviet Union to urge"[14] North Korea to join the Nuclear Proliferation Treaty (NPT).

To build on the efforts of President Reagan, his successor President Bush "withdrew American tactical nuclear weapons from South Korea."[15] In response to President Bush's unilateral action, on November 8, 1991, "President Roh Tae Woo of South Korea announces the Declaration on the Denuclearization of the Korean Peninsula, under which South Korea promises not to produce, possess, store, deploy, or use nuclear weapons."[16] It should be noted "the declaration unilaterally prohibits South Korea from possessing nuclear reprocessing or uranium enrichment facilities. These promises, if enacted, would satisfy all of North Korea's conditions for allowing IAEA inspections of its nuclear facilities."[17]

On December 31, 1991, "The two Koreas" sign the South-North Joint Declaration on the Denuclearization of the Korean Peninsula. Under the declaration, both countries agree not to "test, manufacture, produce, receive, possess, store, deploy or use nuclear weapons" or to "possess nuclear reprocessing and uranium enrichment facilities."[18] It appeared that President Bush succeeded in preventing nuclear proliferation in the Korean Peninsula.

PRESIDENT BILL CLINTON

North Korean provocations during the administration of President Bill Clinton dramatically increased the tensions in the region. Those actions include concern about North Korea's "continued defiance of [International Atomic Energy Agency] IAEA safeguards."[19] The second concerned North Korea's "March 1993 withdrawal from the NPT"[20] and third, on June 13, 1993, the government of North Korea made the decision to withdraw from the IAEA.[21]

In response to North Korea's quest for nuclear weapons, both President Clinton and President Kim Il Sung engaged in an extended period of harsh statements that pushed their countries on the path to war. As the crisis deepened, President Clinton dispatched military reinforcements to South Korea in preparation for war.

Was the Clinton administration prepared to go war? The answer is yes. In the view of Robert Gallucci, then the State Department's point man on Korea in 1994, he made the following statement: "I believe it would have resulted almost certainly in war. We demonstrated we were prepared to go down the military route if we needed to, but that was clearly not something that was a preferred course."[22]

Clinton's Secretary of Defense William Perry provided this inside perspective of the crisis: "We knew we were poised on the brink of a war that might involve weapons of mass destruction. When the president entered the room, he was more somber than usual; Indeed, everyone there recognized the gravity of the situation."[23] In an interview with Perry, Jamie McIntyre, provided additional information:

> In a 1999 interview two years after he left the Pentagon, Perry told me he was convinced the US could have taken out the Yongbyon facility without the risk of nuclear contamination but said he didn't brief that option to Clinton that day. "I concluded that was too likely to start a war," Perry told me. Instead, he kept those plans in reserve, an ace-in-the-hole, if tough new sanctions failed to bring Pyongyang around.[24]

Leon V. Sigal, a consultant for the Social Science Research Council, offered this analysis of the incident: "The June 1994 crisis was a turning point in US nuclear diplomacy with North Korea. For nearly three years, starting in late 1991, the United States had tried to coerce Pyongyang into halting its nuclear weapons program, and failed."[25] Sigal noted the Clinton administration "Then . . . tried cooperation and succeeded. In the end, it was the high-level diplomatic intercession of former President Jimmy Carter that diffused the immediate crisis and allowed Washington and Pyongyang to peacefully resolve their nuclear stalemate."[26]

After four months of tense negotiations, conducted by former president Jimmy Carter, the parties signed the Agreed Framework in Geneva Switzerland in June 1994. The agreement required "North Korea to freeze and eventually eliminate its nuclear facilities, a process that will require dismantling three nuclear reactors, two [at the time were] still under construction. North Korea also allows the IAEA to verify compliance through "special inspections."[27] In addition, "it agrees to allow 8,000 spent nuclear reactor fuel elements to be removed to a third country."[28] Lastly, the Clinton administration agreed to provide "two Light Water Reactors (LWRs) to North Korea along with "annual shipments of heavy fuel oil during construction of the reactors."[29]

President Clinton moved to quickly deescalate tensions in the region, in a speech on October 18, 1994, Clinton informed the American people that he was "pleased that the United States and North Korea . . . reached agreement on the text of a framework document on North Korea's nuclear program."[30] Additionally, President Clinton revealed, "This agreement represents the first step on the road to a nuclear-free Korean Peninsula. . . . Compliance will be certified by the International Atomic Energy Agency. The United States and North Korea have also agreed to ease trade restrictions and to move toward establishing liaison offices in each other's capitals."[31]

PRESIDENT GEORGE W. BUSH

In office for the less than a month, "President Bush suspended the Agreed Framework, pending the results of an internal review of the US policy toward North Korea."[32] The decision to suspend the controversial agreement remained in place until the completion of the policy review in June 2001.

In the wake of the policy review, in a speech on June 6, 2001, President Bush directed senior officials to engage in "serious discussions with North Korea on a broad agenda to include: improved implementation of the Agreed Framework relating to North Korea's nuclear activities; verifiable constraints on North Korea's missile programs and a ban on its missile exports; and a less threatening conventional military posture."[33] Bush made this important statement: "Our approach will offer North Korea the opportunity to demonstrate the seriousness of its desire for improved relations."[34] The president subsequently informed the North Korean government that "a positive reaction could lead to productive relations and an easing of sanctions."[35]

The Bush administration's initial policy was interpreted this way: they "linked future dialogue with North Korea on Pyongyang's willingness to permanently dismantle its nuclear power facilities; to eliminate its medium and long-range missile programs; to reduce the size of its conventional force; to improve its human rights performance; and to begin economic reforms."[36]

Prior to and in the wake of President Bush's January 2002 State of the Union address, the US-North Korean relationship declined considerably. During the address "President Bush branded North Korea a member of an 'axis of evil' alongside Iraq and Iran."[37] After the "US Nuclear Posture Review was leaked to the press, revealing that the US might consider launching a preemptive nuclear attack upon North Korea,"[38] the relationship continued to decline.

The Bush administration pursued a new course, a significant departure from President Clinton's approach. Beginning in August of 2003, President Bush made a complete break from the Clinton approach. During this same month, President Bush pursued the Six-Party diplomatic initiative. Bush included China, Japan, North Korea, Russia, South Korea, along with the United States in a multilateral approach aimed at eliminating North Korea's nuclear program and restoring stability to the region. After the end of the first round of talks, "North Korea agreed to abandon its nuclear weapons and nuclear program."[39]

An analysis of the progress of the Six-Party Talks is as follows: "In between periods of stalemate and crisis, those talks arrived at critical breakthroughs in 2005, when North Korea pledged to abandon 'all nuclear weapons and existing nuclear programs' and return to the NPT, and in 2007, when the parties agreed on a series of steps to implement that 2005 agreement."[40]

The Bush administration's approach faltered for several reasons. Given the expanding insurgency in Iraq, President Bush no longer considered North Korea a priority. The absence of consistent Chinese pressure permitted North Korea with the necessary wiggle room to commence a new period of provocations that undermined the Six-Party negotiations. Thus, the negotiations "broke down in 2009 following disagreements over verification and an internationally condemned North Korea rocket launch. Pyongyang has since stated that it . . . is no longer bound by their agreements. The other five parties . . . remain committed to the talks and have called for Pyongyang to recommit to its 2005 denuclearization pledge."[41]

President Bush's approach and the failure to achieve denuclearization invited criticism. An example is found in the following excerpt: "The net result of Bush's hawkish policies was little better, if not worse, than those of the Clinton administration. . . . Bush clearly underestimated the North Korean regime. . . . What we learned from the Bush years is that North Korea will not yield to pressure easily."[42]

PRESIDENT BARACK OBAMA

During the 2008 presidential campaign, then candidate Senator Obama promised he would engage Americas enemies, whether in North Korea, Iran, Cuba, or in Syria. Once in office, Iran, and not North Korea, was the immediate focus of the president's engagement activities. In early February of 2009, the administration quietly used China as a diplomatic instrument to open a dialogue with the regime of Kim Jung Il.

Within a matter of months, President Obama's engagement rhetoric met the reality of the unpredictable and provocative actions of the North Korean regime. The initial dilemma that President Obama had to confront is the North Korean demand the US government recognized Pyongyang "as a nuclear weapons state and [second] that a peace treaty with the United States must be a prerequisite to denuclearization."[43] The Obama administration did not recognize North Korea as a nuclear weapons state and equally significant they viewed Pyongyang's "possession of nuclear weapons as 'unacceptable.'"[44]

At another level, "despite the overtures for engagement after Obama took office, a series of provocations from Pyongyang halted progress on furthering negotiations. These violations of international law initiated a periodic cycle of action and reaction in which the United States focused on building a consensus"[45] at the UN Security Council. Subsequent ballistic missile tests "spurred the passage of UNSC Resolution 1874, which outlines a series of sanctions to deny financial benefits to the Kim regime."[46]

The Obama administration's North Korea problem remained consistent. That is, "Three years later, this cycle repeated itself: North Korea launched two long-range missiles in 2012, the UNSC responded with rebukes, North Korea tested a nuclear device in February 2013, and the United States again wrangled yet harsher sanctions through the UNSC (Resolutions 2087 and 2094)."[47]

There are several significant questions still unanswered: what is the Obama administration's policy? How did the administration respond to the provocations of the government of North Korea? The Obama administration's two-pronged approach to North Korea consisted of strategic patience and the use of sanctions in an attempt to force Pyongyang to pursue denuclearization. The sanctions came in two forms, multilateral and unilateral. The multilateral sanctions involved those that were imposed by the United Nations. The unilateral sanctions are comprised of the executive orders that were implemented by President Obama. For example, President Obama signed Executive Order 13551 which targeted entities in North Korean engaged "in money laundering, arms sales, narco-trafficking, luxury goods" that "exported into and out of the country."[48]

In the final analysis, strategic patience amounted to the administration's diplomatic initiative to restart the stalled Six-Party Talks, a process initiated by President Bush. A critical component of President Obama's policy is to employ China to increase pressure to force North Korea to the bargaining table and aid in the reduction of tensions in the region. These efforts embodied the administration's engagement efforts with North Korea.

There are many that assert that President Obama should have made Iran and North Korea equal priorities. That is, each of the rogue states and their nuclear saber rattling caused instability in their respective regions. Others assert that President Obama should have focused exclusively on the North Korean threat.

David Straub, an author and expert on the Korean Peninsula and US-Korea relations, argued "there is a 'rogue' regime with an active nuclear weapons program about which Americans these days [have expressed] concerned. It is of course Iran, but one could be forgiven for thinking we should be focused on North Korea instead."[49]

Straub provided a wealth of evidence to support his argument. In the case of North Korea, they have already conducted two nuclear tests involving the use of plutonium by the end of 2009.[50] During this same period, the Iranian government had not conducted any such tests. As of November 2010, the North Korean regime revealed that it had constructed a uranium enrichment facility.[51] At this stage, the evidence indicates that Iran's facility was still in the development stages.[52] In an important argument, Straub asserted that the North Korean regime assisted Iran in developing "their missile technology."[53] Yet, for these and many other examples that Straub listed, the Obama administration engaged in direct negotiations with the government in Iran that was previously considered implausible by the administration.[54] Equally troubling to Straub is that he, along with many other experts, viewed North Korea (due their level of testing and possession of nuclear weapons) as a far more significant threat to international security than the Iranian regime.[55]

Following the death of Kim Jong-Il, the Obama administration's policy continued to flounder. With the tenure of Kim Jong-Il over, President Obama and his senior advisors did not know how to react to Kim Jung-Un, the son of the departed leader. Thus, engagement stalled further and there was little hope for a diplomatic breakthrough.

Early in the second term of the Obama administration, it is clear that engagement failed. Charles Pritchard, the former special envoy for negotiations with North Korea during the Bush administration and a special assistant to Bill Clinton on national security, made the following statement about

President Obama's engagement policy: "It is essentially in tatters. They made a calculation. They reached out to North Korea and it fell apart. I think the US will be essentially regrouping on an international basis. They're not going to go back to a bilateral engagement with the North Koreans any time soon."[56]

Ben Rhodes, Obama's deputy national security adviser, offered this defense of the president's policy: "What this administration has done is broken the cycle of rewarding provocative actions by the North Koreans that we've seen in the past. . . . North Korea was removed from the terrorism list, even as they continued to engage in provocative actions. Under our administration we have not provided any assistance to North Korea."[57] Rhodes provided this statement in another defense of the Obama administration's policy: "The message that we've been delivering is that North Korea is wasting its money on these weapons as many of their people starve and as their economy is one of the most backward in the world."[58] What Rhodes did not comprehend is that Kim Jong-Un, like his father, viewed President Obama as a weak leader and thus the young leader of North Korea was willing to test the American leader. This is a recognition that the Obama administration would not unleash a tough military response. It is for this reason that North Korea was willing to continue nuclear tests to improve their nuclear capabilities.

In the final year of his presidency, in recognition of limited options, and in response to another North Korean provocative nuclear test, President Obama "pressed for and won stringent new economic sanctions at the United Nations. . . . It sought to further choke off North Korea's access to the world financial system by designating the country a 'primary' money launderer."[59] Additionally, the State Department "took the unusual step of naming Mr. Kim and 14 other senior officials it said were responsible for grave human rights abuses in a five-page report detailing repression in North Korea."[60] These measures did not end the provocative actions of the North Korean government. As the president's tenure in office concluded, Obama was not prepared to end the North Korean nuclear problem. Rather, it "kicked the can down the road." Translation, North Korea became the problem of his successor.

PRESIDENT DONALD TRUMP'S UNPREDICTABILITY AND THE NEW DANGEROUS OPTIONS

There are a host of commonalities about the behavior of the government of North Korea and some of its similarities associated with the American response. Three previous presidents, Clinton, Bush, and Obama pursued diplomacy with the hopes of ending North Korea's nuclear program. Expressing concern about the burgeoning North Korean nuclear threat, the same three

American presidents, "considered preemptive military strikes against North Korea's nuclear sites and all eventually decided against it."[61] There is this additional analysis of the American response covering the previous presidents:

> Past US administrations have attempted bilateral deal-making and multilateral implementation (the Clinton administration's Agreed Framework), neglect (first George W. Bush administration, 2001–2004), and bilateral engagement within the context of Six Party Talks (second George W. Bush administration, 2005–2008). None of these approaches was successful in deterring North Korea from pursuit of its nuclear program.[62]

The excerpt indicated that North Korea is a persistent challenge for the United States and the international community.[63] There is something equally troubling—problematic presidential responses and "the deficiencies of the international responses."[64]

With this backdrop, a series of questions developed. For example, why did experts argue North Korea represented a nightmare for President Trump? Additionally, are North Korean provocations combined with the "unpredictability" of President Trump suggestive that a crisis with Kim Jung-Un could be far more dangerous than those with previous American presidents? Finally, in the event of a crisis with North Korea, is the Trump response likely to include a military response, one that could set the stage for a full-scale war?

TRUMP'S EARLY COMMENTS ABOUT NORTH KOREA: AN ASSESSMENT OF THE NUCLEAR THREAT

Long before his White House bid, in the book *The America We Deserve*, Trump made the following declaration: "North Korea would suddenly discover that its worthless promises of civilized behavior would cut no ice. I would let Pyongyang know in no uncertain terms that it can either get out of the nuclear arms race or expect a rebuke similar to the one Ronald Reagan delivered to Gaddafi in 1986."[65] Trump offered this provocative statement: "I don't think anybody is going to accuse me of tiptoeing through the issues or tap-dancing around them either. Who else in public life has called for a preemptive strike on North Korea?"[66]

In response to North Korea's hydrogen bomb test on January 6, 2016, in an interview on *Fox News*, Trump remarked, "China has . . . total control over North Korea. And China should solve that problem. And if they don't solve the problem, we should make trade very difficult for China."[67] Concerned that North Korea might be developing technology to target the United States, Trump indicated he would respond with military action: "We got to close it down [North Korea's nuclear program], because he's getting too close to doing something. Right now, he's probably got the weapons, but he doesn't have the transportation system. Once he has the transportation system, he's sick enough to use it. So, we better get involved."[68]

During the Eighth Republican Presidential Primary Debate in New Hampshire on February 6, 2016, candidate Trump provided a detailed statement concerning how he would respond to North Korea. Trump remarked: "China says they don't have that good of control over North Korea. They have ... absolute control ... of North Korea. ... I would ... let China solve that problem. They can do it quickly and surgically. That's what we should do with North Korea."[69]

This statement represented a window into one component of Trump's strategy for confronting North Korea—rely heavily on China to reign in North Korea's nuclear ambitions. Once in office, President Trump had to quickly embrace a certain reality. In North Korea the new president inherited a nightmare.

North Korea's nuclear threat continued to cause instability in the Korean Peninsula, but one that is likely to include an arsenal of weapons capable of targeting the United States. It is important however to provide a perspective on North Korea's nuclear threat and the dilemma it represented for President Trump.

James Clapper, the former US director of national intelligence, offered the following statement during remarks before the Senate Select Committee on Intelligence on January 29, 2014: "Because of deficiencies in their conventional military forces, North Korean leaders are focused on deterrence and defense. We have long assessed that, in Pyongyang's view, its nuclear capabilities are intended for deterrence, international prestige, and coercive diplomacy."[70]

On February 25, 2016, in testimony before the House Permanent Select Committee on Intelligence, Clapper provided a far more alarming testimony. Clapper testified that "North Korea has also expanded the size and sophistication of its ballistic missile forces—from close range ballistic missiles to intercontinental ballistic missiles (ICBMs)—and continues to conduct test launches."[71]

Evans J. R. Revere, a senior fellow at the Center for East Asia Policy Studies at the Brookings Institution, provided an important assessment of the leader of North Korea and the burgeoning nuclear threat. According to Revere, Kim "provided Mr. Trump with a blunt statement of North Korea's nuclear and missile goals, just as the new American president was beginning to grapple with the question that has bedeviled each of his four predecessors: What to do what about North Korea's nuclear weapons and their threat to America and its allies?"[72]

Revere concluded the North Korean leader provided an unmistakable message to President Trump: "Kim Jong Un's personal reiteration of his regime's game plan so soon before the American presidential inauguration signaled that he has made up his mind about how he intends to deal with an inexperienced new US president."[73]

There are those that assessed North Korea's nascent nuclear program in far more alarming terms. Jeffrey Lewis, the director of the East Asia Nonproliferation Program at the Middlebury Institute of International Studies at Monterey, articulated, "North Korea has started launching Scuds and Nodongs from different locations all over the damn country. These aren't missile tests, they are military exercises. North Korea knows the missiles work. What the military units are doing now is practicing—practicing for a nuclear war."[74] Lewis then made this highly provocative statement: "North Korea is developing an offensive doctrine for the large-scale use of nuclear weapons in the early stages of a conflict."[75] Lewis left this stunning warning: "When combined with what we know about US and South Korean war plans, this fact raises troubling questions about whether a crisis on the Korean peninsula might erupt into nuclear war before President Donald Trump has time to tweet about it."[76]

The available information suggested North Korea currently maintains a nuclear arsenal of approximately twenty-plus nuclear bombs. Robert Litwak, Director of International Security Studies at the Woodrow Wilson Center, asserted North Korea is "on the verge of nuclear breakout."[77] This is a reference to Pyongyang's increasing ability to enhance the technology of miniaturization.

Well-known expert, Victor Cha, the former adviser on North Korea during the Bush administration and currently serving as the Korea chair at the Center for International Security Studies (CSIS), provided this disturbing analysis: "This is no longer about a . . . dictator crying for attention or demanding negotiations. This is now a military testing program to acquire a proven capability."[78]

In his analysis Cha observed that during a period covering eight years, the regime in Pyongyang "spurned any serious and substantive diplomacy with all neighbors."[79] Second, despite the intentions of the US and international community, the regime continued their aggressive "military testing program of ballistic missiles and nuclear devices."[80] Third, the regime continued to engage in gross human rights abuses.[81] Cha offered this additional data which further demonstrated the seriousness of the threat: "Between 1994 and 2008, North Korea conducted 17 missile tests and 1 nuclear test. However, in the past eight years, these numbers have increased to 62 missile tests and 4 nuclear tests, including 20 (missile) and 2 (nuclear) respectively in the past year alone."[82]

If the above information is not enough to demonstrate the threat posed by North Korea, the following excerpt further clarified the nightmare that is associated with North Korea's quest to further upgrade their nuclear arsenal.

Harry J. Kazianis, the Director of Defense Studies at the Center for the National Interest, offered this sobering perspective:

> While Washington, Moscow or Beijing might have mastered the Jedi arts of nuclear weapons decades ago, North Korea is still in padawan mode—but making slow and steady progress. And that is where the danger lies. Kim's testing schedule will only escalate if he really wants to deter America and its allies through atomic means. If Kim is serious about building missiles that can hit the US homeland he will need to thoroughly test them. . . . But the cost for such a weapon comes at a steep price. With every [missile] launch tensions will rise. As each missile goes further and further afield, more demands for action—military action, that is—will be made.[83]

The experts saliently demonstrate that North Korea's evolving nuclear program does indeed represent a nightmare for the Trump administration. There is something equally alarming. North Korea's nuclear saber rattling dramatically increased tensions within the Korean Peninsula. And given that multiple North Korean test missiles have landed in waters near Japan, such tests have increased the tensions between Pyongyang and Tokyo.

THE TRUMP ADMINISTRATION'S RESPONSE AND SEARCH FOR A STRATEGY

During the early months of the administration, President Trump and his senior advisors continued the harsh rhetoric towards North Korea. For his part, President Trump asserted the threat posed by North Korea expanded under the watch of President Obama. Trump provided this statement of condemnation of his successors failure: "We have a big problem. We have somebody that is not doing the right thing [referring to North Korean dictator Kim Jong Un] and that's going to be my responsibility. But I'll tell you, that responsibility could have been made a lot easier if it was handled years ago."[84]

During a joint news conference with visiting NATO Secretary General Jens Stoltenberg, President Trump issued a warning to China. The United States welcomed assistance from China on the North Korea problem, but should Beijing falter, "we're just going to go it alone."[85]

Vice President Mike Pence provided this statement that caught the attention of leaders around the world during his visit to South Korea. Pence warned Pyongyang "not to test [Trump's] resolve or the strength of the armed forces of the United States in this region."[86] Concerned about the bellicose language, North Korea's deputy UN ambassador to the United Nations, Kim In-Ryong, asserted the Trump administration is fostering "a dangerous situation in which a thermonuclear war may break out at any moment."[87]

Secretary Tillerson made this statement which provided a window into how the administration was prepared to deal with North Korea: "Let me be very clear. The policy of strategic patience has ended. We are exploring a new range of diplomatic, security and economic measures. All options are on the table."[88] For those concerned the administration was on a path to war, Tillerson issued this statement: "Certainly, we do not want for things to get to a military conflict."[89] Tillerson subsequently issued a warning to Pyongyang: "Obviously, if North Korea takes actions that threaten South Korean forces or our own forces, that would be met with appropriate response. If they elevate the threat of their weapons program to a level that we believe requires action, that option is on the table."[90]

Secretary Mattis was tasked with the responsibility of clarifying the North Korean threat. In remarks delivered to an audience at the International Security Conference in Singapore, Mattis remarked, "North Korea's continued pursuit of nuclear weapons and the means to deliver them is not new. . . . Its nuclear weapons program is maturing as a threat to all. As a matter of national security, the United States regards the threat from North Korea as a clear and present danger."[91]

An important question needs to be addressed immediately. Does the Trump administration have a policy for dealing with North Korea? In the opening moments of the administration, no policy exited. Instead, several senior officials put forward a series of statements that when taken collectively illustrate the Trump administration intends to respond in a more forceful way than previous American presidents. That said, "Trump's problem is not just that the [North Korea problem is] . . . tough. It's that his administration is unable to articulate what American policy even is."[92]

The issue of administration policy was again on display during a background briefing on the "First 100 Days." A senior administration official was asked to address whether North Korea should be placed back on the state sponsor of terrorism list. The response by the official is as follows: "That is one of the things we're considering. We're looking at a broad range of options, obviously, across all elements of national power and multinational power in connection with North Korea. You've seen . . . an integrated effort to prioritize diplomatic and informational aspects of national power."[93] In addition, the official that conducted the briefing acknowledged "what you'll see soon is using the economic dimension of national power, as well as the military preparations that are underway."[94]

The official failed to address a rudimentary query. When asked to provide a timeline for potential military response, the official offered this confusing reply: "Well, we have timelines in mind for what we would like to see changed, but it's mainly event-driven. It depends on the actions of North

Korea. It depends on the actions of others whose help we're looking for in resolving this problem and moving toward the goal of denuclearization of the Korean Peninsula."[95]

The search for a policy continued well into the opening months of the Trump administration. Following an internal review of US strategies against North Korea, the administration in April of 2017 unveiled is new strategy.

The Trump administration settled on a strategy of "maximum pressure" to curtail and eventually eliminate North Korea's illicit nuclear weapons program. The critical aspects of the administration strategy called for working through China to reign in Kim's nuclear ambitions. In addition, the administration relied on "the combined might of punishing sanctions, diplomatic isolation,"[96] and the threat to use force to coerce North Korea into pursuing denuclearization.

To ensure the successful implementation of the president's strategy, the administration recognized that China had to understand that maximum pressure would be directed at Beijing to ensure its support in reigning North Korea. On this point, Walter Lohman, the director of the Asian Studies Center at the Heritage Foundation, offered this statement: "Trump is going to be forceful with China over North Korea. He is not going to ask for help anymore. We are going to demand help. The time for talk is over. The US can impose secondary sanctions on Chinese companies if China doesn't cooperate."[97]

To get the attention of the Kim regime, the Trump administration imposed strict sanctions. This is a critical component of the strategy—eliminating Kim's external sources of revenue. The strategy of maximum pressure "is designed to shut down all sources of revenue to the Kim regime."[98]

The most difficult component of the strategy—military coercion—is the most difficult aspect to implement. Any discussion of military options or verbiage calling for the annihilation of the North Korea fed into the Clinton campaign caricature of Trump as a war monger and played supportive cable outlets throughout the presidential campaign.

The administration had to walk a fine line. On the one hand the president and senior military officials had to produce credible military options to induce Kim to the diplomatic table, but so options could not be perceived as "regime threatening" or one that indicated the administration was pursuing preemptive strikes. The latter would have increased tensions in the peninsula, raised concerns in South Korea and Japan, and unleashed domestic criticism not to mention "I told you so outcry" statements from the left or the resistance.

Often mistaken for regime change, maximum strategy is more about pursuing engagement rather than confrontation and regime removal. Indeed, as one senior White House official noted, "The administration's priority is to end the threat of a North Korean regime armed with nuclear weapons. That is our goal."[99]

Trump policy of maximum pressure quickly morphed into the Trump Doctrine. This shift to a doctrine is based on the fact that the Trump administration applied to Iran and their ambitious nuclear program. The termination of the Iran nuclear agreement and the reinstitution of sanctions, and administration threats to sanction EU states for trade with Tehran, illustrates this version of maximum pressure.

THE AUGUST MISSILE CRISIS OVER GUAM AND ITS AFTERMATH

The Defense Intelligence Agency (DIA) issued an important report on North Korea's missile development on July 28, 2017. The analysis by the DIA asserts, "The IC [intelligence community] assesses North Korea has produced nuclear weapons for ballistic missile delivery, to include delivery by ICBM-class missiles."[100] The report also stressed that North Korea surpassed the threshold of miniaturizing "a nuclear warhead that can fit inside its missiles."[101] In an earlier report, it was suggested that North Korea could possess up to 60 nuclear missiles.[102]

Another critical component that set the stage for the August crisis is the twin provocative missile tests that were launched by North Korea in late July and the swift international response. In the wake of multiple missile tests, the Trump administration requested an emergency meeting of the United Nations Security Council. In response to the North Korean missile provocations, on August 5 the Security Council passed UNSCR 2317 by a vote of 15-0. The resolution "Expands financial sanctions by prohibiting new or expanded joint ventures and cooperative commercial entities with the DPRK and clarifies that companies performing financial services are considered financial institutions for the purpose of implementing the relevant sanctions measures."[103]

Expressing a sense of optimism that Russia and China joined the international condemnation of North Korea's provocative missile tests, US ambassador to the United Nations, Nikki R. Haley, remarked it is clear "we're not playing anymore."[104]

In response to the sanctions, during a ministerial meeting in the Philippines, North Korean Foreign Minister Ri Yong-ho issued this terse statement: "We will, under no circumstances, put the nukes and ballistic rockets on the negotiating table."[105]

The North Korean military subsequently announced plans that they intended to launch missile strikes near Guam, a territory of the United States and home to Anderson Air Base where the B-1 bomber is stationed. The government-run *Korean Central News* (KCNA) announced the North's Strategic Force is "Now carefully examining the operational plan for making an enveloping fire at the areas around Guam with medium-to-long-range strategic ballistic rocket Hwasong-12."[106]

On August 9, 2017, while on a working vacation at the Bedminster National Golf Club in New Jersey, and in a response to a reporter's question on the administration's reaction to the government of North Korea's threat to launch missiles near Guam, President Trump issued this combative statement: "Let's see what he does with Guam. [If] He does something in Guam, it will be an event the likes of which nobody has seen before—what will happen in North Korea. . . . He's not getting away with it."[107]

A day earlier, President Trump issued the following statement that caught the attention of the government of North Korea, the international community, and most certainly the American media: "North Korea best not make any more threats to the United States. . . . They will be met with fire, fury and frankly power the likes of which this world has never seen before."[108]

Tensions between North Korea and the United States continued to rise. The mini-crisis never reached the level of the June 1994 crisis where President Clinton threatened to launch a preemptive strike against Pyongyang's nuclear installations. In the United States, those on the left believed that President Trump's language and unpredictability set the stage for war, perhaps a nuclear war with North Korea. From another perspective, the South Korea government expressed concern about the possibility of war and that their citizens could be caught up in the conflict and up to a million people in Seoul could perish in the opening day of hostilities.

In an op-ed piece in *the Wall Street Journal*, Secretary Mattis and Secretary Tillerson sent another message to the Kim regime that argued "We're Holding Pyongyang to Account." Tillerson used the message to assert:

> While diplomacy is our preferred means of changing North Korea's course of action, it is backed by military options. The US will continue to work with our allies and partners to deepen diplomatic and military cooperation, and to hold nations accountable to their commitments to isolate the regime. That will include rigorous enforcement of sanctions, leaving no North Korean source of revenue untouched. . . . As always, we will embrace military preparedness in the defense of our homeland, our citizens and our allies, and in the preservation of stability and security in Northeast Asia. And we will say again here: Any attack will be defeated, and any use of nuclear weapons will be met with an effective and overwhelming response. North Korea now faces a choice. Take a new path toward peace, prosperity and international acceptance, or continue further down the dead alley of belligerence, poverty and isolation.[109]

In recognition that the regimes rhetoric did not dissuade the Trump administration, "the government of North Korea blinked." In an evaluation of the North Korean response, Ankit Panda, an expert on North Korea, noted, "By deciding not to proceed with the launch, Kim appears to have expressed an intent to deescalate."[110] For now, a showdown in the Korean Peninsula had been averted. Kim Jong Un's credibility took a major hit during the crisis and maximum pressure worked.

THE POTENTIAL FOR A NEW REALITY-PATH TO PRODUCTIVE US-NORTH KOREAN RELATIONSHIP

After a year-plus period of implementing the strategy of maximum pressure, the Trump administration shifted their approach towards North Korea. What is behind the administration's salient shift in their approach to relations with North Korea?

The answer is complicated. The Korean rapprochement during the Olympics is a critical starting point. Not only did Kim Jong Un and the leader of South Korea Moon Jae-in set the stage for more a peaceful path, but it is the fact that the North Korean government came to terms with two realities that is equally relevant. Those realities include a rapprochement with the South and a choice between potential conflict with the United States or direct negotiations with the Trump administration.

President Trump's verbiage and demeanor set him apart from previous American presidents. And when combined with Trump's willingness to use force, the North Korean government recognized that previous acts of defiance would not alter the Trump administration's approach. Second, the Trump administration-led sanctions crippled the North Korean economy. This alone caused the Kim government to consider a diplomatic approach not with South Korea but also with the United States. Kim's recognition of the two realities, his willingness to pursue diplomacy, along with the South Korean President Moon's delicate diplomatic dance assisted in the path to the summit between the United States and North Korea cannot be overlooked as another significant variable.

There are several corollary variables that contributed to Kim's shift. Trump's hardline approach to China, particularly the implementation of restrictive sanctions because of Beijing's failure to alter Kim's quest for a nuclear deterrent undermined their relationship with the United States. Because of the impact of the sanctions, the government of China was so concerned about the Trump administration's threats to use force, willingness to introduce cycle after cycle of new sanctions directed toward Beijing, and Trump's success in obtaining international support, assisted in enabling China to rebuke Kim with the objective of forcing the North Korean leader to reconsider nuclearization.

This decision resulted in the not-so secret Xi-Kim summits (The initial summit occurred during the period March 25–March 28, 2018. The second meeting covered the period May 7–8, 2018.).[111] The summits between allies represented another critical variable to further comprehend the ever-changing North Korean behavior. The Kim government in effect was forced to come terms with Trump's demand. That is, the impact of the harsh round of US-led international sanctions, and Trump's sustained pressure directed at China convinced Kim that diplomacy rather brinksmanship with the American president represented a far better course of action.

There is another perspective on the summit that was completely overlooked: the summit not only ensured that Kim would end the threats and potentially curtail his nuclear program, but it also permitted Xi and Kim to remain on the "same page." Shannon Tiezzi, the editor-in-chief of *The Diplomat*, provided details of what was really accomplished during the two meetings. According to Tiezzi, "In light of the ongoing diplomatic efforts, the goal here was for Xi and Kim to present a united front. Xinhua reiterated that Kim and Xi had 'fully exchanged views and reached important consensus' on the Korean Peninsula issue at their first meeting."[112] Tiezzi provided this additional perspective: "Those views were repeated . . . at this meeting. Xi restated China's support for North Korea's 'adherence to the denuclearization of the peninsula' as well as 'the dialogue and consultation between the DPRK and the United States for resolving the peninsula issue.'"[113]

There is another significant corollary variable to consider. The secret meeting between the director of the CIA Mike Pompeo and Kim Jong Un which set the stage for "the potential of a new direction" in US-North Korean relations.[114] The Pompeo-Kim meeting is critical in that it allowed the North Korean leader an opportunity to present his case for a US-North Korea summit and it permitted Trump to confirm that Kim is serious about a path towards the dissipation of North Korea's quest for a nuclear deterrent.

The Pompeo-Kim secret meeting offered a supplementary surprise to experts and those in the media. The surprise centered on the mystery man that accompanied Pompeo to North Korea. Accompanying Pompeo on the historic trip was none other than Andrew Kim, head of CIA's Korea Mission Center, an organization designed to track and collect intelligence in the Korean Peninsula.

The use of an individual from the year-plus old spy center for a major diplomatic mission appeared odd and out of place to most observers. Indeed, many among the ever-increasing anti-Trump partisans and many within the foreign policy establishment itself viewed the decision to conduct a major diplomatic negotiation without a major role for the State Department represented for the president's detractors of conspicuous evidence that Trump is undermining State's traditional role and perhaps decreasing the opportunity to produce stability in the region.

The criticism however is without supporting evidence. In fact, the use of the mission center, with Kim's direct participation, may turn out to be a pivotal decision connected to Trump's efforts to negotiate an agreement on denuclearization with North Korea. On the critical decision to make use of Kim, elements within the White House national security staff and the CIA privately lobbied the president that no one is more suited to represent the administration in pursuit of this mission than Kim. Why is Kim's selection viewed so positively among White House officials and the president?

Born in South Korea, Kim is fluent in his native language, and maintains direct connections with senior officials within the South Korean government. That is, Kim attended "the prestigious Seoul High School, whose alumni include Suh Hoon, now the head of South Korea's intelligence agency, and Chung Eui-yong, South Korea's national security adviser. He is also Chung's cousin."[115] Additionally, Kim's influence extended beyond the secret Pompeo-Kim meeting. The exceprt below exemplifies the point:

> He [Kim] took part in President Donald Trump's Oval Office meeting with a senior North Korean envoy last week and has helped prepare the president for his June 12 summit with Kim Jong Un in Singapore. The unusual public role has given Kim, who was raised in South Korea, extraordinary influence over the administration's approach to the summit and the North Korean nuclear threat more broadly. Just as Pompeo has become Trump's right-hand man on the Korean talks, twice meeting with Kim Jong Un this year, Andrew Kim has found himself in a similar role for the secretary of state.[116]

The summit was canceled by over reactions by both parties. The North Korean government objected to being referred to as the Libyan Model and publicly reacted to previously announced planned US-South Korean war games. On the Trump administration's role or actions that set the stage for the summit's cancellation, the president unveiled a series of statements indicating his objections to the strident language used by North Korean officials and the fact that many of their diplomats did not attend prearranged diplomatic meetings with officials in the US government.

These actions set the stage for President Trump's decision to cancel the summit. Trump's letter to Kim Jung Un clarified the president's reasons to halt summit preparations. As stated by President Trump, "I was very much looking forward to being there with you. Sadly, based on the tremendous anger and open hostility displayed in your most recent statement, I feel it is inappropriate, at this time, to have this long-planned meeting."[117] In a subsequent portion of the letter, Trump unveiled his administration's intentions for American participation in a future summit: "I felt a wonderful dialogue was building up between you and me, and ultimately, it is only that dialogue that matters. Someday, I look very much forward to meeting you."[118]

Kim expressed regret about the cancellation, and in the immediate aftermath the leader quietly informed senior aides in the North Korean government to make use of the good office of the South Korean president to press their point that the summit should proceed. Following the personal diplomacy of President Moon, the two parties worked to reopen discussions for the summit.

Following two critical meetings, one with Secretary Pompeo and former North Korean intelligence chief Kim Yong Chol in New York[119] and a subsequent meeting between Chol and Trump which was attended by Pompeo and other senior officials to include Andrew Kim and former chief of staff John F. Kelly, the euphoric president, after receiving a private letter from Kim Jong Un, announced the summit was back on track and scheduled to take place at its original location in Singapore on June 12, 2018.

Consistent with previous moments during the administration, following the announcement of details of a successful event which proved favorable to the Trump White House, the president undermined the positive media coverage "by stepping on his message." In this case, following overwhelming media coverage of the announcement that the summit would resume, President Trump confidently stated, "I do not think I need to prepare very much"[120] for the summit. The statement not only undermined the positive vibes about the pending summit, but it forced Secretary Pompeo to clarify the president's statement.

On the clarification, Pompeo articulated, "There were few days that I left the Oval Office after having briefed the president that we didn't talk about North Korea. I am very confident the president will be fully prepared when he meets with his North Korean counterpart."[121]

In a strange twist, oddly in the end there were those that felt that while the president's statement is awkward, he was nonetheless correct. Joseph Y. Yun, a former high ranking official in the State Department who resigned over the president's hawkish approach to dealing with North Korea, argued, "This is something [preparing to meet Kim Jong Un] that Trump has thought about for a long time, even before the election. In that sense, he is . . . well prepared."[122] After this brief sideshow, speculation about the summit and its outcome resumed.

On June 7, just four days prior to the summit, Secretary Pompeo endeavored to reassure the international community that productive meetings were well underway ahead of the Trump-Kim summit. Additionally, he used remarks to warn Kim about yet another broken promise by the North Korean government. Pompeo asserted:

> American leadership rallied the international community to send a strong message to Chairman Kim Jong Un and the world that we would not stand for the DPRK's illegal weapons programs. The President's bold decision to meet with Chairman Kim Jong Un grew from this incredibly strong and targeted campaign. The President's policy directly led to the historic summit that will take place on June 12th in Singapore. Back on March 8th, Chairman Kim Jong Un expressed his desire to meet with President Trump as soon as possible. And

then on May 9th, I met with Chairman Kim Jong Un in Pyongyang and explained America's expectations for denuclearization. . . . The United States and North Korea have been holding direct talks in preparation for a summit, and North Korea has confirmed to us its willingness to denuclearize. A comprehensive whole-of-government effort in support of President Trump's upcoming summit is under way. White House and State Department-led advance teams are finalizing logistical preparations and will remain in place in Singapore until the summit begins. The President continues to follow every development closely and is getting daily briefings from his national security team.[123]

Following the historic summit, President Trump and Kim Jong Un agreed to a joint statement that read in part: "Convinced that the establishment of new US–DPRK relations will contribute to the peace and prosperity of the Korean Peninsula and of the world and recognizing that mutual confidence building can promote the denuclearization of the Korean Peninsula."[124] The discourse between the two leaders and their representatives yielded the following areas of agreement:

The United States and the DPRK commit to establish new US–DPRK relations in accordance with the desire of the peoples of the two countries for peace and prosperity; second, the United States and the DPRK will join their efforts to build a lasting and stable peace regime on the Korean Peninsula; third, Reaffirming the April 27, 2018 Panmunjom Declaration, the DPRK commits to work toward complete denuclearization of the Korean Peninsula, and fourth, The United States and the DPRK commit to recovering POW/MIA remains, including the immediate repatriation of those already identified.[125]

The closing portion of the joint statement included these words: "The US–DPRK summit was an epochal event of great significance in overcoming decades of tensions and hostilities between the two countries and for the opening up of a new future, President Trump and Chairman Kim Jong Un commit to implement the stipulations in this joint statement fully and expeditiously."[126] The United States and the DPRK agreed to follow-on negotiations.

Few doubted the historic nature of the summit. However, many Trump critics, particularly among the never-Trumpers on the right and the resistance on the left that despise the president, questioned the vagueness of the agreement and whether President Trump conceded too much to the North Korean government. This is a reference to the fact that Trump, in a brief press conference, notified the media the administration agreed to a pause in US–South Korean war games. Critics question if the administration consulted with the South Korean government.

One of the more interesting aspects in the post-summit period is the battle over the narrative. That is, many on the left argued that Trump was not a winner, but rather China won. Others on the left argued that Trump lost because he did not achieve the complete and immediate denuclearization. Those loyal to the president in the Republican party, among his base, and those in the flyer-over states that were critical to his electoral victory, overwhelming believed that Trump is the salient winner in the post-summit politicization of a major moment in the history of American foreign policy.

The clear issue not discussed is that Trump did not morph into the campaign presidential caricature narrative that then candidate Hillary Clinton and her surrogates used successfully in the media during the presidential campaign: that Trump's rhetoric and his hawkish agenda would lead to war in the Korean Peninsula. The reality of the completion of the summit and its positive outcome should have ended that narrative. Strangely it continued, only this time in segments of the media that oddly are incessantly pushing the narrative.

Preparation for the Trump-Kim February 2019 summit in Hanoi, Vietnam provided fresh momentum for a substantial agreement. Many observers argued that President Trump must achieve definitive results. To be clear, the president must ensure there is a workable and verifiable timetable for denuclearization, one that can be verified by the United Nations International Atomic Energy Agency (IAEA) and American intelligence.

In spite of the optimism both parties departed Vietnam without an agreement. What is the key issue behind the collapse of the diplomatic negotiations? In a word, sanctions. To place the dispute over sanctions in context, the available information suggests Kim was prepared to offer the dismantling of North Korea's Yongbyon complex, to include all structures or facilities connected to the nuclear reactor.[127] In exchange, the government of North Korea demanded the complete dismantling of US and UN sanctions. For its part, the Trump administration countered there had to be substantial progress toward a framework of denuclearization before agreeing to a sanctions relief. Additionally, the Trump administration rejected Kim's offer. Secretary Pompeo argued even with the formal end of the facility at Yongbyon, that "still leaves missiles, still leaves warheads and weapons system"[128] in place. With the major components of Kim's nuclear program still in place, the fear is that lifting sanctions would only lead to the production of new weapons and "the continued production of uranium."[129] With Kim's insistence on sanctions relief and no further movement consistent with what the Trump administration desired, the talks collapsed. At present, the presumption is talks for a subsequent summit will resume. Does that mean that a third summit is likely? For the Kim government it has suggested the Trump administration rejected an opportunity of a lifetime—the complete dismantling of the central infrastructure behind North Korea's nuclear program. The Kim government argued that it may require intervention by the South Korean government or other entities, acting as intermediaries, could be used to get talks back on track.

In the wake of the second summit, few can debate that a new reality exists in US-North Korean relations. In its own way, the Hanoi summit aided in defining the next stage of the relationship—another round of diplomacy with the objective of producing a definitive agreement. The diplomatic process represents a salient demonstration of progress in US-North Korean relations. Confirmation of the long-term, big picture of the relationship, will be enhanced if both sides agree to a framework for denuclearization.

NOTES

1. Author interview with State Department official in the administration of President Barack Obama.
2. F. Seib, Gerald, Solomon, Jay, and Lee, Carol E., "Barack Obama Warns Donald Trump on North Korea Threat," *The Wall Street Journal*, November 22, 2016. https://www.wsj.com/articles/trump-faces-north-korean-challenge-1479855286. Accessed on January 16, 2019.
3. Crowley, Michael, "North Korea Defies Trump," *Politico*, April 28, 2017. http://www.politico.com/story/2017/04/28/trump-north-korea-237778. Accessed on January 16, 2019.
4. Seib, Solomon, and Lee, "Barack Obama Warns Donald Trump on North Korea Threat."
5. Leventhal, Paul and Dolley, Steven, "The North Korean Nuclear Crisis," *Medicine & Global Survival* (1994) Vol. 1, No. 3. http://www.ippnw.org/pdf/mgs/1-3-leventhal.pdf. Accessed on January 16, 2019.
6. Ibid.
7. Szalontai, Balázs, "The International Context of the North Korean Nuclear Program, 1953–1988," in Ostermann, Christian F., Series Editor, *The Wilson Center*, Cold War International History Project Working Papers Series, August 2006. https://www.wilsoncenter.org/sites/default/files/WP53webfinal1.pdf. Accessed on January 16, 2019.
8. Ibid.
9. Ibid.
10. Ibid.
11. Ibid.
12. Ibid.
13. Leventhal and Dolley, "The North Korean Nuclear Crisis."
14. Ibid.
15. Straub, David, "The Obama Administration's North Korea Policy: An Assessment," Shorenstein APARC Seminar Series, The Korean Studies Program, Stanford University. February 10, 2012. https://fsi.stanford.edu/sites/default/files/evnts/media/North_Korea_Policy_Assessment.pdf. Accessed on January 16, 2019.
16. Ibid.
17. Davenport, Kelsey, "Chronology of US-North Korean Nuclear and Missile Diplomacy," *Arms Control Association*, April 2017. https://www.armscontrol.org/factsheets/dprkchron. Accessed on January 16, 2019.
18. Ibid.
19. Leventhal and Dolley, "The North Korean Nuclear Crisis."
20. Ibid.
21. Ibid.
22. McIntyre, Jamie, "Washington Was on Brink of War with North Korea 5 Years Ago," *CNN*, October 4, 1994. http://www.cnn.com/US/9910/04/korea.brink/. Accessed on January 16, 2019.
23. As quoted in McIntyre, Jamie, "The Last Korean Meltdown: Bill Clinton on the Brink of War," *The Daily Beast*, November 24, 2010. http://www.thedailybeast.com/the-last-korean-meltdown-bill-clinton-on-the-brink-of-war. Accessed on January 17, 2019.
24. Ibid.

25. Sigal, Leon V., "The North Korean Nuclear Crisis: Understanding the Failure of the 'Crime-and-Punishment' Strategy," *Arms Control Association*, May 1, 1997. https://www.armscontrol.org/act/199705/sigal. Accessed on January 17, 2019.
26. Ibid.
27. Davenport, "Chronology of US-North Korean Nuclear and Missile Diplomacy."
28. Ibid.
29. Ibid.
30. Remarks on the Nuclear Agreement with North Korea, October 18, 1994. President Bill Clinton, 1993–2001. The American Presidency Project. http://www.presidency.ucsb.edu/ws/index.php?pid=49319&st=north+korea&st1. Accessed on January 17, 2019.
31. Ibid.
32. Minnich, James M., Chapter 14 "Resolving the North Korean Nuclear Crisis: Challenges and Opportunities in Readjusting the US-ROK Alliance" [No Date] http://apcss.org/Publications/Edited%20Volumes/turningpoint/CH14.pdf. Accessed on January 17, 2019.
33. Statement on Completion of the North Korea Policy Review, President George W. Bush. The American Presidency Project, June 6, 2001. http://www.presidency.ucsb.edu/ws/?pid=45819. Accessed on January 17, 2019.
34. Ibid.
35. Ibid.
36. Minnich, Chapter 14 "Resolving the North Korean Nuclear Crisis"
37. Ibid.
38. Ibid.
39. Thiessen, Marc A., Editor, *A Charge Kept: The Record of the Bush Presidency, 2001–2009*. https://georgewbush-whitehouse.archives.gov/infocus/bushrecord/documents/charge-kept.pdf. Accessed on January 17, 2019.
40. Davenport, "Chronology of US-North Korean Nuclear and Missile Diplomacy."
41. Ibid.
42. Lohschelder, Sarah, "Three Presidents Facing North Korea-A Review of US Foreign Policy," *Huffingtonpost.com*, [No Date] http://www.huffingtonpost.com/young-professionals-in-foreign-policy/three-presidents-facing-nb9335546.html. Accessed on January 17, 2019.
43. Chanlett-Avery, Emma, Rinehart, Ian, and Nikitin, Mary Beth, "North Korea: US Relations, Nuclear Diplomacy, and Internal Situation," *Congressional Research Service* (CRS) Report, January 15, 2016. https://fas.org/sgp/crs/nuke/R41259.pdf. Accessed on January 17, 2019.
44. Ibid.
45. Ibid.
46. Ibid.
47. Ibid.
48. Executive Order 13551—Blocking Property of Certain Persons with Respect to North Korea," Obamawhitehouse.gov, August 30, 2010. https://obamawhitehouse.archives.gov/the-press-office/2010/08/30/executive-order-president-blocking-property-certain-persons-with-respect.
49. Straub, David, "The Obama Administration's North Korea Policy: An Assessment," Shorenstein APARC Seminar Series, The Korean Studies Program, Stanford University. February 10, 2012. https://fsi.stanford.edu/sites/default/files/evnts/media//North_Korea_Policy_Assessment.pdf. Accessed on January 17, 2019.
50. Ibid.
51. Ibid.
52. Ibid.
53. Ibid.
54. Ibid.
55. Ibid.
56. McGreal, Chris, "Obama Engagement Policy in Tatters After North Korean Rocket Defiance," *The Guardian*, April 13, 2012. https://www.theguardian.com/world/2012/apr/13/obama-north-korea-engagement-policy. Accessed on January 17, 2019.
57. Ibid.

58. Ibid.

59. Davis, Julie Hirschfeld, "Obama Places Sanctions on Kim Jong-un and Other Top North Koreans for Rights Abuses," *New York Times*, July 7, 2016. https://www.nytimes.com/2016/07/07/world/asia/obama-puts-sanctions-on-north-korean-leaders-for-human-rights-abuse.html?mcubz=2. Accessed on January 17, 2019.

60. Ibid.

61. Friedman, Uri, "What Are America's Options on North Korea?" *The Atlantic*, April 7, 2017. https://www.theatlantic.com/international/archive/2017/04/trump-options-nuclear-north-korea/522075/. Accessed on January 17, 2019.

62. Pritchard, Charles L., Tilelli Jr., John H., and Snyder, Scott A., "US Policy Toward the Korean Peninsula," Council on Foreign Relations, Independent Task Force Report No. 64, June 2010. https://www.cfr.org/content/publications/attachments/Korean_PeninsulaTFR64.pdf. Accessed on January 17, 2019.

63. Ibid.

64. Ibid.

65. Trump, Donald, *The America We Deserve* (Los Angeles, CA: Renaissance Book, 2000), p. 274.

66. Ibid.

67. Campbell, Colin, "Donald Trump: Here's How I'd Handle That 'Madman' in North Korea," *Business Insider*, January 6, 2016. http://www.businessinsider.com/donald-trump-north-korea-china-nuclear-2016-1. Accessed on January 17, 2019.

68. Ibid.

69. "Transcript of the New Hampshire GOP Debate, Annotated," *The Washington Post*, February 6, 2016. https://www.washingtonpost.com/news/the-fix/wp/2016/transcript-of-the-feb-6-gop-debate-annotated/?utm_term=802b20d32&nodirect=on. Accessed on January 17, 2019.

70. Cordesman, Anthony H., "North Korean Nuclear Forces and the Threat of Weapons of Mass Destruction in Northeast Asia," Center for Strategic and International Studies (CSIS), July 25, 2016. https://csis-prod.s3.amazonaws.com/s3fs-public/publication/160725_Korea_WMDReport0.pdf. Accessed on January 17, 2019.

71. Ibid.

72. Revere, Evans J. R., "2017: Year of Decision on the Korean Peninsula," *The Brookings Institution*, February 8, 2017. https://www.brookings.edu/wp-content/uploads/2017/03/fp20170208evansreverekrins.pdf. Accessed on January 17, 2019.

73. Ibid.

74. Lewis, Jeffrey, "North Korea is Practicing for Nuclear War," *Foreign Policy*, March 9, 2017. http://foreignpolicy.com/2017/03/09/north-korea-is-practicing-for-nuclear-war/. Accessed on January 18, 2019.

75. Ibid.

76. Ibid.

77. Warrick, Joby, "Anxiety Grows Over North Korea's Arsenal: 'Danger Now is Miscalculation,'" *Chicago Tribune*, March 11, 2017. http://www.chicagotribune.com/news/nationworld/ct-north-korea-weapons-arsenal-20170311-story.html. Accessed on January 18, 2019.

78. Ibid.

79. Statement Before the House Foreign Affairs Committee, "Countering the North Korean Threat: New Steps in US Policy." Testimony by Victor Cha, Washington, DC. February 7, 2017. https://csis-prod.s3.amazonaws.com/s3fs-public/congressional_testimony/ts170207_victor_Chatestimonykorea.pdf?r7FvI3JKotcvocJ3crNTVlElSTfeOBL. Accessed on January 18, 2019.

80. Ibid.

81. Ibid.

82. Ibid.

83. Kazianis, Harry J., "The North Korea Nightmare Continues," *National Interest*, April 28, 2017. http://nationalinterest.org/feature/the-north-korea-nightmare-continues-20413. Accessed on January 18, 2019.

84. Lucas, Fred, "*National Interest* (Blog), April 5, 2017. http://nationalinterest.org/blog/the-buzz/us-china-summit-the-4-big-issues-donald-trump-xi-jinping-20043. Accessed on January 18, 2019.

85. Dromi, Uri, "Trump Should Avoid Any Knee-Jerk Reactions with North Korea," *Miami Herald*, April 24, 2017. http://www.miamiherald.com/opinion/op-ed/article146526734.html. Accessed on January 18, 2019.

86. Ibid.

87. Ibid.

88. "US Policy of 'Strategic Patience' with North Korea Over: Tillerson," CNBC.com, March 17, 2017. http://www.cnbc.com/2017/03/17/us-policy-of-strategic-patience-with-north-korea-over-tillerson.html. Accessed on January 18, 2019.

89. Owen, Jim, "Tillerson and Trump Slam North Korea: All Options Are on the Table," AllThatsNews.com, March 19, 2017. http://www.allthatsnews.com/articles/politics/tillerson-and-trump-slam-north-korea-all-options-are-table. Accessed on January 18, 2019.

90. Ibid.

91. Burns, Robert, "James Mattis Calls North Korea a 'Clear and Present Danger,'" *Time*, June 3, 2017. http://time.com/4804124/james-mattis-north-korea-china/. Accessed on January 18, 2019.

92. Graham, David, "The Many North Korea Policies of the Trump Administration," *The Atlantic*, April 28, 2017. https://www.theatlantic.com/international/archive/2017/04/the-many-north-korea-policies-of-rex-w-tillerson/524736/. Accessed on January 18, 2019.

93. Background Briefing on the First 100 Days. The White House, Office of the Press Secretary, April 16, 2017. https://www.whitehouse.gov/the-press-office/2017/04/26/background-briefing-first-100-days. Accessed on January 18, 2019.

94. Ibid.

95. Ibid.

96. Nasr, Vali, "Trump's 'Maximum Pressure' Strategy for North Korea and Iran Will Fail," *DefenseOne*, October 4, 2018. https://www.theatlantic.com/international/archive/2018/10/trump-iran-north-korea-nuclear-sanctions/572080/. Accessed on January 18, 2019.

97. As quoted in Lucas, Fred, "4 Issues Trump Will Likely Confront Chinese Leader About," *The Daily Signal*, April 5, 2017. http://dailysignal.com/2017/04/05/4-issues-trump-will-likely-confront-chinese-leader-about/. Accessed on January 18, 2019.

98. Blumenthal, Daniel, "Give Maximum Pressure a Chance," *Foreign Policy*, February 15, 2018. https://foreignpolicy.com/2018/02/15/maximum-pressure-needs-more-time-trump-pence-united-states-north-korea/. Accessed on January 18, 2019.

99. Rogin, Josh, "Trump's North Korea Policy is 'Maximum Pressure' but Not 'Regime Change,'" *Washington Post*, April 17, 2017. https://washingtonpost.com/news/josh-rogin/wp/2017/04/14/trumps-north-korea-policy-is-maximum-pressure-but-not-regime-change/?utm_term=.b187c01a0eae. Accessed on January 18, 2019.

100. Warrick, Joby, Nakashima, Ellen and Fifield, Anna, "North Korea Now Making Missile-Ready Nuclear Weapons, US Analysts Say," *Washington Post*, August 8, 2017. https://www.washingtonpost.com/world/national-security/north-korea-now-making-missile-ready-nuclear-weapons-us-analysts-say/2017/08/08/e14b882a-7b6b-11e7-9d08-79f191668edstory.html?utmterm=3f5a969fe6ab. Accessed on January 18, 2019.

101. Ibid.

102. Ibid.

103. Security Council Resolution 2371. August 5, 2017. https://www.un.org/sc/suborg/en/sanctions/1718/resolutions. Accessed on January 18, 2019.

104. Perlez, Jane and Gladstone, Rick, "North Korea Rails Against New Sanctions. Whether They Will Work Is Unclear," *New York Times*, August 7, 2017. https://www.nytimes.com/2017/08/07/world/asia/north-korea-responds-sanctions-united-states.html. Accessed on January 18, 2019.

105. Ibid.

106. "North Korea Threatens Missile Strike Near Guam," *Yonhap News Agency*, August 9, 2017. http://english.yonhapnews.co.kr/news/2017/08/09/0200000000AEN20170809001051315.html. Accessed on January 18, 2019.

107. Pappas, Alex, "Trump Turns Up Heat on North Korea, Warns of Unprecedented Response if Guam Attacked," *Fox News*, August 10, 2017. http://www.foxnews.com/politics/2017/08/10/trump-turns-up-heat-on-north-korea-warns-unprecedented-response-if-guam-attacked.html. Accessed on January 18, 2019.

108. Zelany, Jeff, Merica, Dan, and Liptak, Robert, "Trump's 'Fire and Fury' Remark Was Improvised but Familiar," *CNN*, August 9, 2017. http://www.cnn.com/2017/08/09/politics/trump-fire-fury-improvise-north-korea/index.html. Accessed on January 18, 2019.

109. Mattis and Tillerson: "We're Holding Pyongyang to Account." The White House, Office of the Press Secretary. August 14, 2017. https://www.whitehouse.gov/the-press-office/2017/08/14/mattis-and-tillerson-were-holding-pyongyang-account. Accessed on January 18, 2019.

110. Harris, Bryan and Manson, Katrina, "North Korea Backs Away from Guam Strike," *Financial Times*, August 15, 2017. https://www.ft.com/content/2de5c7ce-815f-11e7-a4ce-15b2513cb3ff.

111. [No Author] "The Xi-Kim Summit and Kim Jong Un's Gambit," Asia Society.org, March 28, 2018. https://asiasociety.org/policy-institute/xi-kim-summit-and-kim-jong-uns-gambit. Accessed on January 18, 2019.

112. Tiezzi, Shannon, "China, North Korea Hold Second Summit," *The Diplomat.com*, May 9, 2018. https://thediplomat.com/2018/05/china-north-korea-hold-second-summit/. Accessed on January 18, 2019.

113. Ibid.

114. Macias, Amanda, "White House Releases Photos of Mike Pompeo Meeting with North Korea Leader Kim Jong Un," CNBC.com, April 26, 2018. https://www.cnbc.com/2018/04/26/photos-mike-pompeo-meeting-with-north-korea-leader-kim-jong-un.html. Accessed on January 18, 2019.

115. Fifield, Anna and Kim, Min Joo, "South Korea Asks: Who Is That Mystery Man with Pompeo and Kim?" *Washington Post*, May 17, 2018. https://www.washingtonpost.com/world/asia_pacific/south-korea-asks-who-is-thatmystery-man-with-pompeo-and-kim/2018/05/17/0d4281b4-58f6-11e8-8b9245fdd7aaef3c_story.html?noredirect=on&utmterm=426520e2610e. Accessed on January 18, 2019.

116. Wadhams, Nick, "Mystery CIA Officer Thrust into Spotlight as Korea Summit Looms," Bloomberg.com, June 6, 2018. https://www.bloomberg.com/news/articles/2018-06-06/mystery-cia-officer-thrust-into-spotlight-as-korea-summit-looms. Accessed on January 18, 2019.

117. Sanger, David E., "Trump's Letter to Kim Canceling North Korea Summit Meeting, Annotated," *New York Times*, May 24, 2018. https://www.nytimes.com/2018/05/24/world/asia/read-trumps-letter-to-kim-jong-un.html. Accessed on January 18, 2019.

118. Ibid.

119. Gaoutte, Nicole, "North Korean Ex-Spy Chief Meets with Pompeo in New York," *CNN*, May 30, 2018. https://www.cnn.com/2018/05/30/politics/kim-yong-chol-new-york/index.html. Accessed on January 18, 2019.

120. Fabian, Jordan, "Trump: Don't Have to Prepare Very Much for North Korea Summit," *The Hill*, June 7, 2018. http://thehill.com/homenews/administration/391193-trump-dont-have-to-prepare-very-much-for-north-korea-summit. Accessed on January 18, 2019.

121. Landler, Mark, "No Need to Prepare to Meet Kim Jong-un? Trump Has a Point," *New York Times*, June 9, 2018. https://www.nytimes.com/2018/06/09/us/politics/trump-north-korea.html. Accessed on January 18, 2019.

122. Ibid.

123. "Press Briefing by Secretary of State Mike Pompeo," White House.gov, June 7, 2018. https://www.whitehouse.gov/briefings-statements/press-briefing-secretary-state-mike-pompeo-060718/. Accessed on January 18, 2019.

124. Joint Statement of President Donald J. Trump of the United States of America and Chairman Kim Jong Un of the Democratic People's Republic of Korea at the Singapore Summit. White House, June 12, 2018. https://www.whitehouse.gov/briefings-statements/joint-statement-president-donald-j-trump-united-states-america-chairman-kim-jong-un-democratic-peoples-republic-korea-singapore-summit/. Accessed on January 18, 2019.

125. Ibid.

126. Ibid.

127. Ripley, Will, "How Trump and Kim Summit Dream Fell Apart," CNN.com, March 2, 2019. https://www.cnn.com/2019/03/02politics/trump-kim-summit-dream-ripley-int/index.html. Accessed on March 3, 2019.

128. Sanger, David and Wong, Edward, "Failed: Big Threats, Big Egos, Bad Bets," *New York Times*, March 2, 2019. https://www.nytimes.com/2019/03/02/world/asia/trump-kim-jong-un-summit.html. Accessed on March 3, 2019.

129. Ibid.

Chapter Six

Confronting Chaos

Trump and the Middle East

The Middle East has long been recognized as the most volatile region in the world. The Arab Spring and the emergence of the Islamic State, Al Qaeda's continuing threat, Iran's attempt to create a regional Shiite order, instability in Iraq and Syria, the Russian presence, and the ongoing impasse in the Israeli-Palestinian negotiations, represent some of the divisive issues that exist in the region. These issues notwithstanding, as Diego Pagliarulu, an international affairs analyst, asserts, "Dealing with the many crises that tragically still torment the Middle East is likely to be a defining challenge for the . . . Trump administration."[1] Historically, Americans have understood the "religious and cultural relevance, a strategically pivotal location, huge oil reserves, interlocked and intractable conflicts, and the persistence of major security threats such as . . . the risk of nuclear proliferation."[2] To succeed in the always tempestuous and turbulent region, Trump must create "a mission statement,"[3] a comprehensive policy for the region to have any hope of success. At issue, is the unpredictable and controversial American president prepared for the challenge?

TRUMP, THE MIDDLE EAST, AND THE PRESIDENTIAL CAMPAIGN[4]

In a speech delivered before an audience at the Center for National Interest on April 26, 2016, Trump continued the "America First" theme. In the words of Trump, "It's time to shake the rust off America's foreign policy. It's time to invite new voices and new visions into the fold. . . . My foreign policy will always put the interests of the American people and American security above all else. It has to be first."[5]

On American policy during the Obama administration in the Middle East, Trump asserted, "Logic was replaced with foolishness and arrogance."[6] The result, in the words of Trump produced "one foreign policy disaster after another. . . . We went from mistakes in Iraq to Egypt to Libya, to President Obama's line in the sand in Syria."[7] Trump argued that Obama's policies resulted in the chaos in the region and ultimately produced the environment that ushered in the Islamic State.[8]

Trump scolded the Obama administration for the mistreatment of Israel, a historical ally in the region. In the words of Trump, "Israel, our great friend and the one true democracy in the Middle East has been snubbed and criticized by an administration that lacks moral clarity. . . . President Obama has not been a friend to Israel."[9] Trump argues Obama's policies made Iran "a great power."[10] Equally problematic, in the view of Trump, is that this occurred at "the expense of Israel."[11]

As to how the candidate would confront the region, Trump argued that it is important to confront and defeat radical Islamic terrorism. Stability cannot occur if the region is unprepared and unwilling to defeat the Islamic State and like-minded transnational terrorist groups. On relationships with states in the region, friendship, said Trump, is a two-way street. He opined that his administration would "extend generosity to states in the region, but only to those countries that are truly friends of the United States."[12]

David Aaron Miller, Middle East analyst, and advisors to previous American secretaries of state from both parties, offered this evaluation of Trump's position in Syria and Iraq. Trump's analysis of "Syria and Iraq seem in keeping with those who have a broad wariness of getting involved in military adventures in conflicts"[13] that are not directly linked to threats to the interests of the United States.

Miller makes use of Trump's book, *The America We Deserve*, to capture the evolution of when Trump believed intervention proved necessary. He uses this excerpt to make the point: "obvious that most Americans will know where the hot spot is . . . and will quickly understand why we're getting involved."[14]

On the Iraq War, Miller's argument is that "he has also blasted the"[15] conflict and "made clear the Iraqis should pay for it (shades of Mexico and the wall) and hammered Jeb Bush for the mess the Iraq War created. He then struggled to summarize the candidates' position on Iraq and the use of force: "So, beneath Trump's reckless rhetoric about seizing Iraqi oil and killing the families of ISIS fighters."[16] Miller asserted his real views might be better reflected by this statement: "We have to get smart. We can't continue to be the policemen of the world."[17]

Former CIA director and one-time Trump campaign advisor, James Woosely, provided an interesting analysis of the candidates' positions in the turbulent region. Woosely contends that in "the Middle East, generally, Trump calls for less, but calls for aggressive intervention against ISIS at the same time."[18] With respect to "reforming Middle Eastern countries,"[19] Woosely observed that Trump "criticizes intervening in the Middle East"[20] whether in Iraq and later in Libya as a waste of taxpayer money on issues that are not interests of the United States.

WILL THE PRESIDENT MEET FOUR TRANSFORMATIVE CAMPAIGN FOREIGN POLICY PLEDGES?

Aaron Miller and Richard Sokolsky, a non-resident fellow at the Carnegie Endowment for International Peace, questioned if Trump would meet his four transformative campaign foreign policy pledges. Miller and Sokolsky asserted, "When it comes to the Middle East, President Donald Trump"[21] failed to provide the priorities of his administration in the region, "but he certainly made a number of transformative promises on the campaign trail about what he would like to do."[22] Candidate Trump made four bold commitments. Those commitments include: (1) "We will move the American Embassy to . . . Jerusalem"; (2) "I will utterly destroy ISIS"; (3) "My number priority is to dismantle the disastrous Iran deal"; and (4) "A lot of people tell me . . . it's impossible [to make Middle East peace]. I have reason to believe I can do it."[23]

In a highly charged and polarizing statement which is part of an address before American Israel Public Affairs Committee (AIPAC) in Washington, DC on March 21, 2016, Trump articulated, "when the United States stands with Israel, the chances of peace . . . rises exponentially. That's what will happen when Donald Trump is president of the United States."[24] This decision, the movement of the US embassy to Jerusalem, said the candidate, "Will send a clear signal that there is no daylight between America and our most reliable ally, the state of Israel."[25]

The promises received predictable responses. Trump's campaign promise to relocate the US embassy to Jerusalem received praise from the Israeli government of Benjamin Netanyahu. In the Arab world, the response was negative. The former Jordanian foreign minister, Kamel Abu Jaber, asserted there would be a dual reaction: Trump's statement would provoke an Arab and Muslim backlash across the region.[26] Abu Jaber's interpretation of Trump's statement included the following analysis: "The man is a businessman. And a realist. I don't think he wants to see any more flames in the Middle East. It would be just like . . . poking a stick into a beehive."[27]

There is another reason why the responses in the Arab world and the reaction in Israel proved to be predictable: this scenario represented the third iteration whereby a US president used a presidential campaign to promise the movement of the American embassy to Jerusalem.

In previous examples, "Bill Clinton and George W. Bush both promised during their presidential campaigns to move the embassy to Jerusalem. . . . Convinced by Middle East experts that doing so would prejudge negotiations for a final settlement between Israelis and Palestinians,"[28] Clinton and Bush did not implement the campaign pledge.

In an interesting move, the US legislative branch also weighed into the debate. In 1995, the Congress of the United States "passed a law declaring Jerusalem to be Israel's capital and requiring the embassy be moved there by 1999—or else the State Department building budget would be cut in half."[29] The legislation did provide an important provision that viewed as an "an opt out-clause" The provision allowed "presidents to waive its requirement for six months if they determined it was in the national interest. So, every six months, Mr. Clinton, Mr. Bush and eventually President Obama signed such waivers, fearing a violent response in the Arab world if the embassy moved."[30]

Should we anticipate that Trump's campaign promise will suffer the same fate? In June of 2017, the Trump administration, consistent with the Jerusalem Embassy Act, issued the following statement on June 1, 2017: "While President Donald J. Trump signed the waiver under the Jerusalem Embassy Act and delayed moving the US Embassy in Israel from Tel Aviv to Jerusalem, no one should consider this step to be in any way a retreat from the President's strong support for Israel and for the United States-Israel alliance."[31] President Trump, according to the statement, "repeatedly stated his intention to move the embassy, the question is not if that move happens, but only when."[32]

In the opening year of the administration, consistent with his predecessor's campaign statements, Trump's pledge to Israel appeared unlikely to be implemented. As Dennis Ross, the former envoy to the Middle East pointed out, there is another significant reason why Trump will move on from the March 2016 statement to other administration foreign policy priorities: "Every president who reversed his campaign promise did so because he decided not to take the risk. Jerusalem has historically been an issue that provoked great passions—often as a result of false claims—that did trigger violence."[33]

In a bold move during year two of his presidency, Trump met his campaign pledge. The decision to formally transfer the American embassy to Jerusalem shocked and confounded domestic critics and offended allies in the region and emboldened an already expanding Palestinian uprising.

In a statement in December of 2017, President Trump directed the State Department "to begin preparation to move the American embassy from Tel

Aviv to Jerusalem. This will immediately begin the process of hiring architects, engineers, and planners, so that a new embassy, when completed, will be a magnificent tribute to peace."[34]

On May 14, 2018 the preparation shifted to the actual opening of the US embassy in Jerusalem. On that day, Ivanka Trump and White House Envoy Jerod Kushner presided over the formal ceremony that represented the formal opening of the American embassy in Jerusalem. In an effort that captured the reaction of the *Washington Post*. Two reporters, Anne Gearan and Ruth Eglash, argued the Palestinian leadership viewed the embassy opening as a "betrayal and an abdication of the US role as a neutral broker in the Israeli-Palestinian conflict."[35] Though President Trump continued to offer statements about peace in the region, there are those, Hamas in particular, that argued diplomacy is not likely after the administration's decision to open the embassy.

In what Palestinian organizers in the Gaza Strip dubbed "The Great Right of Return," a reference to the right of all Palestinians to return to what is now Israel, the campaign which began on March 30, 2018, incessantly challenged Israeli security forces. Unfortunately, the protests and Israeli reaction to them, resulted in Palestinian deaths.

The images of the protest garnered significant media attention. An article in *Reuters* attempted to capture the perspectives of the parties in the dispute. The article asserts, "groups of youths waved Palestinian flags and burnt hundreds of tires and Israeli flags near the fenced-off border after Friday prayers. At one camp east of Gaza City, youths carried on their shoulders a coffin wrapped in an Israeli flag bearing the words 'The End of Israel.' Israel has declared a no-go zone close to the Gaza border fence."[36] The Israeli government accused Hamas, the Islamist movement that ruled Gaza largely since Israeli soldiers and settlers withdrew in 2005, of having instigated the protests and of using them as cover to launch attacks."[37] On the Israel response, a spokesman from the foreign ministry offered this comment: "Israel will continue to defend its borders and its citizens. Your country would do the same."[38]

The Trump White House strongly supported the Israeli position. The efforts by Hamas to coopt what is widely viewed as a "grassroots movement" undermined the Palestinian protests. Taken collectively, there is no peace initiative likely to succeed in the current political environment. For now, the parties are unlikely to engage in any meaningful discourse on a peace settlement. At this stage, the Trump administration should engage the Israelis and Palestinians in confidence building measures that could serve as a bridge to future serious talks on the outstanding issues.

Chapter 6

TRUMP AND MIDDLE EAST PEACE

In an interview with the *New York Times* on November 22, 2016, President-elect Trump confidently stated, "A lot of people tell me . . . that it's impossible [reaching an accord in the Middle East]—you can't do it. I disagree. I think you can make peace. I have reason to believe I can do it."[39]

Miller and Sokolsky, previously stated, "Of all Trump's campaign promises related to the Middle East, this is the one that is perhaps most marked by magical thinking. If there is any issue in the dysfunctional Middle East that is not ready for prime time, it is surely the Israeli-Palestinian peace process."[40] Miller and Sokolsky articulate a major obstacle makes peace unlikely:

> The key issue blocking an impasse in the search for a two-state solution—which is probably the least bad outcome—is not the absence of US leadership or the negotiating talents of this or that president or secretary of state. Rather, it is the politically inconvenient fact that neither the Israeli government nor the leadership of the Palestinian Authority is willing or able to make the kind of decisions required on the core issues (Jerusalem, territory, refugees) that would enable an effective mediator to get close enough to bridge the gaps.[41]

This statement is symptomatic of the increasing perspective that asserts the Trump administration is unlikely to succeed in Middle East diplomacy. There are additional arguments that offer similar assessments.

In an equally dismissive account, Gregg Carlstrom, a Middle East correspondent for *The Economist*, argued, "Trump has so far dashed their hopes that his administration plans to increase pressure on Netanyahu to issue a settlement freeze and publicly endorse the two-state solution. In fact, the Trump administration appears to be moving in the opposite direction: Trump made six public statements during his 28 hours in the Holy Land—but not once did he utter the words 'two-state solution.'"[42] The Israelis took note. More problematic in the view of Carlstrom, "Trump's top officials also do not appear emotionally or intellectually invested in this issue. Obama and George W. Bush both had secretaries of state who were deeply committed to bringing peace in the Holy Land."[43] Under Trump, Secretary Tillerson "has evinced little interest in the conflict."[44]

David Graham, a writer for *The Atlantic*, provided an interesting take on President Trump's opportunity to succeed in the always difficult issue of Middle East Peace. The following excerpt details Graham's assessment of Trump and Middle East Peace:

> One of Donald Trump's great strengths is his ability to project confidence and bravado nearly constantly. The president is sometimes peevish, and he sometimes lashes out, but he seldom seems glumly resigned. Who else, in the middle of a rough stretch of his presidency (one that, arguably, has persisted

since Inauguration Day) could blithely assert that he would solve the most famously unsolvable problem in international diplomacy? Yet there was Trump ... appearing with Palestinian President Mahmoud Abbas and promising to bring peace in the Middle East. "We want to create peace between Israel and the Palestinians. We will get it done," Trump said. "We will be working so hard to get it done. I think there is a very good chance and I think we will." At a lunch later on, he was even bolder: "It is something that I think is frankly, maybe, not as difficult as people have thought over the years. . . . As Dennis Ross, who worked on Israeli-Palestinian issues for Presidents Clinton and Obama, notes, Trump is not the first president for whom the supposed intractability of the conflict has created the attraction. But none of the others has offered so many contradictory signals in such a short time, nor have they offered so little guidance on what they want to see in the process."[45]

There are always critics of presidential administrations on Middle East Peace. One of the early issues that further illustrates the presence of hyper partisanship is that President Trump's detractors leaped at any opportunity to criticize the president's overtures in the region. It is too often dismissed that nearly every post-World War II administration confronted criticism for the failure to develop a coherent Middle East peace proposal, and worse, a Middle East strategy.

There are those that argue the Trump administration's approach does offer promise on the always turbulent issue of Middle East Peace. Hussein Ibish, the senior resident scholar at the Arab Gulf States Institute in Washington (AGSIW), argued there is reason for optimism about and agreement between the Israelis and Palestinians, as the president unveils details about the "outside-in" strategy.[46]

Trump visited Israel as part of his initial foreign trip. It is during this portion of the trip that Ibish argued, "Trump made the strongest public link thus far between two important initiatives: reviving Israeli-Palestinian peace and creating an Israeli-Arab alliance to confront Iran."[47] During an event with Prime Minister Benjamin Netanyahu, Trump ad-libbed about Saudi King Salman's potential role in brokering a peace agreement, saying the monarch "would love to see peace with Israel and the Palestinians."[48] At the center of this agenda, according to Ibish, "is the 'outside-in' strategy for resuscitating Israeli-Palestinian negotiations."[49] The discussions "linked to the development of a broader Middle Eastern coalition to oppose Iran's ongoing expansion of influence in the Middle East and prepare for the day of reckoning when the nuclear agreement expires."[50] Most interesting is that this strategy represents "the only approach that anyone has posited in many years that might break the deadlock, potentially offering a win-win-win scenario for Israel, the Palestinians, and the Arab states."[51]

To produce an agreement between the parties, "Trump, the reality TV veteran, will need to craft a script for Israelis, Palestinians, and Arabs that somehow combines *Let's Make a Deal* with *The Price is Right*."[52] Ibish is one of the few commentators that recognizes the Trump era potentially offers a glimmer of hope of peace between Israel and the Palestinians.

In the final analysis, Middle East Peace is one of many consequential issues in the region. Sadly, there is a shameful carryover of partisan politics into an area of great significance to US foreign policy. The shame is that all too often, it appears commentators on the left are rooting for Trump's failure. The criticism is of course tied to Trump's presidential victory, one which in the venue of the Middle East, represents another area where there will be no Democratic Party continuity, one that President Obama, Hillary Clinton, and their minion of supporters believed would lead to a major legacy—peace between the Israelis and Palestinians. Trump changed that. Now it appeared commentators on the left have a clear agenda—expand the resistance movement into the realm of Middle East policy.

TRUMP'S CONFRONTATION WITH THE ISLAMIC STATE

During a campaign address in Akron, Ohio, on August 22, 2016, Trump made the following statement: "We are going to work with our allies to crush, defeat, and utterly destroy ISIS."[53] In previous statements about the Islamic State, the candidate provided several statements about how he would deal with ISIS. This time the candidate offered no specifics. Critics of the candidate charged, "Trump has declined to lay out a coherent strategy for doing so. . . . Trump insists that he has a plan but says it must remain secret to avoid tipping off the enemy."[54] Previously, the candidate spoke about "bombing the hell out of ISIS"[55] but this, like other anti-ISIS statements, according to critics, did not represent a credible plan to defeat the transnational network.

As president, the Trump administration made substantial progress in their counter anti-ISIS campaign. Working with the coalition, most notably Iraq's Security Forces, the Trump administration assisted in the retaking of Mosul, the second largest city in the country. The administration assisted Iraq's security forces in reclaiming Tal Afar. Additionally, increasing the tempo of operations and deploying more American forces both in Iraq and Syria, the coalition recaptured territory formerly under the control of the Islamic State. The Islamic State however is far from defeated. It is too soon to evaluate whether the president will defeat the Islamic State; the network still exists in twenty-plus states around the world.

Miller and Sokolsky assert Trump is unlikely to defeat ISIS. They provide convincing evidence to support their position. Miller and Sokolsky contend, "In military terms, destroying an enemy means destroying permanently its ability to resist. This is a realistic goal in conventional conflicts, but not in a conflict against an enemy like the Islamic State."[56] The Trump administration thus far has ended the caliphate, but the transnational network is far from defeated. The Islamic State has morphed into an insurgency. As mentioned earlier, the insurgency has produced a "resurrection" in parts of Iraq, Syria, Libya, and Afghanistan. The likely result of the conflict is that like the conflagration with Al Qaeda, the war with the Islamic State will continue, particularly as the administration's focus shifts to other foreign and domestic priorities. There is another reality that Trump and the anti-ISIS coalition is learning: "degrading that resilience requires decisions and actions that America's partners have shown no interest in taking."[57]

TRUMP AND THE IRANIAN NUCLEAR DEAL

Trump used another segment of the AIPAC address to discuss President Obama's nuclear deal with Iran (the Joint Comprehensive Plan of Action or JCPOA). In this portion of the address, Trump bluntly claimed, "My number one priority is to dismantle the disastrous Iran deal."[58] The agreement, said Trump, "Is catastrophic for America, for Israel and for the whole of the Middle East."[59]

Trump later acknowledged the agreement revealed a major problem. As stated in the address, "the problem is [Iran] . . . can keep the terms and still get the bomb by simply running out the clock. And of course, they'll keep the billions and billions of dollars that we so stupidly and foolishly gave them."[60]

President-Elect Trump received what many commentators interpreted as a warning from outgoing President Obama on the eve of the inauguration. During the last week of his presidency, the statement from the Obama White House argued "The United States must remember that this agreement was the result of years of work."[61] Additionally, nearly a few days short of the initial anniversary, the statement read, it "must be measured against the alternatives—a diplomatic resolution that prevents Iran from obtaining a nuclear weapon is far preferable to an unconstrained Iranian nuclear program or another war in the Middle East."[62]

During the transition period, the president-elect received options that if implemented could possibly lead to the dismantling of the agreement. In one example, it is suggested that, "The wise course would be to undertake a review of the JCPOA and allow Congress to ratchet up sanctions."[63]

Once in the office, Trump used Twitter to undermine the agreement. On February 2, 2017, in response to Iran's test firing a ballistic missile, the president stated, "Iran has been formally PUT ON NOTICE for firing a ballistic missile. Should have been thankful for the terrible deal the US made with them!"[64] One day later, the president issued another tweet: "Iran is playing with fire—they don't appreciate how "kind" President Obama was to them. Not me!"[65]

On April 19, 2017, Tillerson informed Congress the Iranian government complied with the provisions of the JCPOA.[66] Despite that statement, Tillerson announced the Trump administration is engaged in a 90-day inter-agency review of the agreement to determine if the government of Iran is cheating. On this point, at a press conference, White House Press Secretary Sean Spicer acknowledged, "That's why he's [the president] is asking for this review. . . . If he didn't, if he thought everything was fine, he would have allowed this to move forward. I think he's doing the prudent thing by asking for a review of the current deal and what's happening."[67]

In early July, a tense meeting occurred between senior officials to determine if the administration would certify the agreement in the future. In a report in the *New York Times*, "all of the president's major security advisers recommended he preserve the Iran deal for now."[68] According to the report a source familiar with the deliberations stated President Trump "spent 55 minutes of the meeting telling them"[69] he opposed recertification.

On July 19, 2017, the Trump administration decided to once again recertify the Iranian nuclear deal. In addition to recertification, the administration announced, "They intended to toughen enforcement of the deal, apply new sanctions on Iran for its support of terrorism and other destabilizing activities, and negotiate with European partners to craft a broader strategy to increase pressure on Tehran."[70]

The Senate passed a bill (a version of which was passed out of the House of Representatives) which represented ". . . one of the first major bipartisan pieces of legislation passed during Trump's presidency."[71] The legislation "effectively ties the hands of the President when it comes to easing Russia sanctions. The bill also includes new sanctions on Iran and North Korea and was a product of lengthy negotiations between the House and Senate."[72] President Trump eventually signed the legislation into law, but the administration subsequently delayed its implementation. That decision unleashed criticism from Democratic members of Congress, with the majority suggesting the failure to implement the legislation is an indication of the president's ties to the Russian's and perhaps that he is soft and not prepared to implement a hardline policy against Moscow.

In addition to the congressional legislation, the Trump administration imposed their own unilateral sanctions against Iran. The Treasury Department sanctioned 16 entities and individuals for their support of "illicit Iranian actors or transnational criminal activity."[73] According to Secretary of the Treasury Steven Mnuchin, "This administration will continue to aggressively target Iran's malign activity, including their ongoing state support of terrorism, ballistic missile program, and human rights abuses."[74] Mnuchin argued the sanctions "send a strong signal that the United States cannot and will not tolerate Iran's provocative and destabilizing behavior. We will continue to target the [Iranian Revolutionary Guard Council] IRGC and pressure Iran to cease its ballistic missile program and malign activities in the region."[75]

The Trump administration's dismantling of the Iranian nuclear agreement will require shrewd diplomacy. Politically, the base of Trump's support remembered the candidate confidently touted that his "number one priority is to dismantle the disastrous Iran deal." Informing the American people, not to mention the Israelis and Saudis, that the president's intentions to accept the agreement would undermine his fragile standing with his domestic and foreign policy allies.

Any early attempts to dismantle the agreement could be equally perilous for President Trump. The Trump administration may learn that "Much like Obamacare, dismantling the JCPOA without thinking through the costs, particularly if there is nothing to replace it, may not appear as attractive in the White House as it did on the campaign trail."[76] The administration did understand a significant reality. That is, France, Britain, Germany, Russia, China, and others are unlikely to implement a subsequent sanctions-regime against Iran. Therefore, Trump's use of unilateral American sanctions is unlikely to have the same impact (at the time that was the view of many analysts; the reality however indicated that US sanctions under Trump did significantly impact Iran's economy) as those that were implemented under the Bush-led and Obama-led United Nations sanction's regimes. The Trump administration did have one advantage: time.

After months of internal debates among the president and key advisers, Trump made the decision to withdraw from the JCPOA with Iran. After several State Department announcements that Iran complied with the agreement, President Trump announced, "his Administration would cease implementing US commitments under the 2015 multilateral Joint Comprehensive Plan of Action (JCPOA) with Iran and reimpose all U.S. sanctions that were in place prior to the JCPOA."[77]

In a statement on May 8, 2018, President Trump met another foreign policy campaign pledge. The critical passages included the following words: "The Iran deal is defective at its core. If we do nothing, we know exactly what will happen. In just a short period of time, the world's leading state sponsor of terror will be on the cusp of acquiring the world's most dangerous weapons."[78] President Trump later stated, "I am announcing . . . the United States will withdraw from the Iran nuclear deal."[79] In addition, the president acknowledged "I will sign a presidential memorandum to begin reinstating US nuclear sanctions on the Iranian regime. We will be instituting the highest level of economic sanction."[80] The president then issued a warning to the international community: that his administration is prepared to implement harsh sanctions against any country found to be assisting Iran develop nuclear weapons.[81]

The other significant passage involved a statement on the importance of the Trump administration keeping their word and how the decision could impact future US-North Korean relations. On these issues, President Trump stated: "Today's action sends a critical message: The United States no longer makes empty threats. When I make promises, I keep them. In fact, at this very moment, Secretary Pompeo is on his way to North Korea in preparation for my upcoming meeting with Kim Jong-un."[82]

President Trump delivered a clear message to North Korea: he hoped that stability, security, and prosperity could result from the summit.[83] Additionally, the president relayed another message to Iran: "As we exit the Iran deal, we will be working with our allies to find a real, comprehensive, and lasting solution to the Iranian nuclear threat. This will include efforts to eliminate the threat of Iran's ballistic missile program; to stop its terrorist activities worldwide; and to block its menacing activity across the Middle East."[84]

After the announcement of the American withdrawal from the JCOP, several objectives surfaced in the wake of the decision. Critics asserted that the decision undermined American credibility, a reference that in future situations requiring an agreement, states around the world would question US veracity and commitment. Second, because the decision undermined US allies that were party to the agreement with Iran, critics charged allies may be reluctant to participate in other major accords. Third, few believed the administration was serious about initiating discussions with Iran on a new nuclear agreement.

President Trump ignored his critics. Instead, the president and administration senior foreign policy advisers quietly prepared for the unveiling of Trump's new Iranian strategy. After a period of internal administration deliberations, Secretary Pompeo informed the media the new strategy would be revealed soon. In an address delivered at the Heritage Foundation in Washington, DC, Secretary of State Pompeo announced the details of the administration's new Iran strategy.

The address contained the standard administration rhetoric. For example, Pompeo spoke of the negatives contained in the agreement. In the words of Pompeo: "the weak sunset provisions of the JCPOA merely delayed the inevitable nuclear weapons capability of the Iranian regime."[85] Iran, said Pompeo is prepared to allow the "countdown clock" to run "out on the deal's sunset provisions" and then "Iran would be free for a quick sprint to the bomb, setting off a potentially catastrophic arms race in the region."[86]

Despite criticism of the agreement, Secretary Pompeo used the address to offer an olive branch to the government of Iran. The excerpt below underscores Pompeo's attempt to reach out to the Iranian government while simultaneously demonstrating to the international community the administration's willingness to engage in diplomacy as opposed to the use of harsh rhetoric:

> In exchange for major changes in Iran, the United States is prepared to take actions which will benefit the Iranian people. . . . Once this is achieved, we're prepared to end the principal components of every one of our sanctions against the regime. We're happy at that point to reestablish full diplomatic and commercial relationships with Iran. . . . But relief from our efforts will come only when we see tangible, demonstrated, and sustained shifts in Tehran's policies. . . . [87]

The new strategy represented a three-fold approach.[88] First, the initial objective is to force Iran to rethink their foreign policy objectives. Translating the new strategy represents an effort to end Tehran's quest for a Shiite order in the region, end state sponsorship of terrorism, end threats and aggressive behavior toward Israel, end support for the regime in Syria, and end support for Hezbollah and other Shiite militias in the region. These are critical issues that are aimed at curbing Iran's adventurism within and beyond the region.[89] The second approach of the administration's new strategy calls for the dissipation of Iranian efforts to enrich uranium. The third aspect of the strategy calls for the implementing of new American sanctions on Iran. Taken collectively, these components are designed to ensure a path to a better nuclear deal with Iran and increase security for the region.

The Iranian government responded harshly to Pompeo's address. In the view of the Iranian government, they argued the Trump administration's decision to abrogate the agreement is a violation of international law and undermines regional security. The Iranian government moved swiftly to seek assurances from European governments that they intend to continue to support the agreement. The objective of the Iranian strategy is designed to drive a wedge between the Trump administration and their European allies.

Allied states in the Atlantic alliance argue the Iranian nuclear agreement represents the best path to the management of Iran's quest for a nuclear weapon. Many argued Trump's decision to withdraw from the nuclear deal undermined the agreement. The European governments engaged in quiet diplomacy with the Trump and other administration officials with the objective of convincing the American president to accept the agreement. The following words provide details of the European diplomacy and the outcome:

> The other powers that negotiated the accord with Iran—Russia, China, France, Britain, and Germany—have consistently asserted that the JCPOA is succeeding in its core objectives and that its implementation should not be jeopardized. Several European countries have sought to address President Trump's demands in negotiations with US officials. In late April 2018 visits to Washington, DC, the President of France and the Chancellor of Germany told President Trump they want to work with the United States to formulate joint action that would address his concerns, but they urged that he keep the United States in the accord as a foundation on which to build additional restrictions on Iran. The leaders of Britain, France, and Germany, as well as the European Union,

expressed "regret" about the US decision and pledged to work with Iran to continue implementing the JCPOA.[90]

At the time of this writing, there is yet no evidence of increased tensions or worsening relations. The rhetoric increased on both sides. Anticipated areas of increased discord between Washington and Tehran are likely to occur in Syria or Iraq. Experts will also analyze Iran's reaction to the re-imposition of American sanctions. For example, if the sanctions are working, will Iran open negotiations over a new agreement with the Trump administration? From another perspective, if administration pressure is used on the European allies to curtail or eliminate trade with Iran, how will Tehran react to another intense effort to undermine their economy and contain the regimes adventurism? What future actions will the Trump administration implement should Iran accelerate testing (break out of the agreement)? The answers to these and other questions will provide a sense of the path of the US-Iranian relationship.

TRUMP AND SYRIA

Syria is an issue that will at times overshadow the president's foreign policy agenda. President Trump will have to address how to end the civil war, end the regime of President Bashar al-Assad, deal with Russian and Iranian influence in the country, and confront the Islamic State and Al Qaeda in Syria. These issues represent the cauldron of problems that await the attention of President Trump.

One of the bold moves of the Trump presidency concerned the president's decision to launch 59 cruise missiles that targeted the Shayrat air base in Syria after American intelligence confirmed Syrian President Assad ordered a chemical weapons attack that killed innocent civilians.

In a brief televised address, President Trump stated, "Tonight, I ordered a targeted military strike on the airfield in Syria from where the chemical attack was launched. It is in this vital national security interest of the United States to prevent and deter the spread and use of deadly chemical weapons."[91] The president then pivoted to the civil war: "Tonight, I call on all civilized nations to join us in seeking to end the slaughter and bloodshed in Syria, and also to end terrorism of all kinds and all types."[92]

The strike received bipartisan praise in the United States. Around the world, particularly in the Middle East, commentators asserted the strike demonstrated that American leadership and credibility returned. There is another important reality associated with the strike: Russia, China, Iran, and North Korea understood that Trump is not Obama and a new era in Washington may be underway.

On June 25, 2017, President Trump launched another strike against the same air base in Syria. The US intelligence community indicated activity that a chemical weapons attack appeared imminent in the previously attacked Shayrat air base.[93]

Speaking about the warning, Sean Spicer, the former White House press secretary stated, "The US has identified potential preparations for another chemical weapons attack by the Assad regime that would likely result in the mass murder of civilians, including innocent children."[94] Additionally, Spicer, reiterated US policy in the country: "As we have previously stated, the US is in Syria to eliminate the Islamic State of Iraq and Syria [ISIS]. If, however, Mr. Assad conducts another mass-murder attack using chemical weapons, he and his military will pay a heavy price."[95]

Other Trump administration officials offered additional clarifying comments. US ambassador to the United Nations, Haley, articulated the strike sent a powerful message: "I believe that the goal is, at this point, not just to send Assad a message but to send Russia and Iran a message that if this happens again we are putting you on notice."[96] In the final analysis, the Syrian government did not launch a subsequent chemical weapon air strike. President Trump's threat did produce desired results.

Another issue of significance in Syria concerned the future of territory liberated from the Islamic State. In advance of the G-20 meeting, Secretary Tillerson "appeared to be trying to influence those talks"[97] to forge cooperation between the United States and Russia. For Tillerson, Syria represented one issue where he believed both sides could fine commonality.

Tillerson noted, "The United States is prepared to explore the possibility of establishing with Russia joint mechanisms for ensuring stability, including no-fly zones, on the ground cease-fire observers, and coordinated delivery of humanitarian assistance."[98] Tillerson believed that if there is success in the aforementioned areas, "a foundation for progress on the settlement of Syria's political future."[99]

In addition to the above statement, Tillerson stated, "no faction in Syria illegitimately retakes or occupies areas liberated from ISIS."[100] Graham Langtree, a national security reporter with *Newsweek*, interpreted the statement this way: "That means that the Syrian autocrat would not be able to reoccupy the Islamic State (ISIS) terrorist group's stronghold in the city of Raqqa without some sort of agreement between all parties."[101] Langtree insisted the Trump administration is in a precarious position because the president has yet to provide an overt and coherent Syrian policy.[102]

Steven Heydemann, a fellow at Brookings' Center for Middle East Policy, offered an interesting take on Trump and Syria. Heydemann argued, "That Trump will not have a Syria policy, he will have a Russia policy."[103] The point is the future of Syria, to include ending the civil war and ending the future government of the country, will come through cooperation with

Russia. Heydemann's comments followed Tillerson's statement where the secretary stated he "wants the US and Russia to run joint operations in Syria to increase cooperation between the two nations."[104]

Though not endorsing the Heydemann approach, Tillerson did inform the press that cooperation in Syria is well underway: "The United States and Russia have already achieved progress in establishing de-confliction zones in Syria that have prevented mutual collateral damage.... If our two countries work together to establish stability on the ground, it will lay a foundation for progress on the settlement of Syria's political future."[105] Another avenue of cooperation could be in the elimination of the Islamic State from the country as well as Al Qaeda in Syria (AQS). However, Russian interference in the 2016 presidential election undermined opportunities for comprehensive efforts to combat terrorism in Syria.

President Trump and Russian President Vladimir Putin met for an extended period during the G-20 gathering in Germany. The two leaders announced on July 8, 2017 that a ceasefire agreement had been reached "on curbing violence in southwest Syria."[106]

Several administration officials spoke on the significance of the agreement. Secretary Tillerson stated, "This is our first indication of the US and Russia being able to work together in Syria," and that there were "lengthy discussion of other areas in Syria where we can work together."[107] White House national security adviser McMaster argued the "de-escalation zones" are central to US policy.[108] In addition, McMaster stated, "We're encouraged by the progress made to reach this agreement"[109] and he noted "The United States remains committed to defeating ISIS, [ending] . . . the conflict in Syria, reducing suffering, and enabling people to return to their homes. This agreement is an important step toward these common goals."[110]

On the agreements enforcement, Russian Foreign Minister, Sergei Lavrov, informed reporters at the G-20 meeting the Russian military police would coordinate with the US and Jordanian governments to ensure that all sides adhere to the accord.[111] Lavrou also stated that humanitarian access would be provided in "the de-escalation zone" and he "promised to ensure that all groups there comply with the ceasefire."[112]

There are important aspects of the agreement that few have discussed publicly. For example, "The pact is aimed at addressing demands by Israel and Jordan—the latter is a party to the agreement—that Iranian forces and their proxies, including Hezbollah, not be permitted near the Israeli-occupied Golan Heights, which separates Syria from Israel, or along the Jordanian border."[113] There are several problems. Is the agreement enforceable? In addition to this issue, many "diplomats and observers" expressed "doubts that Russia could act as a reliable guarantor for a cease-fire involving the Syrian regime, Iran, and its proxies."[114]

Gerald Feierstein, a retired American diplomatic, represented a chorus of critics that questioned the feasibility of the agreement. Feierstein argued, "The question is, 'Who is going to enforce that?' Is Russia going to take on the responsibility for telling Iran what to do? Iranians are much closer to Assad's position on the way forward in Syria than the Russians are. It's the Iranians and their proxies who are doing a bulk of the fighting inside Syria."[115] There are a host of commentators that have questioned the enforcement of the agreement. However, despite the negative statements, the accord remains in force.

The Trump administration monitored the clash between Iran and Israel in Syria in May of 2018. In response to the Iranian Rocket attacks that initiated the crisis, White House spokesperson Sarah Huckabee Sanders, responded by acknowledging the "provocative rocket attacks from Syria against Israeli citizens."[116] Sanders also observed the Israeli governments counter strike is consistent Israel's right to act in self-defense."[117]

At issue, could the crisis be contained? The *Wall Street Journal* reported, "The direct military conflict between Israel and Iran has already begun, with a series of increasingly bold (and usually unacknowledged) Israeli strikes on Iranian bases in Syria in recent weeks."[118] The article poses an important set of questions: "Whether this clash could be contained within Syria—or whether violence could spread to Israeli, Iranian and maybe Lebanese territory, unleashing a regional war."[119]

Despite concerns of a conflict between Iran and Israel, tensions quickly dissipated in part because Iran (facing pressure from Russia and recognition that the escalation of conflict with Israel at that time is not in its best interest), never responded to the wide-ranging Israeli counter attack which hit most of the Iranian infrastructure in the Golan Heights.

Many critics questioned if the Trump administration should have done more to prevent or contain Israeli military actions. Other's questioned if the administration is engaged at all. Many critics argued that "Unless the United States steps in with a plan for Syria, Israel and Iran will continue to clash there."[120] Thus far, the Trump administration has not unveiled a comprehensive American strategy for Syria. Another crisis in an already chaotic region, for now, ended without it spiraling to wider conflict. A potential set of issues remain on the horizon: will Israel and Iran clash at a later point and how will the Trump administration respond?

TRUMP'S TRIP TO SAUDI ARABIA – THE QUEST FOR COUNTERTERRORISM IN THE MUSLIM WORLD

In advance of President Trump's trip to Saudi Arabia, the administration in late April and in early May, formerly began to debate the future of US counterterrorism. An internal White House memo leaked to *Reuters* indicated the administration is seriously examining the future of US counterterrorism policy.[121]

There are several critical points that provide a window into the Trump administration's counterterrorism strategy. Examples contained in the eleven-page draft include the following excerpts:

- "We need to intensify operations against global jihadist groups while also reducing the costs of American 'blood and treasure' in pursuit of our counterterrorism goals"[122];
- "We will seek to avoid costly, large-scale US military interventions to achieve counterterrorism objectives and will increasingly look to partners to share the responsibility for countering terrorist groups."[123]

Addressing some of the contents of the new strategy, Michael Anton, the spokesman for the White House National Security Council, asserted, consistent with the approach, administration "is taking a fresh look at the entire US national security strategy, to include the counterterrorism mission, which is especially important since no such strategy has been produced publicly since 2011."[124] In the end, a central tenet of the administration strategy is to avoid "open-ended"[125] military engagements.

The trip to Saudi Arabia and President Trump's desire to construct an Arab-NATO coalition to confront terrorism is very much consistent with the administration's approach to counterterrorism strategy. With the ongoing domestic problems, the Middle East trip represented an opportunity to meet with world leaders, improve relationships with regional allies, and reset the anti-ISIS coalition. Administration officials understood that with a series of successful trips, upon return to the United States, President Trump could then restart his stalled domestic agenda.

Susan B. Glasser, a reporter from *Politico* asserted, "Russia won in Syria thanks to President Barack Obama's inaction. The Middle East unraveling of the past decade is due in no small part to America not listening to her allies in the region. Never mind President Donald Trump's Muslim-bashing rhetoric, he may just be a better partner."[126] Glasser then provided this critical analysis of the region: "leaders of America's Arab allies in the Mideast . . . telegraphed this view of the world, and it helps explain why the gilded palaces of the troubled, war-torn region are the few places on the planet—outside Russia—where Trump has been more popular than the president he succeeded."[127] In the addition, Glasser acknowledged, "[There is] . . . hope for a more decisive approach is the reason why . . . Arab leaders prefer Trump."[128]

President Trump issued this statement to set the tone for a critical speech in Saudi Arabia: In the Kingdom, "I will speak with Muslim leaders and challenge them to fight hatred and extremism, and embrace a peaceful future for their faith."[129] The administration's priorities in Saudi Arabia include an improved regional counterterrorism cooperation against the Islamic State, a strengthened US relationship with the Muslim community, and a restored American leadership in the region.

The "love affair" expressed by Arab leaders was on display throughout President Trump's visit to Saudi Arabia. Trump used his address "to reset his relationship with the Muslim world, strained by his own Islamophobic rhetoric."[130] A problematic and divisive statement such as "I think Islam hates us,"[131] that Trump made offended the Muslim community within the United States and undermined the candidates' standing with Muslims around the world.

Dismissed by the media and critics of Trump's horrific campaign statements is the reality that prior to the trip, the president privately repaired relationships with key Muslim leaders. In one example, long before the president's trip to Middle East, Trump spoke to Salman bin Abdulaziz Al Saud, the King and then leader of Saudi Arabia by phone on January 29, 2017. The outcome of the conversation indicated both leaders established a productive relationship. Both leaders agreed on an approach to deal with Iran, on how to confront regional terrorism, and the need for safe zones in Syria.[132]

In a second example, President Trump and the Egyptian leader Abdel Fattah el-Sisi worked to improve relations between their two countries. The following statement clarified the state of the relationship: "The two presidents may differ ideologically, Trump has an ally in Sisi that is willing to support the fear-mongering his team has been dishing out since he first announced he would run for US president. In Trump, Sisi has also found support for the image he wishes to project of himself: that of the strongman fighting terrorism."[133]

On March 21, 2017, the day of President Trump's keynote address, this date represented an opportunity for redemption. Speaking before leaders representing 55 Sunni majority states around the world, President Trump asserted, "America is prepared to stand with you in pursuit of shared interests and common security. But nations of the Middle East cannot wait for American power to crush this enemy for them. . . ."[134] The president then issued this charge to the gathering of leaders: "The nations of the Middle East . . . have to decide what kind of future they want for themselves, for their countries and frankly for their families and for their children. Terrorism has spread across the world. But the path to peace begins right here, on this ancient soil, in this sacred land."[135]

Across the region, and even within the not so non-partisan American media, the speech was reviewed positively. Within the administration, there was little time for "triumphalism." In short order, "Trump was taken through the Global Center for Combating Extremist Ideology after delivering a major speech to a number of Arab leaders about collaboration in the fight against terrorism."[136] In the view of Mohammed al-Issa, the secretary general of the Muslim World League, he noted "the counterterrorism center is significant because leaders understood that force alone would not defeat terrorism."[137] To defeat the extremists, according to al-Issa, one must be prepared "defeat their ideology."[138]

In another sign of the significance of the counterterrorism cooperation, "The US and Saudi Arabia signed a joint declaration . . . that called for the creation of a special commission to coordinate both country's efforts on combating extremism by cutting off groups' financing, countering their messaging and applying military force."[139]

The joint statement also added this significant point: "The two leaders expressed their support for the Iraqi government's efforts to eradicate ISIS, uniting the Iraqis to combat terrorism that poses a threat to all Iraq, and preserving the unity and integrity of Iraqi territory."[140] There are two additional points of significance. The United States and Saudi Arabia pledged to end Iranian interference in the internal affairs of the government of Iraq.[141] Second, both parties recognized that there is continuing need for productive relations between Saudi Arabia and Iraq.[142]

Long after the return to Washington, DC, the president and senior administration officials were recharged after the highly successful Middle East trip. Months later, counterterrorism, a regular feature in the Trump era, took center stage.

In the wake of the celebratory environment following the recapture of Mosul, Iraq's second largest city in July, critics questioned if the Trump administration had developed a comprehensive counterterrorism strategy. Similarly, many within the counterterrorism community argued that unless there is post-conflict and stabilization funding to rebuild the war-ravaged city, provide shelter and food to citizens returning to their homes, the disaffected citizens, in the area populated by Sunni Muslims, could join extremist movements that could set the stage for the return of the Islamic State.[143]

Josh Rogin, a reporter from the *Washington Post,* asserted, "The Trump administration doesn't seem to have learned that lesson."[144] Rogin then paraphrases Richard Clarke, former White House counterterrorism adviser, noting the Trump administration did not develop reconstruction plans for Iraq and Syria."[145] Later in the article, Rogin makes use of this quote from Clarke, who stated, "The best breeding ground for terrorists is a city without services. The short-termism in our counterterrorism policy is baffling, because we will have to come back and do it all again."[146]

This statement indicated that Trump provided a winning strategy that forced the collapse of the Islamic States' Caliphate, but the administration had not spent an inordinate amount of time on post-conflict stabilization. The dilemma confronting Trump is that if he fails to "get things right" in the

Levant, it is possible that US forces could be in Syria, and possibly Iraq, for an extended period of time.

CRISES IN THE GULF

Fresh off the successful trip to Saudi Arabia where President Trump created a strong Arab coalition against the Islamic State, where the participants agreed to confront radical Islam in the region around the world and achieve cooperation among member states to roll back Iranian regional influence, the administration watched as the positive headlines vanished. What was behind the absence of positive headlines? Within weeks those headlines instead were supplanted by a Saudi-led movement to confront Qatar's embrace of Iran and their strong support for radical Islamist movements.

In a major decision, in early June 2017, "Saudi Arabia, Egypt, the United Arab Emirates, Yemen, Libya, [and] Bahrain . . . severed their ties with Qatar . . . accusing it of supporting terrorism and opening up the worst rift in years among some of the most powerful states in the Arab world."[147] Additionally, the Saudi-led coalition issued "13 demands for Doha to comply with to lift the blockade, expanding the scope of the dispute beyond the initial emphasis on terrorism financing."[148] One of the most important demands required that Qatar sever "diplomatic ties with Iran and sever links to terrorist organizations—like the Muslim Brotherhood."[149]

The crisis in the Gulf involving Qatar and other American allies in the region have been exasperated by the "Trump Administration's Discord, Dysfunction."[150] Rather than remain neutral, President Trump instead made the following statement that deepened the crisis: "Nations . . . spoke to me about confronting Qatar. I decided . . . the time had come to call on Qatar to end its funding. The nation of Qatar . . . has historically been a funder of terrorism at a very high level."[151]

The president's statement emboldened Saudi Arabia and their allies and embarrassed Qatar. In a recognition of a worsening crisis, Tillerson and Mattis worked to bring the parties of the dispute together to resolve the crisis.[152] The actions implemented by these officials gave the appearance of discord between the president and two of his senior advisors.[153] Even though "President Donald Trump, who has on two occasions condemned and mocked Qatar, a longtime US partner," the administration made the case no descension existed.[154]

The problematic statement by the president ignited an uproar inside the United States and in select states in the Arab world. Among NATO partners, some openly criticized the president's decision to sell arms to states in the region. In one example, German Foreign Minister Sigmar Gabriel criticized what he called the "Trumpification" of the Middle East. Gabriel asserted,

"The recent massive arms deals President Trump made with the Gulf monarchies exacerbate the risk of a new arms race. This policy is completely wrong, and it is certainly not Germany's policy."[155] This decision is what the foreign minister argued is behind the crisis involving Qatar and their gulf neighbors. In addition, Gabriel noted, "I am very concerned by the dramatic escalation of the situation and the consequences for the whole region."[156]

Diplomatically, experts asserted the situation in the Gulf is further complicated because Qatar is home to the largest American air base in the region. The base is home to "More than 11,000 US and coalition forces at al-Udeid air base outside Doha, which is the center for US air operations over Syria, Iraq, Yemen and Afghanistan."[157] Despite the tensions in the relationship with the United States, "Qatar . . . called on Trump to intervene decisively, saying he was "crucial" to resolving the crisis."[158]

In July of 2017, Secretary Tillerson's shuttle diplomacy with representatives of the government of Saudi Arabia and representatives of the government of Qatar represented another administration attempt to reduce regional tensions. The diplomatic effort resulted in an accord with Qatar on July 11, 2017. On the significance of the accord, Tillerson noted, "The agreement . . . represents weeks of intensive discussions between experts and reinvigorates the spirit of the Riyadh summit."[159] In addition, Tillerson stated, "The memorandum lays out a series of steps that each country will take in coming months and years to interrupt and disable terror financing flows and intensify counter terrorism activities globally."[160]

The Trump administration acknowledged the agreement is significant, and the memorandum of understanding represented an important first step. A problem remained: until the Saudi-led bloc signed the accord, tensions in the region will persist.

Critics complained President Trump's deference to the Saudi's undermined diplomatic initiatives by Tillerson. In addition, the overt pressure on Qatar, combined with "inconsistent messages from within his administration—reflecting concerns that Washington not place Riyadh's priorities above its own and absence of a coordinated greater Middle East strategy—hamper his efforts to lead."[161] This is not the first time that critics and allies of the administration questioned when the president would implement a strategy for the region. In the absence of a strategy which alerts allies inside and outside the region about administration interests, Trump administration officials are likely to adopt an ad hoc approach when a dispute develops. This is what occurred during the Qatar disagreement.

TRUMP AND THE CIVIL WAR IN YEMEN

During the administration of President Obama, US policy in Yemen dramatically changed in 2015 following two critical decisions. In the wake of the capture of the capital by Iranian-backed Houthis rebels, the US government shut down their embassy and subsequently withdrew American Special Forces (many of which returned in small numbers months later) which were targeting Al Qaeda in the Arabian Peninsula (AQAP).[162]

Since that time, a proxy war assumed center stage. In this not so shadow conflict, Saudi Arabia, Jordan, Morocco, Bahrain, Kuwait, Qatar, Egypt, Sudan, the UAE, the United States, the EU, and Pakistan and other states, supported the minority anti-government Sunni groups which are opposed by Iran and their Shia Houthis allies.[163]

Former secretary of defense and CIA director, Leon Panetta, made the following critical statement: "The Obama administration frankly did not pay enough attention to Iran's support to terrorism in that region particularly at the time they were negotiating with the Iranians. I think it's very important for President Trump not to simply bounce to the other extreme."[164]

The Trump administration accelerated the US role in the dispute in Yemen which produced this analysis: The president "Is trying to intensify its efforts to counter Al Qaeda in the Arabian Peninsula and the Houthi maritime threat because those efforts are in the interests of the United States."[165] The Trump administration is attempting to "convince both Saudi Arabia and the United Arab Emirates—the two most important US partners in the Gulf—that the United States takes seriously their fears about spreading Iranian influence."[166]

Trump's policy in Yemen is aimed at reducing Iran's role in the country. To implement this policy the Trump administration "signed off on the precision-guided munitions"[167] to Saudi Arabia. Mattis subsequently requested the White House "approve US surveillance, intelligence, refueling and operational planning for a United Arab Emirates-led offensive on Hodeida, a Red Sea port held by the Houthis."[168]

Second, the administration notified the Senate Foreign Relations Committee "that it approved a $5 billion sale of 19 F-16 fighter jets and related equipment to Bahrain, which is part of the Saudi coalition."[169] The Obama administration previously "halted the sale over concerns about Bahrain's human rights record."[170] Third, "General Joseph Votel, commander of US Central Command, told the House Armed Services Committee [for those] concerned about Iran making a 'chokepoint' in the Bab al-Mandab Strait between Yemen and the Horn of Africa, similar to Iran's behavior in the Strait of Hormuz."[171] Taken collectively, these efforts indicated the Trump administration is determined to prevent Iran from restricting this vital waterway. One of the salient weaknesses associated with the administration policy is that Saudi Arabia and their allies launched air strikes that resulted in civilian casualties. At another level, these attacks and the Saudi-led effort to restrict badly needed aid to civilians increased the humanitarian situation in the country.

The Trump administration is actively engaged in the Yemeni civil war. In addition, during the transition period, a decision was made to increase counterterrorism drone strikes, raids, and other mechanisms of activities against the AQAP. The administration approved several US SOF-led raids and increased drone and other conventional strikes against the Al Qaeda affiliate. In addition, "a small contingent of US troops"[172] were "involved in a Yemeni operation to push al Qaeda militants from one of their key strongholds in central Yemen."[173]

In another illustration of the increasing American presence in Yemen, the Pentagon announced that US forces "are engaged in intelligence sharing" and "the United States is providing midair refueling and overhead reconnaissance for forces involved in the operation. The Bataan Amphibious Ready Group, a collection of US Navy ships loaded with Marines, is in the region and is probably assisting the operation with aircraft and personnel. In the past, amphibious groups much like the Bataan's have been integral in supporting US-led operations against al Qaeda in Yemen."[174]

There is increasing opposition to Trump's administration's involvement in the civil war in Yemen. In an illustration of the opposition, Senator Chris Murphy (D-Conn.), forcefully stated, "It sounds like we've learned absolutely no lessons from the last 15 years in the Middle East. We're engaged in a rapid military escalation with no political strategy. This is a recipe for disaster, and I'm prepared to use whatever tools I have at my disposal to try to force Congress to weigh in on this question."[175]

MIDDLE EAST STRATEGY AND THE JAMAAL KASHOGGI AFFAIR

Administration critics incessantly complained the absence of a coherent strategy is evident in Syria, Middle East Peace, Yemen, and elsewhere in the region. In August 23, 2018, the Trump administration quietly unveiled their regional approach. The approach is titled the Joint Regional Strategy-Middle East and North Africa (MENA). The strategy is composed of four parts. Each of the components embodies the Trump administration's objectives for MENA. The initial component stressed the need for "enhanced security, stabilization, and conflict resolution."[176] The second component involves the advancement of Arab-Israeli Peace.[177] The third component involved the "promotion of inclusive economic growth, socio-economic development, open markets," which would pave the way for increased American exports across MENA.[178] And finally, the administration stressed the requirement of good governance, "strengthen[ing of] Democratic Institutions and Processes, and support and engage civil society."[179] The Bureau of Near Eastern Affairs (NEA) is charged with implementing the Trump administration's regional strategy. The NEA offered this statement in the roll-out of the strategy: "Our engagements and programming are restricted in critical areas of the region which are troubled by conflict and instability."[180]

One of the contradictory features of the president's strategy is Trump campaigned on limiting US military intervention and involvement in the region. During the campaign candidate Trump criticized previous administrations for the overextension of American forces which engaged in expensive operations in the region. Based on the campaign statements, many experts assumed President Trump would disengage from the region. Other experts assert the Trump administration is instead pursuing a policy of "selective engagement" in the Middle East. An illustration of selective engagement is demonstrated by the multiple cruise missile strikes against Syrian government forces suspected of launching chemical weapons attacks against civilians and American counterterrorism operations in Yemen, Libya, and in Syria where the administration launched numerous air strikes against Islamic State fighters.

The administration quietly implemented another unspoken component—the embrace of Israel, Egypt, and Saudi Arabia—which represented what one fiercely outspoken critic of Trump's foreign policy, Stephen M. Walt, the distinguished Professor in International Relations from Harvard University, argued is an illustration of the president's "Middle East strategy on Steroids."[181] Walt and others expressed concern that President Trump is investing political capital in our traditional allies, whether in Israel, Egypt, or Saudi Arabia, when the reality suggests the president should not have done so. This approach represents an illustration of realism—when American interests assumed prominence, the president overlooked conspicuous failings in the leaders of the three regional allies.

Leon Hadar, a geopolitical analyst for The RANE Network, a risk management consulting group, argued there are several successes associated with the trajectory of the president's regional approach despite the potential of the perils.[182] In the case of Israel, President Trump's policies have reestablished a previously tattered relationship with America's most indispensable ally in the region.[183] There are those that believe the president should force the Benjamin Netanyahu-led Israeli government to institute "a freeze" on settlement activities. Instead, President Trump has not provided any indication that he is willing to halt settlement construction in Palestinian territories.

Egyptian leader Abdel Fattah el-Sisi is engaged in an on-going overt policy to undermine freedom of speech and freedom of the press, and he jails political prisoners. Despite these obvious threats to democracy in the country

President Trump embraced el-Sisi and the administration views the Egyptian leader as an ally against regional extremism, one that could potentially assist in Israeli-Palestinian diplomatic efforts, and act as a buffer against Iran.

In the case of Saudi Arabia, a previously stalled and declining relationship under President Obama, is witnessing a rebirth. Trump and Saudi leader Mohammed Bin Sultan have forged a strategic relationship whereby both leaders have agreed to work to confront Iran's quest for a nuclear program and have pledged to challenge Tehran's vision of a Shia-dominated region. The relationship is evident in the Trump administration's support of Saudi Arabia and their Gulf allies in the struggle with Iran and its allies in Yemen. On the Islamic State, and other transnational networks, Washington and Riyadh have pledged to advance counterterrorism cooperation to confront extremism across MENA.[184]

Despite the perils associated with these problematic relationships, the Trump administration is gambling that the utilization of the three critical allies provides an "opportunity" to reestablish US credibility with each, restore American leadership, and provide a semblance of stability in the region.

On another level, there is another benefit associated with the Trump administration's strategy—forging an approach whereby the United States is not likely to engage in a costly and lengthy intervention in Syria. These are issues that Russia's President Putin must confront. Put more plainly, the Trump administration, unlike President Bush in Iraq or President Obama in Afghanistan, is not "at the center of civil war and being forced to pay a high military and financial costs"[185] in Syria. President Trump's decision to withdraw some of the US forces from Syria is consistent with the approach. However, the short-term and long-term consequences could unleash Syrian-Russian efforts to retake territory formally held by the Islamic State, Turkey may be emboldened to attack US-backed Kurdish forces, and ISIS and Al Qaeda in Syria will most certainly welcome the absence of American forces as an opportunity to regroup. In the future there are those that assert that if there is a complete withdrawal of US forces from Syria, the scramble to fill the power vacuum will commence.

THE KHASHOGGI AFFAIR

The murder of outspoken Saudi-born journalist Jamal Khashoogi threatened to unravel the Trump administration's carefully orchestrated efforts to forge a strategic partnership with Saudi Arabia. Khashoggi's comments about the government of Saudi Arabia's human rights record, gender inequity, press freedom, and the slow-paced efforts of democratic reform represents some of the numerous issues highlighted by the journalist. An activist journalist, Khashoggi is well-known in media circles and, equally important, he represents a conspicuous force for change and a thorn in the side of the Saudi government. The premeditated murder, and purported evidence of the participation by Crown Prince bin Salman, instantaneously created a cloud over US-Saudi relations.

How did the Trump administration respond to the Khashoggi affair? Noah Phillips, a fellow from the Begin-Sadat Center for Strategic Studies, articulated the murder and subsequent cover-up of the outspoken journalist's murder put the Trump administration in an uncomfortable position.[186] The administration had to strike a balance between human rights and the rule of law, foundational principles of the American system and navigating domestic and external pressures to "issue a harsh response" if the Saudis were found complicit in a murder purportedly authorized by Bin Salman. This not being enough, the Trump administration had to consider ways to preserve the strategic partnership.

The Turkish government and the additional information obtained by the US intelligence community provided overwhelming evidence of an operation designed to kidnap and subsequently murder and then "dump" Khashoggi's body in a yet undetermined location.

In the days after meetings with Pompeo, who privately met with the crown prince, and CIA Director Gina Haspel, who reviewed classified evidence gathered by the Turkish government of the murder of Khashoggi, President Trump spoke about the necessity of implementing a tough response if the Saudi government was found to be complicit in the murder. President Trump made the fatal mistake of publicly mentioning "the mega-arms deal" which is estimated at $450 billion. There are other aspects of the cultivated relationship that include "strong economic ties with the desert kingdom and . . . much stock in the diplomatic relationship" which assisted in development of Saudi Arabia as "a key strategic Sunni ally."[187]

From the outset, President Trump and Secretary Pompeo spoke about the need to "preserve the strategic relationship." On November 20, 2018, President Trump issued this statement in defense of the Saudi leader that alarmed his detractors and allies: "It could very well be that the Crown Prince had knowledge of this tragic event—maybe he did and maybe he didn't!"[188] Three days later, on November 23, 2018, President Trump provided this statement, "The crime against Jamal Khashoggi was a terrible one, and one that our country does not condone."[189] Based on intelligence community assessments, Trump announced, "We have sanctioned 17 Saudis known" to have participated "in the murder of Mr. Khashoggi, and the disposal of his body."[190] The president then agued the US-Saudi relationship will survive the tragic death of Khashoggi.

David Remnick, editor of *The New Yorker*, offered this critique of President Trump's open support for the embattled leader of Saudi Arabia: "The Khashoggi affair has alarmed and outraged Republicans and Democrats in equal measure."[191] The embrace of bin Salman underscores a problem "with the Trump Presidency: the president's fondness for autocrats."[192]

The administration continued its focus on the strategic relationship despite the criticism from both sides of the political spectrum. In the wake of his return from a meeting with Bin Salman, Pompeo privately expressed to the president the Saudi leader claims that he did not have knowledge of murder. In a presser at "the foggy bottom," Pompeo then provided statements that demonstrated the synergy between the White House and the state department on the American response to the murder of Khashoogi. Pompeo asserted, "As the President said today, the United States will continue to have a relationship with the Kingdom of Saudi Arabia."[193] He spoke of the fact that the Saudi's are an "important partner."[194] He then argued the administration has already issued a tough response. He then stated, "At the same time [the administration] is committed to making sure . . . America's national security interests . . . continues to . . . grow."[195]

The negative reaction to the Trump administration's response reached a fever pitch. Congressional leaders spoke of passing legislation condemning the Saudi government for their direct participation in the murder. White House officials scrambled to prevent the consideration of legislation, the passage of which could undermine the president's authority in foreign policy. Those efforts failed.

On December 13, 2018 by a vote of 56-41, the US Senate passed a nonbinding joint legislation that formally condemned the government of Saudi Arabia for their role in the murder of Khashoggi and subsequent legislation that ended American military assistance to the kingdom in its war in Yemen. The action in Yemen limits the president's war powers.[196]

The Khashoggi affair will forever cast a shadow over relations between the United States and Saudi Arabia. Amazingly, "there is a crisis in US-Saudi relations, yet neither government seems to realize it."[197] There is something equally significant: Anger in Congress over the Khashoggi killing has been compounded by the "Trump administration's inept response to it."[198] There are those that expressed the viewed that "President Trump has an opportunity to pressure the Saudi leadership to incorporate journalistic freedom into its program of domestic reform."[199] Given the overwhelming upheaval over the killing of well-known journalist, and evidence of the Saudi government's role, with substantial leverage afforded to him in the wake of the affair, President Trump did consider the opportunity afforded to him and the administration. It represented an opportunity to do what is right; a response to protect journalists around the world. Now the American president will have to deal with the unfolding peril for the failure to correct an injustice. The affair will linger, and it will no doubt shape the perception of US policy in the region.

The situation in Yemen, like the Gulf crisis involving Qatar, the nascent Arab anti-ISIS counterterrorism coalition, the collapse of the caliphate in Syria and Iraq, and the subsequent emergence of the Islamic States' insurgent movement and resurrection, the Khashoggi affair, and pursuit of Israeli-Palestinian peace all remain in flux. Though the Trump administration has made progress in the region, particularly in changing the perception of American leadership, the Middle East remains turbulent. Armed with a coherent strategy for the region, it will prove interesting to watch the Trump administration's response to the certain crises that will develop in the always chaotic region.

NOTES

1. Pagliarulu, Diego, "Donald Trump, the Middle East, and American Foreign Policy," *E-International Relations*, January 3, 2017. http://www.e-ir.info/2017/01/03/donald-trump-the-middle-east-and-american-foreign-policy/. Accessed on April 3, 2018.
2. Ibid.
3. Springborg, Robert, "The New US President: Implications for The Middle East and North Africa," *Future Notes*, October 2016. http://www.iai.it/sites/default/files/mena-ra_fn_2.pdf. Accessed on April 3, 2018.
4. In most chapters in this study there is a section that explores Trump's campaign statements and the topic to be addressed, such as Russia, China, or North Korea, for example. With respect to the Middle East, the bulk of Trump's statements are principally directed at exposing the flaws in President Obama's policies in one country or another in the region. Trump offers few specifics on how he would tackle most of the problems (of which there are many in the region) in the area if he would become president. Thus, the section provides an overview of the candidates' positions in those cases where significant campaign statements/speeches were made.
5. "Transcript: Donald Trump's Foreign Policy Speech," *New York Times*, April 27, 2016. https://www.nytimes.com/2016/04/28/us/politics/transcript-trump-foreign-policy.html. Accessed on April 3, 2018.
6. Ibid.
7. Ibid.
8. Ibid.
9. Ibid.
10. Ibid.
11. Ibid.
12. bid.
13. Miller, Aaron David, "Trump on the Middle East: Where Does He Really Stand?" *CNN*, March 20, 2016. http://www.cnn.com/2016/03/20/opinions/trump-aipac-meeting-miller/index.html. Accessed on April 4, 2018.
14. As quoted in the previous source.
15. Ibid.
16. Ibdid.
17. Ibid.
18. Wooley, James, "The Foreign Policy Views of Donald Trump," *Foreign Policy Research Institute*, August 6, 2016. http://www.fpri.org/article/2016/11/foreign-policy-views-donald-trump/. Accessed on April 4, 2018.
19. Ibid.
20. Ibid.
21. Miller, Aaron David and Sokolsky, Richard, "Donald Trump's Middle East Promises: Can He Keep Them?" *Realclear Politics*, December 5, 2016. http://www.realclearworld.com/

articles/2016/12/05/donald_trumps_middle_east_promises_can_he_keep_them112133.html. Accessed on April 4, 2018.
  22. Ibid.
  23. Ibid.
  24. Begley, Sarah, "Read Donald Trump's Speech to AIPAC," *Time*, March 21, 2016. http://time.com/4267058/donald-trump-aipac-speech-transcript/. Accessed on April 4, 2018.
  25. Ibid.
  26. Details of the Jordanian foreign ministers' response is found in "Trump Favors Moving US Embassy to Jerusalem, Despite Backlash Fears," *NPR*, November 15, 2016. http://www.npr.org/sections/parallels/2016/11/15/502195135/trump-favors-moving-u-s-embassy-to-jerusalem-but-many-worry. Accessed on April 4, 2018.
  27. Ibid.
  28. Baker, Peter, "An Embassy in Jerusalem? Trump Promises, But So Did Predecessors," *New York Times*, November 18, 2016. https://www.nytimes.com/2016/11/19/world/middleeast/jerusalem-us-embassy-trump.html. Accessed on April 4, 2018.
  29. Ibid.
  30. Ibid.
  31. Statement on the American Embassy in Israel. The White House Office of the Press Secretary, Washington, DC, June 1, 2017. https://www.whitehouse.gov/briefings-statements/statement-american-embassy-israel/. Accessed on April 4, 2018.
  32. Ibid.
  33. Baker, "An Embassy in Jerusalem? Trump Promises, But So Did Predecessors."
  34. Statement by President Trump on Jerusalem, Washington, DC. White House, Diplomatic Reception Room, December 6, 2017. https://www.whitehouse.gov/briefings-statements/statement-president-trump-jerusalem/. Accessed on April 4, 2018.
  35. Gearan, Anne and Eglash, Ruth, "Trump's Decision to Open Jerusalem Embassy Complicates Promise to Seek Middle East Peace," *Washington Post*, https://www.washingtonpost.com/politics/trumps-decision-to-open-jerusalem-embassy-complicates-promise-to-seek-peace-in-the-region/2018/05/12/86113024-5557-11e8-9c91-7dab596e8252story.html?utmterm=5530b2db0184. Accessed on April 4, 2018.
  36. "Thousands of Palestinians Protest at Gaza-Israel Border, One Dead," *Reuters*, https://www.reuters.com/article/us-israel-palestinians-protests/palestinians-wounded-at-gaza-israel-border-protests-idUSKBN1HK1E7. Accessed on April 4, 2018.
  37. Ibid.
  38. Ibid.
  39. Shear, Michael D., Hirschfeld, Julie and Haberman, Maggie, "Trump, in Interview, Moderates Views but Defies Conventions," *New York Times*, November 22, 2016. https://www.nytimes.com/2016/11/22/us/politics/donald-trump-visit.html. Accessed on April 4, 2018.
  40. Miller and Sokolsky, "Donald Trump's Middle East Promises: Can He Keep Them?"
  41. Ibid.
  42. Carlstrom, Greg, "Donald Trump Playacts Peace in the Middle East," *Foreign Policy*, May 23, 2017. http://foreignpolicy.com/2017/05/23/donald-trump-playacts-peace-in-the-middle-east/. Accessed on April 4, 2018.
  43. Ibid.
  44. Ibid.
  45. Graham, David, "Trump: Middle East Peace Is 'Not as Difficult as People Have Thought,'" *The Atlantic*, May 3, 2017. https://www.theatlantic.com/international/archive/2017/05/trump-middle-east-peace-is-not-as-difficult-as-people-have-thought/525267/. Accessed on April 4, 2018.
  46. Ibish, Hussein, "Trump's Plan for Middle East Peace Could Actually Work," *Foreign Policy*, May 25, 2017. http://foreignpolicy.com/2017/05/25/trumps-plan-for-middle-east-peace-could-actually-work/. Accessed on April 5, 2018.
  47. Ibid.
  48. Ibid.
  49. Ibid.
  50. Ibid.

51. Ibid.
52. Ibid.
53. Read Full Transcript of Donald Trump Speech in Akron, Ohio. Heavy.com, August 22, 2016. http://heavy.com/news/2016/08/read-full-transcript-donald-trump-rally-speech-akron-ohio-text/. Accessed on April 5, 2018.
54. Johnson, Jenna and DelReal, Jose A., "Trump Vows to 'Utterly Destroy ISIS'—But He Won't Say How," *Washington Post*, September 24, 2016. https://www.washingtonpost.com/politics/trump-vows-to-utterly-destroy-isis-but-he-wont-say-how/2016/09/24/911c6a74-7ffc-11e6-8d0c-fb6c00c90481story.html?utm_term=2d6db1dc165b. Accessed on April 5, 2018.
55. Ibid.
56. Miller and Sokolsky, "Donald Trump's Middle East Promises: Can He Keep Them?"
57. Ibid.
58. Read Full Transcript of Donald Trump Speech in Akron, Ohio.
59. Ibid.
60. Ibid.
61. Pengelly, Martin, "Obama Warns Against Ditching Iran Nuclear Deal on First Anniversary," *The Guardian*, January 16, 2016. https://www.theguardian.com/world/2017/jan/16/iran-nuclear-deal-anniversary-trump-warning. Accessed on April 5, 2018.
62. Ibid.
63. Miller and Sokolsky, "Donald Trump's Middle East Promises: Can He Keep Them?"
64. Beggin, Riley, "Trump Administration Will Review Iran Nuclear Deal Despite Compliance," *ABCnews.go.com*, April 21, 2017. http://abcnews.go.com/Politics/trump-administration-review-iran-nuclear-deal-compliance/story?id=46890406. Accessed on April 5, 2018.
65. Ibid.
66. Wideman, Paul, "Trump Administration Grudgingly Faces Reality on the Iran Nuclear Deal," *Washington Post*, April 19, 2017. https://www.washingtonpost.com/blogs/plum-line/wp/2017/04/19/trump-administration-grudgingly-faces-reality-on-the-iran-nuclear-deal/?utm_term=1c44923e2111. Accessed on April 5, 2018.
67. Ibid.
68. Baker, Peter, "Trump Recertifies Iran Nuclear Deal, But Only Reluctantly," *New York Times*, July 17, 2017. https://www.nytimes.com/2017/07/17/us/politics/trump-iran-nuclear-deal-recertify.html. Accessed on April 7, 2018.
69. Ibid.
70. Ibid.
71. Herb, Jeremy, "Senate Sends Russia Sanctions to Trump's Desk," *CNN*, July 27, 2017. http://www.cnn.com/2017/07/27/politics/russian-sanctions-passes-senate/index.html. Accessed on April 7, 2018.
72. Ibid.
73. Williams, Katie Bo, "Trump Administration Unveils New Iran Sanctions," *The Hill*, July 18, 2017. http://thehill.com/policy/national-security/342505-us-hits-iran-with-new-sanctions-over-ballistic-missiles. Accessed on April 7, 2018.
74. Ibid.
75. Ibid.
76. Miller and Sokolsky, "Donald Trump's Middle East Promises: Can He Keep Them?"
77. Katzman, Kenneth, Kerr, Paul K. and Heitshusen, Valerie, "US Decision to Cease Implementing the Iran Nuclear Agreement," *Congressional Research Service*, May 9, 2018. https://fas.org/sgp/crs/nuke/R44942.pdf. Accessed on April 7, 2018.
78. President Trump Says the Iran Deal is Defective at Its Core. A New One Will Require Real Commitments. White House.gov, May 11, 2018. https://www.whitehouse.gov/articles/president-trump-says-iran-deal-defective-core-new-one-will-require-real-commitments/. Accessed on April 7, 2018.
79. Ibid.
80. Ibid.
81. Ibid.
82. Ibid.
83. Ibid.

84. Ibid.
85. "After the Deal: A New Iran Strategy." The Department of State. May 28, 2018. https://www.state.gov/secretary/remarks/2018/05/28230.htm. Accessed on April 7, 2018.
86. bid.
87. Ibid.
88. Gordon, Michael, "US Lays Out Demands for New Iran Deal," *Wall Street Journal*, May 21, 2018. https://www.wsj.com/articles/mike-pompeo-lays-out-next-steps-on-iran-1526909126. Accessed on April 7, 2018.
89. Ibid.
90. Katzman, Kenneth, Kerr, Paul K., and Heitshusen, Vaalerie, "US Decision to Cease Implementing the Iran Nuclear Agreement," *Congressional Research Service*, May 9, 2018. https://fas.org/sgp/crs/nuke/R44942.pdf. Accessed on April 7, 2018.
91. Statement by President Trump on Syria, Mar-a-Lago, Florida. The White House, Office of the Press Secretary. April 6, 2017. https://www.whitehouse.gov/the-press-office/2017/04/06/statement-president-trump-syria. Accessed on April 7, 2018.
92. Ibid.
93. Mason, Jeff and Solovyov, Dmitry, "US Says it Saw Preparations for Possible Syria Chemical Attack," *Reuters*, June 26, 2017. https://www.reuters.com/article/us-mideast-crisis-syria-usa-idUSKBN19I083. Accessed on April 8, 2018.
94. Sevastopulo, Demetri and Solomon, Erika, "Trump Warns Syria Over Suspected Chemical Attack Plan," *Financial Times*, June 27, 2017. https://www.ft.com/content/b2ca1dac-5af2-11e7-9bc8-8055f264aa8b. Accessed on April 8, 2018.
95. Ibid.
96. Mason and Solovyov, "US Says It Saw Preparations for Possible Syria Chemical Attack."
97. Toosi, Nahal, "Tillerson Urges Russia to Cooperate on Syria Ahead of Trump-Putin Meeting," *Politico*, July 5, 2017. http://www.politico.com/story/2017/07/05/tillerson-russia-syria-240250. Accessed on April 8, 2018.
98. Ibid.
99. Ibid.
100. Langtree, Graham, "Trump to Putin: Syrian President Assad Can't Have Land Liberated From ISIS," *Newsweek*, July 6, 2017. http://www.newsweek.com/trump-tell-putin-assad-cant-seize-syrian-land-liberated-isis-632850. Accessed on April 8, 2018.
101. Ibid.
102. Ibid.
103. Ibid.
104. Ibid.
105. Ibid.
106. Cohen, Zachary and Liptak, Kevin, "Tillerson: Trump, Putin: Reach Syria Ceasefire Agreement," *CNN*, July 8, 2017. http://www.cnn.com/2017/07/07/politics/syria-ceasefire-us-russia-tillerson/index.html. Accessed on April 9, 2018.
107. Ibid.
108. Ibid.
109. Ibid.
110. Ibid.
111. Ibid.
112. Ibid.
113. Lynch, Colum, Cramer, Robbie, De Luce, Dan, and McLeary, Paul, "Secret Details of Trump-Putin Syria Cease-Fire Focus on Iranian Proxies," *Foreign Policy*, July 11, 2017. http://foreignpolicy.com/2017/07/11/exclusive-trump-putin-ceasefire-agreement-focuses-on-iranian-backed-fighters-middle-east/. Accessed on April 9, 2018.
114. Ibid.
115. Ibid.
116. Tarnopolsky," Noga, "In Most Serious Military Clash in Decades, Israel Hits Iranian Targets in Syria," *LA Times*, May 10, 2018. http://www.latimes.com/world/middleeast/la-fg-israel-strikes-iranian-targets-20180510-story.html. Accessed on April 9, 2018.

117. Ibid.
118. Trofimov, Yaroslav, "Can Israel's Clash with Iran Be Contained in Syria?" *Wall Street Journal*, May 3, 2018. https://www.wsj.com/articles/can-israels-clash-with-iran-be-contained-to-syria-1525339800. Accessed on April 9, 2018.
119. Ibid.
120. Katib, Lina, "Only the US Can Prevent More Clashes Between Israel and Iran in Syria," *The Guardian*, https://www.theguardian.com/commentisfree/2018/may/11/us-israel-iran-clashes-syria-war. Accessed on April 9, 2018.
121. Landay, Jonathan and Strobel, Warren, "Exclusive: Trump Counterterrorism Strategy Urges Allies to Do More," *Reuters*, May 5, 2017. http://www.reuters.com/article/us-usa-extremism-idUSKBN1812AN. Accessed on April 9, 2018.
122. Ibid.
123. Ibid.
124. Ibid.
125. Ibid.
126. Glasser, Susan B., "Why the Middle East Hated Obama But Loves Trump," *Politico*, July 31, 2017. http://www.politico.com/magazine/story/2017/07/31/donald-trump-middle-east-barack-obama-215441. Accessed on April 9, 2018.
127. Ibid.
128. Ibid.
129. Nahmen, Alexandra von, "Trump in Saudi Arabia—Counterterrorism and Weapons Deals," *Deutsche Welle* (DW), May 19, 2017. http://www.dw.com/en/trump-in-saudi-arabia-counterterrorism-and-weapons-deals/a-38900168. Accessed on April 10, 2018.
130. [No Author] "What did Donald Trump Achieve in the Middle East?" *The Economist*, May 25, 2017. https://www.economist.com/news/middle-east-and-africa/21722632-not-much-saudi-and-israeli-governments-are-delighted-what-did-donald. Accessed on April 10, 2018.
131. Ibid.
132. Holland, Steve, "Saudi King Agrees in Call with Trump to Support Syria, Yemen Safe Zones: White House," *Reuters,* January 29, 2017. http://www.reuters.com/article/us-usa-trump-saudi-idUSKBN15D14L. Accessed on April 10, 2018.
133. Magid, Pesha, "Trump and Sisi Bond Over Counterterrorism Ambitions," Madamasr.com, April 10, 2017. https://www.madamasr.com/en/2017/04/10/opinion/u/trump-and-sisi-bond-over-counter-terrorism-ambitions/. Accessed on April 10, 2018.
134. "President Trump to Arab Leaders: 'Drive Out' Terrorism," *Fortune* (From *Reuters*), May 21, 2017. http://fortune.com/2017/05/21/president-donald-trump-middle-east-saudi-arabia-speech/. Accessed on April 10, 2018.
135. Ibid.
136. Siciliano, John, "Trump Tours Saudi Counterterrorism Complex," *Washington Examiner*, May 21, 2017. http://www.washingtonexaminer.com/trump-tours-saudi-counter-terrorism-complex/article/2623767. Accessed on April 10, 2018.
137. Ibid.
138. Ibid.
139. Ibid.
140. Joint Statement Between the Kingdom of Saudi Arabia and the United States of America. The White House, Office of the Press Secretary. May 23, 2017. https://www.whitehouse.gov/the-press-office/2017/05/23/joint-statement-between-kingdom-saudi-arabia-and-united-states-america. Accessed on April 10, 2018.
141. Ibid.
142. Ibid.
143. Rogin, Josh, "The Trump Administration's Shortsighted War on Terrorism," *Washington Post*, July 16, 2017. https://www.washingtonpost.com/opinions/global-opinions/the-trump-administrations-shortsighted-war-on-terrorism/2017/07/16/4be64cdc-68c1-11e7-a1d7-9a32c91c6f40story.html?utm_term=36ab526c8f67. Accessed on April 10, 2018.
144. Ibid.
145. Ibid.
146. Ibid.

147. "Saudi Arabia, Egypt Lead Arab States Cutting Qatar Ties, Iran Blames Trump," *CNBC*, June 5, 2017. https://www.cnbc.com/2017/06/04/saudi-arabia-bahrain-and-egypt-cut-diplomatic-ties-with-qatar.html. Accessed on April 10, 2018.

148. Woody, Christopher, "Mattis and Tillerson Are Trying to Soothe a Crisis in the Persian Gulf, But Trump Keeps Picking on a US Ally," *Business Insider*, July 1, 2017. http://www.businessinsider.com/mattis-and-tillerson-try-to-sooth-gulf-crisis-as-trump-fights-qatar-2017-6. Accessed on April 11, 2018.

149. Ibid.

150. Shinkman, Paul, "Qatar-Saudi Crisis Shows Trump Administration's Discord, Dysfunction," *USNews.com*, July 17, 2017. https://www.usnews.com/news/world/articles/2017-07-17/qatar-saudi-crisis-shows-trump-administrations-discord-dysfunction-experts-say. Accessed on April 11, 2018.

151. Woody, "Tillerson Are Trying to Soothe a Crisis in the Persian Gulf, But Trump Keeps Picking on a US Ally."

152. Ibid.

153. Ibid.

154. Ibid.

155. Huggler, Jason, "Donald Trump's Middle East Policy is 'Completely Wrong,' Says Germany," *The Telegraph*, June 7, 2017. http://www.telegraph.co.uk/news/2017/06/07/donald-trumps-middle-east-policy-completely-wrong-says-germany/. Accessed on April 11, 2018.

156. Ibid.

157. Smith, David and Siddiqui, Sabrina, "Gulf Crisis: Trump Escalates Row by Accusing Qatar of Sponsoring Terror," *The Guardian*, June 9, 2017. https://www.theguardian.com/us-news/2017/jun/09/trump-qatar-sponsor-terrorism-middle-east. Accessed on April 11, 2018.

158. Ibid.

159. Finn, Tom, "US, Qatar Sign Agreement on Combating Terrorism Financing," Theglobeandmail.com, July 11, 2017. https://www.theglobeandmail.com/news/world/us-politics/us-qatar-sign-agreement-on-combating-terrorism-financing/article35654060/. Accessed on April 11, 2018.

160. Ibid.

161. Tanter, Raymond and Stafford, Edward, "The Qatar Crisis Is an Opportunity for Trump," *National Interest*, July 6, 2017. http://nationalinterest.org/feature/the-qatar-crisis-opportunity-trump-21446. Accessed on April 11, 2018.

162. Griffin, Jennifer and Tomlinson, Lucas, "Trump Foreign Policy: American Military Increasingly Involved in Yemen Civil War," *Fox News*, June 29, 2017. http://www.foxnews.com/politics/2017/06/29/trump-foreign-policy-american-military-increasingly-involved-in-yemen-civil-war.html. Accessed on April 11, 2018.

163. Shakdam, Catherine, "Yemen at War: The New Shia-Sunni Frontline That Never Was," Foreign Policy Journal.com, April 10, 2015. https://www.foreignpolicyjournal.com/2015/04/10/yemen-at-war-the-new-shia-sunni-frontline-that-never-was/. Accessed on April 11, 2018.

164. Griffin and Tomlinson, "Trump Foreign Policy: American Military Increasingly Involved in Yemen Civil War."

165. Exum, Andrew, "What's Really at Stake for America in Yemen's Conflict," *The Atlantic*, April 14, 2017. https://www.theatlantic.com/international/archive/2017/04/yemen-trump-aqap/522957/. Accessed on April 11, 2018.

166. Ibid.

167. Kheel, Rebecca, "Trump Signals Deeper US Involvement in Yemen," *The Hill*, March 1, 2017. http://thehill.com/policy/defense/326767-trump-signals-deeper-us-involvement-in-yemen. Accessed on April 11, 2018.

168. Ibid.

169. Ibid.

170. Ibid.

171. Ibid.

172. Gibbons-Neff, Thomas, "US Troops are on the Ground in Yemen for Offensive Against Al-Qaeda Militants," *Washington Post*, August 4, 2017. https://www.washingtonpost.com/

news/checkpoint/wp/2017/08/04/u-s-troops-are-on-the-ground-in-yemen-for-offensive-against-al-qaeda-militants/?utmterm=390bbb341d87. Accessed on April 11, 2018.
173. Ibid.
174. Ibid.
175. Kheel, "Trump Signals Deeper US Involvement in Yemen."
176. Joint Regional Strategy-Middle East and North Africa. Department of State, Washington, DC, August 23, 2018. Accessed on September 8, 2018.
177. Ibid.
178. Ibid.
179. Ibid.
180. Ibid.
181. Walt, Stephen M., "This is America's Middle East Strategy on Steroids," *Foreign Policy*, October 15, 2018, https://foreignpolicy.com/2018/10/15/this-is-americas-middle-east-strategy-on-steroids/. Accessed on October 15, 2018.
182. Hadar, Leon, "Trump's Strategy for the Middle East is Working," *National Interest*, May 17, 2018. https://nationalinterest.org/feature/trumps-strategy-the-middle-easst-working-25869. Accessed on April 11, 2018.
183. Ibid.
184. Ibid.
185. Ibid.
186. Phillips, Noah, "How Trump Should Handle the Jamal Khashoggi Killing," Begin-Sadat Center for Strategic Studies, October 2018. https://besacenter.org/perspectives-papers/jamal-khashoggi-trump/. Accessed on October 15, 2018.
187. Ibid.
188. Statement from President Donald J. Trump on Standing with Saudi Arabia, The White House, November 20, 2018. https://www.whitehouse.gov/briefings-statements/statement-president-donald-j-trump-standing-saudi-arabia/. Accessed on November 21, 2018.
189. Ibid.
190. Ibid.
191. Remnick, David, "The Jamal Khashoggi Affair," *The New Yorker*, December 17, 2018. https://www.newyorker.com/books/double-take/sunday-reading-the-khashoggi-affair. Accessed on December 19, 2018.
192. Ibid.
193. Remarks Secretary of State by Michael R. Pompeo, Press Briefing Room, Washington, DC. November 20, 2018. https://www.state.gov/secretary/remarks/2018/11/287487.htm. Accessed on December 19, 2018.
194. Ibid.
195. Ibid.
196. Hirschfield Davis, Julie and Schmitt, Eric, "Senate Votes to End Aid for Yemen Fight Over Khashoggi Killing and Saudi's War Aims, *New York Times*, December 13, 2018. https://www.nytimes.com/2018/12/13/us/politics/yemen-saudi-war-pompeo-mattis.html. Accessed on December 15, 2018.
197. Mckeon, Brian P., "Neither US Senators nor the Trump's Team is Lying About Khashoggi Killing," *Foreign Policy*, December 14, 2018. https://foregnpolicy.com/2018/12/14/neither-trumps-team-nor-u-s-senators-is-lying-about-khashoggos-killing/. Accessed on December 15, 2018.
198. Ibid.
199. Phillips, "How Trump Should Handle the Jamal Khashoggi Killing."

Chapter Seven

The Reckoning

Trump, Russia, and China

Throughout history great powers have had to confront challengers. In the post-World War II period, the United States envisaged a two-generational challenge from the Soviet Union. The United States persevered and survived the communist ideological challenge. Currently, the United States is confronting twin challenges, one from Russia and the other from China. These twin challenges represent a watershed moment in the American quest to sustain their global dominance. The twin threats represent a reckoning, an opportunity to preserve American dominance or a period that could result in the continuing and perhaps precipitous decline of US supremacy.

At this pivotal period in American history, a political and foreign policy novice is it at the helm. How will President Trump manage this critical period? Is it possible that Trump could unleash a period of unprecedented diplomacy to create "new rules" to sustain US global leadership which would manage US-Russian and US-China relations and simultaneously create a period of stability in international security? Or, in the absence of "rules," is the president prepared to deal with instability and incessant challenges from Russia and China, that if mismanaged, could lead to conflict?

TRUMP'S CAMPAIGN STATEMENTS ABOUT RUSSIA

One year prior to the announcement of his candidacy for President of the United States, during an interview with Eric Bolling of the *Fox Business Network* on April 12, 2014, Donald Trump offered his analysis of Russia's invasion of Crimea in the Ukraine. In his assessment, Trump praised Russia's invasion, noting "Well, he's done an amazing job of taking the mantle. And he's taken it away from the President, and you look at what he's doing. . . . When you see the riots in a country because they're hurting the Russians, OK, 'We'll go and take it over.' And he really goes step by step by step, and you have to give him a lot of credit."[1] Trump's statement is revealing in that he demonstrated no command of the facts and worse he praised Putin's illegal invasion and subsequent annexation of an area comprising a major naval port and facilities in a sovereign state.

A few months after formally declaring his candidacy, Trump expressed his view of whether Russia would at some point target Islamic State forces in Syria and not just the anti-Assad rebel forces. Trump stated, "He doesn't want ISIS going into Russia and so he's going to want to bomb ISIS."[2] In a second point, Trump argued, "Vladimir Putin is going to want to really go after ISIS, and if he doesn't it'll be a big shock to everybody."[3]

Nearly a month later, during a Republican presidential debate on November 15, 2015, the candidate described his assessment of Russian aggression. In a response to a query from the moderator, Trump issued this statement: "Well, first of all, it's not only Russia. We have problems with North Korea where they actually have nuclear weapons. You know, nobody talks about it, we talk about Iran, and that's one of the worst deals ever made. . . . So, we have [problems with] more than just Russia."[4] This statement identified a problematic trend, one that extended into his presidency—Trump's refusal to criticize the Russian government's aggression and unlawful behavior in the Ukraine or Syria. His response drew derision among his fellow Republican presidential candidates and sharp criticism from the media.

In a revealing interview with *ABC*'s George Stephanopoulos on *This Week* on July 31, 2016, Trump issued a statement that identified that he lacked knowledge of a major issue in international affairs. The issue in question is Russian intervention in Ukraine. Trump stated, "He's [Putin] not going into Ukraine. . . . You can mark it down. You can take it anywhere you want."[5] Moments after Trump's astonishing statement, Stephanopoulos informed the candidate, "Well, he's already there, isn't he?"[6]

The point of the clarification is that Russia intervened and subsequently annexed Crimea in March of 2014. In a problematic attempt to recover from the error, Trump made this comment: "OK—well, he's there in a certain way. But I'm not there [in the White House]. You have Obama there. And frankly, that whole part of the world is a mess under Obama with all the strength that you're talking about and all of the power of NATO and all of this. In the meantime, he's going away. He takes Crimea."[7] Subsequent tweets by the candidate could not undo the damage that ensued in the wake of the interview.

After winning the election and becoming the leader of the United States, irrespective of the problematic statements concerning the admiration of Putin, the prevailing view of Dmitry Gorenburg and Michael Kofman, research scientists at CNA, a non-profit research organization, is that President Trump is afforded a monumental opportunity. That said, the assessment of Gorenburg and Kofman is replete with caveats: "Donald Trump's victory has the potential to fundamentally reshape US-Russian relations, but whether such a realignment will actually take place will depend on how Trump" learns from "the past failures of several US attempts to engage Russia. It remains to be seen whether he will be willing to follow the advice of professionals, or if he will strike off on his own."[8] The scientists then point to several weaknesses of the president. They assert "Trump's first problem will be that other than a small number of close advisers who share his instincts to engage Putin, most of the policy establishment is likely to hold hardened views of Putin's Russia, ranging from distrustful to confrontational."[9] Another problem that Trump must deal with is a foreign policy bureaucracy will council against any attempts to quickly normalize relations with Russia.[10]

Despite the opportunity, President Trump indicated that he still believed that a productive relationship with Russia is still a goal of his administration. In a speech on April 27, 2017 in Washington, DC, President Trump reaffirmed that position: "I believe an easing of tensions, and improved relations with Russia—from a position of strength only—is possible, absolutely possible. Some say the Russians won't be reasonable. I intend to find out."[11]

Members of the NATO alliance remained unnerved by President Trump's on-going fascination with establishing a positive relationship with Russia. In fact, the prevailing position among alliance partners is that a hardline approach is what is required to combat Russian aggression and future adventurism in Europe and outside the continent. There are however other significant concerns that have been expressed within the alliance about President Trump's intentions.

Many in Western Europe expressed concern that President Trump endangers not just the alliance but post-World War II frameworks. Trump continues to "express doubts about NATO and showed allegiance to Brexit and similar anti-European movements."[12] Put succinctly, several alliance partners questioned if the president "can be counted on."[13]

There is another issue that greatly concerns the alliance: Trump's inability to provide a signature statement whereby he is critical of Russian aims and their ongoing negative behavior around the world. General Sir Richard Shirreff, the former deputy supreme allied commander of NATO addressed another potential dilemma: "The great fear is the neutering of NATO and the decoupling of America from European security. If that happens, it gives Putin all kinds of opportunities. . . . You're beginning to see the collapse of institutions built to insure our security."[14]

There are those that assert that during the Trump presidency there is serious concern the United States may lose the next Cold War. Strobe Talbott, and the former adviser of President Bill Clinton, represented an example of an established foreign policy official that expressed anxiety about whether President Trump understood the current geopolitical environment.[15] Talbott also asserted the president's embrace of Putin could ensure an American defeat in a subsequent Washington-Moscow ideological clash. As articulated by Talbott, "There is a very real danger not only that we are going to lose a second Cold War—or have a redo and lose—but that the loss will be largely because of a perverse pal-ship, the almost unfathomable respect that Trump has for Putin."[16] On the consequences of losing Talbott argues, "The not quite apocalyptic answer is that it is going to take years and years and years to get back to where we the United States and we the champions of the liberal world order—were as recently as five years ago."[17]

THE REALITY OF PRESIDENT TRUMP'S RUSSIA POLICY

President Trump's Russia policy in many ways is inconsistent with the candidates' campaign rhetoric. While president Trump continued to speak about a desire for strong US-Russian relations, senior Trump officials have relied upon stringent rhetoric in discussing the threat posed by Russia. Secretary of Defense Mattis asserted, "We are not in a position right now to collaborate on the military level, but our political leaders will engage and try to find common ground."[18] Mattis made this additional statement: "Russia's aggressive actions have violated international law and are destabilizing."[19] Mattis did note that cooperation with Russia is conditional, stating, "We remain open to opportunities to restore a cooperative relationship with Moscow, while being realistic in our expectations and ensuring our diplomats negotiate from a position of strength."[20]

Former Secretary of State Tillerson also expressed caution about a cooperative relationship with Russia. During the confirmation hearing before the Senate Foreign Relations Committee, Tillerson provided several statements that demonstrated he is prepared to engage in strident anti-Russian verbiage. Said Tillerson, "We must also be clear-eyed about our relationship with Russia."[21] In a more detailed analysis of the threat, Tillerson provided this statement: "Russia today poses a danger, but it is not unpredictable in advancing its own interests. It has invaded Ukraine, including the taking of Crimea, and supported Syrian forces that brutally violate the laws of war. Our NATO allies are right to be alarmed at a resurgent Russia."[22]

The external alliance pressure, domestic-political pressure associated with the alleged Trump campaign collusion with Russian efforts to undermine US elections, and senior officials that are pushing a hardline Russia policy collectively appeared to have had an effect: President Trump reversed his earlier views of Russia. In a conspicuous example, during a White House news conference with NATO Secretary-General Jens Stoltenberg, President Trump characterized the state of US-Russia relations this way: "Right now, we're not getting along with Russia at all. We may be at an all-time low in terms of relationship with Russia."[23] The collective view of President Trump, Secretary Mattis, and Secretary Tillerson and others in the administration is the prevailing administration perspective that Russia cannot be trusted, and they are currently not a partner the United States can count on to defeat the Islamic State.

How can President Trump "reshape US-Russian relations"[24] and avoid increasing tensions in an already declining relationship? The answer is that it will require deft diplomacy. On the importance of diplomacy, Hans Binnendijk, an adjunct political scientist at the RAND Corporation, and William Courtney, the Executive Director of the RAND Business Leaders Forum, offer this analysis: "Trump's interest in improving relations with Russia is fraught with risk unless his diplomacy is up to snuff. But if executed properly, Trump's diplomacy could help reverse a destabilizing downward spiral in relations and create a vision of what normal relations might entail. Only Russia's withdrawal from eastern Ukraine would allow progress toward normalized relations."[25]

What are the issues that are responsible for the current state of affairs between the United States and Russia? The issues that have caused tension in the relationship include Russian intervention in Ukraine and the annexation of Crimea, on-going Russian efforts to undermine NATO, Russian support for Syria, and Russian meddling in the 2016 presidential election and the 2018 midterm elections and the elections in NATO countries.

Many commentators assert that when Trump meets with Putin, the American president must address the Russian intervention of Ukraine. In these discussions, "Trump should begin by underlining the West's opposition to Russia's aggression in Ukraine and its support of broad economic sanctions until Russian forces and proxies are withdrawn from the war-torn Donbas region in the country's east. The European-led Minsk peace process is stalled. Trump should add US heft to the negotiation and boost military support for Ukraine, while reaffirming that Donbas-related sanctions will be lifted if Russia fulfills Minsk obligations."[26] It is clear from the analysis, the diplomacy over the Ukraine dispute will remain the most contentious.

The administration continues to strengthen military cooperation with Poland, Croatia, and other NATO states near Russia.[27] The presence of US military personnel and the increase in joint military exercises with those NATO countries have only increased tensions between Moscow and Washington. (It its certain that Putin is using the old "encirclement argument" to rally domestic support.) Equally important, any future Russian efforts to undermine NATO will decrease the likelihood of cooperation between Trump and Putin.

One of the best illustrations of an issue that is likely to widen the gulf between Moscow and Washington is the future of Syria and by extension the regime of President Bashar al-Assad. The Russian government continues to protect their ally, and in doing so they preserve their influence and military assets (bases and port access) in the country. The numerous ceasefires, conferences, and efforts to vanquish anti-government rebels are aimed at the preservation of the Assad government.

On the future of Assad, in the opening months the Trump administration did not present a coherent policy. That is, previously, several members of the administration mentioned in a press report that "removing Assad was not a top priority."[28] In the end, in the words of Nikki Haley, US ambassador to the United Nations, is more representative of administration policy: "We don't see a peaceful future with Assad in there."[29]

With the international rollover the future status of Assad behind them, a military action by the administration in response to the Syrian government's use of chemical weapons further eroded US-Russian relations. The US military strike occurred prior to a scheduled meeting between Tillerson and his counterpart Russian Foreign Minister Sergey Lavrov. The meeting between the chief diplomats in Washington and Moscow was described as "frank" and "chilly."

Reports of the details of the meeting only clarified the tensions. The following is a detailed report of the meeting:

> Tillerson's trip to Moscow . . . was further evidence of how low Russian-American relations have sunk since Mr. Trump, reversing earlier opposition to intervening in Syria's civil war, launched 59 cruise missiles against a Syrian air base after President Bashar al-Assad used chemical weapons against civilians. The Russians have strongly supported Mr. Assad despite his brutality. Tillerson wondering for most of the day whether an encounter with Mr. Putin would take place. Once they did meet—it was the first between Mr. Putin and a top Trump administration official—the results were not encouraging. Mr. Putin said bilateral trust has "degraded," while Mr. Tillerson said relations were "at a low point." Back in New York, Russia vetoed a United Nations Security Council resolution condemning Syria's chemical attack, the eighth time it has protected Mr. Assad from diplomatic action.[30]

The Trump administration's criticism of Putin's government further exacerbated tensions: "Since the airstrikes. . . . The White House accused Russia of a cover-up. On Wednesday, Mr. Trump weighed in, saying Russia most likely knew of Mr. Assad's plan to gas his own people and promising that Mr. Putin will come under increasing pressure to abandon Mr. Assad."[31]

Given the state of relations between the United States and Russia, it is appropriate to ask what must be done to improve relations? For starters, a formal diplomatic plan by the Trump administration is required to engage

Putin's Russia. That plan will require "new rules" to govern US-Russian relations. It is overlooked that during the Cold War there were formal rules to govern US-Soviet relations. Once that superpower ideological schism dissipated, during the unipolar euphoria the United States enjoyed unprecedented political, economic, and military power from 1991 and into the new millennium. Covering three US presidencies, Bill Clinton, George W. Bush, and Barack Obama, US power eroded. During three successive presidencies, Clinton, Bush, and Obama each endeavored to "reset" US-Russian relations. Each of the reset efforts resulted in failure.[32] In addition, one conspicuous issue is present in the three previous administrations: no rules existed and no American president (e.g., no rules existed prior to the Russian intervention in Georgia, the Ukraine, or Syria) informed the Russian government about the price of adventurism. Such statements occurred in the wake of Russian interventions; by then it was too late.

The pursuit of a productive relationship with Russia through diplomacy will continue to fail until the United States recognizes rules are required (and the willingness to enforce them) to rebalance US-Russia relations. President Trump is offered a grand opportunity to reap the benefits of a relationship constructed "in a rules-based environment." The businessman universally recognized for *The Art of Deal* is uniquely positioned to cash-in. Equally important, a rules-based relationship will benefit the Russians as well.

The objective in the implementation of new rules is to produce what Thomas Graham of the Kissinger Associates referred to as "A New Equilibrium In US-Russian Relations."[33] That is the objective, getting there will be a long hard slog. How to get there? First and foremost, the administration will have to overcome the hyper partisan environment over the congressional investigations surrounding alleged Trump campaign collision with Russia (several congressional hearings have thus far concluded no collusion existed between the Trump campaign and Russia) and the politics that are well underway in the wake of the release of Special Counsel Robert Mueller's Report.

Jack Matlock, a former US ambassador to the Soviet Union from 1987 to 1991, offered this assessment on the partisanship and the delay in "restarting" US-Russian diplomacy. According to ambassador Matlock,

> Our press seems to be in a feeding frenzy regarding contacts that President Trump's supporters had with Russian Ambassador Sergei Kislyak and with other Russian diplomats. The assumption seems to be that there was something sinister about these contacts, just because they were with Russian diplomats. As one who spent a 35-year diplomatic career working to open up the Soviet Union and to make communication between our diplomats and ordinary citizens a normal practice, I find the attitude of much of our political establishment and of some of our once respected media outlets quite incomprehensible. What in the world is wrong with consulting a foreign embassy about ways to

improve relations? Anyone who aspires to advise an American president should do just that.[34]

Only when the Trump administration navigates the domestic political landmines can the diplomatic process commence. In the interim, President Trump and his senior foreign policy advisors must develop a coherent Russia policy. The significance of this point is buttressed by the following argument made by Paul J. Saunders: "President Trump will face no more urgent foreign-policy task than developing a Russia policy. . . . The President is correct in his intuition that the United States needs a new approach to Russia, breaking with the bipartisan consensus that has guided policy since the Cold War."[35]

The framework of the Trump administration's Russia policy is linked to several critical documents. Those documents include the National Security Strategy of the United States (NSS) which was released in December 2017 and the National Defense Strategy (NDS) which was released in early 2018.

The NSS documents acknowledges the United States is engaged in an era of great power competition from states that are determined to alter the pyramid of power arrangements that existed since the creation of the post-World War II liberal international order. The administration acknowledges that Russia and China are hell-bent on challenging American power, interests, and global leadership. In the case of Russia, the federation seeks to challenge the United States in the militarily sphere, create discord within NATO, extend their power political and military influence in the Middle East, assist rogue regimes whether in the case of Iran, North Korea, or Syria to sustain regional influence, and Moscow continues to utilize cyberspace to undermine Western elections.

To meet these challenges, the administration asserts it will rely heavily on sanctions, diplomacy, and when required, military power in support of diplomatic actions in the words of A. Wess Mitchell, President Trump's Assistant Secretary of State, in the Bureau of European and Eurasian Affairs, to "degrade Putin's ability to conduct aggression by imposing costs on the Russia state."[36] Mitchell also stated the administration's approach, in order to be effective, recognizes the Russian threat is "not just external or military" but it includes "influence operations"[37] that are directed from the highest levels of the Russian Federation which includes the direct participation of Putin. The administration, according to Mitchell, is prepared to confront the Russian challenge "by systematically strengthening the military, economic and political [aspects] of American power."[38]

The NDS illustrated the Trump administration is prepared to engage and to defeat Russia in strategic military competition whether conventional or nuclear. In the competition in these areas, the Defense Department is required to increase and sustain "investment of the magnitude of threats they pose to US security and prosperity."[39] The Trump administration is determined "to reverse years of cuts to the defense budgets."[40] With respect to the NATO alliance, the administration is prepared to increase US military preparedness in defense of its partners and is asking members to increase their share to ensure the longevity and survivability of the partnership.

THE NEED FOR RULES TO STABILIZE US-RUSSIA RELATIONS

Long before the rules can be established, a critical phase of diplomacy is required: there must be an exchange between both participants to acknowledge and accept the current "power status" of the other. The United States, despite a period of relative decline, remains the unquestioned superpower in the international system and the country with considerably more global interests than any other state and the military machine to protect American far-flung interests.

The Russia government is seeking to reestablish a power capability that existed during the zenith of their dominance during the old Soviet Union. Critics charge, and I would agree, that such a power capability does not exist in present day Russia and is unlikely to be achieved under Putin. That said, Putin is working to achieve capabilities that will expand Russia's interests into areas of the world beyond their traditional post-Cold War orbit. Additionally, Putin is using information warfare to undermine the unity of NATO, interfere in US and allied partner elections, and the Russian government is utilizing cyberspace to undermine the sovereignty of states near the Russia border.

The Trump administration is reasserting US power, much of which remained dormant during the Obama years, while simultaneously ending Russian adventurism in Europe and in the Middle East. The reality that the relationship is at the lowest point at any period during the post-Cold War and post-9/11 worlds is alarming. In the final analysis, President Trump and President Putin must find a way to create a more cooperative relationship or both sides risk the path to war. William Danvers of the Center for American Progress offered this analysis:

> The detritus of the US-Soviet Union relationship remains a part of the US-Russian relationship. During the Cold War, US policy went from containment to détente to confrontation. Today, the vicissitudes of Russian President Vladimir Putin's engagement with the United States range from the productive—the Iran nuclear deal is one example—to confrontation—Ukraine is a good example—to doing a bit of both—Syria is an example of this. Putin wants Russia to not only have a seat at the table where decisions are made about global international issues but also wants the seat once held by the former Soviet Union. In other words, Putin wants a return to the great power politics of the Cold War and a free hand in the territory that was part of the Soviet Union. In this regard,

Putin needs the United States as an adversary, though not necessarily as an enemy. The approach of the Trump administration toward Russia should be based on American interests, not on what will appease the Russians. Moreover, engagement with Russia will not be an option . . . it is a necessity.[41]

Until both sides reach an understanding on what constitutes the areas of interests and respects those interests, then one should anticipate, particularly in the case of Putin, efforts to meddle or attempt to undermine those interests. Put another way, Putin will test Trump, time and time again. However, the cruise missile strike in the wake of the Syrian governments chemical weapons attack on their civilians and the use of the Massive Ordinance Air Blast (MOAB) in Afghanistan have informed the Russian government that Trump is not Obama. Thus, Putin is aware that Trump is reasserting American leadership and unafraid to meet any challenge. Still, will both leaders respect the other?

Confronting these dynamics is critical for the next stage: a formal series of Summits whereby the leaders of the United States and Russia along with their delegations meet on multiple occasions. Unlike the initial Trump-Putin Summit, which is discussed later, a "real summit(s)" is likely not to occur until perhaps the fourth year of the Trump presidency. The results of these summits could set in motion a process of change in the relationship and establish norms of behavior for both Moscow and Washington.[42]

The next phase of diplomacy concerns the issues around which the rules will be established. At issue, what are the issues that have caused instability in the US-Russia relationship? Second, if rules or a semblance thereof are established will that set the stage for cooperation?

Danvers, argued, there are three areas that require immediate attention: Syria; the Ukraine; and "the Russian disinformation campaign and cyberattacks. If each of these issues are dealt with firmly, they could steer US-Russian relations in a productive direction."[43] The issues outlined by Danvers represent a small sample of the issues that await Trump-led diplomacy to establish a series of rules to potentially establish a cooperative relationship with the government of Russia. This section closes with a subsequent subset of issues around which rules should be established in the US-Russia relationship.

The initial set of rules are naturally based on several current and recurring issues that intersect US-Russian relations. These issues include (1) the ongoing civil war in Syria; (2) confronting Russian intervention in Ukraine; and (3) the Russian disinformation campaign and information warfare, specifically those directed towards influencing the 2016 presidential election, the 2018 midterm elections, and the 2020 presidential election.

At issue, why would rules regarding the above issues assist in establishing productive relations between the US and Russia? On the issue of the Syrian civil war, for example, assuming a conference whereby the US and Russia are participants, how will both states work to resolve the dispute, work to move beyond the Assad government, and work to establish a framework of understanding of US and Russian interests in Syria and how they should be managed in a post-Assad Syria?

Ukraine is an issue of great disagreement and a subject that caused consternation from NATO because of the direct and ongoing indirect Russian intervention in that country. Putin asserts that Ukraine is still within the Russian orbit and thus an area of great interest to Moscow for legitimate political and military reasons. The United States and their NATO partners assert that Russia cannot violate a sovereign state and subsequently annex territory within that state.

There is another issue of great significance: fear. There is a genuine concern within NATO and certainly inside the US government that Russia may use the intervention in Ukraine as a pretext for subsequent intervention in Poland or perhaps in the Baltic states. Clear rules must be established to preclude Russia from subsequent interventions. The problem with such rules is that new demarcations in select areas of Europe will need to be erected. Another way to make the case for rules is this: "The challenge is to develop a set of [rules] . . . that reassure allies and address Russia's security concerns."[44]

The Russian government's decision to seize three Ukrainian vessels (two armored boats and a tug boat) in route to the Kerch Straight in November of 2018 provided yet another reason why Trump and Putin should intensify direct discussion on what should be done to end Russian intervention in Ukraine and the need to rollback Moscow's annexation of Crimea. The incident increased tensions between Russia and Ukraine.

With respect to talks between Trump and Putin, because of Russia's blatant disregard for international law, the American president correctly announced the cancellation of the planned meeting with the Russian leader at the G-20 gathering in Argentina. In further evidence of discord between Washington and Moscow, Ambassador Haley, in a statement delivered at an emergency session of the United Nations Security Council, bluntly stated the Russian action represented an "outrageous violation of sovereign Ukrainian territory."[45] NATO followed by denouncing the Russian action asserting they "fully support Ukraine's sovereignty and its territorial integrity, including its navigational rights in its territorial waters."[46]

One of the important outcomes of the incident is that NATO and the Trump administration displayed unity. During the July 2018 NATO meeting, Trump and leaders of the alliance traded insults leaving many to question the state and direction of the alliance. Russia's salient violation of international law in the seizure of Ukrainian vessels in their sovereign waters temporarily quieted those concerns.

Establishing rules on the matter of Russian disinformation campaign and interference in Democratic Elections and the curtailment of cyberattacks will be most interesting. The US intelligence community asserts there is overwhelming evidence the Russian government conducted their campaigns and cyberattacks inside the homeland and among NATO and other states in Europe. President Obama claims to have informed Putin "to cut it out, there [are] . . . going to be serious consequences if he did not."[47] However, given Putin's perception that Obama is a weak leader, the admonition was quickly dismissed. A strong leader must be willing to make such a statement directly to Putin and then alert him there will be consequences. Frank verbiage may be used to set up the necessity for a rule that alerts Moscow that meddling in the affairs of a Democratic state constitutes a violation of US sovereignty. At issue, will Trump, and if necessary, the hawkish Mattis, be willing to ensure the message is heard loud and clear?

What are the other issues of concern around which rules may be established to assist in the mending or creating cooperative relations between the United States and Russia? Rules are more likely to be established in the following areas: (1) opening new lines of communication between the United States and Russia; (2) confronting international terrorism (e.g., dealing with ISIS and Al Qaeda in Syria); (3) what Graham refers to as "maintaining strategic stability [and] preventing the proliferation of weapons of mass destruction,"[48] which is a reference to North Korea and Iran; (4) rules surrounding the renewal of the role of Great Power Summits; and (5) the improvement of military to military cooperation. Taken collectively, the establishment of rules in the above areas enhances the opportunities for fruitful US-Russian relations in the future. At issue, is President Trump up to the task?

Trump's national security advisor, John Bolton, met with Putin. During the meeting which took place on June 27, 2018, the participants clarified their country's position on a range of issues, whether in the form of nuclear arms control, Syria, and potential areas of cooperation. Most importantly, Washington and Moscow agreed to a summit.[49]

The Trump-Putin summit in Helsinki, Finland produced no major breakthroughs. Trump, who engaged the Russian leader in a private session, one that included only translators, argued "Our relationship has never been worse than it is now." Still, the president stated of his private session with Putin, "We had direct, open, deeply productive dialogue. It went very well."[50]

In a subsequent session that included the senior foreign policy representatives of both countries, the leaders spent considerable time on Crimea, nuclear issues, the need to reconstruct Syria and the future of Assad, and trade between Washington and Moscow, and energy issues, particularly the Russian gas pipeline that would run through the Baltic Sea and into Germany.

The complete details and outcomes associated with these issues remain shrouded in secrecy.

The media's coverage (and that of the president's critics) of the summit centered on Trump's decision to accept Putin's denial that Russia engaged in the meddling in the 2016 presidential election, despite the voluminous evidence presented by the American intelligence community. Those in opposition to Trump unleashed strongly worded condemnation of the president's performance. In a well-publicized example, former CIA director John Brennan, stated the president's performance was "nothing short of treasonous."[51]

The summit produced no major agreements. However, the summit produced confidence building measures that both parties believed could set the stage for a more productive relationship in the future. The Trump administration made it clear that no concrete developments in US-Russian relations can occur unless "Russia addresses and resolves the problem they created by invading Ukraine."[52]

In the end, the summit produced no "new set of rules" to govern relations between long-time revivals. In the wake of the Russian seizure of the Ukrainian ships and ongoing Russian contravention of the Intermediate Range Nuclear Force (INF) Treaty, and President Trump's decision to withdraw from the agreement on February 1, 2019,[53] the relationship continued to spiral downward. The need for rules to govern the relationship may be required to prevent the relationship from shifting towards future conflict.

TRUMP'S STATEMENTS ABOUT CHINA

President Xi Jinping of China quickly understood that Donald Trump did not view his country in the same way he did Russia. That is, candidate Trump repeatedly spoke of his desire for a positive relationship with Vladimir Putin. President Xi did not receive words of praise from Trump. Additionally, the American presidential candidate did not issue direct statements about the likelihood of improved Sino-American relations.

Rather during Republican debates, foreign policy speeches, and campaign rallies and throughout the general election, Trump incessantly used harsh and often bellicose language that was directed at China. To underscore Trump's harsh criticism of the Chinese government, it is important to review some of the candidates' statements.

An excerpt from his book, *Crippled America: How to Make America Great Again*, Trump indicated that confronting China would be a focus of his presidential campaign. In the book Trump perceived China "as our enemy."[54] Trump then argued China "destroyed entire industries by utilizing low-wage workers, cost us tens of thousands of jobs, spied on our businesses, stolen our technology, and have manipulated and devalued their currency, which makes importing our goods more expensive—and sometimes, impossible."[55]

During the announcement of his candidacy for president on June 15, 2015, Trump used the opportunity to again address his view of US-China trade relations. This time the president softened the rhetoric:

> I love China. The biggest bank in the world is from China. You know where their United States headquarters is located? In this building, in Trump Tower. I love China. People say, Oh, you don't like China? No, I love them. But their leaders are much smarter than our leaders, and we can't sustain [ourselves]. . . with that. There's too much—it's like—it's like take the New England Patriots and Tom Brady and have them play your high school football team. That's the difference between China's leaders and our leaders.[56]

This statement indicated a duality. President Trump appears to respect China's rise. At the same time, Trump expresses his disdain for how the government of China achieved that status. The candidate additionally expresses concern that Beijing's ascent occurred through overt problematic policies that undermined American exports that produced China's expansive trade surplus.

On the campaign trail, bashing China quickly developed into a campaign theme. Speaking at a campaign rally in Bluffton, South Carolina on July 15, 2015, Trump chastised the government of China over the trade imbalance and unfair trade practices. Additionally, Trump argued that he is the candidate that possessed the skills to confront China. On this point, during the rally Trump made the following statement, "I win against China. You can win against China if you're smart. But our people don't have a clue. We give state dinners to the heads of China. I said why are you doing state dinners for them? They're ripping us left and right. Just take them to *McDonald's* and go back to the negotiating table."[57]

In an interview on Good Morning America on November 3, 2015, Trump addressed why labeling China as an enemy is appropriate: "Because it's an economic enemy, because they have taken advantage of us like nobody in history. . . . They've taken our jobs."[58]

A series of statements on the campaign trail further indicated Trump's desire to reverse the state of the US-China relationship that he inherited from President Obama. During a campaign rally in Staten Island, New York on April 17, 2016, the candidate mused "China's upset because of the way Donald Trump is talking about trade with China. They're ripping us off, folks, it's time. I'm so happy they're upset."[59] Well into a campaign rally in Fort Wayne, Indiana on May 2, 2016, the candidate made this highly provocative statement: "We can't continue to allow China to rape our country and that's what they're doing. It's the greatest theft in the history of the world."[60]

Trump addressed an issue in US-China trade relations that most Americans are unfamiliar with or did not view as a pivotal campaign issue. During a gathering in Manchester, New Hampshire on June 20, 2016, Trump used the issue as a part of an ongoing populist message: "The single biggest weapon used against us and to destroy our companies is devaluation of currencies, and the greatest ever at that is China."[61]

During the transition period, President-Elect Trump sent US-China relations spiraling out of control after the contents of a phone conversation with the President of Taiwan Tsai Ing-wen were leaked to the press. In the wake of the phone conversation initiated by the leader of Taiwan, Trump issued this statement on Twitter—"The President of Taiwan CALLED ME today to wish me congratulations on winning the Presidency"—the government of China reacted angrily to the disclosure. In response, China's Foreign Minister Wang Yi offered this statement: "China firmly opposes any official interaction or military contact between [the] US and Taiwan."[62]

The significance of the incident is the US government maintained a "One-China policy" since 1979. From the perspective of the government of China, the exchange between Trump and the President of Taiwan violated the long-standing policy and immediately US-China relations spiraled downward. Trump's subsequent statement that he may no longer adhere to the policy, only increased the rift between Washington and Beijing. However, once in office, in the wake of a phone conversation between President Trump and President Xi, the White House agreed the United States would adhere to the One-China policy.[63] The impasse thereafter dissipated.

Unknown to most, Trump's campaign statements did have an impact on the government of China. In fact, the leadership in China did not know how to react to Trump. With Hillary Clinton, there is an established relationship and an understanding of her tendencies. With Trump, Chinese leaders did not know how to handle Trump's bluntness and his unpredictability. It is for this reason the Chinese government examined the candidate closely, assessing the candidates' tendencies, but they never developed a formal plan to deal with Trump.

Journalist Sara Hsu, a writer for *Forbes* covering China's economy and business sector, offered a detailed analysis of the Chinese government's clumsy and uncertain reaction to the Trump candidacy. According to Hsu, "Despite US President-elect Donald Trump's popularity among some ordinary Chinese, Chinese policy makers and media are wary of his proposed policies on trade and climate change."[64] Hsu noted ". . . China's leadership has reservations about Trump's presidency. Chinese President Xi Jinping himself appears to hold a cautious view of Trump. In a phone call between the two on November 14, the Chinese President reportedly said, "cooperation is the only correct choice for China and the US."[65] She then noted that "Xi felt he had to make this comment, in light of Trump's many criticisms of

China."[66] Hsu argued the statement is "as close as" Xi would commit to Trump's opinion of China and his anti-globalization message.[67] Still she noted, "China's wariness of the US President-elect is justified." However, she expressed the desire that officials in the government of China, along with the "media warnings" might "temper some of Trump's policies; if not, Chinese warnings, now reserved, will become louder."[68]

Reuters provided additional evidence of Trump's victory and its impact on US-China relations: "Donald Trump's upset election victory cracks open pressing strategic and economic questions in US-China ties, and has likely surprised and worried Chinese leaders, who prize stability in relations between the two powers. . . . That unpredictability is not an ideal election outcome for China's stability-obsessed Communist Party."[69]

Privately, the government of China continued to assess the incoming American president. The president's perception of the government of China, his views on Sino-American trade relations, and Trump's unpredictability set the stage for rocky a relationship and rough waters which the Xi-led government would find difficult to manage.

PRESIDENT TRUMP AND US-CHINA RELATIONS

Andreas Bøje Forsby, a scholar with Danish Institute for International Studies, offered this description of the state of US-China relations: "[They] seem to be in a league of their own on the international stage, but rather than forming an axis of stability, Beijing and Washington have in recent years often found themselves at loggerheads over bilateral trade, the South China Sea or human rights issues."[70]

One of the critical issues before the Trump administration is the need to develop a China policy. In the initial year, the administration lacked a coherent approach to dealing with China's challenge. Critics quickly addressed the dilemmas of dealing with China in the absence of a sound policy. Mira Rapp-Hooper, a fellow at the Center for a New American Security, offered this comment about what would constitute a sound approach. She noted "a thoughtful US approach to China would be rooted in a broader Asia strategy."[71] That approach had to include "the relative shifts in military, diplomatic, and economic power."[72] In the opening months of the administration, Rapp-Hooper, asserted President Trump "adopted a transactional approach to China that is both narrow in its scope and . . . is a perilous way to fashion US foreign policy in Asia."[73]

In a subsequent example, Rush Doshi, in an article that appeared in the *National Interest* argued, "President Trump's [lacks a] . . . policy for dealing with China. So far, that policy is both inchoate and inscrutable. His administration appears to be careening unexpectedly between two possible China policies: one that is dangerously escalatory and another that is curiously naïve."[74]

From China's perspective, the initial Trump-Xi meeting provided a grand opportunity to size-up the new American president. Put another way, the meeting with Trump confirmed and alarmed China's fears. Fred Fleitz, the senior vice president for the Center for Security Policy, provided this assessment of the meeting: "China is coming here to try to figure Trump out. He's not like a president they've ever seen before. He's not a president they can walk all over like Obama."[75]

The meeting between President Trump and President Xi at the Mar-a-Lago Club in Florida represented the government of China's opportunity to indeed evaluate the American leader. The problem for China is that while the meeting may have been replete with traditional protocol, the president moved quickly to insert issues from the campaign. For example, the president "brought up the chronic trade imbalance between China and the United States."[76] Similarly, "Tillerson said Mr. Trump . . . told the Chinese leader that there needed to be concrete steps to level the playing field for American workers."[77]

President Trump's decision to launch a cruise missile strike against a Syrian air base deemed by the administration as the location for the introduction of chemical weapons against innocent civilians overshadowed the meeting between the leaders of the United States and China. The *New York Times* characterized the military strike this way: "[The] first meeting . . . ended up being less about great-power collaboration than a chance for the Chinese leader to witness a raw display of American military might. [Then] Mr. Trump ordered Tomahawk cruise missiles to be fired on a Syrian airfield, [and] he pressed Mr. Xi to use China's leverage to curb another rogue government, North Korea."[78]

In the aftermath of the meeting, the prevailing view is the Chinese leader expressed anger about the American display of force. The position of China "on Syria is much closer to Russia's than to the US."[79] It is also understood the strike had a second target—North Korea. The subliminal message and the strike itself certainly "ruffled the feathers" of the leader of China. The following quote clarified the above points: "And the Chinese government will guess that the timing of the American missile strike was a blunt message that without more robust Chinese help on dismantling Kim Jong-Un's nuclear program, the next target for preemptive American military action might be North Korea."[80] The abruptness of the missile strike from the perspective of Beijing violated Chinese diplomatic protocol, which argues "sudden moves disrupting set piece occasions are avoided wherever possible, and in private, President Xi is likely to be angry that President Trump chose to strike on the very night of his visit."[81]

On the positive front, President Trump's decision to end the rhetoric that "he won't brand China a currency manipulator, retreating from a core campaign promise, though he argued that a strong dollar is hampering the ability of American firms to compete,"[82] represented, in the eyes of many observers a short-term victory for China. The president's decision not to honor the campaign pledge meant the US president signaled to the leadership of China that he is prepared to pursue cooperative relations.

The meeting between President Trump and President Xi identified that China wanted to work to build trust and cooperation with the United States. In the weeks after the gathering in Florida, those efforts culminated in a trade agreement with the United States on May 12, 2017. The deal is viewed as an opportunity to reset trade relations between the two countries. US Secretary of Commerce Wilbur Ross stated the agreement represented a win for the president. Ross also acknowledged, "This will help us to bring down the deficit for sure. You watch and you'll see."[83] In addition, the Trump administration asserted that long-term American businesses and companies "benefit from the agreement, particularly those in the Beef and Poultry Producers, Agro-Bio Tech companies, Credit Card providers, Credit Ratings agencies and financial institutions."[84]

There are however those that dispute the significance of the agreement. In one notable example, James Zimmerman, a Beijing-based lawyer and former chairman of the American Chamber of Commerce in the Chinese capital, offered this assessment of the agreement: "Meaningful, yes. All progress on market access is well-received by the business community. However, many of these issues have been part of ongoing bilateral discussions for years and many more barriers need to be resolved."[85] In a subsequent perspective, Joerg Wuttke, the President of the European Chamber of Commerce in China, noted, "This is a very selected list. We have to see if the Chinese live up to their promises. [The American Chamber of Commerce] and we had all hoped for a broad opening of the market, not a piecemeal opening due to political pressure."[86]

The meeting between the leaders of the United States and China did not resolve a rudimentary issue: "Prior to and in the wake of the meeting, it exposed the need for the Trump administration to engage in a 'comprehensive reassessment of US-China policy.'"[87]

As stated earlier, Rapp-Hooper asserted that President Trump followed a transactional approach until a formal policy was created.[88] Transactionalism is an approach that asserts that assumes that because Trump lacks a vision, or a set of ideas, and views "policy issues on a case-by-case basis very much like a business transaction."[89]

Additionally, Rapp-Hooper asserts there are inherent dilemmas associated with Trump's transactional approach. To begin with, "Xi is likely to want to be only cooperative enough to satisfy any bargain, while Trump is likely to expect Beijing's cooperation to grow with the situation. . . . ."[90] Second, "by fixing his gaze on North Korea and trade issues alone, the Trump approach artificially narrows a highly complex relationship . . . to [the] advantage China."[91] And third, a "related danger of Trump's transactionalism towards China is that it circumscribes the role of allies in decision-making. This puts US interests at risk."[92]

After much internal debate and input from multiple officials spanning State, CIA, Defense, Treasury, Commerce, and the FBI, the Trump administration finally settled on an approach to confront China's challenge. The Trump administration strategy is a hardline "whole of government approach" aimed at challenging China's encroachment in traditional areas of American dominance (trade and investment and political-military advantages in Asia).

Beginning in the fall of 2017, the Trump administration intensified the already harsh language directed against Chinese government policies the administration believed undercut American exports. Vice President Mike Pence and National Security Advisor Bolton continued this theme. Pence and Bolton promised "protracted counterefforts" (sanctions) would be utilized to reiterate previous administration warnings that China's theft of intellectual property, trade barriers, the institution of unfair practices that undermined American businesses operating in China illustrate the Trump administration is prepared for a long-term response to challenge China in these areas.[93]

A second component of the administration strategy is to respond to the challenge of Chinese economic espionage. During a presentation of evidence before a congressional committee, FBI Director Christopher Ray delivered a stern warning that challenged China's decades-old policy of economic espionage. Ray warned the administration is prepared to confront China's economic espionage and to disrupt their cyber activities which he asserts is a blatant attempt to decrease American technological advantages.[94]

In a demonstration of the third component of the administration strategy, Secretary of State Pompeo in October of 2018 shifted the focus to another previously unchallenged area of China's accelerated quest for dominance— the One Belt, One Road Initiative. Pompeo warned China's global investment initiative "presents risks to American interests, and we intend to oppose them at every turn."[95] The administration's response to One Belt, One Road is found in the BUILD Act, legislation enacted by Congress that provided "$60 billion in investment and financing projects"[96] around the globe. This administration strategy "is in direct competition" with the One Belt, One Road initiative.[97] Additionally, Pompeo quietly sought and received assistance from "Japan, Australia, and India" which collectively instituted "parallel measures of their own that worked against" China's One Road initiative.[98]

The fourth component of Trump's administration strategy is directed at China's increasingly destabilizing arsenal of conventional intermediate range missile fleet. The Trump administration threatened and later withdrew from the INF Treaty due to salient Russian contravention of the agreement. In addition, the decision to withdraw from the INF Treaty represents a warning to China. The message is clear: the administration is prepared to respond to China's missile threat in Asia. Beijing's intermediate range missiles represent a threat to US naval vessels and troops and allied interests across Asia. The administration promised to respond to this challenge, which includes the threat to deploy capabilities (naval ship building and anti-ballistic missiles) in response to China's intermediate missiles. In addition, there is a consideration to upgrade antiquated American intermediate missiles and to deploy the weapons to the region.

On the trade front, the Trump administration informed China that the old trade arrangements would have to be altered and that if the Xi government is not prepared to make the necessary adjustments, particularly regarding trade barriers that Beijing uses to undercut American exports, the administration is prepared to engage in an expanded trade war. Secretary of Commerce Ross and the Special Trade Representative Robert Lighthizer are leading this component of the administration strategy. In the wake of China's failure to respond appropriately to administration demands, the Trump administration instituted $200 billion dollars in tariffs aimed at Chinese exports. The Xi government launched less punitive tariffs at the American agricultural sector. An extended trade war is now in full swing. The administration claims it is prepared to win the trade war, even if that means facing short-term consequences to the American economy. Thus far, the consequences to the American economy have been minimal. In contrast, China's economy which was already suffering from a downturn, continues to decline under the weight of the American tariffs.

Trump's "whole of government approach" represents a hardline strategy that is directed at China from multiple levels. The strategy counters China's political gains in Asia and elsewhere around the world. The strategy responds to China's military provocations and in response to incessant threats in the South China Sea, and finally, the strategy is aimed at reshaping the Sino-American trade relationship. This collective "push-back" is ultimately designed to reshape the US-China relationship and preserve American interests and power capabilities in Asia.

CHINA AND THE NORTH KOREAN THREAT

At various points during the Trump presidency, the administration repeatedly warned the old regional approaches in confronting the threat posed by North Korea must be altered if not eliminated altogether. There is little doubt the administration's message is directed at China. Outside the administration, a host of scholars have been more direct. In an example that is consistent with administration thinking, Walter Lohman, the Director of the Asian Studies Center at the Heritage Foundation, argued: "Trump is going to be forceful with China over North Korea. He is not going to ask for help anymore. We are going to demand help. The time for talk is over. The US can impose secondary sanctions on Chinese companies if China doesn't cooperate."[99]

North Korea's missile tests predate the Trump administration. That said, the fact that Pyongyang accelerated their capabilities to hit the continental United States during the early months of the administration alarmed officials across the American government. The 21st Century China Center suggested the administration should "encourage China to use more of its economic and political leverage to convince North Korea's leaders to halt development of their nuclear and missile programs, the Trump administration should work in close coordination with South Korea to propose an omnibus negotiation."[100] Additionally, they suggest the administration should negotiate "a formal peace treaty replacing the Korean War armistice."[101] This should be done "in return for a verified freeze of North Korean nuclear and missile programs and a pledge to denuclearize."[102]

The administration, consistent with three previous presidents, recognizes China is a pivotal player in administration hopes to thwart North Korea's nuclear ambitions. The difference is that the Trump administration warned that they are prepared to go it alone. This is a reference to the reality the president is not willing to wait for China's assistance over an extended period to resolve the North Korea crisis. For many of the president's senior foreign policy advisors, solving the North Korea problem is central to US-China relations. However, a senior official made this statement, "the clock is now very, very quickly running out."[103]

CHINA'S THREAT IN THE SOUTH CHINA SEA

During the transition period, US allies in Asia expressed several concerns. Would the new American president implement his campaign promise to withdraw US support for the Trans-Pacific Partnership (TPP)? Another salient query is this: how would President Trump confront the evolving threat posed by North Korea? Finally, there is another issue that most allies in the region considered a high priority: how would Trump confront China's quest for hegemony in the South China Sea?

President Trump did of course withdraw from the Trans-Pacific Partnership, although the American leader did flirt with establishing a framework for US participation in the TTP. Almost from the start, officials in the administration understood that North Korea would become a high priority, high stakes issue. Perhaps more alarming is the president and senior officials consistently, on and off the record, offered statements that suggested "the military option" is on the table. Such statements, though associated with coercive diplomacy, alarmed members of foreign policy elite, leaders within Congress, parties in the Korean Peninsula, and states around the world.

In the opening months, the Trump administration did not have a formal strategy to deal with the instability in the South China Sea. And in those cases when statements were made about the issue, subsequent comments were quickly watered-down. As a case in point, during the Senate Confirmation hearing of Tillerson on January 11, 2017, he made this provocative statement: "We're going to have to send China a clear signal that first, the island-building stops, and second, your access to those islands also is not going to be allowed."[104] The media and Democratic members on the Senate Foreign Relations Committee expressed concern the Trump administration may be too hawkish in dealing with Beijing in the South China Sea. These same Democratic committee members openly expressed that it would be hard to vote for Tillerson's confirmation. To calm the waters, Tillerson, in response to written inquiries from committee members, offered another statement that closely approximated the position of the Obama administration. That position contained the following words: "The United States will uphold freedom of navigation and overflight by continuing to fly, sail and operate where international law allows."[105] Tillerson, after concerns the administration appeared too soft on the issue, issued a subsequent statement that included the following language: the US government "must be willing to accept risk if it is to deter further destabilizing actions [in the South China Sea] and reassure allies and partners."[106]

In the early months of the Trump presidency, allies in the region expressed another concern: at what point is the administration willing to initiate naval patrols in the South China Sea? In response to this concern, a senior White House official stated, "The United States will certainly continue to fly and sail where international law allows."[107]

Nearly two months after the Trump-Xi meeting, in late May of 2017, the Navy initiated their first American patrol in the South China Sea.[108] The operation allayed allied fears and simultaneously increased US-China tensions. Since that time, the American Navy consistently launched patrols across the South China Sea. As to be anticipated, China warned the patrols violated their sovereignty. In the final analysis, US Freedom of Navigation Patrols (FONOP) in the South China Sea play a pivotal role in upholding the International Court of Justice (ICJ) ruling against China's illegal claims in the region.[109]

US-CHINA TRADE RELATIONS

Trump campaigned on restoring the US economy and increasing jobs for American workers. To achieve both Trump must reverse the US trade deficit with China. Data released by the administration argued, "the US trade deficit more than doubled from 2000 to 2016, from $317 billion to $648 billion" and that "our trade deficit in goods and services with China soared from $81.9 billion in 2000 to almost $334 billion in 2015."[110]

During the campaign Trump argued that China's trade barriers undermined fair trade between Washington and Beijing. These "obstacles . . . make it difficult for US companies to operate and sell there."[111]

Another issue Trump addressed during the campaign is China's illegal dumping assisted in the expansion of Chinese export in the United States. Once in office President Trump signed two executive orders. The initial executive order called "for stricter enforcement of so-called anti-dumping laws along with increasing punitive duties on goods deemed to have been dumped."[112] A second executive order "calls on the Commerce Department and US Trade Representative to conduct a comprehensive study on the cause of the US trade deficit."[113]

On the significance of the executive orders, President Trump asserted, "We're going to get these bad trade deals straightened out. The jobs and wealth have been stripped from our country, year after year, decade after decade, trade deficit upon trade deficit reaching more than $700 billion last year alone and lots of jobs."[114]

On dealing with China's dumping, a bipartisan report—US Policy Toward China: Recommendations for a New Administration—urged "Trump to slap more tariffs on those Chinese goods determined to have been dumped on the US market and to deny Chinese firms investment opportunities if US firms are not given equal access in China."[115] The Trump administration acknowledged these actions over time should reverse China's trade advantages.

THE NEED FOR RULES TO STABILIZE US-CHINA RELATIONS

As stated by Andreas Forsby, a researcher at the Danish Institute for International Studies, the "simmering great power" US-China rivalry "constitute the single most important set of bilateral relations in the world today."[116] Dingding Chen, an international relations scholar at Jinan University, observes there are consequences for the failure to manage the US-China relations. According to Chen, "There is little doubt that the US-China relationship is one of the most important and most consequential bilateral relationships for the global order in the twenty-first century."[117] He further argues that mismanagement of the relationship could result in the path to conflict.

Previous American presidents, Bill Clinton, George W. Bush, and Barack Obama have implemented diplomatic initiatives aimed at engaging China in the liberal international order and reducing the threat of instability in Asia and beyond. Given the current state of Sino-American relations and tensions in the region, it is safe to argue the previous presidential initiatives did not meet their objectives. Each of these presidents in one form or another had a not so secret objective which called for management of China's rise.

From the perspective of China, President Xi, like his predecessors, is convinced the United States is developing "a containment strategy aimed at preventing China from resuming its historic role as a regional great power."[118] In the final analysis, a "simmering strategic rivalry between the United States and China"[119] continues unabated. The dilemma for the United States and China is this, currently, there are no rules to govern this complex relationship. Is there an opportunity whereby both parties are willing to engage in complex diplomacy to erect a body of rules to govern this complex and often tense relationship?

The areas where formal rules should be established to govern US-China relations include the following: (1) President Trump must immediately engage Chinese President Xi Jinping to "create a new high-level channel dedicated to the joint resolution of [any crisis or potential crisis]"[120]; (2) create a mechanism to manage the volatile claims issues in the South China Sea; (3) create a cooperative environment whereby the United States and China work to resolve North Korea's destabilizing nuclear ambitions; (4) develop short-term and long-term initiatives to manage the pivotal US-China trade relationship; and (5) manage the simmering cyberspace rivalry that threatens to further undermine US-China relations.

It is important to discuss the necessity for rules in some of the above areas. On the initial rule (the creation of a new high-level channel dedicated to preventing the potential of a crisis, or if one did develop work jointly to manage the crisis before it escalates into a conflict), it is important to establish "a direct communication channel" to avoid a crisis or crises from spiraling out of control. The third crisis in the Taiwan Straits during the Clinton administration and the Hainan Island incident in 2001 during the Bush administration are salient examples of previous crises. These incidents pushed the US-Chinese governments to initiate dangerous bellicose language and the threat of the use of force. The point of a high-level channel between the two leaders or a hot line would be to establish "a new communication instrument" to avoid a path to war. Previous attempts to create a hotline ended in failure.[121] This new hotline goes beyond the military-to-military hotline or the space hotline.

A mechanism to manage the volatile claims issues in the South China Sea is central to avoiding a direct confrontation between the United States and China. From the perspective of the United States and its Asian allies in the region, a mechanism already exists—international law. While international law exists, it has not decreased tensions in the region. Even when US conducts freedom of seas naval movements to reaffirm customary principles of international law, China views the presence of American warships as an encroachment on their sovereignty. Such American naval movements must continue, and the Trump administration must employ the "same set of policies . . . in the East China Sea."[122]

The ICJ in June 2016 "delivered a sweeping rebuke" against China's behavior in the South China Sea, including its construction of artificial islands, and "found that its expansive claim to sovereignty over the waters had no legal basis."[123] Even though the ICJ ruled in favor of the claims of the government of the Philippines, the government of China rejected the decision arguing it "is invalid and has no binding force."[124]

It is for this reason that high-level meetings should take place to clearly "establish the principles of rule of law" to the government of China. The Trump administration thereafter will have to "constantly reaffirm" the rule of law through the deployment of the American Navy or other means. The tensions in the South and East China Seas continue unabated. Though the United States understands that international law is on its side, but because China rejects the body of law regarding claims and instead relies on an "ancient claims" argument, the disputes involving several states in the region continue.

In the specific island where China constructed runways and deployed aircraft on the island, tensions may move toward a potential conflict. Thus, the Trump administration must "intensify efforts to encourage a principled, 'rules-based approach' in the management and settlement of Asia-Pacific Maritime disputes."[125]

There is need to establish a rule (or agreement) to create a cooperative environment that deals with North Korea nuclear ambitions or one that curtails their efforts to destabilize the Korean Peninsula. As is known, US-China relations deteriorated substantially during the second term of the Obama administration. Because of the impasse in US-China relations, the United States government is in no position, other than the use of rhetorical statements with the desire of obtaining China's support, to warn North Korea that several of the tests proved provocative and destabilizing. With China as the central entity to curtail those activities, it is necessary that US-China officials ensure a cooperative environment to address North Korean actions. In short, no efforts to resolve future North Korean provocations can work if both parties fail to communicate or if a productive relationship is not established.

There are other issues that require rules. For example, both parties, the United States and China, are using distinctive initiatives that the other considers to be destabilizing. Interestingly, these efforts involve some form of rebalancing. In the case of China, they are likely to continue a rebalancing that commenced during the administration of President George W. Bush. In Bush's war on terrorism, the US president made extensive use of the slogan "you are with us, or against us." Not all states wanted to participate in the US-led war on terrorism. Equally troubling, the Chinese expressed concern that the Bush Doctrine could impact trade relations in the region. In their version of rebalancing, the government of China informed many traditional American allies that Beijing is willing to engage in trade relations and create new partnerships as an alternative to American pressure.[126]

Another form of rebalancing may occur because of President Trump's decision to withdraw from the TPP. China informed states in Asia that they are willing to engage in trade partnerships in the wake of President Trump's America First approach, which many US allies and China view as nothing more than a cover for American protectionism. China is prepared to step in and allay the fears of these states. If China succeeds, this rebalancing strategy will undermine US credibility and leadership in the region. This approach could lead to a counter American strategy that would increase tensions between the United States and China.

The American initiative is quite comprehensive. To confront China's increasing power projection capabilities, the US government will engage in a rebalancing effort which "comprises various diplomatic, economic and not least military-strategic initiatives designed to bind Asian-Pacific states closer to Washington (rather than Beijing) in a 'network of like-minded states that sustains and strengthens a rules-based regional order.'"[127] A critical rule must therefore be instituted to establish the legitimate regional and global interests of each party.

There is another flashpoint that could undermine any legitimate period of cooperation: the status of Taiwan. Taiwan emerged as a flashpoint during the transition period. Each party must work to prevent a major crisis, particularly in the form of the tensions in the Taiwan Straits that developed during the Clinton administration. At issue, is there a mechanism that can be created to prevent a future crisis in the straights? One thing is a near certainty, Taiwan will always serve as an area of contention between the parties.

The implementation of the grand diplomatic initiative depends on an American president known for his business proclivities. As argued by Forsby, "Ultimately, however, Trump's utter lack of any political credentials combined with his anti-establishment attitude should turn his presidency into a highly unpredictable one."[128] With a real estate mogul occupying the White House, "US foreign policy is no longer business-as-usual."[129]

There is another important perspective. Sam Kiley, foreign affairs editor of *Sky News*, wrote, "Donald Trump has shown 'a fine disregard for the rules of the game' in international affairs."[130] There is a paradox, the US president recognized for the "disregard for the rules of the game" is positioned to work for the creation of rules to govern two significant relationships: US-Russian relations and US-China relations. If President Trump is to end the instability in these twin relationships (which have been complicated by congressional sanctions against Russia and a tit-for-tat request by Moscow and Washington to reduce their diplomatic staffs, and not to mention the Trump administration's sanctions directed at China for their failure to curb North Korea's nuclear ambitions and the trade war), he must employ "summits" as the instrument to broker the new rules to govern US-Russian relations and US-China relations. In the final analysis, a comprehensive period of diplomacy will have to commence at a level not witnessed since the Truman administration which culminated in the creation of postwar liberal international order or the Reagan administration whose efforts ushered in the dissipation of the Cold War.

Graham rightly articulates it is in the interest of the United States to pursue diplomacy to achieve a new era of cooperation.[131] Thus, in the words of Graham, "our goal should be to create what we might call a new equilibrium, that is, a balance of cooperation and competition with Russia [and China] and that reduces the risk of great-power conflict, manages geopolitical rivalry and contains transnational threats."[132] To "achieving this equilibrium" the United States will have to "break with some of our traditional diplomatic practices."[133]

Graham also argues that "In diplomacy, dialogue should not be a reward for good behavior, but a means to understand the other side's interests and intentions. It is especially needed when events threaten to spin out of control, as they now do in US-Russian [and US-China] relations."[134]

In the case of US-China relations, there is a formula that the Trump administration should consider: strategic assurance. Writing in *Foreign Affairs*, Eduaro Araral, the Associate Professor and Vice Dean of Research at the Lee Yaun School of Public Policy, provided details on the importance of "strategic reassurance." Araral contends, "China, as the rising power, has to convince the United States, the incumbent power, that it is not a threat to US security and is not out to undermine US core interests. Similarly, the United States has to convince China that Chinese core interests will not be harmed."[135] There is an added problem according to Araral: "The uncertainty, distrust, and fear that underlie US-China relations, both countries may be unable to make and keep credible commitments to each other."[136]

Araral does acknowledge that there is an opportunity for "cooperative equilibrium" in US-China relations. On this point Araral argued, "If the prospects of a cooperative equilibrium depend on trust, what then are the indications that commitments or reassurances from both parties are no longer trustworthy?"[137] In the final analysis, "strategic reassurance has important implications for framing the future of US-China relations."[138]

One thing is certain, a tremendous amount of opportunities awaits President Trump. That is, a grand period of global significance is on the horizon. The grand period is "the reckoning," a moment of truth for great power relations. During this period of reckoning, a period where diplomacy can be used to implement rules of conduct to dramatically improve US-Russia and US-China relations or in the absence of rules and diplomacy, such relations can spiral out of control and shift to the path of war. If Trump is successful, this brand of diplomacy could serve as a critical point to establish a legacy. There is something else. If Trump is successful, subsequent American leaders will follow a strategy created by Trump in the same way that previous American president's followed Truman's implementation of George Kennan's containment doctrine that served as a guide for US-Soviet relations. At issue, is Trump prepared for the challenge? Time will tell.

NOTES

1. Kaczynski, Andrew, Massie, Chris, and McDermott, Nathan, "80 Times Trump Talked About Putin," *CNN*, http://www.cnn.com/interactive/2017/03/politics/trump-putin-russia-timeline/. Accessed on February 2, 2019.

2. Jacobs, Ben, "The Donald Trump Doctrine: Assad is Bad but US must Stop Nation-Building," *The Guardian*, October 13, 2015. https://www.theguardian.com/us-news/2015/oct/13/donald-trump-foreign-policy-doctrine-nation-building. Accessed on February 2, 2019.

3. Ibid.

4. Kaczynski, Massie, and McDermott, "80 Times Trump Talked About Putin."

5. Bradner, Eric and Wright, David, "Trump Says Putin is 'Not Going to go Into Ukraine,' Despite Crimea," *CNN*, July 31, 2016. http://www.cnn.com/2016/07/31/politics/donald-trump-russia-ukraine-crimea-putin/index.html. Accessed on February 2, 2019.

6. Ibid.

7. Ibid.

8. Tucker, Joshua, "Here's How Trump's Election Will Affect US-Russian Relations," *Washington Post*, November 11, 2016. https://www.washingtonpost.com/news/monkey-cage/wp/2016/11/10/heres-how-trumps-election-will-affect-u-s-russian-relations/?utm_term=da3f3ad2257b. Accessed on February 2, 2019.

9. Ibid.

10. Ibid.

11. Paletta, Damian, "Clinton vs. Trump-Where They Stand on Foreign Policy Issues," *Wall Street Journal*, Election 2016. http://graphics.wsj.com/elections/2016/donald-trump-hillary-clinton-on-foreign-policy/. Accessed on February 2, 2019.

12. Osnos, Evan, Remnick, David and Yaffa, Joshua,"Trump, Putin, and the New Cold War," *The New Yorker*, March 6, 2017, https://www.newyorker.com/magazine/2017/03/06/trump-putin-and-the-new-cold-war. Accessed on February 2, 2019.

13. Ibid.

14. Ibid.

15. Ibid.

16. Ibid.

17. Ibid.

18. Masters, James, "Trump Defense Chief Mattis: US Not Ready for Military Cooperation with Russia," *CNN*, February 16, 2017. http://www.cnn.com/2017/02/16/politics/mattis-russia-military-cooperation/. Accessed on February 4, 2019.
19. Ibid.
20. Ibid.
21. Schram, James, "Rex Tillerson Says Russia Poses a 'Danger' to US," *New York Post*, January 11, 2017. http://nypost.com/2017/01/11/rex-tillerson-says-russia-poses-a-danger-to-us/. Accessed on February 4, 2019.
22. Ibid.
23. Moore, Mark and Fredericks, Bob, "Trump: US-Russia Relations May be at 'All-Time Low,'" *New York Post*, April 12, 2017. http://nypost.com/2017/04/12/trump-us-russia-relations-may-be-at-all-time-low/. Accessed on February 4, 2019.
24. Osnos, Remnick, and Yaffa, "Trump, Putin, and the New Cold War."
25. Binnendijk, Hans and Courtney, William, "Can Trump Make a Deal with Putin"? *US-News.com*, December 1, 2016. https://www.usnews.com/opinion/world-report/articles/2016-12-01/how-donald-trump-could-normalize-relations-with-russia-and-vladimir-putin. Accessed on February 4, 2019.
26. Binnendijk and Courtney, "Can Trump Make a Deal with Putin"?
27. See President Trump in Poland. The White House, Donald J. Trump. July 7, 2017. https://www.whitehouse.gov/blog/2017/07/06/president-trump-poland. Accessed on February 4, 2019.
28. Tani, Maxwell, "The Trump Administration Appears Torn Over Whether to Support Removing Syria's Assad from Power," *Business Insider.com*, April 9, 2017. http://www.businessinsider.com/trump-bashar-al-assad-nikki-haley-regime-change-rex-tillerson-mcmaster-2017-4. Accessed on February 4, 2019.
29. Ibid.
30. The Editorial Board, "Mr. Trump's Fickle Diplomacy," *New York Times*, April 12, 2017. https://www.nytimes.com/2017/04/12/opinion/mr-trumps-fickle-diplomacy.html?mcubz=2&r=0. Accessed on February 4, 2019.
31. Ibid.
32. Note: There is commonality associated with the failures. Neither of the US presidents fully understood Russia's quest to return to great power status. US power capabilities declined, and its military monopoly diminished due to US intervention in Afghanistan and Iraq. There is one additional reason for the failure. NATO expansion reinvigorated Russian paranoia about "encirclement." Taken collectively, the Russians perceived the presence of several power vacuums and were prepared to fill them.
33. See Saunders, Paul J., Editor, "A New Direction in US Russia Relations? America's Challenges and Opportunities in Dealing with Russia," The Center for the National Interest, February 2017. https://187ock2y3ejr34z8752m6ize-wpengine.netdna-ssl.com/wp-content/uploads/2017/03/A-New-Direction-in-US-Russia-Relations-CFTNI-2017-Saunders.pdf. Accessed on February 4, 2019.
34. Matlock, Jack, "Risks in Demonizing Diplomacy with Russia," *Consortiumnews.com*, March 6, 2017. https://consortiumnews.com/2017/03/06/risks-in-demonizing-diplomacy-with-russia/?Print=pdf. Accessed on February 4, 2019.
35. Saunders, "A New Direction in US Russia Relations? America's Challenges and Opportunities in Dealing with Russia."
36. Mitchell, A. Wess, Assistant Secretary of State, Bureau of European and Eurasian Affairs, "US Strategy Toward the Russian Federation," Statement Delivered Before Senate Foreign Relations Committee, Washington, DC, August 21, 2018. https://www.state.gov/p/eur/rlsrm/2018/285247.htm. Accessed on February 5, 2019.
37. Ibid.
38. Ibid.
39. As quote in Cordesman, Anthony H., "Trump on Russia: His Strategy Documents vs. His Meeting with Putin," *Center for Strategic International Studies*, July 17, 2018. https//www.csis.org/analysis/trump-russia=his-strategy-documents-vs-his-meeting-putinhtml. Accessed on February 5, 2019.

40. Mitchell, Assistant Secretary of State, Bureau of European and Eurasian Affairs, "US Strategy Toward the Russian Federation."

41. Danvers, William, "US and Russia Relations Under Trump and Putin," Center for American Progress, December 14, 2016. https://www.americanprogress.org/issues/security/reports/2016/12/14/295001/u-s-and-russia-relations-under-trump-and-putin/. Accessed on February 5, 2019.

42. Should Trump not be reelected then the next American president will have to continue what was started under the Trump administration. In short, continuity is important.

43. Danvers, "US and Russia Relations Under Trump and Putin."

44. Saunders, "A New Direction in US Russia Relations? America's Challenges and Opportunities in Dealing with Russia."

45. The Editorial Board, "Russian Attacks Ukrainian Ships and International Law," *New York Times*, November 26, 2018. https://www.nytimes.com/2018/11/26/opinion/russia-ukraine-attack-ships-crimea.html. Accessed on February 6, 2019.

46. [No Author] "Tension Escalates After Russia Seizes Ukraine Naval Ships," *BBC*, November 26, 2018. https://www.bbc.com/news/world-europe-46338671. Accessed on February 6, 2019.

47. Lander, Mark and Sanger, David, "Obama Says He Told Putin: 'Cut It Out' on Hacking," *New York Times*, December 16, 2016. https://www.nytimes.com/2016/12/16/us/politics/obama-putin-hacking-news-conference.html?mcubz=2. Accessed on February 6, 2019.

48. Graham, Thomas, "Toward a New Equilibrium in US-Russian Relations," *National Interest*, February 1, 2017. http://nationalinterest.org/feature/toward-new-equilibrium-us-russian-relations-19281?page=2. Accessed on February 6, 2019.

49. Roth, Andrew and Borger, Julian, "Trump and Putin to Reveal Details of First Official Summit," *The Guardian*, June 27, 2018. https://www.theguardian.com/us-news/2018/jun/27/john-bolton-vladimir-putin-moscow-visit-us-russia. Accessed on February 6, 2019.

50. Remarks by President Trump and President Putin of the Russian Federation in Joint Press Conference, The White House, July 16, 2018. https://www.whitehouse.gov/briefings-statements/remarks-president-trump-president-putin-russian-federation-joint-press-conference/.

51. Vazques, Maegan, "Former Intel Chiefs Condemn Trump's News Conference with Putin," *CNN*, July 17, 2018. https://www.cnn.com/2018/07/16/politics/john-brennan-donald-trump-treasonous-vladimir-putin/index.html. Accessed on February 6, 2019.

52. Taylor, William B., "What's Next for the US and Russia After the Trump-Putin Summit?" USIP.org, July 17, 2018. https://www.usip.org/publications/2018/07/whats-next-us-and-russia-after-trump-putin-summit. Accessed on February 6, 2019.

53. President Donald J. Trump to Withdraw the United States from the Intermediate-Range Nuclear Forces (INF) Treaty, The White House, February 1, 2019. https://www.whitehouse.gov/briefings-statements/president-donald-j-trump-withdraw-united-states-intermediate-range-nuclear-forces-inf-treaty/. Accessed on February 6, 2019.

54. Trump, Donald, *Crippled America: How to Make America Great Again* (New York: Simon and Schuster, 2015), p. 43.

55. Ibid.

56. Key Asia Issues in the 2016 Presidential Campaign, *Asia Matters for America*, http://www.asiamattersforamerica.org/asia/key-asia-issues-in-the-2016-campaign. Accessed on February 6, 2019.

57. Legal View with Ashleigh Banfield, *CNN* Transcripts, July 21, 2015. http://transcripts.cnn.com/TRANSCRIPTS/1507/21/lvab.01.html. Accessed on February 6, 2019.

58. Stracqualursi, Veronica, "10 Times Trump Attacked China and Its Trade Relations with the US," *ABCnews.go.com*, April 6, 2017. http://abcnews.go.com/Politics/10-times-trump-attacked-china-trade-relations-us/story?id=46572567. Accessed on February 6, 2019.

59. Ibid.

60. Gass, Nick, "Trump: We Can't Continue to Allow China to Rape Our Country," *Politico*, May 2, 2016. www.politico.com/blogs/2016-gop/2016/05/trump-china-rape-america-222689. Accessed on February 6, 2019.

61. Earle, Geoff, "Trump Sends Dollar Plunging as He Says He Wants Interest Rates Kept Low-And Won't Be Calling China 'Currency Manipulator,'" *Daily Mail*, April 12, 2017. http://www.dailymail.co.uk/news/article-4406584/Trump-sends-dollar-plunging-comments-currency.html. Accessed on February 6, 2019.

62. Campbell, Charlie, "Donald Trump Angers China with Historic Phone Call to Taiwan's President," *Time*, December 2, 2016. http://time.com/4589641/donald-trump-china-taiwan-call/.

63. Lander, Mark and Forsythe, Michael, "Trump Tells Xi Jinping US Will Honor 'One China' Policy," *New York Times*, February 9, 2017. https://www.nytimes.com/2017/02/09/world/asia/donald-trump-china-xi-jinping-letter.html?mcubz=2&_r=0. Accessed on February 6, 2019.

64. Hsu, Sara, "China Wary of President-Elect Donald Trump," *Forbes*, November 11, 2016. https://www.forbes.com/sites/sarahsu/2016/11/23/china-wary-of-president-elect-donald-trump/#7116a5a7202b. Accessed on February 6, 2019.

65. Ibid.
66. Ibid.
67. Ibid.
68. Ibid.

69. "Donald Trump's Victory Raises Questions in China," *Fortune* (Reuters), November 9, 2016. http://fortune.com/2016/11/09/donald-trump-win-china/. Accessed on February 6, 2019.

70. Boje Forsby, Andreas, "US-China Relations Under Trump: Partners or Rivals?" *Danish Institute for International Studies* (DIIS), June 19, 2017. https://www.diis.dk/en/event/us-china-relations-trump-partners-or-rivals. Accessed on February 6, 2019.

71. As quoted in Fujii, George, "ISSF Policy Roundtable 1-9: US-China Relations and the Trump Administration," *ISSFforum.org*, May 17, 2017. https://networks.h-net.org/node/28443/discussions/179828/issf-policy-roundtable-1-9-us-china-relations-and-trump. Accessed on February 7, 2019.

72. Ibid.
73. Ibid.

74. Doshi, Rush, "Trump's China Policy: A Tale of Two Extremes," *National Interest*, April 7, 2017. http://nationalinterest.org/feature/trump-must-choose-between-hard-line-china-strategy-soft-20002. Accessed on February 7, 2019.

75. Lucas, Fred, "US-China Summit: The 4 Big Issues Donald Trump and Xi Jinping Will Discuss," *National Interest* (Blog), April 5, 2017. http://nationalinterest.org/blog/the-buzz/us-china-summit-the-4-big-issues-donald-trump-xi-jinping-20043. Accessed on February 7, 2019.

76. Lander, Mark, "Airstrike in Syria Overshadows Meeting Between Trump and Xi," *New York Times*, April 7, 2017. https://www.nytimes.com/2017/04/07/us/politics/airstrike-in-syria-overshadows-meeting-between-trump-and-xi.html?mcubz=2&_r=0. Accessed on February 7, 2019.

77. Ibid.
78. Ibid.

79. [No Author] "Trump Hails 'Tremendous' Progress in Talks with China's Xi," *BBC.com*, April 7, 2017. http://www.bbc.com/news/world-us-canada-39517569. Accessed on February 7, 2019.

80. Ibid.
81. Ibid.

82. Mayeda, Andrew, "Trump Drops Campaign Promise to Label China a Currency Manipulation," Bloomberg.com, April 12, 2017. https://www.bloomberg.com/politics/articles/2017-04-12/trump-says-u-s-will-not-label-china-a-currency-manipulator. Accessed on February 7, 2019.

83. Donnan, Shannon, "Trump Administration Hails US-China Trade Deal," *Financial Times*, May 12, 2017. https://www.ft.com/content/9a5ee6b8-36c0-11e7-bce4-9023f8c0fd2e. Accessed on February 7, 2019.

84. Yoon, Eunice, "Here's Who Wins with the New US-China Trade Deals," *CNBC.com*, May 12, 2017. http://www.cnbc.com/2017/05/12/heres-who-wins-with-the-new-us-china-trade-deals.html. Accessed on February 7, 2019.

85. Ibid.
86. Ibid.
87. Fujii, "ISSF Policy Roundtable 1-9: US-China Relations and the Trump Administration."
88. Ibid.
89. Hadar, Leon, "The Limits of Trump's Transactional Foreign Policy," *National Interest*, January 2, 2017. https://nationalinterest.org/feature/the-limits-trumps-transactional-foreign-policy-18898. Accessed on February 7, 2019.
90. Ibid.
91. Ibid.
92. Ibid.
93. Sutter, Robert, "Pushback: America's New China Strategy," *The Diplomat*, November 17, 2018. https://thediplomat.com/2018/11/pushback-americas-new-china-strategy/. Accessed on February 7, 2019.
94. Ibid.
95. Delaney, Robert, "Mike Pompeo Promises US Will Meet China's Strategies with 'Strong and Vigorous Response,'" *South China Morning Post*, October 18, 2018. https://www.scmp.com/news/china/diplomacy/article/2170463/mike-pompeo-promises-us-will-meet-chinas-strategies-strong-and. Accessed on February 7, 2019.
96. Sutter, "Pushback: America's New China Strategy."
97. Ibid.
98. Ibid.
99. Lucas, Fred, "4 Issues Trump Will Likely Confront Chinese Leader About," *The Daily Signal*, April 5, 2017. http://dailysignal.com/2017/04/05/4-issues-trump-will-likely-confront-chinese-leader-about/. Accessed on February 7, 2019.
100. Schell, Orville and Shirk, Susan L., "US Policy Toward China: Recommendations for a New Administration," Task Force Report February 2017. Asia Society, US San Diego, School of Global Policy and Strategy, 21st Century China Center. http://asiasociety.org/files/US-ChinaTask_Force_Report_FINAL.pdf. Accessed on February 7, 2019.
101. Ibid.
102. Ibid.
103. As quoted in Lucas, "4 Issues Trump Will Likely Confront Chinese Leader About."
104. Cook, Malcolm and Storey, Ian, "The Trump Administration and Southeast Asia: Limited Engagement Thus Far," *ISEAS-Yusof Ishak Institute Perspective*, Singapore, April 2017. https://www.iseas.edu.sg/images/pdf/ISEAS_Perspective_2017_27.pdf. Accessed on February 7, 2018.
105. Ibid.
106. Ibid.
107. Lucas, "US-China Summit: The 4 Big Issues Donald Trump and Xi Jinping Will Discuss."
108. Ross, Eleanor, "US Will Still Challenge Beijing's Claims to South China Sea Under Donald Trump," *Newsweek*, March 9, 2017. http://www.newsweek.com/us-china-south-china-sea-claim-beijing-test-challenge-engaged-605858. Accessed on February 7, 2018.
109. Perlez, Jane, "Tribunal Rejects Beijing's Claims in South China Sea," *New York Times*, July 12, 2016. https://www.nytimes.com/2016/07/13/world/asia/south-china-sea-hague-ruling-philippines.html?mcubz=2&r=0. Accessed on February 7, 2018.
110. Fred, "4 Issues Trump Will Likely Confront Chinese Leader About."
111. Yu, Roger, "US-China Trade Scorecard: Advantage China," *USA Today*, April 4, 2017. https://www.usatoday.com/story/money/2017/04/04/united-states-china-trade-relations/999891116/. Accessed on February 7, 2019.
112. Wallace, Charles, "Crunch Time for Trump on China Trade," *Forbes.com*, April 3, 2017. https://www.forbes.com/sites/charleswallace1/2017/04/03/crunch-time-for-trump-on-china-trade/#7e65e7305d99. Accessed on February 7, 2019.
113. Ibid.
114. Ibid.

115. Pomfret, John, "How Trump Could Put US-China Relations on the Right Track," *Washington Post*, February 6, 2017. https://www.washingtonpost.com/news/global-opinions/wp/2017/02/06/how-trump-could-put-u-s-china-relations-on-the-right-track/?utm-term=a22357e9589b. Accessed on February 8, 2019.

116. Bøje Forsby, Andreas, "Donald Trump and US-China Relations: Putting America First Could China the Edge," *Danish Institute for International Studies* (DIIS), *DIIS Policy Brief*, November 2016. http://pure.diis.dk/ws/files/691386/US_Chinese_relations_WEB.pdf.

117. Fujii, "ISSF Policy Roundtable 1-9: US-China Relations and the Trump Administration."

118. Forsby, "Donald Trump and US-China Relations: Putting America First Could China the Edge."

119. Ibid.

120. Schell and Shirk, "US Policy Toward China: Recommendations for a New Administration."

121. Paper, Robert, "A Hotline to Cool Asian Crises," *Washington Post*, April 29, 2014. https://www.washingtonpost.com/news/monkey-cage/wp/2014/04/29/a-hotline-to-cool-asian-crises/?utm_term=bc095f0d01be. Accessed on February 9, 2019.

122. Schell and Shirk, "US Policy Toward China: Recommendations for a New Administration."

123. Perlez, Jane, "Tribunal Rejects Beijing's Claims in South China Sea," *New York Times*, July 12, 2016. https://www.nytimes.com/2016/07/13/world/asia/south-china-sea-hague-ruling-philippines.html. Accessed on February 9, 2019.

124. Ibid.

125. Ibid.

126. See Ness, Peter Van, "China's Response to the Bush Doctrine," *World Policy Journal*, Vol. 21, No. 4 (Winter, 2004/2005), pp. 38–47.

127. Forsby, "Donald Trump and US-China Relations: Putting America First Could China the Edge."

128. Ibid.

129. Ibid.

130. Kiley, Sam, "How Will the Trump Presidency Affect World Affairs?" *Sky News*, 2017. http://news.sky.com/story/how-will-the-trump-presidency-affect-world-affairs-10732131. Accessed on February 9, 2019.

131. Graham, "Toward a New Equilibrium in US-Russian Relations."

132. Ibid.

133. Ibid.

134. Ibid.

135. Araral, Eduaro, "US-China Relations: A Game of Strategic Reassurance," *Foreign Affairs*, August 7, 2017. https://www.foreignaffairs.com/sponsored/us-china-relations-game-strategic-reassurance. Accessed on February 9, 2019.

136. Ibid.

137. Ibid.

138. Ibid.

Conclusion

President Trump continues to wrestle with the "Obama dilemma"—the extensive unfinished foreign policy issues that were bequeathed to him—well into the administration. Those issues, confronting Russia, China, North Korea, Iran, a chaotic Middle East, the Islamic State, Al Qaeda, and other terrorist groups, the sputtering international economy, represent a sample of the Obama era issues that President Trump will incessantly have to manage if not resolved during his stewardship of American foreign policy.

This not being enough, President Trump is attempting to implement an expansive and controversial foreign policy agenda that encompasses America First and the refinement of multilateralism, rebuilding the military, renovation of the war on terrorism, restoration of American leadership, and Middle East Peace represent just a sample of the issues the administration seeks to advance. The pages that follow represent a "progress report" and the "state of US foreign policy" under Trump through the prism of the Obama dilemma, the president's agenda, and increasing discord in the international community over the course and direction of the administration's foreign policy.

REBUILDING THE MILITARY

Rebuilding the military is certainly an issue that was bequeathed to President Trump from his predecessor President Obama. Throughout the presidential campaign "rebuilding the armed forces" remained a major campaign issue. For candidate Trump, he promised to fix the "depleted military" and restore respect for the United States.

Once in office, President Trump had to deal with the reality that there would be no significant increase in defense spending in 2017. Critics of "Trump's military rebuilding effort" charged the appropriations requested for the armed forces budget is inconsistent with the president's campaign rhetoric. To a degree, the critics are correct. However, they missed a critical point. That is, if you examine the first year of President Ronald Reagan and President George W. Bush's defense budgets, the previous two examples of major increases in defense spending, there is an increase in defense spending. That said, it is during the second and third years that the defense authorizations during the Reagan and Bush administrations were commensurate with their campaign rhetoric.

There are however other dilemmas associated with the Trump administration's rebuilding efforts. Several salient issues occupy the rebuilding program. For example, one can anticipate an increase in fighter jets for the Air Force, increase in troops for the Army and Marines, and the Navy will receive an increase in vessels across the inventory, whether in the form of surface ships, carriers, or submarines.

However, there are several issues still to be resolved. First and foremost, speaking before Air Force personnel at Joint Base Andrews, President Trump stated, "I'm calling on Congress to end the defense sequester once and for all and to give our military the tools, training, equipment and resources that our brave men and women in uniform so richly deserve."[1] The president's statement came in response to a Democrat effort that defeated a Republican-sponsored bill that would have ended sequestration. It is unlikely that substantial increases in military spending consistent with what the president or the Republican congressional leadership desires will occur especially under the Democrat-controlled House of Representatives. One should anticipate incremental increases in defense spending as opposed to the substantial increases the president desires.

Thus far, this aspect of the president's foreign policy agenda is sputtering. That is, there will be increases in defense spending. At issue, will those increases reach the level commensurate with President Trump's vision? There is another important question: will the failure to achieve major defense spending imperil the administration's efforts to confront the threats posed by China in Asia, and confront a host of other evolving issues (e.g., Russia, North Korea, Iran, and Afghanistan)? Domestically, there is another challenge that Trump is confronting—managing his domestic and foreign policy agendas in era of divided government. Put more succinctly can the president achieve the transformation of the military during a period where the Democrats control the House of Representatives? The answer to these questions will provide a window into whether the administration will be able to confront current and future threats and continue to restore American leadership.

AMERICA FIRST AND MULTILATERALISM

Multilateralism represented a critical instrument for President Trump's foreign policy. It is useful in resolving crises, whether in the form of North Korea, working with the anti-ISIS coalition that ended the Islamic States' caliphate, and containing China's adventurism in the South China Sea are just few examples. The Obama dilemma is itself problematic, but the president must overcome critics—the resistance and the never-Trumpers that charge Trump's America First policy is endangering a host of multilateral frameworks that encompass economic, military, or the diplomatic venues of US interests around the globe. At issue, are the critics correct?

One of the critical issues during both the presidential campaign and now well into the presidency of Donald Trump is what constitutes America First? During the campaign, there was a litany of statements associated with America First, but it was not until the early months of the Trump presidency whereby experts, at home and abroad, began to comprehend the meaning and breath of this aspect of administration foreign policy. The dilemma for the Trump administration is coherency which is linked to its implementation. That is, there have been several iterations of America First. The purpose of each iteration represented an attempt to clarify the meaning of the slogan or what many pundits assert is doctrine and others boast "is grand strategy." Candidate Trump unveiled the initial version of the slogan. Trump incessantly argued America First represented a central pillar of his foreign policy.[2]

In a speech to State Department employees on May 3, 2017, former Secretary of State Tillerson offered the second iteration. In the address Tillerson provided this extensive clarification: "I approach it really that it's America First for national security and economic prosperity, and that doesn't mean it comes at the expense of others."[3] Tillerson then addressed the importance of alliances in era of America First. Said Tillerson, US-long held alliances will remain essential to American interests and economic prosperity.[4]

A third explanation of America First was articulated by former National Security Advisor H. R. McMaster and former White House Director of the National Economic Council, Gary D. Cohn. In the *Wall Street Journal* opinion piece, McMaster and Cohn asserted, President Trump's America First approach safeguards the interests of the country and its restores "confidence in American leadership."[5]

Given the unmistakable evidence the post-World War II "rule-based global order"[6] has undergone consequential shifts in the geopolitical balance of power, which has witnessed the arrival of new powers, namely China, Russia, Japan, and the European Union, it is appropriate to ask if the failure of previous administrations to adjust the "rules" to retain or enhance US primacy represented the logic behind Trump's employment of America First? George Friedman offered this analysis: "Trump is proposing a redefinition of

US foreign policies based on current realities, not those of 40 years ago. It is a foreign policy in which American strength is maximized in order to achieve American ends. . . ."[7] Additionally, he noted, Trump rightly challenges the commitment of several US presidents to outmoded international arrangements.[8]

The dilemma for Trump is that after multiple iterations of America First, the president has yet to provide "a blueprint" for a way forward. Most notably, what adjustments to current multilateral arrangements and perhaps the need for the creation of new ones is the Trump administration proposing? There is little doubt "the three-quarters century old" post-World War II arrangements have sustained the United States as the dominate state in the international system. However, Trump argued that while President Obama's failed policies may be associated with the conspicuous decline of American leadership, the president is also asserting the antiquated arrangements offered declining benefits to the American economy and jobs for the American worker.

Many have characterized Trump's America First as a transition to a new vision of world order. Jason O'Brien, a reporter, as found in an article titled, "America First: Trump's New World Order Begins," which appeared in the *Independent,* used an excerpt from President Trump's inaugural address to set up his argument. In the address Trump stated, "From this day forward a new vision will govern our land."[9] Then O'Brien offered this characterization: "America First extended to foreign policy too, as he vowed every decision on trade, taxes, immigration, and on foreign affairs will be made "to benefit American workers and American families."[10]

Boston Globe reporter, James Pindell, asserted Trump's decision to withdraw from the Paris Accord is an indication the president is "announcing a new world order."[11] In addition, Pindell argued, "Trump has hardly been shy about his call to put 'America First,' but until today few here or abroad knew what Trump actually meant by this in terms of a worldview."[12]

There are others that assert that America First is not necessarily an instrument that will act as a tool for the president's transition to a new world order. Michael Claire, author and professor of Peace and World Security Studies at Hampshire College, argued the source of the transition in world order may be connected to the president himself. In the words of Claire, "That Donald Trump is a grand disruptor when it comes to international affairs is now a commonplace observation in the establishment media."[13] Additionally, Claire asserted, many of Trump's statements against NATO and the removal of the United States from the Paris climate agreement, were perceived actions that undermined FDR's liberal world order created. Claire then argues the president is "not only trying to obliterate the existing world order, but also attempting to lay the foundations for a new one."[14] Most important, America First is a "grand strategic design is evident in virtually everything

Trump has done . . . abroad."[15] Robert Samuelson, columnist for *Investor Business Daily*, argued "there is a larger issue here."[16] Samuelson then uses Henry Kissinger to make his point. Samuelson articulated that Kissinger in his book *World Order* "that the world is at its greatest peril when the international order is moving from one system to another."[17]

To negate what the Trump White House asserted represented the misperceptions of the slogan, the president will have to provide subsequent speeches about the objectives of America First. That is, there is no longer a need to consistently correct what the administration believes are false statements that America First threatens the liberal international order, trade wars, and allied arrangements. Instead, the president must constantly remind the American people, the media, and the international community that America First represents an alternative option that details the purpose of the slogan. And to illustrate that it represents a tool to reimagine the current multilateral frameworks and why it serves as a secondary purpose which calls for the creation of new frameworks not just to restore stability in the international order but also assist in establishing "new rules" to protect American interests and its primacy.

From another perspective, the administration has not jettisoned any traditional frameworks. If one examines the administration's efforts to confront the Islamic State, for example, the grand global coalition remains intact, but it has undergone a refinement. In the ever-evolving crises with North Korea, the administration utilized the United Nations to implement stiffer sanctions against the Kim regime. In addition, the Trump administration strengthened the regional alliance with the United States, Japan, and South Korea in the event conflict occurred with North Korea. The administration pushed for increased NATO involvement in the fight against global terrorism and announced adherence to Article 5. The overall record indicated the Trump administration thus far did not shift away from or undermine multilateralism (as critics of administration policy would have you believe) which remains a critical instrument of US diplomacy.

FOREIGN ECONOMIC POLICY

One of the least discussed issues that will remain an albatross that will hover over the Trump presidency is how to reverse the absence of American competitiveness in international trade. Because of the worsening trade imbalances that accrued over multiple presidencies, the slow GDP growth, and the sputtering job growth at home, the American economy sputtered along. Trump inherited this problem from Obama. In fairness, President Obama's policies ended the financial crisis at home (which Obama inherited from President Bush) and increased jobs for American workers, but his policies could not overcome the economic maladies in Asia, Europe, and elsewhere around the world which impacted US exports.

At this stage, foreign economic policy is a long way from producing the desired benefits the Trump administration envisioned. However, the Trump administration has made significant progress. First, the administration engaged in several high-profile "renegotiations." Under President Trump the United States appeared headed for multiple trade disputes that critics charged could undermine American trade relationships and impair international trade. However, after the tremendous efforts of the Treasury and Commerce departments, the work of the Office of the United States Trade Representative, and the intermittent role of President Trump, the United States reached new trade agreements with South Korea (September 24, 2018), the European Union (an interim agreement signed on July 25, 2018), and Mexico and Canada (USMCA signed by the parties on December 1, 2018).

China is considered a critical component of the administration's foreign economic policy. Throughout the presidential campaign, Trump lambasted China from dumping cheap steel on the US market, for its credit manipulation, China's engagement in a host of other unfair trade practices, and the candidate campaigned on improved access for American businesses in China.

This component haunts the administration's foreign economic policy—trade negotiations with China which have been hampered by the North Korean nightmare. During a series of provocative actions by the Kim regime, President Trump and administration officials have been prepared to unleash a "get tough" trade policy with China. The policy is designed to make it clear to China the "old days are over"; that trade relations should be altered to ensure greater access for American businesses in China's market. There is a supplemental objective: a reduction if not elimination of the annual trade surplus. This position is consistent with the populist America First slogan. An extended trade war is well underway. Both sides did reach a pause in the dispute to engage in diplomatic discussions to end the trade war, however neither party thus far has been willing to commit to significant changes making it unlikely that an immediate agreement would be produced.

Another critical piece of the administration's foreign economic policy is linked to President Trump's campaign pledge to reform the American tax code. The administration understood that its domestic agenda could pay dividends on the international trade front and advance US foreign economic objectives. The Republican controlled Congress passed legislation from each chamber on December 20, 2017 that provided a dramatic overhaul of the tax code. With this legislative victory President Trump is hoping to use the achievement to meet one of the administration's signature objectives: to "Grow the American economy by discouraging corporate inversions, adding a huge number of new jobs, and making America globally competitive again."[18]

The Trump administration's foreign economic policy is still evolving. Along with the trade renegotiations discussed above, and the attempts to reset US-China trade relations, the administration is still dealing with the fallout over the decision to withdraw from the TTP, backlash from the perception associated with America First and its potential trade implications, and the withdrawal from the Transatlantic Trade and Investment Partnership (TTIP) negotiations[19] with European partners. Taken collectively, the reality indicates the foreign economic component of the Trump administration's external agenda has yet to achieve success envisioned by administration officials in some areas, but many others remain outstanding.

There is another issue: Trump signaled his desire to rejoin the Trans-Pacific Partnership. Will the administration be successful in rejoining the partnership? What happens if the administration is unsuccessful? How will Trump react? How will the failure of the United States to rejoin the TPP impact regional and potential global trade?

On the trade war with China, is the Trump administration viewing the Washington-Beijing trade relationship through the prism of the trade imbalance with Japan. During the 1980s, the Reagan administration, which desired to reverse the US trade imbalances with Japan, the Republican president instituted a host of policies designed to rebalance the relationship. The Reagan administration's solution called for quotas on Japan's imports, forcing Tokyo to build cars in the United States, and a reduction in trade barriers on American imports. Over time, Japan lost its economic superpower status (this decline was additionally aided by the East Asian economic crisis).

The Trump administration is pursuing a similar strategy—one that is predicated on reversing China's annual trade surpluses and reducing if not ending the trade barriers that impacted US imports. These and other issues are critical in the Trump administration-led trade war with China. There are several scenarios connected with the Trump administration's strategy. Is the trade war an approach designed to contain China, to undermine their economic superpower status? Some argue the strategy represents an effort to inform Beijing this administration is not like previous presidents and actions that undermine American interest will be challenged.

The administration strategy is forcing counter reactions by the Xi-led government. The government in China's response to US trade tariffs in one salient illustration. There are others that can be best understood in the form of questions. Will China permit the Trump administration to continue to implement harsh trade policies designed to end Beijing's trade surplus? Worse, if a solution is reached will China permit the Trump administration to obtain outcomes that place Beijing in a situation that strips the country of their economic superpower status? What are the likely or potential showdowns in trade that could devolve into a potentially military showdown? Of equal importance, is Washington and Beijing prepared to separate economic and national security issues? The latter is of critical importance, particularly since there is increasing concern among allies and enemies about President Trump's apparent decisions to combine the two. The following quote is indicative of the anxiety:

> President Trump is merging his national security and trade goals in a blur of tactical improvisation that risks alienating US allies and opening American businesses to costly retaliation. The president holds an expansive view of national security, describing imported products like steel or passenger sedans as worrisome threats to the United States. Yet he also engages in freewheeling bargaining that treats vital strategic considerations as the equivalent of commercial factors, leaving negotiating partners unsure of his true priorities.[20]

Criticism of the president's combined view of national security is that his strategy is too expansive and the outcome uncertain. That is, Trump conducted multiple trade wars simultaneously. Thus, critics of the administration trade policy assert it is impossible to provide an immediate short-term analysis, and worse there is the belief that in the long term the US economy and allies could pay a substantial price. From another perspective, there is the belief that the American trade relationship with China could be damaged for the foreseeable future.

This negative perspective aside, there is potential for a dramatic shift in the way the United States conducts its trade policies. During the presidential campaign Trump warned that he would adopt a radical approach to trade policy—one that in the words of the president would put "America First." There is no doubt that he has succeeded. There is something of far greater consequence that has been overlooked by critics of administration policy. For the first time an American president is placing all aspects of US relationships under intense scrutiny. In the venue of trade this has forced states around the world to consider righting the relationship (often by accepting administration demands) or opting for a more confrontational approach, which translates into an expansive trade war. This option will likely result in access to a major trade market (the United States), loss of jobs, and undermining of a relationship (in the short and perhaps long term). The Trump administration is betting that those states under the president's crosshairs are more likely than not to opt for concessions that are more beneficial to the United States. There will be an aberration—a country that will likely counter administration tariffs and threats (China exemplifies this point). The dilemma with this approach is that the state invites being used as an example of what could happen to a state if they fail to make concessions.

REVISION OF THE WAR ON TERRORISM: THE NEXT THREAT

The Trump administration inherited the war on terrorism, most notably the threat posed by the Islamic State. The Trump administration rapidly and quietly deployed conventional combat forces and SOFs with the objective of ending the Islamic States' caliphate. After the loss of Mosul and Tal Arar,[21] the major components of the caliphate that existed in Iraq have been dissolved. That does not mean that ISIS will be defeated in Iraq. In Syria, the last stronghold in Baghouz was liberated, ending the last remaining territory of the caliphate. However, in Iraq and Syria and elsewhere, the terrorist organization commenced long ago the transition to an insurgency.

A report compiled by the Combating Terrorism Center at West Point argued that "Pushing the Islamic State out as the formal governing party in a territory is not a sufficient development when it comes to ending the group's ability to enact violence against individuals in Iraq and Syria."[22] Translation, the surviving leadership and thousands of fighters of the Islamic State will go underground in Iraq and Syria, and many will relocate to sanctuaries controlled by the transnational entity around the world. The purpose of the organization is to retain control over other sanctuaries while attempting to create new ones. In addition, members of the organization have returned long ago to areas in Iraq where cells are hiding in Sunni-controlled cities and towns and continue to launch attacks against government security forces in Iraq and began the process of reconstituting the organization through the establishment of fresh recruits. The reality is simple: as the caliphate collapsed "the Islamic State lives on"[23] and it is resurging in the Levant.

The threat of ISIS-inspired terrorism entered a pivotal period long before the collapse of the caliphate. During this period, several critical events will force the Trump administration to alter their strategy. One of the major periods of upheaval induced a struggle for the leadership of the jihadist movement. Beginning in early 2014, following the consolidation of Islamic States' caliphate, the prevailing view is that Al Qaeda is sidelined and no longer dominated the jihadist movement.

There is another prism to view the ISIS-Al Qaeda schism. The Islamic State established sanctuaries in over 30 countries around the world and used social media to recruit, to radicalize new foot soldiers, and then employed those forces to target Western Europe and the United States. For its part, Al Qaeda constructed emirates in Yemen, elsewhere in the Middle East, and in locales in various areas in Africa. Additionally, Al Qaeda quietly coopted anti-regime movements in Syria. Most importantly, Al Qaeda established their own recruitment of jihadists and there is another development: the emergence of Osama bin Laden's son, Hamza bin Laden, who is seeking revenge against the United States for the death of his father and he is assuming a not yet defined leadership role within the transnational organization.[24]

After losing Mosul, and with only a host of small sanctuaries remaining in Iraq in the weeks after the loss of control over Iraq's second largest city, and Raqqa, the Islamic States' operational hub, along with Deir al-Zior in Syria, the struggle between ISIS and Al Qaeda entered yet another phase. With the collapse of the Islamic States' caliphate, and some of their sanctuaries under assault from US, British, and French special operation forces, and confronting increased US air strikes, many observers argued this represented Al Qaeda's opportunity to reclaim supremacy of the global jihadist movement. At some point, one must ask when the Trump administration will launch a full-scale assault on Al Qaeda in Syria?

There is another phase—this one involves the United States. This phase identifies the requirement for the Trump administration to adjust their approach. The following excerpt clarifies the phase and dilemma that awaits the American president:

> The United States will soon reach a crossroads in its struggle against terrorism. The international coalition fighting the Islamic State (also known as ISIS) has driven the group out of . . . territory it once held and, sooner or later, will militarily defeat it by destroying its core in Iraq and Syria. But military victory over ISIS will not end the global war on terrorism that the United States has waged since 9/11. Some of ISIS's provinces may outlive its core. Remnants of the caliphate may morph into an insurgency. Al Qaeda and its affiliates will still pose a threat. Moreover, the conditions that breed jihadist organizations will likely persist across the greater Middle East. So, the United States must decide what strategy to pursue in the next stage of the war on terrorism.[25]

The adjustment in the administration's approach will prove significant in several ways. Will the Trump administration increase US combat forces in the Middle East and in North Africa to deal with the Islamic State/Al Qaeda threats? Will the administration increase special operation missions to confront the predictable period of ISIS's insurgency? Will air strikes and special operation missions work to reverse Al Qaeda's increasing influence? Another question is imperative: will President Trump withdraw all of its US forces from Syria? The answers to most of these questions will go a long way toward defining the contours of the war on terrorism and the Trump administration's ability to adapt to what remains a rapidly changing security environment.

Deir al-Zior is the front in the war on terrorism that is least discussed in the media. It represented a significant front that will require the Trump administration to deal with an evolving conflict. The author previously described the situation this way:

The struggle inside Deir al-Zior will create an extended period of danger for the United States. That is, conflict in the area could involve an indirect struggle between Russia and its proxies which include Iran, Hezbollah and Syrian government forces for control of this strategic region of the country. On this point, Louisa Loveluck and Zakaria Zakaria make a significant statement: "For Iran, securing a land route across the Syria-Iraq border to its Lebanese proxy, Hezbollah, is a key motivation. The United States, which lists Hezbollah as a terrorist organization because of its attacks on Israel, would oppose such a conduit."[26]

A question begs, how much political and military capital is President Trump prepared to use in a potential conflict to come after ISIS is defeated in Deir al-Zior? This is a critical issue. Why? Trump stated his Syrian policy calls for the defeat of the Islamic State. However, as indicated above, there are a host of players in Syria that will seek the territory formally held by the Islamic State. Will Trump address this challenge or after the defeat of the Islamic State in Syria will he withdraw all US forces? Withdrawing from Syria could have far greater consequences then Obama's misguided decision to leave Iraq. The United States cannot turn over territory lost by the Islamic State to Iran, to Russia, and equally problematic to the Al Qaeda in Syria. Is another extended conflict on the horizon in Syria? How will the Trump administration confront this issue? Then there is the next phase of the war on terrorism in Syria, confronting Al Qaeda in Syria. Privately, there is no doubt these are issues the Pentagon is already pondering. At issue, is President Trump prepared to make the political decision to engage Russia, Iran, Hezbollah, and Al Qaeda in Syria to prevent a Shiite crescent controlled by Tehran? In the final analysis, irrespective of the ruminations about the land-grab in Deir al-Zior, one thing is certain, as the Syrian portion of the caliphate collapsed, the Islamic State will live on to fight another day.[27]

President Trump's decision to withdraw most of the US forces from Syria induced an intense period of criticism. After the president announced the defeat of ISIS in Syria, Trump wanted to withdraw US forces immediately. The president's statement was not supported by senior commanders on the ground and by civilian or military leaders in the Pentagon which asserted the Islamic States' resurrection in the form of an insurgency remains a critical problem. One of the signature events connected with the crisis that erupted after Trump's decision to withdraw is the resignation of Secretary Mattis. The resignation produced another debate inside the Beltway and around the world. The discourse focused attention on how Mattis's departure exposed a major dilemma—there is one less senior advisor with authority to check President Trump's impulsive behavior.

THE NORTH KOREAN NIGHTMARE
AND THE CHANGING REALITY

Weeks after the dissipation of the crisis over North Korea's threat to launch an attack on the American territory of Guam, the rogue regime issued another destabilizing provocation. This time, the regime conducted a successful test of a hydrogen bomb. Not surprisingly, a new crisis unfolded.

In a subsequent statement, the regime issued another threat to the United States. Speaking at the UN-sponsored Conference on Disarmament, Han Tae-Song, the Democratic People's Republic of Korea's (DPRK) Ambassador to the United Nations in Geneva, provided details about the nuclear test and then issued this threat:

> I am proud of saying that just two days ago on the 3rd of September, DPRK successfully carried out a hydrogen bomb test for intercontinental ballistic rocket under its plan for building a strategic nuclear force. The recent self-defense measures by my country, DPRK, are a gift package addressed to none other than the US. The US will receive more gift packages from my country as long as it relies on reckless provocations and futile attempts to put pressure on the DPRK.[28]

In response to the hydrogen test, the Trump administration issued a new set of warnings. This time, however, the statements, particularly from President Trump, were more measured. Trump issued the following statement: "Military action would certainly be an option. We've had presidents for 25 years now, they've been talking . . . and the day after an agreement is reached, new work begins in North Korea" on its rogue nuclear weapons program, Trump said. "So, I would prefer not going the route of the military, but it's something certainly that could happen."[29]

On September 11, 2017, the Trump administration pushed for and received a new round of restrictive UN-led sanctions. The administration did not receive the complete ban on oil imports on North Korea it sought. Instead, the administration agreed to a cap on oil imports at the 2016 level. The administration did achieve unanimous Security Council support for a resolution that an administration official asserted prohibited up to "90 percent of North Korea's"[30] exports.

The rhetoric and counter-Kim Jung Un diplomatic response reached a new level during the opening of the General Assembly session at the United Nations. As anticipated, President Trump used the address to again claim North Korea's nuclear saber-rattling flouted international norms:

> No one has shown more contempt for other nations and for the well-being of their own people than the depraved regime in North Korea. It is responsible for the starvation deaths of millions of North Koreans, and for the imprisonment,

torture, killing, and oppression of countless more. . . . If this is not twisted enough, now North Korea's reckless pursuit of nuclear weapons and ballistic missiles threatens the entire world with unthinkable loss of human life. It is an outrage that some nations would not only trade with such a regime, but would arm, supply, and financially support a country that imperils the world with nuclear conflict. . . . It is time for North Korea to realize that the denuclearization is its only acceptable future. . . . It is time for all nations to work together to isolate the Kim regime until it ceases its hostile behavior.[31]

One day after the well-received address, and during a meeting with the leaders of Japan and South Korea, President Trump issued an executive order that increased the diplomatic pressure on the North Korean regime.[32] The new administration sanctions are aimed at "any state" that is trading with the Kim regime. Though not mentioned by name in the executive order, the sanctions were directed at China and Russia. On the significance of the new sanctions, President Trump acknowledged, "It is unacceptable that others financially support this criminal rogue regime"[33] and "tolerance for this disgraceful practice must end now."[34]

The Trump administration's tough rhetoric and US-led sanctions forced the government of China to initiate sanctions that were designed to alter the reckless path of the Kim regime. In response to the Trump administration's pressure, President Xi ordered China's Central Bank to end assistance to the North Korean regime. The Central Bank issued this statement to clarify their position: "Our bank is fulfilling our international obligations and implementing United Nations sanctions against North Korea. As such, we refuse to handle any individual loans connected to North Korea."[35]

Trump's "North Korea Nightmare" will continue until the administration ends the ongoing American reaction to threats from the rogue regime. That is, covering four US presidents, Bill Clinton, George W. Bush, Barack Obama, and now Donald Trump, North Korea incessantly forced the American government to react to their provocations. Imagine a rogue regime forcing the unquestioned superpower to react to their provocations for multiple decades.

One thing is certain, reversing the two-decade plus ability of the government of North Korea to force the United States into a reactionary mode will not be easy. If the administration fails to create a "package of options" to thwart the North Korean provocations, and place the regime on the defensive, then President Trump will have to confront a series of nightmares that will come in the form of "packages."

Well into the presidency of Donald Trump, the anti-establishment president exceeded the expectations of most foreign policy experts. Indeed, with the awkward and at times alarming controversial statements, there are those that anticipated a host of foreign policy blunders, setbacks, and perhaps even the misapplication of force. The peril associated with this reality is great and could possibly lead to a conflict. The opportunity is significant: end the nightmare and restore stability in the Korean Peninsula.

Most surprisingly, the diplomatic track (most specifically the stringent sanctions and the impact on the North Korean economy), along with the administration's hawkish "maximum pressure" approach, which includes a military option, produced a series of diplomatic openings.

The initial diplomatic opening occurred during the Winter Olympics which were held in Pyongchang in 2018. Most observers commented on the decline in tensions and the talks between the "two Koreas" on how to combine two separate entities that would "operate as one" on select teams. That said, the real diplomacy unfolded in other ways. The North Korean charm offensive captured headlines in the Western media outlets. At another level, the efforts of President Moon Jae-in of South Korea to push for talks between the North Korean leader and the American president represented the most significant breakthrough in the talks between the Korean entities. The final diplomatic initiative came in the form of an invitation from the North Korean leader Kim Jong Un who requested to meet President Trump to discuss "the denuclearization of the Korean Peninsula" during a summit in Singapore on June 12, 2018. In short order, President Trump accepted the invitation from Kim.

The summit did occur and in the final analysis many experts concluded that Trump is the decisive winner. It is important to begin with Kim's stature in the wake of the summit. The summit increased Kim's standing on the world stage. The very fact that he agreed to participate in the summit, met with the American president and agreed to a comprehensive statement that if implemented could lead to denuclearization also represents an accomplishment.

Why was Trump a winner? Critics overlooked the fact that it is the president's policy that forced North Korea to pursue diplomacy. That is, it was administration pressure and diplomacy that undermined the China-North Korea relationship, put the Xi government on notice that it could no longer flout international will, and continue to support the Kim regime without paying a heavy price. There is another significant aspect: there were many that asserted the president would unleash a war in the Korean Peninsula—thus far the president's actions have proven that his critics have been incorrect.

There is another important perspective. Some of the president's most ardent critics, those from the resistance, the never-Trumpers, and those from the foreign policy establishment, offered praise for the president in the wake of the summit in Singapore. This proved most interesting. Especially since many on the left argued the biggest winner of the Trump-Kim summit was none other then President Xi of China.

The most important winner is the prospect for a nuclear free Korean Peninsula. This point is captured in the following quote: Around the world,

"The deal between President Trump and North Korean leader Kim Jong Un was met by world leaders with optimism and praise for the prospect of denuclearization."[36]

What then are the prospects for denuclearization? It is a pipe dream to think that North Korea will negotiate away its deterrent without significant concessions from the United States, South Korea, and perhaps even China. Second, it is almost certain that Kim will adopt the all-too-familiar strategy of insisting that Pyongyang retain possession of peaceful civilian application of their nuclear capacity. The path to achieve this scenario was articulated this way:

> Odd as it might seem at first glance, the best way to do that is for the United States and South Korea to help North Korea convert its military nuclear and missile programs for civilian use rather than insisting on total denuclearization. Pyongyang will almost surely insist on maintaining civilian programs, because it has in the past stressed that these programs are its sovereign right, not one that Washington can choose to grant or withhold.[37]

Despite the positives that have been gained since the two summits, the Trump administration, with emphasis on the president and Secretary Pompeo, is entering a pivotal moment. Trump made the correct decision to walk away from the Hanoi summit after Kim demanded the United States lift "all sanctions." The president is now envisaging major pressure, one that can be summed up in this question: Can the administration broker a deal that implements a plan for denuclearization in the Peninsula and ensure that a future treaty is verifiable? The answer to this question will provide an important watershed in defining Trump's stewardship of American foreign policy in the region. For example, if President Trump is successful in obtaining a negotiated solution to the ever-evolving crises in the Korean Peninsula, there is little doubt that the American president will use the experience of the summits with the North Korean leader as practice for subsequent summits with Xi of China and Putin of Russia.

CHAOS IN THE MIDDLE EAST

The Middle East remains as chaotic as ever. A negotiated settlement between Israel and the Palestinian Authority is not likely to occur anytime soon. The administration's decision to formally open the US Embassy in Jerusalem further undermined the ability of the administration to reach a negotiated solution on the intractable Israeli-Palestinian dispute. Oddly, many experts argued that any presidential decision to open an embassy in Jerusalem would unleash violence across the region and threaten American interests in the region. Thus far, there is no evidence of any instability that is threatening to US interests in the region.

The Syrian civil war is on-going, and millions of civilians remain displaced, hundreds of thousands have been killed, Assad remains in power, and Russia and Iran retain their influence. There are several additional challenges. The Islamic States' caliphate dissipated; however, the transnational network morphed into an insurgency. In this insurgent capacity the Islamic States' resurrection is in full-swing. It is estimated there are between 20,000 and 30,000 ISIS fighters in Iraq and Syria. Equally troubling, other resurrections are occurring in Libya, Afghanistan, and beyond.

Within Syria in the wake of the president's decision to withdraw most of the US forces of the country, we are still awaiting word on which "allied entities" or coalition of regional states will assume the mantle of confronting ISIS in the country. Another significant issue is the future of the US-backed SDF. Is the Trump administration prepared to provide air support to protect its ally? Will US SOFs be used to assist the SDF in the event of a Turkish assault or will the president rely on direct diplomacy with the leader of Turkey? The president's decision to commit a force for stabilization in Syria is an important one, and one that will prevent a slaughter of the SDF.

In Iraq, the Islamic State can no longer refer to Mosul, the second largest city in the country, as a component of their caliphate. The process of rebuilding the country is underway, but Kurdistan's quest for a referendum to create an independent state threatens to create another period of instability and perhaps a civil war in Iraq. Thus far, the governments of Turkey and Iran have pledged to prevent the creation of an independent Kurdish state.

There are other illustrations of tumult in the region. One of the more conspicuous crises involves multiple Gulf states. The crisis involving Qatar and the Saudi-led Gulf states was already spiraling out of control in the wake of repeated warnings that Qatar end their financial support for Islamist terrorist organizations and refusal to terminate its relationship with Iran. However, the situation in the Gulf was exacerbated by President Trump who issued several tweets condemning Qatar, an ally of the United States.

Critics charged the president's ill-advised statements unnecessarily endangered a relationship with an ally which permits the United States to operate aircraft from the Al Udeid Air Base. Additionally, "The US Combined Air Operations Center is located there, providing command and control of US and allied air power throughout the region, especially over Iraq, Syria and Afghanistan."[38]

Thanks to former Secretary Tillerson's shuttle diplomacy, the chief American diplomat restored the US-Qatar alliance. One would hope that a vital lesson was learned: solve a dispute among allies, do not choose sides, and be aware of "strategic relationships," particularly those involving the use of a vital forward military base.

Following separate telephone conversations with the leaders of Saudi Arabia and Qatar, it appeared that a "dialogue" was in place that could be used to resolve the crisis. Subsequently, after the American presidential intervention, the Saudi and Qatari leaders spoke by phone and it appeared the tensions were subsiding. Oddly, it was the "terms of what they discussed that have created a new dispute."[39] Jon Campbell of the *Associated Press* provided further details about the fallout of the telephone conversation.

> The Saudi and Qatari leaders stressed the need to resolve this crisis by sitting down to the dialogue to ensure the unity and stability of Gulf nations, the *Qatar News Agency* account read. Saudi Arabia reacted angrily to the Qatari statement, issuing a second message saying Doha's statement did not have "any relevance to truth. This proves that the authority in Qatar is not serious in dialogue and continues its previous policies," the *SPA* said. "The Kingdom of Saudi Arabia declares that any dialogue or communication with the authority in Qatar shall be suspended until a clear statement explaining its position is made in public."[40]

The crisis continues unabated. At this point, the Trump administration is no longer willing to pursue any direct diplomatic intervention to resolve the dispute among American gulf allies. There are private US diplomatic activities that have not produced an end to hostilities among the parties to the dispute. The dispute is one that will linger for the foreseeable future.

The civil war and the equally troubling proxy war in Yemen collectively symbolized the instability that continues to haunt the region. The Iranian government, for example, supplies weapons and military advisers to their Houthi allies. The United States provides intelligence and weapons to the Saudi government which supports their Sunni-Yemeni allies. Underneath the radar of the proxy war in Yemen, AQAP, the Al Qaeda terrorist group in the country, quietly expanded their territorial reach and increased membership in their organization. In short, AQAP filled a power vacuum in the country. In response to this threat, the Trump administration made the decision to end many Obama-era created rules of engagement. The administration thereafter increased the number of special forces raids and drone strikes against the terrorist organization. Currently, there has been both a decline in the territory formally controlled by the AQAP and the organization has suffered heavy losses.

There is an issue that surfaced in the wake of the resignation of Mattis that may impact the future of hostilities in the country. Prior to his departure, Mattis privately worked with many regional partners to assist the UN in creating a ceasefire in December of 2018.[41] In Mattis's absence, the acting Secretary of Defense Patrick Shanahan appointed John Rood, the current number three individual in the Pentagon's civilian hierarchy, as the person charged with working with the UN to resurrect another ceasefire between the combatants. Unfortunately, Rood lacked the clout of Mattis, and many argue not having a more high-profile official leading the administration engagement in seeking a peaceful solution to the ongoing proxy war in Yemen[42] could result in unremitting hostilities.

Iran, a pivotal state, is by far the single-greatest threat to regional security. It is only a matter of time before Iran's quest for the bomb becomes a reality. Rest assured the Shiite Theocracy is monitoring the Trump administration's reaction to the provocations unleashed by North Korea and the subsequent diplomatic initiatives. In the meantime, the theocratic regime extended their influence in Iraq, Syria, Qatar, Yemen, and Lebanon. Put another way, the Iranian constructed Shiite Crescent continues to expand.

The government of Iran foments instability in other ways as well. It is a state-sponsor of terrorism, supporting Hezbollah, Hamas, the Houthis, and it supplies weapons and training to Iraqi-Shiites in the southern portion of the country and assists multiple groups in Afghanistan. The weapons supplied to the groups in Afghanistan and Iraq resulted in the death of hundreds of US military personnel in both countries. At issue, will Trump confront Iran, a country that continues to undermine US interests, and whose government has been in a state of war with the United States for over thirty years?[43] Will President Trump follow the path of previous presidents (from President Carter to President Obama) and "kick the can down the road"?

Trump made the decision to withdraw from the Iran nuclear deal. Is he prepared for the consequences? That is, Iran is attempting to use President Trump's decision to withdraw from the Obama administration brokered deal to drive a wedge between the United States and many of their key NATO allies. Thus far, EU states have openly warned the Trump administration that they are prepared to fight American sanctions aimed at undermining EU trade agreements with Iran. There are other potential issues on the horizon. For example, if Iran resumes full-scale nuclear testing designed to achieve weaponization, is the Trump administration prepared for a military solution to circumvent Iranian efforts to obtain a nuclear deterrent? Is the administration prepared for an Iranian response to American use of force? Is the administration prepared for a conflict with Iran? These are scenarios that the Pentagon is wrestling with. At issue, how real or likely is a military conflict between Washington and Tehran?

The Middle East, along with a host of problems in North Africa, are far too numerous for the Trump administration to tackle and resolve in one or perhaps two presidential terms. The president will have to receive extraordinary cooperation from regional and non-regional allies just to make a dent in resolving some of the issues outlined above.

THE RECKONING: TRUMP, RUSSIA, AND CHINA

Management of bilateral relationships remains an essential component of US foreign policy. Covering President Clinton, President Bush, President Obama, and now President Trump, bilateral relations with Russia and China continue to spiral out of control. Most interesting, each of the four post-Cold War presidential administrations have sought but have been unable to secure better relations with both Russia and China.

The three previous administrations made statements about the need for improved relations, but such efforts have ultimately ended in failure. President Clinton previously argued, "Nowhere is [US] . . . engagement more important than in our policies toward Russia. It presents the greatest security challenge for our generation and offers one of the greatest economic opportunities of our lifetime."[44] On China, President Clinton, in defense of constructive engagement, stated, "The emergence of a China as a power that is stable, open and non-aggressive . . . rather than a China turned inward and confrontational, is deeply in the interests of the American people."[45] Constructive engagement, said Clinton, represented "our best hope to secure our own interest and values and to advance China's."[46]

President Bush spoke of a relationship with Russia based on "friendship." In fact, Bush used that word to link China and Russia to a goal of productive bilateral relationships. During a foreign policy address in Simi Valley, California, Bush stated, "China and Russia, are powers in transition. . . . If they become America's friends, that friendship will steady the world. But if not, the peace we seek may not be found."[47]

Speaking before an audience at Moscow's New Economic School, President Obama articulated US-Russia relations this way: "America wants a strong, peaceful and prosperous Russia . . . on the fundamental issues that will shape this century, Americans and Russians share common interests that form a basis for cooperation. That is why I have called for a 'reset' in relations between the United States and Russia."[48] With respect to US-China relations, President Obama, offered this statement: "The relationship between the United States and China is the most important bilateral relationship of the 21st century" and "the United States welcomes the rise of China."[49] Beyond that President Obama offered no coherent statement on US policy with China.

Candidate Trump incessantly posed this question on the campaign trail, "Wouldn't it be nice if we got along with Russia?"[50] During the transition, President-Elect Trump issued this statement via Twitter: "Having a good relationship with Russia is a good thing, not a bad thing. . . . When I am President, Russia will respect us far more than they do now and both countries will, perhaps, work together to solve some of the many great and pressing problems and issues of the WORLD!"[51]

Once in office, with congressional hearings on Russian meddling in the presidential election and other investigations that examined whether Trump and campaign officials colluded with Moscow (not to mention the Mueller investigation which examined but did not believe there was evidence of collusion and punted on the issue of obstruction of justice), the president recognized productive relations with Russia are not likely for the foreseeable future. During his tenure as secretary of state, Tillerson provided a more declarative statement on the state of US-Russia relations: "There is a low level of trust between our two countries. The world's foremost two nuclear powers cannot have this kind of relationship."[52]

It is well understood that actions by Russia, whether in the form of invading Georgia or the annexation of Crimea, along with Putin's decision to overtly interfere in a US presidential election and the 2018 midterm elections combined with the decision to deploy aircraft and troops to Syria to demonstrate their support for the ruthless Assad regime, represent a few additional reasons that provide subsequent motivations behind the decline of US-Russia relations.

Similarly, the instigation of several crises (the Taiwan Straits and in the skies above Hainan Island), the continuous crises in the South China Seas, cyberattacks against the United States, burgeoning trade imbalance with the United States and now a trade war, are just a sample of the issues that negatively impact US-China relations.

That said, what is behind the failure to create new rules to govern the twin relationships? The answer to the query is that it has much to do with post-Cold War American arrogance and the failure of imagination. The post-Cold War arrogance is associated with two realities. On the first, the United States won the bipolar superpower conflict. In the post-Cold War period, the United States recognized that no state possessed the military power or capability to challenge the unrivaled American supremacy. Second, the arrogance itself is linked to the unrivaled US supremacy. That is, the post-Cold War period represented the "unipolar moment."[53] During this "era of supremacy" the United States represented "the only country with the military, diplomatic, political and economic assets to be a decisive player in any conflict in whatever part of the world it chooses."[54] Successive US administrations understood that with such capabilities, and as the last superpower, America represented "the center of world power."[55]

Accompanying the understandable American triumphalism in winning the Cold War is the unprecedented increase in the use of force. Lost among leaders during this period is that there is a noticeable decline in US-led diplomatic activity and an increased willingness to use force, particularly covering the years 1991–2017.[56] It is during this period that each of the post-Cold War American presidents obtained a false sense of security. That is, under the umbrella of its new status as the sole superpower, US leaders incorrectly and arrogantly assumed that Russia and China would accept the US-dominated post-Cold War world.

There are multiple issues that have not been addressed during this period. Most notably, American leaders never instituted rules to govern a new era without the Soviet Union and the superpower rivalry. There were rules that governed the Cold War epoch.[57] The rules were often agreed upon during the superpower summits that occurred during and in the wake of crises. However, a failure of imagination existed among US leaders to create rules to ensure its supremacy and the protection of the ever-increasing far-flung interests during the unipolar moment. Worse, covering the period 1991 through 2017, none of the three previous presidents understood the need to manage relations with Russia and China through a rules-based process. Thus, it should not come as a surprise that during the evolving ascendancy of Russia and China multiple crises arose, each testing American resolve and willingness to protect their interests. In each case, American presidents and their senior foreign policy advisers are concerned about "the rise" of the challengers and the threats they posed to US supremacy. In the absence of rules, the cycle continues.

To prevent "the reckoning"—a major conflict—between the United States and Russia or one involving the United States and China, as previously argued, President Trump is afforded an opportunity to do what his predecessors failed to do, create rules to govern two great power relationships. Time will tell if the president is up to the task. If Trump is up to the task a host of positive opportunities exist with Russia and China. Those benefits exist in the security and trade venues. If the president fails to secure new rules, he risks a downward trend in relations with Russia and China. The resulting peril could lead to potential conflicts that would further undermine already unproductive relationships and increase instability in an existing chaotic international order.

VARIABLES FOR ASSESSMENT OF TRUMP'S STEWARDSHIP OF US FOREIGN POLICY

There are multiple issues that will serve as additional variables that can be utilized to assess President Trump's stewardship of US foreign policy. Some of those variables include the following: (1) management of potential crises with rogue states (North Korea, Iran, Syria, and Venezuela); (2) the president's temperament and unpredictability; (3) international trade, particularly the trade war with China or the outcome of TTIP negotiations between the United States and the European Union; and (4) the restoration of American leadership.

MANAGEMENT OF POTENTIAL CRISES WITH ROGUE STATES

There are several rogue states and their actions (and Trump's management of them) that are critical variables in measuring the president's stewardship of US foreign policy. Among the rogue states, North Korea, Iran, and potentially even Venezuela are all potential flashpoints.

Due to the provocative missile tests and hydrogen bomb tests, North Korea represents a potential source of conflict. Given the rhetoric and threats from the leader of North Korea, President Trump countered "the Rocket Man is on a suicide mission for himself and for his regime."[58] Does this mean that a conflict is likely? This is a critical question, particularly since President Trump previously stated, "all military options are on the table."[59] The outcome of the management of the situation in the Korean Peninsula is an issue that will dominate the Trump administration. Similarly, the use of coercive diplomacy and perhaps a preemptive strike arguably in response to the North Korean nightmare represents one of the significant threats to security in the region and a major test of presidential leadership. The initial Trump-Kim summit provided momentum for a new relationship between the United States and North Korea. However, in the wake of the gathering there has been no significant progress toward denuclearization. Additional progress during the second summit in Hanoi in February 2019 was achieved. However, Kim's request for sanctions relief forced President Trump to end the summit after the North Korean leader refused to retract his demand. The planned signing ceremony never took place, but both sides agreed to continue talking.

Regarding Iran, President Trump argued the oil profits of the regime are now being used to "fund Hezbollah . . . [and] goes to shore up Bashar al-Assad's dictatorship [and] fuel Yemen's civil war. . . . It is time for the entire world to join us in demanding that Iran's government end its pursuit of death and destruction."[60] Trump's decision to terminate the Iranian nuclear deal and reinstall US sanctions met a campaign promise. Now the American president must manage the fallout. Thus far, the rhetoric between Washington and Tehran has increased but there is no indication that a conflict is imminent. There are multiple areas that represent critical barometers of the president's ability to manage a series of potential crises with Iran. Those areas include Iraq where the Trump administration seeks to curtail Iranian influence in the country. Syria is where Iran is expanding their influence (a direct confrontation is not likely given the withdrawal of most US forces). However, the US does have to worry about a potential Iranian-Israeli conflict if the hostilities expand beyond rockets and Israeli counterattacks.

The brutal Syrian regime is not presently a major issue on the Trump foreign policy agenda. Removing the Islamic State from the country is the top priority of the administration in that country. With the caliphate of ISIS destroyed, the administration will have to wrestle with several issues. The Islamic States' territory in Syria has been recaptured by the SDF and with the withdrawal of US forces underway, the Trump administration is confronting an ISIS insurgency, the need to protect their Kurdish ally, potentially the requirement to reduce Iranian influence in the country and prevent Turkey from attacking or potentially slaughtering the US-backed SDF. These and other issues indicate that this rogue state which is also failed state now and in the foreseeable future will remain a source of regional instability and potential threat to US interests in the region. How the Trump administration deals with Syria and the multiple internal threats will prove interesting.

Venezuela is another rogue state, and one that received significant administration focus since the final months of 2018. Venezuela was declared a rogue state under the tenure of President Hugo Chavez. Venezuela's alliances with Russia, Iran, the Cuban government, and the leftist communist entity Revolutionary Armed Forces of Columbia and the salient involvement in the conspicuous export of narcotics across the hemisphere made Chavez (and later Nicolas Maduro) an enemy of the United States and most countries in the Western hemisphere.

Several American presidents, George W. Bush and Barack Obama, denounced the shift to the left and Chavez's not so salient dalliance with the left, undermining stability in the region and incessantly denouncing the United States in public speeches. In addition, American leaders from Bush to Trump, have denounced Venezuela's shift to a socialist dictatorship, destruction of democracy in the country, and completing the destruction of the economy.

In a speech at the United Nations on September 19, 2017 President Trump warned the "situation is completely unacceptable." The president then spoke of the goal of his administration in dealing with this rogue entity: to assist the people of Venezuela in regaining "their freedom, recover their country, and restore democracy."[61] The fact that President Trump spoke of human rights, a willingness to fight for the resurrection of democracy in a country undermined those from the resistance and the never-Trumpers that repeatedly argued the president has surrendered US leadership in the struggle for the export and maintenance of democracy around the world.

There is little doubt that Trump's policy continued to unfold during the tenure of Nicolas Maduro, who supplanted Chavez after his death. In what has been described as the "refreshing foreign policy approach," the president "launched another remarkable diplomatic initiative that sets the United States on a refreshing new path of hemispheric relations."[62]

The Trump administration's approach and subsequent recognition of opposition leader Juan Guaido, who declared that he is the interim president, now has the backing of the majority of countries in the Organization of

American States (OAS) and the international community. The president warned that "everything is on the table," a reference to the notion that the introduction of American military forces is an option. Taken individually or collectively, it is clear the president is not afraid to challenge the rogue states, whether in the form of North Korea, Iran, or Venezuela. What remains unclear is whether there are opportunities to advance the administration's agenda or induce a period(s) of instability or peril.

TRUMP'S TEMPERAMENT AND UNPREDICTABILITY

Two character traits, temperament and unpredictability, represent twin issues that Republican presidential primary challengers and the Democratic presidential nominee Hillary Clinton used to undermine the candidacy of Trump. Many experts concluded that both characteristics could undermine Trump's foreign policy.

In a statement on the president's temperament, Derek Chollett, the executive vice president for security and defense policy at the German Marshall Fund of United States, asserted, "Donald Trump will enter the White House with less experience and more foreign policy uncertainties and contradictions than any incoming commander-in-chief in modern history. Trump will be a very different American leader: prickly, impulsive, unpredictable, and at times openly vindictive."[63]

As a candidate, Trump stated, "We must as a nation be more unpredictable. We are totally predictable. We tell everything. We're sending troops? We tell them."[64] Trump argued, in foreign policy, "We have to be unpredictable."[65] As president, unpredictability represented a double-edged sword. By not announcing key foreign policy decisions, the administration's counter-ISIS strategy, troop deployments, and key policy pronouncements, President Trump kept enemies and allies guessing. In the case of the enemies of the United States, unpredictability is replete with positive benefits, most notably ISIS and other transnational terrorist groups are afforded little time to adjust to the new American tactics. The dilemma for allies of the United States is that they feel they may not have a role in the administration strategy. Worse, some believe they are more likely to find out about Trump's administration strategy once the results of US military actions are unveiled through the media or subsequent administration press conferences.

As one would anticipate, there is criticism linked to the president's unpredictability. Michael Fuchs of *The Guardian* argued, "Donald Trump's doctrine of unpredictability has the world on edge."[66] In another example, British journalist Gideon Rachman asserted, "Donald Trump's unpredictability is destabilizing the world."[67]

Conversely, there are several individuals that argued Trump's unpredictability represented a critical variable which the president can use to his advantage. In a notable example, "During an interview with Bill O'Reilly back in January [of 2016], Trump was asked whether, as president, he might bomb Iran's nuclear facilities. Again, Trump responded with what's becoming one of his favorite words. "Bill, I'm gonna do what's right," he said. "I want to be unpredictable."[68] From another perspective, "There can often be a great advantage to doing the unexpected in politics."[69] There is little doubt Iran is questioning what they can and cannot get away with in the age of Trump.

The president's temperament and unpredictability will be easier to evaluate as more crises emerge. For now, both variables have tangible benefits and drawbacks. In the final analysis, the data will validate whether the positions of Secretary Clinton, the never-Trumpers, and the foreign policy establishment are correct that taken individually or collectively whether Trump's temperament and unpredictability are measures that confirm suspicions that undermine the president's leadership of foreign policy.

INTERNATIONAL TRADE

Throughout the presidential campaign, Trump made international trade a pivotal issue. As president, Trump already met a campaign pledge by signing an executive order withdrawing the United States from the TTP. The administration signed several trade agreements with China. There are other significant international trade issues that could serve as variables when evaluating the president's US foreign policy. Below the radar, the outcome of TTIP negotiations between the US and the European Union will provide another measure of the president's foreign economic policy.

From the beginning, progress on the TTIP negotiations "was delayed by public distrust."[70] That is, the "TTIP was a highly divisive issue even before Trump became president."[71] Since the end of the Obama administration, there was reported progress with TTIP negotiations. President Trump scuttled negotiations. Renegotiations took place but little progress toward agreement was made during talks in October 2018. A truce prevented a trade war between the United States and the EU. Oddly, "the US government trades more with the EU than China."[72] If the EU trade barriers are removed the administration argued the United States could significantly expand American exports. Yet, the Trump administration has not made the TTIP negotiations an administration priority. Is this a smart or bad strategy?

The renegotiations between the United States and South Korea resulted in an amended agreement. This agreement will not require congressional approval. Subsequently, President Trump concluded an agreement with Mexico and later Canada (USMCA) that once passed by the legislatures of the parties will supplant NAFTA. These agreements along with the US-EU trade agreement in July of 2018 are achievements for the president and the administration.

The outstanding issue is the trade war with China. There is little doubt this trade conflict could have short- and long-term consequences for trade between the parties of the dispute and potentially regional and international trade. The Xi government is the most likely party to "blink" in this dispute because they export far more goods to the United States than America does to China. There has been a pause in the dispute to allow for a negotiated settlement. Is an agreement possible during the "pause" or will another round (or two) of tariffs be required before a settlement is reached?

These and other potential agreements could significantly impact the American economy and US jobs. Given that Trump campaigned on improving the American position in international trade, expanding the GDP and creating American jobs, a negative outcome on US-China trade relations could derail a major component of the president's foreign policy agenda.

AMERICAN LEADERSHIP

A host of commentators argued that President Trump's foreign policy is undermining US leadership. From the conclusion of the 2016 election, most characterizations of US leadership under Trump have been decidedly negative. In an illustration of the point, with Trump not yet in office, many commentators pronounced "the era of American global leadership is over."[73] In an astonishing assessment, Ian Bremmer, the founder of the Eurasia Group, argued, "The new President will recite his lines carefully, smile broadly and change history. And American international leadership, a constant since 1945, will end with the presidential inauguration of Donald J. Trump on January 20, 2017."[74]

In a subsequent example, President Trump's decision to withdraw from the Paris Accord and TTP represent two cases where commentators asserted the president "surrendered US leadership."[75] These twin decisions by Trump produced the following assessment: "Mr. Trump has revolutionized our ideas of what the US stands for. We live in the world the US made. Now it is unmaking it. We cannot ignore that grim reality."[76]

There is one thing to say about the previous assessments, they will prove to be meaningless or perhaps correct. The reality thus far is that US leadership is in transition. That transition thus far is favorable toward President Trump. In the always chaotic Middle East, for example, President Trump's decision to launch several cruise missiles that targeted a Syrian base which unleashed a chemical weapon's attack against innocent civilians demonstrated President Trump is prepared to attack the regime of Assad even in the presence of Russian, Iranian, and Hezbollah's allies. Within Syria (among anti-Assad forces), in the region, and elsewhere around the world, the decision was well received.

There is little doubt that Israel recognizes and is a beneficiary of the restoration of American leadership under Trump. This is also true from the perspective of Saudi Arabia, following the creation of an Arab Coalition to confront radical Islamists in the region. The Trump administration's overt support for the Kingdom's quest to defeat Iran and their allies in Yemen and elsewhere in the region also assisted in the restoration of American leadership. There are those however that argue the Trump administration's relationship with Saudi Arabia in the wake of the murder of Jamal Khashoggi undermined American leadership.

In Afghanistan, President Trump's decision to order the use of the MOAB against Islamic State-K forces in the Khorasan Province caught the attention of the internationally community. The subsequent decision to deploy up to 3,500 US forces to the country signalled to the world at that moment in time that America will not abandon their allies. The subsequent decision to launch a subsequent strike at a Syrian chemical weapons facility, and the targeting of the infrastructure of the base, is another example of Trump's leadership. The point being the president spoke of "a red line"—Syrian use of chemical weapons against innocent civilians—that would prompt an American response. There are few leaders around the world at this point who will doubt this president's statement(s) on the administration's threat to use force.

In the end, there are positive examples of the restoration of American leadership. Still, it is important to state that there is considerable time available to evaluate the restoration of American leadership during the Trump presidency. That is, a host of unknown events could easily change the perception of American leadership at home and abroad. Rest assured, this is a critical variable in measuring President Trump's stewardship of US foreign policy.

There is another subset of variables that can assist in evaluating President Trump's foreign policy—the agenda. The president's agenda is one of sweeping change. At one level, the agenda endeavors to confront the Sino and Russo great power challenges. One query is critical in evaluating the twin relationships: In the absence of rules, can the president be successful in containing these twin threats?

The president's maximum pressure strategy against North Korea forced an end to Kim's nuclear tests and ended provocative threats to the United States, South Korea, and Japan. Through diplomacy, both Trump and Kim are in the midst of transition to a new relationship. However, in the wake of two summits the American president has been unable to work with Kim on building a path toward a framework for denuclearization and a path to a more cooperative relationship. The clock is ticking on Trump's patience. From another perspective, the president's reputation as a deal maker is on the line. An agreement, one with a framework for denuclearization, and one that includes verification, can preserve and advance the president's reputation.

The president revamped American counterterrorism strategy to meet a diverse set of threats. The Islamic States' caliphate has dissipated, now the American president must adapt US strategy to deal with an insurgency and a resurgence of ISIS in Iraq, Syria, and beyond. It has confronted many affiliates of Al Qaeda, most prominently Al Shabab in Somalia and AQAP in Yemen. However, the Trump administration must confront Al Qaeda central and Al Qaeda in Syria. The latter two terror threats "represent critical nodes" in evaluating the president's counterterrorism strategy. One thing is clear, the president has no doubt discovered there is a constant dilemma associated with presidential counterterrorism strategies: transnational terrorists are always adapting, introducing tactics of their own designed to circumvent US approaches. The Trump administration must be prepared to adapt as well. For students, scholars, and ordinary citizens at home and abroad, the president's counterterrorism strategy represents a major source of information in the evaluating Trump.

In the Middle East, the president invested significant political capital in Israel and Saudi Arabia. In both cases, President Trump is repairing relationships that declined considerably during the tenure of President Obama. As a first step in the improvement of relations between Israel and the United States, President Trump moved the American embassy from Tel Aviv to Jerusalem.

In the case of Saudi Arabia, President Trump proposed that the kingdom assume an active counterterrorism role against radical Islamic terrorism, Islamic extremism in the region, and act as a partner in containing Iran. The murder of Jamal Khashoggi, and the domestic and international fallout, is testing the administration's commitment to that relationship and to longstanding American human rights principles. These two relationships, and potentially a third, the revamping of the US-Egyptian relationship, represent critical pillars of the administration strategy in the always turbulent Middle East.

On the trade front, the Trump administration embarked on a two-pronged strategy. The initial pillar involves the renegotiation of agreements with trade partners that have proven disadvantageous to the United States and the American worker. The second pillar called for direct economic confrontation with a state (China) which has undermined international trade rules, employed cyber espionage, engaged in unfair trade practices, and instituted domestic policies that hampered US businesses operating in China. These and other misdeeds, have produced a staggering trade imbalance with the United States. Trump is engaged in a trade war with the Xi-led government which at the time of this writing is likely to produce a major trade agreement that will correct China's unfair advantages and ensure a more balanced trade relationship between Washington and Beijing. All of these are activities that are consistent with the Trump administration's foreign economic policy. The policy represents another variable in evaluating the president's foreign policy. Several questions are of interest. After renegotiations with multiple countries around the world, multiple new trade accords, did the American trade position improve? How many new jobs are associated with the president's strategy? Conversely, did the president's strategy negatively impact jobs for the American worker?

Another critical component of administration foreign policy is rebuilding "the depleted military." This slogan was constantly used during the campaign. The armed forces are being outfitted with new equipment, recruitment is improving, training is at levels consistent with readiness, and the president even created a new service, the Space Force. In short, the reconstruction of the military is well underway, but future increases in military spending will face stiff opposition from the Democrat-controlled House of Representatives. Consistent with the revamping of the military, President Trump cajoled US NATO allies into increased burdened sharing which is a reference to a two percent increase in Atlantic partner military spending. Among members of the anti-ISIS coalition, the president demanded that they increase their respective roles in the ongoing struggle against the Islamic State. There are several queries that provide a window into the success (or failure) of the president's rebuilding efforts. Did the president achieve the objective of expanding the force levels across the services? Is the reconstruction, and the administration's defense strategy, sufficient to meet the Sino-Russo threats? In the research and development area, will "future weapons systems" enter the inventory during the Trump administration or a subsequent administration? One of the successes of the Reagan defense build-up is the research and development efforts ultimately produced multiple weapons systems that entered service during and long after the president's tenure. Critics no doubt will evaluate Trump's build-up through a similar prism.

At the international level, President Trump is altering international frameworks that he argued hampered US leadership and power capabilities (in the political, economic, and military realms). Secretary Pompeo boldly proclaimed that President Trump is seeking a new world order[77] to resurrect and preserve US leadership and power capabilities. In addition, Pompeo asserted the new order is about the "prevention of war" and "achieves greater prosperity for all."[78] This aspect of administration effort embodies one of the most significant aspects of the president's foreign policy—America First.

President Trump promised sweeping changes in defense of American interests and in altering antiquated international frameworks that undermined US leadership. This study provides the reader with the agenda and other variables to begin the process of evaluating the most divisive epoch in US foreign policy and simultaneously one of the pivotal periods in American history.

NOTES

1. Remarks by the President and First Lady on the 70th Anniversary of the US Air Force. The White House, Office of the Press Secretary. Joint Base Andrews, Camp Springs, Maryland. September 15, 2017. https://www.whitehouse.gov/the-press-office/2017/09/15/remarks-president-and-first-lady-70th-anniversary-us-air-force. Accessed on February 12, 2019.
2. "Donald J. Trump Foreign Policy Speech." DonaldJTrump.com. April 27, 2016. https://www.donaldjtrump.com/press-releases/donald-j.-trump-foreign-policy-speech. Accessed on February 12, 2018.
3. Secretary of State Rex Tillerson. Remarks to US Department of State Employees, Dean Acheson Auditorium, Washington, DC, May 3, 2017. https://www.state.gov/secretary/remarks/2017/05/270620.htm. Accessed on February 12, 2019.
4. Ibid.
5. McMaster, H. R. and Cohn, Gary D., "America First Doesn't Mean America Alone," *Wall Street Journal*, May 30, 2017. https://www.wsj.com/articles/america-first-doesnt-mean-america-alone-1496187426. Accessed on February 12, 2019.
6. Raymond, Greg, Nasu, Hitoshi, Tan, See Seng, and McLaughlin, Rob, "Prospects for A "Rule-Based Global Order," Strategic and Defense Studies Centre, The Centre of Gravity Series Paper Number 34, 2017. http://bellschool.anu.edu.au/sites/default/files/uploads/2017-06/cog_34_global_rules_based_order.pdf. Accessed on February 12, 2019.
7. Friedman, George, "Donald Trump Has a Coherent, Radical Foreign Policy Doctrine," *Realclearworld.com*, January 20, 2017. http://www.realclearworld.com/articles/2017/01/20/Donaldtrumphasacoherentradicalforeignpolicydoctrine112180.html. Accessed on February 12, 2019.
8. Ibid.
9. O'Brien, Jason, "America First: Trump's New World Order Begins," *Independent*, January 21, 2017. http://www.independent.ie/world-news/north-america/us-election-2016/america-first-trumps-new-world-order-begins-35385919.html. Accessed on February 12, 2019.
10. Ibid.
11. Pindell, James, "With Paris decision, President Trump could unveil new world order" *Boston Globe*, June 1, 2017. https://www.bostonglobe.com/news/politics/2017/06/01/with-paris-decision-president-trump-could-unveil-new-world-order/GOVepNceoNVZB2RSBJp37L/story.html. Accessed on February 12, 2019.
12. Ibid.
13. Clare, Michael T., "Is Donald Trump Launching A New World Order?" *Huffington Post*, June 1, 2017. http://www.huffingtonpost.com/entry/is-donald-trump-launching-a-new-world-orderus593eb1e6e4b0c5a35ca1861f. Accessed on February 15, 2019.
14. Ibid.
15. Ibid.
16. Samuelson, Robert J., "The New World Order, 2017," *Washington Post*, January 1, 2017. https://www.washingtonpost.com/opinions/the-new-world-order/2017/01/01/fc54c3e6-ce9d-11e6-a747-d03044780a02story.html?utm_term=c560acecf002. Accessed on February 15, 2019.
17. Ibid.
18. The Goals of Donald J. Trump's Tax Plan. https://assets.donaldjtrump.com/trump-tax-reform.pdf. Accessed on February 15, 2019.
19. LaRocco, Lori Ann, "Wilbur Ross Says He's 'Open to Resuming' Talks on Mega-Trade Deal with Europe," *CNBC.com*, May 30, 2017. https://www.cnbc.com/2017/05/30/exclusive-wilbur-ross-says-hes-open-to-resuming-ttip-negotiations.html. Accessed on February 15, 2019.

20. Lynch, David and Paletta, Damian, "Trump's Fluid Approach to National and Economic Security is Leaving his Allies Baffled," *Washington Post*, May 28, 2018. https://www.washingtonpost.com/business/economy/trumps-fluid-approach-to-national-and-economic-security-is-leaving-his-allies-baffled/2018/05/28/b08c5908-5f95-11e8-9ee3-49d6d4814c4cstory.html?u tmterm=b9a123f26348. Accessed on February 18, 2019.

21. For more on the liberation of Tal Afar, see Alkhshali, Hamdi, Smith-Spark, Laura, and Tawfeeq, Mohammed, "Iraqi Prime Minister: Tal Afar 'Liberated' from ISIS," *CNN*, August 31, 2017. http://www.cnn.com/2017/08/31/middleeast/iraq-tal-afar-isis/index.html. Accessed on February 18, 2019.

22. Schmitt, Eric, "ISIS Reverts to Insurgent Roots to Pose Long-Term Threat, Study Says," *New York Times*, June 29, 2017. https://www.nytimes.com/2017/06/29/world/middleeast/isis-attacks-syria-iraq-study.html. Accessed on February 18, 2019.

23. Davis, John, "After Raqqa: The Islamic State Lives On," http://www.editor-in-chieftheglobalwaronterrorism.com/, July 30, 2017. http://www.editor-in-chieftheglobalwaronterrorism.com/raqqa-islamic-state-lives/. Accessed on February 18, 2019.

24. Warrick, Joby and Mekhennet, Souad, "Bin Laden's Son Steps into Father's Shoes as Al Qaeda Attempts a Comeback," *Washington Post*, May 27, 2017. https://www.washingtonpost.com/world/national-security/bin-ladens-son-steps-into-fathers-shoes-as-al-qaeda-attempts-a-comeback/2017/05/27/0c89ffc0-4198-11e7-9869-bac8b446820astory.html?utmterm=4a7f3127e508&wpisrc=nldraw&wpmm=1. Accessed on February 18, 2019.

25. Feaver, Peter and Brands, Hal, "Trump and Terrorism," *Foreign Affairs*, March/April 2017. https://www.foreignaffairs.com/articles/2017-02-13/trump-and-terrorism. Accessed on February 18, 2019.

26. Davis, John, "The Battle For Raqqa And Deir Al-Zour," http://www.editor-in-chieftheglobalwaronterrorism.com/, June 16, 2017. http://www.editor-in-chieftheglobalwaronterrorism.com/battle-raqqa-deir-al-zour/. Accessed on February 18, 2019.

27. See Davis, "After Raqqa: The Islamic State Lives On."

28. "North Korea: 'More Gift Packages' Coming for the US," *Al Jazeera*, September 5, 2017. http://www.aljazeera.com/news/2017/09/north-korea-gift-packages-coming-170905134153254.html. Accessed on February 18, 2019.

29. Gearan, Anne and Rauhala, Emily, "Trump Renews Threat of Force Against North Korea Over Nuclear Weapons," *Washington Post*, September 7, 2017. https://www.washingtonpost.com/world/china-will-back-fresh-un-sanctions-on-north-korea-over-nuclear-tests/2017/09/07/afc6ac52-93a9-11e7-b9bc-b2f7903bab0dstory.html?utmterm=d885191131f6. Accessed on February 19, 2019.

30. As quoted in Morello, Carol, "UN Agrees to Toughest-Ever Sanctions Against North Korea," *Washington Post*, September 11, 2017. https://www.washingtonpost.com/world/in-the-push-for-oil-embargo-on-north-korea-china-is-reluctant-to-sign-off/2017/09/11/3a5b56fe-96e5-11e7-a5273573bd073e02story.html?utmterm=4f5823d9949f&wpisrc=alalert-COMBO-world%252Bnatioion&wpmk=1. Accessed February 18, 2019.

31. Remarks by President Trump to the 72nd Session of the United Nations General Assembly. United Nations, New York, New York. The White House, Office of the Press Secretary. September 19, 2017. https://www.whitehouse.gov/the-press-office/2017/09/19/remarks-president-trump-72nd-session-united-nations-general-assembly. Accessed on February 18, 2019.

32. Presidential Executive Order on Imposing Additional Sanctions with Respect to North Korea. September 21, 2017. The White House, Office of the Press Secretary. https://www.whitehouse.gov/the-press-office/2017/09/21/presidential-executive-order-imposing-additional-sanctions-respect-north. Accessed on February 18, 2019.

33. Ibid.

34. Ibid.

35. "China's Central Bank Tells Banks to Stop Doing Business with North Korea: Sources," *Reuters*, September 21, 2017. https://www.reuters.com/article/us-northkorea-missiles-banks-china/chinas-central-bank-tells-banks-to-stop-doing-business-with-north-korea-sources-idUSKCN1BW1DL. Accessed on February 18, 2019.

36. Steinbuch, Yaron, "World Leaders Come Out in Support of Historic Trump-Kim Summit," *New York Post*, June 12, 2018. https://nypost.com/2018/06/12/world-leaders-come-out-in-support-of-historic-trump-kim-summit/. Accessed on February 19, 2019.

37. Hecker, Siegfried S., Serbin, Elliot A., and Carlin, Robert L., "Total Denuclearization Is an Unattainable Goal. Here's How to Reduce the North Korean Threat," *Foreign Policy*, June 25, 2018. https://foreignpolicy.com/2018/06/25/total-denuclearization-is-an-unattainable-goal-heres-how-to-reduce-the-north-korean-threat/#39;sPicksOC. Accessed on February 19, 2019.

38. McCarthy, Niall, "Where US Troops Are in the Middle East," *Forbes*, June 7, 2017. https://www.forbes.com/sites/niallmccarthy/2017/06/07/qatar-hosts-largest-u-s-base-in-the-middle-east-despite-allegedly-funding-extremism-infographic/#27f95763dc7e. Accessed on February 19, 2019.

39. Campbell, Jon, "Qatari, Saudi Leaders Have a Phone Call, Start New Dispute," *Associated Press*, September 10, 2017. http://www.msn.com/en-us/news/world/qatari-saudi-leaders-have-a-phone-call-start-new-dispute/ar-AArwNjt?li=AA4Zpp&ocid=spartanntp. Accessed on February 19, 2019.

40. Ibid.

41. Detsch, Jack, "Mattis Departure Risks US Policy Void as Yemen Pact Falls Apart," *Al Monitor*, January 28, 2019. www.al-monitor.com/pulse/originals/2019/01mattis-departure-risks-policy-void-yemen-pact.html?utm_camapign=20190129&utm_source=sailthru&utm_medium=email&utm_term=Daily%20Newsletter. Accessed on February 19, 2019.

42. Ibid.

43. For more details on the US-Iranian Cold War, See Crist, David, *The Twilight War: The Secret History of America's Thirty-Year Conflict with Iran* (New York: Penguin Books, 2012).

44. Remarks to the American Society of Newspaper Editors in Annapolis, Maryland. William J. Clinton, April 1, 1993. The American Presidency Project. http://www.presidency.ucsb.edu/ws/?pid=46392. Accessed on February 19, 2019.

45. "Clinton Defends 'Constructive Engagement' of China," *CNN*, October 24, 1997. http://www.cnn.com/ALLPOLITICS/1997/10/24/clinton.china/. Accessed on February 19, 2019.

46. Ibid.

47. Crowley, Candy, "Bush Lays Out Foreign Policy Vision," *CNN*, November 19, 1999. http://edition.cnn.com/ALLPOLITICS/stories/1999/11/19/bush.speech/. Accessed on February 19, 2019.

48. Weaver, Matthew, "Barack Obama Calls for 'Reset' in US-Russia Relations," *The Guardian*, 2009. https://www.theguardian.com/world/2009/jul/07/barack-obama-russia-moscow-speech. Accessed on February 20, 2019.

49. Li, Cheng, "Assessing US-China Relations Under the Obama Administration," Brookings.edu August 30, 2016. https://www.brookings.edu/opinions/assessing-u-s-china-relations-under-the-obama-administration/. Accessed on February 20, 2019.

50. Collinson, Stephen and Diamond, Jeremy, "The Good, Bad and Ugly of Warmer US-Russia Relations," *CNN*, December 14, 2016. http://www.cnn.com/2016/12/14/politics/russia-us-trump-reset-pros-cons/index.html. Accessed on February 20, 2019.

51. Shelbourne, Mallory, "Trump: Only Stupid People Don't Want A Good Relationship with Russia," *The Hill*, January 7, 2017. http://thehill.com/homenews/administration/313164-trump-only-stupid-people-dont-want-a-good-relationship-with-russia. Accessed on February 20, 2019.

52. Collinson, Stephen, "Trump's Hope for Good Relations with Russia in the Deep Freeze," *CNN*, April 12, 2017. http://www.cnn.com/2017/04/12/politics/russia-trump-putin-cold-war/index.html. Accessed on February 20, 2019.

53. Krauthammer, Charles, "The Unipolar Moment," *Foreign Affairs*, America and the World (1990/1991), pp. 23–33.

54. Ibid.

55. Ibid.

56. It should be noted that the use of force accelerated again following the events on September 11, 2001.

57. For an illustration of the "some of the rules" that were erected during the Cold War, see Jackson, Patrick, "What the Real Cold War Meant," *BBC News*, July 18, 2007. http://news.bbc.co.uk/2/hi/europe/6902345.stm. Accessed on February 20, 2019.

58. Remarks by President Trump to the 72nd Session of the United Nations General Assembly.

59. Green, Miranda, "Trump: Kim Jong Un a 'Madman' Who 'Will be Tested Like Never Before,'" *CNN*, September 22, 2017. http://www.cnn.com/2017/09/22/politics/donald-trump-north-korea-tweet/index.html. Accessed on February 20, 2019.

60. Ibid.

61. Full Transcript of Trump's Speech at UNGA. New York, September 2017. https://qz.com/1081446/unga-2017-donald-trump-full-vide0-and-transcript-at-united-nations-general-assembly/. Accessed on February 21, 2019.

62. See, Malcolm, Andrew, "Trump's Venezuela Approach Refreshing Foreign Policy Posture," *Miami Herald*, February 5, 2019. https://www.miamiherald.com/article22519360.html. Accessed on February 21, 2019.

63. Chollett, Derek, "As Trump's Foreign Policy Emerges, Watch His Temperament in Washington," *Defense One*, January 4, 2017. http://www.defenseone.com/ideas/2017/01/how-trumps-behavior-washington-will-harm-us-policy-abroad/134348/. Accessed on February 22, 2019.

64. Gallo, William, "Trump Embraces Unpredictability as Foreign Policy Strategy," *Voice of America*. November 25, 2016. https://www.voanews.com/a/trump-foreign-policy-unpredictability/3610582.html. Accessed on February 22, 2019.

65. Ibid.

66. Fuchs, Michael, "Donald Trump's Doctrine of Unpredictability has the World on Edge," *The Guardian*, February 13, 2017. https://www.theguardian.com/commentisfree/2017/feb/13/donald-trumps-doctrine-unpredictability-world-edge. Accessed on February 22, 2019.

67. Rachman, Gideon, "Donald Trump's Unpredictability is Destabilizing the World." *Financial Times*, May 22, 2017. https://www.ft.com/content/b56c7c9c-3ecf-11e7-82b6-896b95f30f58. Accessed on February 22, 2019.

68. Alderman, Mark and Schweitzer, Howard, "Donald Trump's Incoherent Positions Are Part of His Master Plan," *Fortune*, May 13, 2016. http://fortune.com/2016/05/13/donald-trump-policies-unpredictability/. Accessed on February 22, 2019.

69. Ibid.

70. Vincenti, Daniela, "EU, US to Set Up Joint Task Force to Make Progress on Trade in Trump Era," Euractive.com, May 26, 2017. https://www.euractiv.com/section/economy-jobs/news/eu-us-to-set-up-joint-workforce-to-make-progress-on-trade-in-trump-era/. Accessed on February 22, 2019.

71. Ibid.

72. Amadea, Kimberly, "Transatlantic Trade Investment Partnership-Advantages, Disadvantages, Opportunities, Obstacles and Next Steps," TheBalance.com, November 18, 2018. https://www.thebalance.com/transatlantic-trade-and-investment-partnership-ttip-3305582. Accessed on February 22, 2019.

73. Bremmer, Ian, "The Era of American Global Leadership is Over. Here's What Comes Next," *Time*, December 19, 2016. http://time.com/4606071/american-global-leadership-is-over/. Accessed on February 22, 2019.

74. Ibid.

75. See Wolf, Martin, "Donald Trump and the Surrendering of US Leadership." *Financial Times*, May 30, 2017. https://www.ft.com/content/f0b9fba6-4241-11e7-9d56-25f963e998b2. Accessed on February 23, 2019

76. Ibid.

77. Borger, Julian, "Trump is Building a New Liberal World Order, Says Pompeo," *The Guardian.com*, December 4, 2018. https://www.theguardian.com/us-news/2018/dec/04/us-president-donald-trump-is-building-a-new-liberal-world-order-says-mike-pompeo. Accessed on February 23, 2019.

78. Ibid.

Bibliography

Abrams, Elliott. "The Trump National Security Strategy," Council on Foreign Relations, Blog Post, December 26, 2017. Accessed on January 3, 2019. https://cfr.org/blog/-trump-national-security-strategy.

"A Crossroads in Our Country's History," New Hampshire State Legislative Office Building. December 10, 1991. Buchanan for President. http://www.4president.org/speeches/buchanan1992announcement.htm.

Address to the Nation on Defense and National Security, March 23, 1983. https://reaganlibrary.archives.gov/archives/speeches/1983/32383d.htm.

"After the Deal: A New Iran Strategy." The Department of State. May 28, 2018. https://www.state.gov/secretary/remarks/2018/05/28230.htm.

Ahmed, Salman and Bick, Alexander, "Trump's National Security Strategy: A New Brand of Mercantilism?" *Carnegie Endowment for International Peace*, August 17, 2017. http://carnegieendowment.org/2017/08/17/trump-s-national-security-strategy-new-brand-of-mercantilism-pub-72816.

Alderman, Mark and Schweitzer, Howard, "Donald Trump's Incoherent Positions Are Part of His Master Plan," *Fortune*, May 13, 2016. http://fortune.com/2016/05/13/donald-trump-policies-unpredictability/.

Alkhshali, Hamdi, Smith-Spark, Laura, and Tawfeeq, Mohammed, "Iraqi Prime Minister: Tal Afar 'Liberated' from ISIS," *CNN*, August 31, 2017. http://www.cnn.com/2017/08/31/middleeast/iraq-tal-afar-isis/index.html.

Amadea, Kimberly, "Transatlantic Trade Investment Partnership-Advantages, Disadvantages, Opportunities, Obstacles and Next Steps," TheBalance.com, November 18, 2018. https://www.thebalance.com/transatlantic-trade-and-investment-partnership-ttip-3305382.

America First-Beginning a New Chapter of American Greatness, Office of Management and Budget. The White House, https://www.whitehouse.gov/sites/whitehouse.gov/files/omb/budget/fy2018/2018_blueprint.pdf.

America First Foreign Policy. President Donald J. Trump, The White House. January 20, 2017. https://www.whitehouse.gov/america-first-foreign-policy.

American Foreign Economic Policy. American History Oxford Research Encyclopedia. http://americanhistory.oxfordre.com/view/10.1093/acrefore/9780199329175.001.0001/acrefore-9780199329175-e-52.

Araral, Eduaro, "US-China Relations: A Game of Strategic Reassurance," *Foreign Affairs*, August 7, 2017. https://www.foreignaffairs.com/sponsored/us-china-relations-game-strategic-reassurance.

Bibliography

Astore, William J., "What Does an 'America-First' Foreign Policy Actually Mean?" *The Nation*, April 13, 2017. https://www.thenation.com/article/what-does-an-america-first-foreign-policy-actually-mean/.

"At Pentagon, Trump Declares His Aim of 'Rebuilding' The Military," NPR.org, January 27, 2017. http://www.npr.org/sections/thetwo-way/2017/01/27/511970907/trump-heads-to-the-pentagon-with-an-eye-on-the-war-against-isis.

Auslin, Michael, "Logic, But No Guarantees for Trump's Foreign Policy," *National Review*, February 21, 2017. http://www.nationalreview.com/corner/445100/donald-trump-foreign-policy-logic-worldview.

Bacon, Kevin and Weisgerber, Marcus, "New Tactics, Quicker Decisions Are Helping to 'Annihilate' ISIS, Pentagon Says," DefenseOne.com, May 19, 2017. http://www.defenseone.com/threats/2017/05/new-tactics-quicker-decisions-are-helping-annihilate-isis-pentagonsays/138024/.

Baker, Peter, "Trump Abandons Trans-Pacific Partnership, Obama's Signature Trade Deal," *New York Times*, January 23, 2017. https://www.nytimes.com/2017/01/23/us/politics/tpp-trump-trade-nafta.html?_r=0.

Baker, Peter, "Trump Signs New Trade Deal with Canada and Mexico After Bitter Negotiations," *New York Times*, November 30, 2018. https://www.nytimes.com/2018/11/30/world/americas/trump-trudeau-canada-mexico.html.

Baker, Peter, "Trump Recertifies Iran Nuclear Deal, But Only Reluctantly," *New York Times*, July 17, 2017. https://www.nytimes.com/2017/07/17/us/politics/trump-iran-nuclear-deal-recertify.html.

Baker, Peter, "An Embassy in Jerusalem? Trump Promises, But So Did Predecessors," *New York Times*, November 18, 2016. https://www.nytimes.com/2016/11/19/world/middleeast/jerusalem-us-embassy-trump.html.

Barfield, Claude and Levy, Philip I., "In Search of an Obama Trade Policy," American Enterprise Institute (AEI) August 5, 2009. https://www.aei.org/publication/in-search-of-an-obama-trade-policy/.

Baron, Kevin, "The 'Nightmare Scenario' Has Happened and You're to Blame," *Defense One*, December 21, 2018. https://www.defenseone.com/politics/2018/12/nightmare-scenario-has-happened-and-youre-blame/153748/.

Beckwith, Ryan Teague, "Read Hillary Clinton's and Donald Trump's Remarks at A Military Forum." *Time*, September 7, 2016. http://time.com/4483355/commander-chief-forum-clinton-trump-intrepid/.

Beggin, Riley, "Trump Administration Will Review Iran Nuclear Deal Despite Compliance," *ABCnews.go.com*, April 21, 2017. http://abcnews.go.com/Politics/trump-administration-review-iran-nuclear-deal-compliance/story?id=46890406.

Begley, Sarah, "Read Donald Trump's Speech to AIPAC," *Time*, March 21, 2016. http://time.com/4267058/donald-trump-aipac-speech-transcript/.

Bender, Bryan and Johnson, Eliana, "Trump's Campaign Pledges Face Collision in Afghanistan," *Politico*, May 9, 2017. http://www.politico.com/story/2017/05/09/trump-afghanistan-troops-taliban-238179.

Bendix, Aria, "Rex Tillerson Spells Out US Foreign Policy," *The Atlantic*, May 3, 2017. https://www.theatlantic.com/news/archive/2017/05/rex-tillerson-america-first-foreign-policy/525309/.

Bengali, Hashank and Sahi, Aoun, "Pakistan Finds Itself on the Defensive in Trump's Afghan War Strategy," *LA Times*, August 22, 2017. http://www.latimes.com/world/asia/la-fg-afghanistan-trump-reaction-20170822-story.html.

Bergsten, C. Fred, "Foreign Economic Policy for the Next President," *Foreign Affairs*, March/April 2004. http://www.mafhoum.com/press7/185E19.htm.

Bergsten, C. Fred, "Competitive Liberalization and Global Free Trade: A Vision for the Early 21st Century," Peterson Institute for International Economics (PIIE) Working Paper 96-15. January 1996. https://piie.com/publications/working-papers/competitive-liberalization-and-global-free-trade-vision-early-21st.

Bergsten, C. Fred, Chapter 1, "A New Foreign Economic Policy of the United States," Peterson Institute for Economics. https://piie.com/publications/chapterspreview/3802/1iie3802.pdf.

Bierman, Noah and Lauter, David, "In UN Speech, Trump Defines his Foreign Policy Doctrine as Sovereignty for Major Powers," *LA Times*, http://www.latimes.com/politics/la-na-pol-trump-un-analysis-20170919-story.html.

Binnendijk, Hans and Courtney, William, "Can Trump Make a Deal with Putin"? *USNews.com*, December 1, 2016. https://www.usnews.com/opinion/world-report/articles/2016-12-01/how-donald-trump-could-normalize-relations-with-russia-and-vladimir-putin.

Blair, Dennis, "Don't Let Washington's Toxic Partisanship Infect Foreign Policy, Too," *The Hill*, April 18, 2018. https://thehill.com/blog/ongress-blog/foreign-policy/383635-dont-let-washingtons-toxic-partisanship-infect-foreign.

Boje Forsby, Andreas, "US-China Relations Under Trump: Partners or Rivals?" *Danish Institute for International Studies* (DIIS), June 19, 2017. https://www.diis.dk/en/event/us-china-relations-trump-partners-or-rivals.

Boje Forsby, Andreas, "Donald Trump and US-China Relations: Putting America First Could China the Edge," *Danish Institute for International Studies* (DIIS), *DIIS Policy Brief*, November 2016. http://pure.diis.dk/ws/files/691386/US_Chinese_relations_WEB.pdf.

Boot, Max, "Donald Trump's Pivot Through Asia," *ForeignPolicy.com*, December 27, 2016. http://foreignpolicy.com/2016/12/27/the-pivot-to-asia-obama-trump/.

Borger, Julian, "Trump is Building a New Liberal World Order, Says Pompeo," The Guardian.com, December 4, 2018. https://www.theguardian.com/us-news/2018/dec/04/us-president-donald-trump-is-building-a-new-liberal-world-order-says-mike-pompeo.

Boulos, Nabih, "Trump's Speech Draws Mixed Reaction, Including Plenty of Anger, In the Muslim World," *LA Times*, May 22, 2017. http://www.latimes.com/world/la-fg-trump-muslim-react-20170521-story.html.

Bradner, Eric and Wright, David, "Trump Says Putin is 'Not Going to go Into Ukraine,' Despite Crimea," *CNN*, July 31, 2016. http://www.cnn.com/2016/07/31/politics/donald-trump-russia-ukraine-crimea-putin/index.html.

Brand, Hal, *American Grand Strategy in the Age of Trump* (Brookings Institution Press, 2018).

Bremmer, Ian, "The Era of American Global Leadership is Over. Here's What Comes Next," *Time*, December 19, 2016. http://time.com/4606071/american-global-leadership-is-over/.

Brendan, McGarry, "Trump Surges to Become Next Commander-in-Chief," Military.com, November 9, 2016. http://www.military.com/daily-news/2016/11/09/trump-surges-become-next-commander-chief.html.

Brunstrum, David and Lambert, Lisa, "Trump Renegotiating 'Rough' US Trade Deal with South Korea," *Fox Business*, June 30, 2017. http://www.foxbusiness.com/politics/2017/06/30/trump-renegotiating-rough-us-trade-deal-with-south-korea.html.

Burns, Robert, and Baldor, Lolita C., "Pentagon Presenting Counter-ISIS Plan to White House," *Military Times*, February 27, 2017. http://www.militarytimes.com/articles/new-anti-isis-strategy-may-mean-deeper-us-involvement-in-syria.

Byman, Daniel, "Takeaways from the Trump administration's New Counterterrorism Strategy," Brookings, October 5, 2018. https://www.brookings.edu/blog/order-from-choas/2018/10/05/takeaways-from-the-trump-administrations-new-counterterrorism-strategy/.

By Team Fix, "5th Republican Debate Transcript, Annotated: Who Said What and What it Meant," *Washington Post*, December 15, 2015. https://www.washingtonpost.com/news/the-fix/wp/2015/12/15/who-said-what-and-what-it-meant-the-fifth-gop-debate-annotated/?utm_term=341106972edf.

Calamur, Krishnadev, "A Short History of 'America First,'" *The Atlantic*, January 21, 2017. https://www.theatlantic.com/politics/archive/2017/01/trump-america-first/514037/.

Campbell, Charlie, "Donald Trump Angers China with Historic Phone Call to Taiwan's President," *Time*, December 2, 2016. http://time.com/4589641/donald-trump-china-taiwan-call/.

Campbell, Jon, "Qatari, Saudi Leaders Have a Phone Call, Start New Dispute," *Associated Press*, September 10, 2017. http://www.msn.com/en-us/news/world/qatari-saudi-leaders-have-a-phone-call-start-new-dispute/ar-AArwNjt?li=AA4Zpp&ocid=spartanntp.

Carlstrom, Greg, "Donald Trump Playacts Peace in the Middle East," *Foreign Policy*, May 23, 2017. http://foreignpolicy.com/2017/05/23/donald-trump-playacts-peace-in-the-middle-east/.

Carson, Joseph G., "National Defense: is Another Spending Boom on the Horizon?" Allianceberstein.com, February 9, 2017. https://alliancebernstein.com/library/national-defense-is-another-spending-boom-on-the-horizon.htm.

Cassidy, John, "Donald Trump's New World Disorder," *The New Yorker*, January 24, 2017.http://www.newyorker.com/news/john-cassidy/donald-trumps-new-world-disorder.

Cavas, Christopher P. and Gould, Joe, "Top Trump Military Advisers Detail GOP Candidate's Defense Plan," *Defense News*, October 30, 2016. http://www.defensenews.com/articles/trump-defense-plan-detailed.

Chase-Lubitz, Jesse, "NAFTA Talks Off to a Rocky Start," *Foreign Policy*, August 16, 2017. http://foreignpolicy.com/2017/08/16/nafta-talks-off-to-a-rocky-start/?utmsource=Sailthru&utmmedium=email&utm_campaign=edpix%208-16&utm_term=%2AEditors%20Picks.

Cheng Li, "Assessing US-China Relations Under the Obama Administration," Brookings.edu August 30, 2016. https://www.brookings.edu/opinions/assessing-u-s-china-relations-under-the-obama-administration/.

"China's Central Bank Tells Banks to Stop Doing Business with North Korea: Sources," *Reuters*, September 21, 2017. https://www.reuters.com/article/us-northkorea-missiles-banks-china/chinas-central-bank-tells-banks-to-stop-doing-business-with-north-korea-sources-idUSKCN1BW1DL.

Choi, David, "After Multiple Deployments, US Special Forces May Have 'Mortgaged the Future,'" *Business Insider*, May 3, 2017. http://www.businessinsider.com/special-forces-groups-problems-2017-5.

Chollett, Derek, "As Trump's Foreign Policy Emerges, Watch His Temperament in Washington," *Defense One*, January 4, 2017. http://www.defenseone.com/ideas/2017/01/how-trumps-behavior-washington-will-harm-us-policy-abroad/134348/.

"Clinton Defends 'Constructive Engagement' of China," *CNN*, October 24, 1997. http://www.cnn.com/ALLPOLITICS/1997/10/24/clinton.china/.

Cohen, Stephen D., *The Making of United States International Economic Policy-Principles, Problems, and Proposals for Reform, 5th Edition* (New York: Praeger, 2000).

Cohen, Zachary and Liptak, Kevin, "Tillerson: Trump, Putin: Reach Syria Ceasefire Agreement," *CNN*, July 8, 2017. http://www.cnn.com/2017/07/07/politics/syria-ceasefire-us-russia-tillerson/index.html.

Cohen, Zachary, "Trump Proposes $54 Billion Defense Spending Hike," *CNN*, March 16, 2016. http://www.cnn.com/2017/03/16/politics/donald-trump-defense-budget-blueprint/index.html.

Collinson, Stephen, "Trump's Hope for Good Relations with Russia in the Deep Freeze," *CNN*, April 12, 2017. http://www.cnn.com/2017/04/12/politics/russia-trump-putin-cold-war/index.html.

Collinson, Stephen and Diamond, Jeremy, "The Good, Bad and Ugly of Warmer US-Russia Relations," *CNN*, December 14, 2016. http://www.cnn.com/2016/12/14/politics/russia-us-trump-reset-pros-cons/index.html.

Colvin, Jill, "10 Moments from Trumps Iowa," CNSNews.com, November 14, 2015. http://www.cnsnews.com/news/article/10-moments-trumps-iowa-speech.

Cook, Lorne, "NATO Chief Says Allies to Join Anti-ISIS Coalition," Military.com, May 25, 2017. http://www.military.com/daily-news/2017/05/25/nato-chief-says-allies-join-anti-isis-coalition.html.

Cooper, Helene, "In a Flash, US Military Policy Turns Inward and Echoes Across the Globe," *New York Times*, December 21, 2018. https://www.nytimes.com/2018/12/21/us/politics/trump-military-syria-mattis-afghanistan.html.

Cordesman, Anthony, "Trump on Russia: His Strategy Documents vs. His Meeting with Putin," *Center for Strategic International Studies*, July 17, 2018. https//www.csis.org/analysis/trump-russia=his-strategy-documents-vs-his-meeting-putinhtml.

Cordesman, Anthony, "Trump on National Security: Calling for More Spending is Not Enough," Center for Strategic and International Studies (CSIS), March 2, 2017. https://csis-prod.s3amazonaws.com/s3fs-public/publication/170302_Trump-National-Security-full.pdf?X3z74rLdloZBP_rmDvdX_0h84_lj7Et1.

Cordesman, Anthony, "The Wrong Presidential Memorandum on Defeating ISIS and an Uncertain Memorandum on Rebuilding the US Military," The Center for Strategic and International Studies (CSIS), February 2, 2017. https://www.csis.org/analysis/wrong-presidential-memorandum-defeating-isis-and-uncertain-memorandum-rebuilding-us.

"Counterterrorism Pitfalls: What the US Fight Against ISIS and Al Qaeda Should Avoid," International Crisis Group, Special Report Number 3, Middle East and North Africa March 22, 2017. https://www.crisisgroup.org/middle-east-north-africa/gulf-and-arabian-peninsula/iraq/003-counter-terrorism-pitfalls-what-us-fight-against-isis-and-al-qaeda-should-avoid.

Crist, David, *The Twilight War: The Secret History of America's Thirty-Year Conflict with Iran* (New York: Penguin Books, 2012).

Crowley, Candy, "Bush Lays Out Foreign Policy Vision," *CNN*, November 19, 1999. http://edition.cnn.com/ALLPOLITICS/stories/1999/11/19/bush.speech/.

Crowley, Michael, "Trump Fails to Impress Foreign Policy Experts," *Politico*, April 27, 2016. http://www.politico.com/story/2016/04/donald-trump-foreign-policy-speech-reaction-222544.

Crowley, Michael, "Foreign Policy Experts Fret Over Trump's America First Approach," *Politico*, January 20, 2017. http://www.politico.com/story/2017/01/2017-trump-inauguration-foreign-policy-reaction-233924.

Danvers, William, "US and Russia Relations Under Trump and Putin," Center for American Progress, December 14, 2016. https://www.americanprogress.org/issues/security/reports/2016/12/14/295001/u-s-and-russia-relations-under-trump-and-putin/.

Davis, John, "The Islamic State's Resurrection in Iraq and Syria," editor-in-chieftheglobalwaronterrorism.com, September 26, 2018. http://www.editor-in-chieftheglobal waronterrorism.com/the-islamic-states-resurrection-in-iraq-and-syria/.

Davis, John, "Obama, Trump, and Bush's Counterterrorism Infrastructure," editor-in-chieftheglobalwaronterrorism.com, January 23, 2017. http://www.editor-in-chieftheglobalwaronterrorism.com/blog/obama-trump-bushs-counterterorism-infrastructure/.

Davis, John, "Partnerships and the War on Terrorism," editor-in-chieftheglobalwaronterrorism.com, February 28, 2017. http://www.editor-in-chieftheglobalwaronterrorism.com/partnerships-war-terrorism/.

Davis, John, "Diplomacy and the War on Terrorism," editor-in-chieftheglobalwaronterrorism.com, May 15, 2017. http://www.editor-in-chieftheglobalwaronterrorism.com/diplomacy-war-terrorism/.

Davis, John, "After Raqqa: The Islamic State Lives On," http://www.editor-in-chieftheglobalwaronterrorism.com. July 30, 2017. http://www.editor-in-chieftheglobalwaronterrorism.com/raqqa-islamic-state-lives/.

Delaney, Robert, "Mike Pompeo Promises US Will Meet China's Strategies with 'Strong and Vigorous Response,'" *South China Morning Post*, October 18, 2018. https://www.scmp.com/news/china/diplomacy/article/2170463/mike-pompeo-promises-us-will-meet-chinas-strategies-strong-and.

Department of Defense Press Briefing by Secretary Mattis, General Dunford and Special Envoy McGurk on the Campaign to Defeat ISIS in the Pentagon Press Briefing Room, News Transcript. US Department of Defense. May 19, 2017. https://www.defense.gov/News/Transcripts/Transcript-View/Article/1188225/department-of-defense-press-briefing-by-secretary-mattis-general-dunford-and-sp/.

"Document: SECDEF James Mattis' Pentagon Budget Guidance," USNI.org, February 1, 2017. https://news.usni.org/2017/02/01/document-defense-secretary-james-mattis-budget-guidance. Joint Regional Strategy-Middle East and North Africa. Department of State, Washington, DC, August 23, 2018.

Destler, I. M., Chapter 11 "'First, Do No Harm' Foreign Economic Policy Making Under Barack Obama," School of Public Policy, Center for International and Security Studies (CISS) at Maryland, 2011. http://cissmdev.devcloud.acquia-ites.com/sites/default/files/papers/first_do_no_harmdestler.pdf.

Detsch, Jack, "Mattis Departure Risks US Policy Void as Yemen Pact Falls Apart," *Al Monitor*, January 28, 2019. www.al-monitor.com/pulse/originals/2019/01mattis-departure-risks-poli-

cy-void-yemen-pact.html?utm_camapign=20190129&utm_source=sailthru&utm_medium=email&utm_term=Daily%20Newsletter.
DeYoung, Karen and Ryan, Missy, "Trump Administration Weighs Deeper Involvement in Yemen War," *Washington Post*, March 17, 2017. https://www.washingtonpost.com/world/national-security/trump-administration-weighs-deeper-involvement-in-yemen-war/2017/03/26/b81eecd8-0e49-11e7-9d5a-a83e627dc120story.html?utmterm=151d14b3dc55.
Diamond, Jeremy, "Trump Slams Globalization, Promises to Upend Economic Status Quo," *CNN*, June 28, 2016. http://www.cnn.com/2016/06/28/politics/donald-trump-speech-pennsylvania-economy/index.html.
Diamond, Jeremy, "Trump Calls for Military Spending Increase," *CNN*, September 6, 2016. http://www.cnn.com/2016/09/06/politics/donald-trump-defense-spending-sequester/index.html.
Dionne, E. J., "Trump shows 'America First' is Utterly Incoherent," *Washington Post*, September 20, 2017. https://www.washingtonpost.com/opinions/trump-shows-america-first-is-utterly-incoherent/2017/09/20/05462002-9e42-11e7-8ea1-ed975285475e_story.html?utm_term=8a3529269ca4.
Dolan, Chris and Rosati, Jerel, "US Foreign Economic Policy and the Significance of the National Economic Council," *International Studies Perspectives* (2006) 7, pp. 102–123. http://people.cas.sc.edu/rosati/documents/dolanrosati.NEC.pdf.
Donald J. Trump Address: Declaring American Economic Independence. Monessen, Pennsylvania, June 28, 2016. https://www.donaldjtrump.com/press-releases/donald-j.-trump-addresses-re-declaring-our-american-independence.
Donald Trump on Foreign Policy—On The Issues. 2016. www.ontheissues.org/2016/DonaldTrumpForeignPolicy.htm.
Donald J. Trump Foreign Policy Speech. DonaldJtrump.com. April 27, 2016. http://www.donaldjtrump.com/press-releases/donald-j.-trump-foreign-policy-speech.
Donald Trump on Foreign Policy, HugeDomains.com. http://www.ontheissues.org/2012/DonaldTrumpForeignPolicy.htm.
"Donald Trump on his Foreign Policy Strategy," *Fox News*, April 29, 2016. http://www.foxnews.com/transcript/2016/04/29/donald-trump-on-his-foreign-policy-strategy.html.
Donald Trump's Speech on Trade, *Time*, June 28, 2016. http://time.com/4386335/donald-trump-trade-speech-transcript/.
"Donald Trump's Victory Raises Questions in China," *Fortune* (Reuters), November 9, 2016. http://fortune.com/2016/11/09/donald-trump-win-china/.
Donnan, Shannon, "Trump Administration Hails US-China Trade Deal," *Financial Times*, May 12, 2017. https://www.ft.com/content/9a5ee6b8-36c0-11e7-bce4-9023f8c0fd2e.
Doshi, Rush, "Trump's China Policy: A Tale of Two Extremes," *National Interest*, April 7, 2017. http://nationalinterest.org/feature/trump-must-choose-between-hard-line-china-strategy-soft-20002.
Dreyfuss, Richard, "Obama's Afghan Dilemma," *The Nation*, December 2, 2008. https://www.thenation.com/article/obamas-afghan-dilemma/.
Earle, Geoff, "Trump Sends Dollar Plunging as He Says He Wants Interest Rates Kept Low-And Won't Be Calling China 'Currency Manipulator,'" *Daily Mail*, http://www.dailymail.co.uk/news/article-4406584/Trump-sends-dollar-plunging-comments-currency.html.
"Executive Order 13551—Blocking Property of Certain Persons with Respect to North Korea," Obamawhitehouse.gov, August 30, 2010. https://obamawhitehouse.archives.gov/the-press-office/2010/08/30/executive-order-president-blocking-property-certain-persons-with-respect.
Exum, Andrew, "Donald Trump Will Defeat ISIS," *The Atlantic*, February 17, 2017. https://www.theatlantic.com/international/archive/2017/02/donald-trump-will-defeat-isis/517062/.
Exum, Andrew, "What's Really at Stake for America in Yemen's Conflict," *The Atlantic*, April 14, 2017. https://www.theatlantic.com/international/archive/2017/04/yemen-trump-aqap/522957/.

Faiola, Anthony, "'The Germans Are Bad, Very Bad': Trump's Alleged Slight Generates Confusion, Backlash," *Washington Post*, May 26, 2017. https://www.washingtonpost.com/world/trumps-alleged-slight-against-germans-generates-confusion-backlash/2017/05/26/0325255a-4219-11e7-b29f-f40ffced2ddbstory.html?utm_term=39c574e03a14.

Farivar, Masood, "Trump Pledges War on Radical Islam," *Small Wars Journal* (Voice of America), January 18, 2017. http://smallwarsjournal.com/blog/trump-pledges-war-on-radical-islamic-terrorism.

Fattahi, Kambiz, "The Rising Risk of Showdown Between Trump and Iran," *BBC*, February 21, 2017. http://www.bbc.com/news/world-middle-east-38961027.

Feaver, Peter, "Five Takeaways from Trump's National Security Strategy," *Foreign Policy*, December 18, 2017. https://foreignpolicy.com/2017/12/18/five-takaways-from-trumps-national-security-strategy/.

Feaver, Peter and Brands, Hal, "Trump and Terrorism," *Foreign Affairs*, March/April 2017. https://www.foreignaffairs.com/articles/2017-02-13/trump-and-terrorism.

Feffer, John, "The Myth of Trump's Alternative Worldview," *Foreign Policy in Focus (FPIS)*, August 3, 2016. http://fpif.org/myth-trumps-alternative-worldview/.

Feickert, Andrew, "US Special Operations Forces (SOF): Background and Issues for Congress," *Congressional Research Service* (CRS Report), January 17, 2017. https://fas.org/sgp/crs/natsec/RS21048.pdf.

Finch, Asa and Kesling, Ben, "US Forces Attack Al Qaeda in Yemen," *Wall Street Journal*, May 23, 2017. https://www.wsj.com/articles/u-s-forces-attack-al-qaeda-in-yemen-1495531409.

Finn, Tom, "US, Qatar Sign Agreement on Combating Terrorism Financing," Theglobeandmail.com, July 11, 2017. https://www.theglobeandmail.com/news/world/us-politics/us-qatar-sign-agreement-on-combating-terrorism-financing/article35654060/.

Fisher, Max, "What Is Donald Trump's Foreign Policy?" *New York Times*, November 11, 2016. https://www.nytimes.com/2016/11/12/world/what-is-donald-trumps-foreign-policy.html.

Freidan, Jeff, "Sectoral Conflict and Foreign Economic Policy, 1914–1940," *International Organization*, No. 42. 1 (Winter 1988). http://pages.ucsd.edu/~jlbroz/Courses/POLI142B/syllabus/friedensector.pdf.

French, David, "Trump and Clinton—Unfit to be Commander-in-Chief," *National Review*, September 6, 2016. http://www.nationalreview.com/article/439848/foreign-policy-donald-trump-hillary-clinton-unfit-be-commander-chief.

Friedman, George, "Donald Trump Has a Coherent, Radical Foreign Policy Doctrine," *Realclearworld.com*, January 20, 2017. http://www.realclearworld.com/articles/2017/01/20/donald_trump_has_a_coherent_radical_foreign_policy_doctrine_112180.html.

Froman, Ambassador Michael, "Trade, Growth, and Jobs: US Trade Policy in the Obama Administration," Washington International Trade Associate (WITA), February 28, 2017. http://americastradepolicy.com/trade-growth-and-jobs-u-s-trade-policy-in-the-obama-administration/#.WZjMmIWcHIU.

Fuchs, Michael, "Donald Trump's Doctrine of Unpredictability has the World on Edge," *The Guardian*, February 13, 2017. https://www.theguardian.com/commentisfree/2017/feb/13/donald-trumps-doctrine-unpredictability-world-edge.

Fujii, George, "ISSF Policy Roundtable 1-9: US-China Relations and the Trump Administration," *ISSFforum.org*, May 17, 2017. https://networks.h-net.org/node/28443/discussions/179828/issf-policy-roundtable-1-9-us-china-relations-and-trump.

Full Rush Transcript: Donald Trump, Milwaukee Republican Presidential Town Hall. *CNN* March 29, 2016. http://cnnpressroom.blogs.cnn.com/2016/03/29/full-rush-transcript-donald-trump-cnn-milwaukee-republican-presidential-town-hall/.

Full Text: Donald Trump's Speech on Fighting Terrorism. *Politico*, August 15, 2016. http://www.politico.com/story/2016/08/donald-trump-terrorism-speech-227025.

Full Transcript of Trump's Speech at UNGA. New York, September 2017. https://qz.com/1081446/unga-2017-donald-trump-full-vide0-and-transcript-at-united-nations-general-assembly/.

Gallo, William, "Trump Embraces Unpredictability as Foreign Policy Strategy," *Voice of America*. November 25, 2016. https://www.voanews.com/a/trump-foreign-policy-unpredictability/3610582.html.

Garamone, Jim, "Trump Calls for 12-Carrier Navy, Promises Rebuilt Military," Defense.gov, March 2, 2017. https://www.defense.gov/News/Article/Article/1100952/trump-calls-for-12-carrier-navy-promises-rebuilt-military/.

Garamone, Jim, "Mattis Issues Budget Guidance, Say's 2017 Submission Will Rise," *Defense One*, February 1, 2017. www.army.mil/article/181718/mattis_issues_budget_guidance_says_fiscal2017_submission_will_rise.

Gardner, Frank, "Trump Urges Muslim Leaders to Lead Fight Against Radicalization," BBC.com, March 22, 2017. http://www.bbc.com/news/world-us-canada-39989548.

Gardner, Hall, *World War Trump: The Risks of America's New Nationalism* (New York: Prometheus Books, March 2018).

Gass, Nick, Trump: "We Can't Continue to Allow China to Rape Our Country," *Politico*, May 2, 2016. www.politico.com/blogs/2016-gop/2016/05/trump-china-rape-america-222689.

Gearan, Anne and Eglash, Ruth, "Trump's Decision to Open Jerusalem Embassy Complicates Promise to Seek Middle East Peace," *Washington Post*, May 12, 2018. https://www.washingtonpost.com/politics/trumps-decision-to-open-jerusalem-embassy-complicates-promise-to-seek-peace-in-the-region/2018/05/12/86113024-5557-11e8-9c91-7dab596e8252story.html?utmterm=5530b2db0184.

Gearan, Anne and Rauhala, Emily, "Trump Renews Threat of Force Against North Korea Over Nuclear Weapons," *Washington Post*, September 7, 2017. https://www.washingtonpost.com/world/china-will-back-fresh-un-sanctions-on-north-korea-over-nuclear-tests/2017/09/07/afc6ac52-93a9-11e7-b9bc-b2f7903bab0dstory.html?utmterm=d885191131f6.

Geltzer, Joshua A., "Trump's Counterterrorism is Relief," *The Atlantic*, October 4, 2018. https://www.theatlantic.com/internationalachive/2018/10/trump-counterterrorism-strategy/572170/.

Gibbons-Neff, Thomas, "US Troops are on the Ground in Yemen for Offensive Against Al-Qaeda Militants," *Washington Post*, August 4, 2017. https://www.washingtonpost.com/news/checkpoint/wp/2017/08/04/u-s-troops-are-on-the-ground-in-yemen-for-offensive-against-al-qaeda-militants/?utmterm=390bbb341d87.

Gillespie, Patrick, "Trump Administration Seeks to Renegotiate South Korean Trade Deal," *CNN Money*, July 13, 2017. http://money.cnn.com/2017/07/12/news/economy/trump-renegotiate-trade-deal-south-korea/index.html.

Glasser, Susan B., "Why the Middle East Hated Obama But Loves Trump," *Politico*, July 31, 2017. http://www.politico.com/magazine/story/2017/07/31/donald-trump-middle-east-barack-obama-215441.

Gordon, Michael, "US Lays Out Demands for New Iran Deal," *Wall Street Journal*, May 21, 2018. https://www.wsj.com/articles/mike-pompeo-lays-out-next-steps-on-iran-1526909126.

Graham, David, "Trump: Middle East Peace Is 'Not as Difficult as People Have Thought,'" *The Atlantic*, May 3, 2017. https://www.theatlantic.com/international/archive/2017/05/trump-middle-east-peace-is-not-as-difficult-as-people-have-thought/525267/.

Graham, Thomas, "Toward a New Equilibrium in US-Russian Relations," *National Interest*, February 1, 2017. http://nationalinterest.org/feature/toward-new-equilibrium-us-russian-relations-19281?page=2.

Grait, Jonathon, "Trump to Ask Generals, Who Know Less Than Trump, for Plan to Defeat ISIS," *New York Magazine*, September 7, 2016. http://nymag.com/daily/intelligencer/2016/09/trump-isis-plan-devised-by-generals-who-dont-know-much.html.

Green, Miranda, "Trump: Kim Jong Un a 'Madman' Who 'Will be Tested Like Never Before,'" *CNN*, September 22, 2017. http://www.cnn.com/2017/09/22/politics/donald-trump-north-korea-tweet/index.html.

Greenberg, Jon, "Trump Touts Plan to Defeat ISIS," *Politifact*, February 28, 2017. http://www.politifact.com/truth-o-meter/promises/trumpometer/promise/1375/develop-plan-defeat-isis-30-days/.

Griffin, Jennifer and Tomlinson, Lucas, "Trump Foreign Policy: American Military Increasingly Involved in Yemen Civil War," *Fox News*, June 29, 2017. http://www.foxnews.com/politics/2017/06/29/trump-foreign-policy-american-military-increasingly-involved-in-yemen-civil-war.html.

Haas, Lawrence J., "Trump's Troubling Retreat," *US News & World Report*, January 24, 2017. https://www.usnews.com/opinion/world-report/articles/2017-01-24/trumps-america-first-foreign-policy-will-hurt-real-americans.

Haberman, Maggie, "Trump Mollifies Lindsey Graham on Troop Withdrawal from Syria," *New York Times*, December 30, 2018. https://www.nytimes.com/2018/12/30/us/politics/linsey-graham-syria-trump.html.

Hadar, Leon, "The Limits of Trump's Transactional Foreign Policy," *National Interest*, January 2, 2017. https://nationalinterest.org/feature/the-limits-trumps-transactional-foreign-policy-18898.

Haffe, Greg, "The Battle to Define An 'America First' Foreign Policy Divides the Trump White House," *Washington Post*, March 18, 2017. https://www.washingtonpost.com/world/national-security/the-battle-to-define-an-america-first-foreign-policy-divides-the-trump-white-house/2017/03/18/d436acf2-09b3-11e7-93dc-0f9bdd74ed1story.html?utm_term=a76c8fe58ee1.

Harris, Bryan and Manson, Katrina, "North Korea Backs Away from Guam Strike," *Financial Times*, August 15, 2017. https://www.ft.com/content/2de5c7ce-815f-11e7-a4ce-15b2513cb3ff.

Hartmann, Margaret, "I Would Not Allow People to Come in From Terrorist Nations. I Would Do Extreme Vetting," *New York Magazine*, July 15, 2016. http://nymag.com/daily/intelligencer/2016/07/trump-nice.html.

Hayden, Michael V., *The Assault on Intelligence: American National Security in an Age of Lies* (New York: Penguin Press, 2018).

Haynes, Danielle, "Trump Puts 'America First' in Manufacturing, Trade Speech," UPI.com, July 17, 2017. https://www.upi.com/Trump-puts-America-first-in-manufacturing-trade-speech/2081500317847/.

Hecker, Siegfried S., Serbin, Elliot A., and Carlin, Robert L., "Total Denuclearization Is an Unattainable Goal. Here's How to Reduce the North Korean Threat," *Foreign Policy*, June 25, 2018.https://foreignpolicy.com/2018/06/25/total-denuclearization-is-an-unattainable-goal-heres-how-to-reduce-the-north-korean-threat/#39;sPicksOC.

Hendrickson, John, "The Roots of Trump's Economic Policy," *American Conservative*, May 31, 2017. http://www.theamericanconservative.com/articles/the-roots-of-trumps-economic-policy/.

Hendrickson, John, "President Coolidge's Economics Lesson," Coolidgefoundation.org, August 8, 2014. https://coolidgefoundation.org/blog/president-coolidges-economics-lesson/.

Henley, John, "Angela Merkel: EU Cannot Completely Rely on US and Britain Anymore," *The Guardian*, May 28, 2017. https://www.theguardian.com/world/2017/may/28/merkel-says-eu-cannot-completely-rely-on-us-and-britain-any-more-g7-talks.

Hennigan, W. J., "Donald Trump's Latest Idea Could Lead to an Arms Race," Time.com, January 17, 2019. https://time.com/5506284/donald-trump-nuclear-weapons-missile-defense/.

Henniger, W. J., "US Special Operations Forces Face Growing Demands and Increased Risks," *LA Times*, May 26, 2017. http://www.latimes.com/nation/la-na-special-operations-20170525-story.html.

Hensch, Mark, "Saudi King: Trump Visit a 'Turning Point,'" *The Hill*, May 22, 2017. http://thehill.com/homenews/administration/334615-saudi-king-trump-visit-a-turning-point.

Herb, Jeremy, "Senate Sends Russia Sanctions to Trump's Desk," *CNN*, July 27, 2017. http://www.cnn.com/2017/07/27/politics/russian-sanctions-passes-senate/index.html.

Higgins, Sean, "US, Mexico and Canada, Conclude 2nd Round of NAFTA Talks," *Washington Examiner*, September 5, 2017. http://www.washingtonexaminer.com/us-mexico-canada-conclude-2nd-round-of-nafta-talks/article/2633462.

"Hillary Clinton Hammers 'Dangerous' Donald Trump After Vladimir Putin Praise," *Agence France-Presse*, September 9, 2016. http://www.ndtv.com/world-news/hillary-clinton-hammers-dangerous-donald-trump-after-vladimir-putin-praise-1456436.

Hirschfield Davis, Julie and Schmitt, Eric, "Senate Votes to End Aid for Yemen Fight Over Khashoggi Killing and Saudi's War Aims, *New York Times*, December 13, 2018. https://www.nytimes.com/2018/12/13/us/politics/yemen-saudi-war-pompeo-mattis.html.

Hoffman, Frank, "President Trump's Defense Budget: Just a Down Payment," FPRI.org, March 7, 2017. http://www.css.ethz.ch/content/dam/ethz/special-interest/gess/cis/center-for-securities-studies/resources/docs/FPRI-President%20Trump%27s%20Defense%20Budget%20Just%20a%20Down%20Payment.pdf.

Holland, Steve, "Saudi King Agrees in Call with Trump to Support Syria, Yemen Safe Zones: White House," *Reuters*, January 29, 2017. http://www.reuters.com/article/us-usa-trump-saudi-idUSKBN15D14L.

Hsu, Sara, "China Wary of President-Elect Donald Trump," *Forbes*, November 11, 2016. https://www.forbes.com/sites/sarahsu/2016/11/23/china-wary-of-president-elect-donald-trump/#7116a5a7202b.

Huggler, Jason, "Donald Trump's Middle East Policy is 'Completely Wrong,' Says Germany," *The Telegraph*, June 7, 2017. http://www.telegraph.co.uk/news/2017/06/07/donald-trumps-middle-east-policy-completely-wrong-says-germany/.

Hyman, Gerald F., "Trump's New Afghanistan Strategy Isn't Really a Strategy," *National Interest*, November 17, 2017. https://nationalinterest.org/feature/trumps-new-afghanistan-strategy-isnt-really-strategy-23258. Access on April 13, 2018.

Hussein, Ibish, "Trump's Plan for Middle East Peace Could Actually Work," *Foreign Policy*, May 25, 2017. http://foreignpolicy.com/2017/05/25/trumps-plan-for-middle-east-peace-could-actually-work/.

Insinna, Valeria, "Trump's New Space Force to Reside Under Department of the Air Force," DefenseNews.com, December 20, 2018. https://www.defensenews.com/space/2018/12/20/trumps-new-space-force-to-reside-under-department-of-the-air-force/.

Jackson, Patrick, "What the Real Cold War Meant," *BBC News*, July 18, 2007. http://news.bbc.co.uk/2/hi/europe/6902345.stm.

Jacobs, Ben, "The Donald Trump Doctrine: Assad is Bad but US must Stop Nation-Building," *The Guardian*, October 13, 2015. https://www.theguardian.com/us-news/2015/oct/13/donald-trump-foreign-policy-doctrine-nation-building.

Johnson, Jenna and DelReal, Jose A., "Trump Vows to 'Utterly Destroy ISIS'—But He Won't Say How," *Washington Post*, September 24, 2016. https://www.washingtonpost.com/politics/trump-vows-to-utterly-destroy-isis-but-he-wont-say-how/2016/09/24/911c6a74-7ffc-11e6-8d0cfb6c00c90481story.html?utm_term=2d6db1dc165b.

Joint Statement Between the Kingdom of Saudi Arabia and the United States of America. The White House, Office of the Press Secretary. May 23, 2017. https://www.whitehouse.gov/the-press-office/2017/05/23/joint-statement-between-kingdom-saudi-arabia-and-united-states-america.

Kaczynski, Andrew, Massie, Chris, and McDermott, Nathan, "80 Times Trump Talked About Putin," *CNN*, http://www.cnn.com/interactive/2017/03/politics/trump-putin-russia-timeline/.

Kahl, Colin and Brands, Hal, "Trump's Grand Strategic Train Wreck," *Foreign Policy*, January 31, 2017. https://foreignpolicy.com/2017/01/31/trumps-grand-strategic-train-wreck/.

Kalb, Marvin, "Afghan Policy—Suddenly in Serious Trouble," Brookings.edu, February 28, 2012. https://brookings.edu/blog/up-front/2012/28/afghan-policy-suddenly-in-serious-trouble/.

Katib, Lina, "Only the US Can Prevent More Clashes Between Israel and Iran in Syria," *The Guardian*, https://www.theguardian.com/commentisfree/2018/may/11/us-israel-iran-clashes-syria-war.

Katzman, Kenneth, Kerr, Paul K., and Heitshusen, Valerie, "US Decision to Cease Implementing the Iran Nuclear Agreement," *Congressional Research Service*, May 9, 2018. https://fas.org/sgp/crs/nuke/R44942.pdf.

Key Asia Issues in the 2016 Presidential Campaign, *Asia Matters for America*, http://www.asiamattersforamerica.org/asia/key-asia-issues-in-the-2016-campaign.

Kheel, Rebecca, "McCain: Trump Defense Budget Not Enough for 'World on Fire,'" *The Hill*, February 27, 2017. http://thehill.com/policy/defense/321374-mccain-trump-defense-budget-not-enough-for-world-on-fire.

Kheel, Rebecca, "Trump Signals Deeper US Involvement in Yemen," *The Hill*, March 1, 2017. http://thehill.com/policy/defense/326767-trump-signals-deeper-us-involvement-in-yemen.

Kiley, Sam, "How Will the Trump Presidency Affect World Affairs?" *Sky News*, 2017. http://news.sky.com/story/how-will-the-trump-presidency-affect-world-affairs-10732131.

Krauthammer, Charles, "The Unipolar Moment," *Foreign Affairs, America and the World* (1990/1991), pp. 23–33.

Laderman, Charlie, *Donald Trump: The Making of a World View* (Endeavor Media, 2017).

Lamothe, Dan, "Critics Say Trump's Proposed Military Buildup Isn't Happening. Wait Until 2019, the Pentagon Says," *Washington Post*, May 23, 2017. https://www.washingtonpost.com/news/checkpoint/wp/2017/05/23/critics-say-trumps-proposed-military-buildup-isnt-happening-wait-until-2019-the-pentagon-says/?utm-term=42371b9803f3.

Landay, Jonathan and Strobel, Warren, "Exclusive: Trump Counterterrorism Strategy Urges Allies to Do More," *Reuters*, May 5, 2017. http://www.reuters.com/article/us-usa-extremism-idUSKBN1812AN.

Lander, Mark, "Airstrike in Syria Overshadows Meeting Between Trump and Xi," *New York Times*, April 7, 2017. https://www.nytimes.com/2017/04/07/us/politics/airstrike-in-syria-overshadows-meeting-between-trump-and-xi.html?mcubz=2&r=0.

Lander, Mark and Forsythe, Michael, "Trump Tells Xi Jinping US Will Honor 'One China' Policy," *New York Times*, February 9, 2017. https://www.nytimes.com/2017/02/09/world/asia/donald-trump-china-xi-jinping-letter.html?mcubz=2&_r=0.

Lander, Mark and Sanger, David, "Obama Says He Told Putin: 'Cut It Out' on Hacking," *New York Times*, December 16, 2016. https://www.nytimes.com/2016/12/16/us/politics/obama-putin-hacking-news-conference.html?mcubz=2.

Landler, Mark, Cooper, Helene, and Schmitt, Eric, "Trump Withdraws US Forces," *New York Times*, December 19, 2018. https://www.nytimes.com/2018/12/19/us/politics/trump-syria-turkey-troop-withdrawal.html.

Langtree, Graham, "Trump to Putin: Syrian President Assad Can't Have Land Liberated From ISIS," *Newsweek*, July 6, 2017. http://www.newsweek.com/trump-tell-putin-assad-cant-seize-syrian-land-liberated-isis-632850.

LaRocco, Lori Ann, "Wilbur Ross Says He's 'Open to Resuming' Talks on Mega-Trade Deal with Europe," *CNBC.com*, May 30, 2017. https://www.cnbc.com/2017/05/30/exclusive-wilbur-ross-says-hes-open-to-resuming-ttip-negotiations.html.

Larter, David, "US Navy to Add 46 Ships in Five Years, but 355 Ships Won't Come for a Long Time," Defensenews.com, February 12, 2018. https://www.defensenews.com/smr/federal-budget/2018/02/13/us-navy-to-add-46-ships-in-five-years-but-355-ships-is-well-over-the-horizon/.

Lee, Youkyung, Tweed, David, and Leonard, Jenny, "Trump Clinches His First Trade Deal With Revamped South Korea Pact," *Bloomberg News*, September 24, 2018. https://www.bloomberg.com/news/articles/2018-09-24/trump-clinches-his-first-trade-deal-in-revamped-south-korea-pact.

Legal View with Ashleigh Banfield, *CNN* Transcripts, July 21, 2015. http://transcripts.cnn.com/TRANSCRIPTS/1507/21/lvab.01.html.

Liptak, Kevin and Diamond, Jeremy, "Senators: Trump is Reconsidering his Stance on TTP Trade Deal," *CNN*, April 12, 2018. https://www.cnn.com/2018/01/12/politics/trump-tpp-reconsidering/index.html.

Lohaus, Phillip, "The Uncertain Future of Special Ops," *USNews.com*, June 15, 2017. https://www.usnews.com/opinion/world-report/articles/2017-06-15/trump-needs-to-course-correct-on-obamas-special-operations-forces-policy.

Lucas, Fred, "US-China Summit: The 4 Big Issues Donald Trump and Xi Jinping Will Discuss," *National Interest* (Blog), April 5, 2017. http://nationalinterest.org/blog/the-buzz/us-china-summit-the-4-big-issues-donald-trump-xi-jinping-20043.

Bibliography

Lucas, Fred, "4 Issues Trump Will Likely Confront Chinese Leader About," *The Daily Signal*, April 5, 2017. http://dailysignal.com/2017/04/05/4-issues-trump-will-likely-confront-chinese-leader-about/.

Lucas, Fred, "Obama Has Touted Al Qaeda's Demise 32 Times Since Benghazi Attack," CNSNews.com, November 1, 2012. http://www.cnsnews.com/news/article/obama-touts-al-qaeda-s-demise-32-times-benghazi-attack-0.

Lynch, Colum, Cramer, Robbie, De Luce, Dan, and McLeary, Paul, "Secret Details of Trump-Putin Syria Cease-Fire Focus on Iranian Proxies," *Foreign Policy*, July 11, 2017. http://foreignpolicy.com/2017/07/11/exclusive-trump-putin-ceasefire-agreement-focuses-on-iranian-backed-fighters-middle-east/.

Lynch, David and Paletta, Damian, "Trump's Fluid Approach to National and Economic Security is Leaving his Allies Baffled," *Washington Post*, May 28, 2018. https://www.washingtonpost.com/business/economy/trumps-fluid-approach-to-national-and-economic-security-is-leaving-his-allies-baffled/2018/05/28/b08c5908-5f95-11e8-9ee3-49d6d4814c4cstory.html?utmterm=b9a123f26348.

Magid, Pesha, "Trump and Sisi Bond Over Counterterrorism Ambitions," Madamasr.com, April 10, 2017. https://www.madamasr.com/en/2017/04/10/opinion/u/trump-and-sisi-bond-over-counter-terrorism-ambitions/.

Making Our Military Strong Again, The White House, Donald Trump. https://www.whitehouse.gov/making-our-military-strong-again.

Malcolm, Andrew, "Trump's Venezuela Approach Refreshing Foreign Policy Posture," *Miami Herald*, February 5, 2019. https://www.miamiherald.com/article225 19360.html.

Malsin, Jared, "How Trump's Presidency Could Become a Dividing Line in the Middle East," Timeinc.net, https://time.com/4658762/donald-trump-middle-east-saudi-arabia-egypt/.

Mansbach, Richard W. and McCormick, James M., Editors, *Foreign Policy Issues for America: The Trump Years* (New York: Routledge, 2019).

Martin Pengelly, "Obama Warns Against Ditching Iran Nuclear Deal on First Anniversary," *The Guardian*, January 16, 2016. https://www.theguardian.com/world/2017/jan/16/iran-nuclear-deal-anniversary-trump-warning.

Mason, Jeff, "Trump Gives No Timetable for Syria Exit; Wants to Protect Kurds," *Reuters*, January 2, 2019. https://af.reuters.com/article/worldNews/idAFKCN1OW1H.1.

Mason, Jeff and Solovyov, Dmitry, "US Says it Saw Preparations for Possible Syria Chemical Attack," *Reuters*, June 26, 2017. https://www.reuters.com/article/us-mideast-crisis-syria-usa-idUSKBN19I083.

Masters, James, "Trump Defense Chief Mattis: US Not Ready for Military Cooperation with Russia," *CNN*, February 16, 2017. http://www.cnn.com/2017/02/16/politics/mattis-russia-military-cooperation/.

Matlock, Jack, "Risks in Demonizing Diplomacy with Russia," *Consortiumnews.com*, March 6, 2017. https://consortiumnews.com/2017/03/06/risks-in-demonizing-diplomacy-with-russia/?Print=pdf.

Mayeda, Andrew, "Trump Drops Campaign Promise to Label China a Currency Manipulation," Bloomberg.com, April 12, 2017. https://www.bloomberg.com/politics/articles/2017-04-12/trump-says-u-s-will-not-label-china-a-currency-manipulator.

McCann, James, "White House Says 200 Troops Will Remain in Syria," *Stars and Stripes*, February 22, 2019. https://www.stripes.com/news/middle-east/white-house-says-200-troops-will-remain-in-syria.

McCarthy, Niall, "Where US Troops Are in the Middle East," *Forbes*, June 7, 2017. https://www.forbes.com/sites/niallmccarthy/2017/06/07/qatar-hosts-largest-u-s-base-in-the-middle-east-despite-allegedly-funding-extremism-infographic/#27f95763dc7e.

Mckeon, Brian P., "Neither US Senators nor the Trump's Team is Lying About Khashoggi Killing," *Foreign Policy*, December 14, 2018. https://foreignpolicy.com/2018/12/14/neither-trumps-team-nor-u-s-senators-is-lying-about-khashoggos-killing/.

McMaster, H. R. and Cohn, Gary D., "America First Doesn't Mean America Alone," *Wall Street Journal*, May 30, 2017. https://www.wsj.com/articles/america-first-doesnt-mean-america-alone-1496187426.

Miller, Aaron David, "Trump on the Middle East: Where Does He Really Stand?" *CNN*, March 20, 2016. http://www.cnn.com/2016/03/20/opinions/trump-aipac-meeting-miller/index.html.

Miller, Aaron David and Sokolsky, Richard, "Donald Trump's Middle East Promises: Can He Keep Them?" *Realclear Politics*, December 5, 2016. http://www.realclearworld.com/articles/2016/12/05/donald_trumps_middle_east_promises_can_he_keep_them_112133.html.

Mills, Daniel Quinn, *The Trump Phenomenon and the Future of US Foreign Policy* (World Scientific Publishing, 2016).

Mitchell, A. Wess, Assistant Secretary of State, Bureau of European and Eurasian Affairs, "US Strategy Toward the Russian Federation," Statement Delivered Before Senate Foreign Relations Committee, Washington, DC, August 21, 2018. https://www.state.gov/p/eur/rlsrm/2018/285247.htm.

Moore, Mark and Fredericks, Bob, "Trump: US-Russia Relations May be at 'All-Time Low,'" *New York Post*, April 12, 2017. http://nypost.com/2017/04/12/trump-us-russia-relations-may-be-at-all-time-low/.

Morello, Carol, "UN Agrees to Toughest-Ever Sanctions Against North Korea," *Washington Post*, September 11, 2017. https://www.washingtonpost.com/world/in-the-push-for-oil-embargo-on-north-korea-china-is-reluctant-to-sign-off/2017/09/11/3a5b56fe-96e5-11e7-a527-3573bd073e02story.html?utmterm=4f5823d9949f&wpisrc=alalert-COMBO-world%252Bnatioion&wpmk=1.

Moyar, Mark, "America's Dangerous Love for Special Ops," (Opinion Page) *New York Times*, April 24, 2017. https://www.nytimes.com/2017/04/24/opinion/donald-trump-americas-dangerous-love-for-special-forces-ops.html.

Nahmen, Alexandra von, "Trump in Saudi Arabia—Counterterrorism and Weapons Deals," *Deutsche Welle* (DW), May 19, 2017. http://www.dw.com/en/trump-in-saudi-arabia-counterterrorism-and-weapons-deals/a-38900168.

Nakashima, Ellen and Lynch, David, "US Charges Chinese Hackers in Alleged Theft of Vast Trove Confidential Data in 12 Countries," *Washington Post*, December 21, 2018. https://www.washingtonpost.com/world/national-security/us-and-more-than-a-dozen-allies-to-condemn-china-for-economic-espionage/2018/21/20/cdf0338-0455-11e9-b5df-5d387411ac36-story.html.

Nasr, Vali, *The Dispensable Nation: American Foreign Policy in Retreat* (New York: Anchor Books, 2013).

National Counterterrorism Strategy. The White House, October 2018. Washington, DC. National Counterterrorism Strategy. The White House, October 2018. https://www.whitehouse.gov/wp-content/uploads/2018/10/NSCT.pdf.

National Defense Strategy, Washington, DC. 2018. https://dod.defense.gov/Portals/1/Documents/pubs/2018-National-Defense-Strategy-Summary.pdf.

National Security Strategy of the United States, White House, December 2017. https://www.whitehouse.gov/wp-content/uploads/2017/12/NSS-Final-12-18-2017-0905.pdf.

Naylor, Sean, "Will Trump Break the Special Forces?" *The Atlantic*, December 27, 2016. https://www.theatlantic.com/international/archive/2016/12/trump-special-forces-green-beret-iraq-obama-jsoc/511229/.

Ness, Peter Van, "China's Response to the Bush Doctrine," *World Policy Journal*, Vol. 21, No. 4 (Winter, 2004/2005), pp. 38–47.

[No Author, *NPR* Staff] "5 Big Foreign Policy Challenges for President-Elect Trump." *NPR*, November 12, 2016. http://www.npr.org/sections/parallels/2016/11/12/501145459/5-big-foreign-policy-challenges-for-president-elect-trump.

"North Korea: 'More Gift Packages' Coming for the US," *Al Jazeera*, September 5, 2017. http://www.aljazeera.com/news/2017/09/north-korea-gift-packages-coming-170905134153254.html.

O'Brien, Jason, "America First: Trump's New World Order Begins," *Independent*, January 21, 2017. http://www.independent.ie/world-news/north-america/us-election-2016/america-first-trumps-new-world-order-begins-35385919.html.

O'Driscoll Jr., Gerald P., and Cobb, Tyrus W., "Trump on US Foreign and Economic Policy," *CATO Institute*, May 1, 2016. https://www.cato.org/publications/commentary/trump-us-foreign-economic-policy.

"Open Letter from Military Leaders." [No Date]. https://assets.donaldjtrump.com/MILITARY-LETTER.pdf.

Osnos, Evan, Remnick, David, and Yaffa, Joshua, "Trump, Putin, and the New Cold War," *The New Yorker*, March 6, 2017, https://www.newyorker.com/magazine/2017/03/06/trump-putin-and-the-new-cold-war.

Pace, Julie, "Trump Raises Prospect of America More Willing to Act Alone on Global Stage," www.pbs.org. December 27, 2016. http://www.pbs.org/newshour/rundown/trump-signals-shift-obamas-focus-multilateralism/.

Pagliarulu, Diego, "Donald Trump, the Middle East, and American Foreign Policy," *E-International Relations*, January 3, 2017. http://www.e-ir.info/2017/01/03/donald-trump-the-middle-east-and-american-foreign-policy/.

Paletta, Damian, "Clinton vs Trump, Where They Stand on Foreign Policy Issues," *Wall Street Journal* [No Date]. http://graphics.wsj.com/elections/2016/donald-trump-hillary-clinton-on-foreign-policy/.

Paper, Robert, "A Hotline to Cool Asian Crises," *Washington Post*, April 29, 2014. https://www.washingtonpost.com/news/monkey-cage/wp/2014/04/29/a-hotline-to-cool-asian-crises/?utm_term=bc095f0d01be.

Patrick, Stewart M., "Donald Trump's Global Agenda: What Have You Got to Lose?" *Council on Foreign Relations*, November 15, 2016. http://blogs.cfr.org/patrick/2016/11/15/donald-trumps-global-agenda-what-have-you-got-to-lose/.

Paulson, John, "Trump and the Economy," *Foreign Affairs*, March/April 2017. https://www.foreignaffairs.com/articles/united-states/2017-02-13/trump-and-economy.

Pawlyk, Oriana, "Mattis: Trump Empowered Commanders to 'Annihilate ISIS,'" Military.com, May 19, 2017. http://www.military.com/daily-news/2017/05/19/mattis-trump-empowered-commanders-annihilate-isis.html.

Perlez, Jane, "Tribunal Rejects Beijing's Claims in South China Sea," *New York Times*, July 12, 2016. https://www.nytimes.com/2016/07/13/world/asia/south-china-sea-hague-ruling-philippines.html?mcubz=2&r=0.

Phillips, Noah, "How Trump Should Handle the Jamal Khashoggi Killing," Begin-Sadat Center for Strategic Studies, October 2018. https://besacenter.org/perspectives-papers/jamal-khashoggi-trump/.

Pindell, James, "With Paris decision, President Trump could unveil new world order" *Boston Globe*, June 1, 2017. https://www.bostonglobe.com/news/politics/2017/06/01/with-paris-decision-president-trump-could-unveil-new-world-order/GOVepNceoNVZB2RSBJp37L/story.html.

Pomfret, John, "How Trump Could Put US-China Relations on the Right Track," *Washington Post*, February 6, 2017. https://www.washingtonpost.com/news/global-opinions/wp/2017/02/06/how-trump-could-put-u-s-china-relations-on-the-right-track/?utm-term=a22357e9589b.

President Bush: "No Nation Can be Neutral in This Conflict." Remarks by the President to the Warsaw Conference on Combatting Terrorism. President George W. Bush, White House, November 6, 2011. Georgewbush-whitehouse.archives.gov.

Presidential Executive Order on Imposing Additional Sanctions with Respect to North Korea. September 21, 2017. The White House, Office of the Press Secretary. https://www.whitehouse.gov/the-press-office/2017/09/21/presidential-executive-order-imposing-additional-sanctions-respect-north.

Presidential Memorandum on Rebuilding the US Armed Forces. The White House Office of the Press Secretary, January 27, 2017. https://www.whitehouse.gov/the-press-office/2017/01/27/presidential-memorandum-rebuilding-us-armed-forces.

"Presidential Memorandum Plan to Defeat the Islamic State of Iraq and Syria." The White House Office of the Press Secretary, January 28, 2017. https://www.whitehouse.gov/the-press-office/2017/01/28/plan-defeat-islamic-state-iraq.

President Donald J. Trump to Withdraw the United States from the Intermediate-Range Nuclear Forces (INF) Treaty, The White House, February 1, 2019. https://www.whitehouse.gov/briefings-statements/president-donald-j-trump-withdraw-united-states-intermediate-range-nuclear-forces-inf-treaty/.

President Donald J. Trump is Protecting the United States from Terrorism. Whitehouse.gov. October 4, 2018. https://www.whitehouse.gov/briefings-statements/president-donald-j-trump-protecting-america-terrorism.

President Donald J. Trump's Six Months of America First. White House, Office of the Press Secretary. July 17, 2017. https://www.whitehouse.gov/the-press-office/2017/07/20/president-donald-j-trumps-six-months-america-first.

President Donald Trump, "Making Our Military Strong Again." White House, January 27, 2017. https://www.whitehouse.gov/making-our-military-strong-again.

"President Obama's Remarks on New Strategy for Afghanistan and Pakistan," *New York Times*, March 27, 2009. http://www.nytimes.com/2009/03/27/us/politics/27obama-text.html.

President Trump Addresses a Joint Session of Congress: A Call for 'Direct, Robust, and Meaningful Engagement with the World.' DipNote Bloggers, February 28, 2017. https://blogs.state.gov/stories/2017/02/28/en/president-trump-addresses-joint-session-congress-call-direct-robust-and.

"President Trump to Arab Leaders: 'Drive Out' Terrorism," *Fortune* (From *Reuters*), May 21, 2017. http://fortune.com/2017/05/21/president-donald-trump-middle-east-saudi-arabia-speech/.

President Trump Says the Iran Deal is Defective at Its Core. A New One Will Require Real Commitments. White House.gov, May 11, 2018. https://www.whitehouse.gov/articles/president-trump-says-iran-deal-defective-core-new-one-will-require-real-commitments/.

President Trump's Speech to the Arab Islamic American Summit. The White House, Office of the Press Secretary. May 21, 2017. https://www.whitehouse.gov/the-press-office/2017/05/21/president-trumps-speech-arab-islamic-american-summit.

Press Trust of India (PTI), "Clinton Campaign Attacks Trump, Says He is 'Too Divisive', Lacks Presidential Temperament," IndianExpress.com, May 4, 2016. http://indianexpress.com/article/world/world-news/clinton-campaign-attacks-trump-says-he-is-too-divisive-lacks-presidential-temperament-2783586/.

Rachman, Gideon, "Donald Trump's Unpredictability is Destabilizing the World." *Financial Times*, May 22, 2017. https://www.ft.com/content/b56c7c9c-3ecf-11e7-82b6-896b95f30f58.

Rafferty, Andrew, "Obama: Trump Doesn't Know Much About Nuclear Weapons, Or the World," *NBC News*, April 1, 2016. http://www.nbcnews.com/politics/2016-election/obama-trump-doesn-t-know-much-about-nuclear-weapons-or-n549476.

Raymond, Greg, Nasu, Hitoshi, Tan, See Seng, and McLaughlin, Rob, "Prospects for A "Rule-Based Global Order," Strategic and Defense Studies Centre, The Centre of Gravity Series Paper Number 34, 2017. http://bellschool.anu.edu.au/sites/default/files/uploads/2017-06/cog_34_global_rules_based_order.pdf.

Read Full Transcript of Donald Trump Speech in Akron, Ohio. Heavy.com, August 22, 2016. http://heavy.com/news/2016/08/read-full-transcript-donald-trump-rally-speech-akron-ohio-text/.

"Read Trump's Full Remarks on Immigration, 'Space Force,'" *The Boston Globe*, June 18, 2018. https://www.bostonglobe.com/news/politics/2018/06/read-trump-full-remarks-immigration-space-force/QcLtBX1us0LiL2eW5KrajL/story.html.

"Read the Full Text of Trump's Address to Congress," *PBS NewsHour*, February 28, 2017. http://www.pbs.org/newshour/rundown/read-full-text-trumps-address-congress/.

Remarks to the American Society of Newspaper Editors in Annapolis, Maryland. William J. Clinton, April 1, 1993. The American Presidency Project. http://www.presidency.ucsb.edu/ws/?pid=46392.

Remarks by President Trump and First Lady Melania Trump to Troops and Families. Naval Air Base Sigonella, Italy. The White House, Office of the Press Secretary. May 27, 2017. https://www.whitehouse.gov/the-press-office/2017/05/27/remarks-president-trump-and-first-lady-melania-trump-troops-and-families.

Remarks by the President and First Lady on the 70th Anniversary of the US Air Force. The White House, Office of the Press Secretary. Joint Base Andrews, Camp Springs, Maryland. September 15, 2017. https://www.whitehouse.gov/the-press-office/2017/09/15/remarks-president-and-first-lady-70th-anniversary-us-air-force.

Remarks by President Trump to the 72nd Session of the United Nations General Assembly. United Nations, New York, New York. The White House, Office of the Press Secretary. September 19, 2017. https://www.whitehouse.gov/the-press-office/2017/09/19/remarks-president-trump-72nd-session-united-nations-general-assembly.

Remarks by President Trump on the Strategy in Afghanistan and South Asia, Fort Myer, Arlington, Virginia. The White House, Donald J. Trump. Office of the Press Secretary, August 21, 2017. https://www.whitehouse.gov/the-press-office/2017/08/21/remarks-president-trump-strategy-afghanistan-and-south-asia.

Remarks by President Trump and President Putin of the Russian Federation in Joint Press Conference, The White House, July 16, 2018. https://www.whitehouse.gov/briefings-statements/remarks-president-trump-president-putin-russian-federation-joint-press-conference/.

Remarks by President Trump and Vice President Pence Announcing the Missile Defense Review. WhiteHouse.gov, January 17, 2019. The Pentagon, Arlington, Virginia. https://www.whitehouse.gov/issues/national-security-defense/.

Remarks by President Trump to Coalition Representatives and Senior US Commanders. The White House, Office of the Press Secretary. MacDill Air Force Base, Tampa, Florida, February 6, 2017. https://www.whitehouse.gov/the-press-office/2017/02/06/remarks-president-trump-coalition-representatives-and-senior-us.

Remarks by President Trump in Meeting with the National Governors Association. State Dining Room. February 27, 2017. https://historymusings.wordpress.com/2017/02/27/full-text-political-transcripts-february-27-2017-president-donald-trumps-speech-at-meeting-with-the-national-governors-association/.

Remarks by President Trump at NATO Unveiling of the Article 5 and Berlin Wall Memorials—NATO Headquarters. Brussels, Belgium. The White House, Office of the Press Secretary, May 25, 2017. https://www.whitehouse.gov/the-press-office/2017/05/25/remarks-president-trump-nato-unveiling-article-5-and-berlin-wall.

Remarks by Vice President Mike Pence at Kennedy Space Center," White House.gov, December 18, 2018. https://www.whitehouse.gov/briefings-statements/remarks-vice-president-pence-kennedy-space-center/.

Remarks of President Donald J. Trump—As Prepared for Delivery in the Inaugural Address. January 20, 2017, Washington, DC. The White House, Donald J. Trump. https://www.whitehouse.gov/inaugural-address.

Remarks Secretary of State by Michael R. Pompeo, Press Briefing Room, Washington, DC. November 20, 2018. https://www.state.gov/secretary/remarks/2018/11/287487.htm.

Remnick, David, "The Jamal Khashoggi Affair," *The New Yorker*, December 17, 2018. https://www.newyorker.com/books/double-take/sunday-reading-the-khashoggi-affair.

Restussia, Andrew and Cook, Nancy, "Trump's Trade Plan Sets Up Global Clash Over 'America First' Strategy," *Politico*, June 30, 2017. http://www.politico.com/story/2017/06/30/trump-america-first-trade-plan-clash-240123.

Ripley, Will, "How Trump and Kim Summit Dream Fell Apart," CNN.com, March 2, 2019. https://www.cnn.com/2019/03/02politics/trump-kim-summit-dream-ripley-int/index.html.

Rogin, Josh, "The Trump Administration's Shortsighted War on Terrorism," *Washington Post*, July 16, 2017. https://www.washingtonpost.com/opinions/global-opinions/the-trump-administrations-shortsighted-war-on-terrorism/2017/07/16/4be64cdc-68c1-11e7-a1d7-9a32c91c6f40story.html?utm_term=36ab526c8f67.

Ross, Eleanor, "US Will Still Challenge Beijing's Claims to South China Sea Under Donald Trump," *Newsweek*, March 9, 2017. http://www.newsweek.com/us-china-south-china-sea-claim-beijing-test-challenge-engaged-605858.

Roth, Andrew and Borger, Julian, "Trump and Putin to Reveal Details of First Official Summit," *The Guardian*, June 27, 2018. https://www.theguardian.com/us-news/2018/jun/27/john-bolton-vladimir-putin-moscow-visit-us-russia.

Roulo, Claudette, "Space Force to Become Sixth Branch of the Armed Forces," DoDNews.gov, August 9, 2018. https://dod.defense.gov/News./Article/Article/1598071/space-force-to-become-sixth-branch-of-armed-forces/.

Rubino, Rich, "Trump Was Not First to Use the 'America First' Slogan," *Huffington Post*, April 17, 2017. http://www.huffingtonpost.com/entry/the-etymology-of-america-firstus5889767de4b0628ad613de3f.

Rusty [Name Provided], "Military Leaders, Congress Praise Trump's 'Inspiring' Afghanistan Speech," *The Political Insider*, August 22, 2017. http://thepoliticalinsider.com/trump-afghanistan-speech/.

Samuelson, Robert J., "The New World Order, 2017," *Washington Post*, January 1, 2017. https://www.washingtonpost.com/opinions/the-new-world-order/2017/01/01/fc54c3e6-ce9d-11e6-a747-d03044780a02story.html?utm_term=c560acecf002.

"Saudi Arabia, Egypt Lead Arab States Cutting Qatar Ties, Iran Blames Trump," *CNBC*, June 5, 2017. https://www.cnbc.com/2017/06/04/saudi-arabia-bahrain-and-egypt-cut-diplomatic-ties-with-qatar.html.

Saunders, Paul J., Editor, "A New Direction in US Russia Relations? America's Challenges and Opportunities in Dealing with Russia," The Center for the National Interest, February 2017. https://187ock2y3ejr34z8752m6ize-wpengine.netdna-ssl.com/wp-content/uploads/2017/03/A-New-Direction-in-US-Russia-Relations-CFTNI-2017-Saunders.pdf.

Scarborough, Rowan, "With ISIS in Crosshairs, Al Qaeda Makes Comeback," *Washington Times*, April 2, 2017. http://www.washingtontimes.com/news/2017/apr/2/al-qaeda-comeback-widens-terror-war-for-donald-tru/.

Schell, Orville and Shirk, Susan L., "US Policy Toward China: Recommendations for a New Administration," Task Force Report February 2017. Asia Society, US San Diego, School of Global Policy and Strategy, 21st Century China Center. http://asiasociety.org/files/US-ChinaTask_Force_Report_FINAL.pdf.

Schmitt, Eric, "ISIS Reverts to Insurgent Roots to Pose Long-Term Threat, Study Says," *New York Times*, June 29, 2017. https://www.nytimes.com/2017/06/29/world/middleeast/isis-attacks-syria-iraq-study.html.

Schneider, Greg and Merle, Renae, "Reagan's Defense Buildup Bridged Military Eras," *Washington Post*, June 8, 2004. http://www.washingtonpost.com/wp-dyn/articles/A26273-2004Jun8.html.

Schram, James, "Rex Tillerson Says Russia Poses a 'Danger' to US," *New York Post*, January 11, 2017. http://nypost.com/2017/01/11/rex-tillerson-says-russia-poses-a-danger-to-us/.

Schwarz, Jon and Mackey, Robert, "All the Times Donald Trump Said the US Should Get Out of Afghanistan," *The Intercept*, August 21, 2017. https://theintercept.com/2017/08/21/donald-trump-afghanistan-us-get-out/.

Secretary of State Rex Tillerson. Remarks to US Department of State Employees, Dean Acheson Auditorium , Washington, DC, May 3, 2017. https://www.state.gov/secretary/remarks/2017/05/270620.htm.

Seligman, Lara, "Trump's Muscular New Plan to Fend Off Russian and Chinese Missiles," *Foreign Policy*, January 18, 2019. https://foreignpolicy.com/2019/01/17/trumps-muscular-new-plan-to-fend-off-russian-and-chinese-missiles-missile-defense-space/.

Setser, Brad W., "US-China Trade War: How We Got Here," *Council on Foreign Relations*, July 9, 2018. https://www.cfr.org/blog/us-china-trade-war-how-we-got-here.

Sevastopulo, Demetri and Solomon, Erika, "Trump Warns Syria Over Suspected Chemical Attack Plan," *Financial Times*, June 27, 2017. https://www.ft.com/content/b2ca1dac-5af2-11e7-9bc8-8055f264aa8b.

Shakdam, Catherine, "Yemen at War: The New Shia-Sunni Frontline That Never Was," Foreign Policy Journal.com, April 10, 2015. https://www.foreignpolicyjournal.com/2015/04/10/yemen-at-war-the-new-shia-sunni-frontline-that-never-was/.

Shane III, Leo and Tilghman, Andrew, "Trump's Military Will Have More Troops and More Firepower—If He Can Find More Money," *Military Times*, November 20, 2016. http://www.militarytimes.com/articles/donald-trump-military-spending.

Shear, Michael and Steinhauer, Jennifer, "Trump to Seek $54 Billion Increase in Military Spending," *New York Times*, February 27, 2017. https://www.nytimes.com/2017/02/27/us/politics/trump-budget-military.html.

Shear, Michael D., Hirschfeld, Julie, and Haberman, Maggie, "Trump, in Interview, Moderates Views but Defies Conventions," *New York Times*, November 22, 2016. https://www.nytimes.com/2016/11/22/us/politics/donald-trump-visit.html.

Shelbourne, Mallory, "Trump: Only Stupid People Don't Want A Good Relationship with Russia," *The Hill*, January 7, 2017. http://thehill.com/homenews/administration/313164-trump-only-stupid-people-dont-want-a-good-relationship-with-russia.

Shinkman, Paul, "Qatar-Saudi Crisis Shows Trump Administration's Discord, Dysfunction," *USNews.com*, July 17, 2017. https://www.usnews.com/news/world/articles/2017-07-17/qatar-saudi-crisis-shows-trump-administrations-discord-dysfunction-experts-say.

Siciliano, John, "Trump Tours Saudi Counterterrorism Complex," *Washington Examiner*, May 21, 2017. http://www.washingtonexaminer.com/trump-tours-saudi-counter-terrorism-complex/article/2623767.

Simms, Brendan and Laderman, Charlie, *Donald Trump: The Making of a World View* (Independently Published, 2017).

Simon, Steve, "Can the Right War Be Won?" *Foreign Affairs*, July/August 2009. https://www.foreignaffairs.com/reviews/review-essay/2009-07-01/can-right-war-be-won.

Sisk, Richard, "Mattis Gives White House Tentative Plan for Rapid Defeat of ISIS," Military.com, February 28, 2017. http://www.military.com/daily-news/2017/02/28/mattis-gives-white-house-tentative-plan-rapid-defeat-isis.html.

Smale, Alison and Erlanger, Steven, "Merkel, After Discordant G-7 Meeting, Is Looking Past Trump," *New York Times*, May 28, 2017. https://www.nytimes.com/2017/05/28/world/europe/angela-merkel-trump-alliances-g7-leaders.html?r=0.

Smith, Julianne, Rizzo, Rachel, and Twardowski, Adam, "US Election Note: Defense Policy After 2016," Chatham House, US and the Americas Programme, August 2016. https://www.chathamhouse.org/sites/files/chathamhouse/publications/research/2016.

Smith, David and Siddiqui, Sabrina, "Gulf Crisis: Trump Escalates Row by Accusing Qatar of Sponsoring Terror," *The Guardian*, June 9, 2017. https://www.theguardian.com/us-news/2017/jun/09/trump-qatar-sponsor-terrorism-middle-east.

Sonne, Paul and Harris, Shane, "US Military Edge has Eroded 'To a Dangerous Degree,' Study for Congress Finds," *Washington Post*, November 14, 2018. https://www.washingtonpost.com/world/national-security/us-military-edge-has-eroded-to-a-dangerous-degree-study-for-congress-finds/2018/11/13/ea83fd96-e7bc-11e8-bd89-eecf3b178206_story.html?utm_term=ba02ec2e14c5.

Springborg, Robert, "The New US President: Implications for The Middle East and North Africa," *Future Notes*, October 2016. http://www.iai.it/sites/default/files/menara_fn_2.pdf.

Statement by President Trump on Syria, Mar-a-Lago, Florida. The White House, Office of the Press Secretary. April 6, 2017. https://www.whitehouse.gov/the-press-office/2017/04/06/statement-president-trump-syria.

Statement from President Donald J. Trump on Standing with Saudi Arabia. The White House, November 20, 2018. https://www.whitehouse.gov/briefings-statements/statement-president-donald-j-trump-standing-saudi-arabia/.

Statement on the American Embassy in Israel. The White House Office of the Press Secretary, Washington, DC, June 1, 2017. https://www.whitehouse.gov/briefings-statements/statement-american-embassy-israel/.

Steinbuch, Yaron, "World Leaders Come Out in Support of Historic Trump-Kim Summit," *New York Post*, June 12, 2018. https://nypost.com/2018/06/12/world-leaders-come-out-in-support-of-historic-trump-kim-summit/.

Stracqualursi, Veronica, "10 Times Trump Attacked China and Its Trade Relations with the US," *ABCnews.go.com*, April 6, 2017. http://abcnews.go.com/Politics/10-times-trump-attacked-china-trade-relations-us/story?id=46572567.

Sutter, Robert, "Pushback: America's New China Strategy," *The Diplomat*, November 17, 2018. https://thediplomat.com/2018/11/pushback-americas-new-china-strategy/.

Swick, Andrew, "The DoD's 'New' Plans for ISIS," *Georgetown Security Studies Review* (GSSR), March 6, 2017. http://georgetownsecuritystudiesreview.org/2017/03/06/the-dods-new-plans-for-isis/.

Szuplat, Terence, "Why Trump's 'America First' Policy Is Doomed to Fail," *The New Yorker*, February 3, 2017. http://www.newyorker.com/news/news-desk/why-trumps-america-first-policy-is-doomed-to-fail.

Taylor, William B., "What's Next for the US and Russia After the Trump-Putin Summit?" USIP.org, July 17, 2018. https://www.usip.org/publications/2018/07/whats-next-us-and-russia-after-trump-putin-summit.

Tani, Maxwell, "The Trump Administration Appears Torn Over Whether to Support Removing Syria's Assad from Power," *BusinessInsider.com*, April 9, 2017. http://www.businessinsider.com/trump-bashar-al-assad-nikki-haley-regime-change-rex-tillerson-mcmaster-2017-4.

Tankel, Stephen, "Has Trump Read His Own Counterterrorism Strategy," *Foreign Policy*, October 12, 2018. https://foreignpolicy.com/2018/1012/has-trump-read-his-own-counterterrorism-strategy/.

Tanter, Raymond and Stafford, Edward, "The Qatar Crisis Is an Opportunity for Trump," *National Interest*, July 6, 2017. http://nationalinterest.org/feature/the-qatar-crisis-opportunity-trump-21446.

Tarnopolsky, Noga, "In Most Serious Military Clash in Decades, Israel Hits Iranian Targets in Syria," *LA Times*, May 10, 2018. http://www.latimes.com/world/middleeast/la-fg-israel-strikes-iranian-targets-20180510-story.html.

Tastekin, Fehim, "Turkish Army Brass at Odds Over Military Operation in Syria," *Al Monitor*, January 4, 2019. https://www.almonitor.com/pulse/originals/2019/01/turkey-syria-some-in-army-oppose-new-operation-against-kurds.html.

"Tension Escalates After Russia Seizes Ukraine Naval Ships," *BBC*, November 26, 2018. https://www.bbc.com/news/world-europe-46338671.

The Editorial Board, "Russian Attacks Ukrainian Ships and International Law," *New York Times*, November 26, 2018. https://www.nytimes.com/2018/11/26/opinion/russia-ukraine-attack-ships-crimea.html.

The Editorial Board, "Mr. Trump's Fickle Diplomacy," *New York Times*, April 12, 2017. https://www.nytimes.com/2017/04/12/opinion/mr-trumps-fickle-diplomacy.html?mcubz=2&r=0.

The Goals of Donald J. Trump's Tax Plan. https://assets.donaldjtrump.com/trump-tax-reform.pdf.

Thomas, (General) Raymond, The Commander of Special Operations Command in Testimony Before the House Armed Services Committee on Emerging Threats and Capabilities on May 2, 2017. Washington, DC. http://docs.house.gov/meetings/AS/AS26/20170502/105926/HHRG-115-AS26-Wstate-ThomasR-20170502.PDF.

Thommesen, Kjartan, "From Excitement to Burnout in 80 Years the Americanization of Europe (1919–1999)," Master's Thesis, 2008. https://www.duo.uio.no/bitstream/handle/10852/26255/FromxExcitementxtoxBurnoutxinx80xYears.pdf?sequence=1.

Thompson, Loren, "Why Trump Needs a Five-Year Defense Plan on Day One," *Forbes*, December 22, 2016. https://www.forbes.com/sites/lorenthompson/2016/12/22/why-president-trump-needs-a-five-year-defense-plan-on-day-one/2/#781079a93e95.

"Thousands of Palestinians Protest at Gaza-Israel Border, One Dead," *Reuters*, https://www.reuters.com/article/us-israel-palestinians-protests/palestinians-wounded-at-gaza-israel-border-protests-idUSKBN1HK1E7.

Tilghman, Andrew, "Donald Trump Paints a Dismal Picture of Today's Military," *Military Times*, October 3, 2016. http://www.militarytimes.com/articles/trump-paints-dismal-picture-of-todays-military.

Tomlinson, Lucas, "Military Branches Drafting Expansion Plans as Trump Vows to Rebuild 'Depleted' Force," *Fox News*, February 21, 2017. http://azbizopps.org/wp-content/uploads/2017/02/Military-Branches-drafting-expansion-plans-02-21-2017.pdf.

Bibliography

Toosi, Nahal, "Tillerson Urges Russia to Cooperate on Syria Ahead of Trump-Putin Meeting," *Politico*, July 5, 2017. http://www.politico.com/story/2017/07/05/tillerson-russia-syria-240250.

Trade Deals That Work for All Americans. The White House, Donald J. Trump. https://www.whitehouse.gov/trade-deals-working-all-americans.

Transcript: Donald Trump on NATO, Turkey's Coup Attempt and the World. *New York Times*, July 22, 2017. https://www.nytimes.com/2016/07/22/us/politics/donald-trump-foreign-policy-interview.html.

Transcript of Donald Trump's Speech on National Security in Philadelphia. *The Hill*, September 7, 2016. http://thehill.com/blogs/pundits-blog/campaign/294817-transcript-of-donald-trumps-speech-on-national-security-in.

"Transcript: Donald Trump's Foreign Policy Speech," *New York Times*, April 27, 2016. https://www.nytimes.com/2016/04/28/us/politics/transcript-trump-foreign-policy.html.

Trofimov, Yaroslav, "Can Israel's Clash with Iran Be Contained in Syria?" *Wall Street Journal*, May 3, 2018. https://www.wsj.com/articles/can-israels-clash-with-iran-be-contained-to-syria-1525339800.

Trump, Donald, *Crippled America: How to Make America Great Again* (New York: Simon and Schuster, 2015).

Trump, Donald, *Trump: The Art of Deal* (Ballantine Books, 2015).

Trump, Donald, *Time to Get Tough: Make America Great Again!* (Washington, DC: Regnery, 2011).

"Trump Hails 'Tremendous' Progress in Talks with China's Xi," *BBC.com*, April 7, 2017. http://www.bbc.com/news/world-us-canada-39517569.

"Trump's Afghanistan Address Generates Wave of Political Reaction," *Fox News*, August 21, 2017. http://www.foxnews.com/politics/2017/08/21/trumps-afghanistan-address-generates-wave-political-reaction.html.

Trump Speech: Clinton Email Corruption Disqualifies Her from Seeking Presidency, September 6, 2016. North Carolina. https://www.donaldjtrump.com/press-releases/trump-speech-clinton-email-corruption-disqualifies-her-from-seeking-presidency.

Tucker, Joshua, "Here's How Trump's Election Will Affect US-Russian Relations," *Washington Post*, November 11, 2016. https://www.washingtonpost.com/news/monkey-cage/wp/2016/11/10/heres-how-trumps-election-will-affect-u-s-russian-relations/?utm_term=da3f3ad2257b.

USTR Releases NAFTA Negotiation Objectives. Office of the US Special Trade Representative Executive Office of the President. Washington, DC. July 2017. https://ustr.gov/about-us/policy-offices/press-office/press-releases/2017/july/ustr-releases-nafta-negotiating.

Vazques, Maegan, "Former Intel Chiefs Condemn Trump's News Conference with Putin," *CNN*, July 17, 2018. https://www.cnn.com/2018/07/16/politics/john-brennan-donald-trump-treasonous-vladimir-putin/index.html.

Vincenti, Daniela, "EU, US to Set Up Joint Task Force to Make Progress on Trade in Trump Era," Euractive.com, May 26, 2017. https://www.euractiv.com/section/economy-jobs/news/eu-us-to-set-up-joint-workforce-to-make-progress-on-trade-in-trump-era/.

Vladimirov, Nikita, "Trump: US Has 'No Choice but to Bomb' ISIS in Libya," *The Hill*, August 2, 2016. http://thehill.com/blogs/ballot-box/presidential-races/290115-trump-us-has-no-choice-but-to-bomb-isis-in-libya.

Wagner, Daniel, "Trump and the Coming Death of Multilateralism," *The Huffington Post* [No Date]. http://www.huffingtonpost.com/daniel-wagner/trump-and-the-coming-deat_b_12915974.html.

Wallace, Charles, "Crunch Time for Trump on China Trade," *Forbes.com*, April 3, 2017. https://www.forbes.com/sites/charleswallace1/2017/04/03/crunch-time-for-trump-on-china-trade/#7e65e7305d99.

Warrick, Joby and Mekhennet, Souad, "Bin Laden's Son Steps into Father's Shoes as Al Qaeda Attempts a Comeback," *Washington Post*, May 27, 2017. https://www.washingtonpost.com/world/national-security/bin-ladens-son-steps-into-fathers-shoes-as-al-qaeda-attempts-a-commeback/2017/05/27/0c89ffc0-4198-11e7-9869-bac8b446820astory.html?utmterm=4a7f3127e508&wpisrc=nldraw&wpmm=1.

Weaver, Matthew, "Barack Obama Calls for 'Reset' in US-Russia Relations," *The Guardian*, 2009. https://www.theguardian.com/world/2009/jul/07/barack-obama-russia-moscow-speech.

Weisgerber, Marcus, "Trump's Military Buildup Won't Begin Until 2019," *Defense One*, May 23, 2017. http://www.defenseone.com/politics/2017/05/trumps-military-buildup-wont-begin-until-2019/138106/.

"What did Donald Trump Achieve in the Middle East?" *The Economist*, May 25, 2017. https://www.economist.com/news/middle-east-and-africa/21722632-not-much-saudi-and-israeli-governments-are-delighted-what-did-donald.

Wideman, Paul, "Trump Administration Grudgingly Faces Reality on the Iran Nuclear Deal," *Washington Post*, April 19, 2017. https://www.washingtonpost.com/blogs/plum-line/wp/2017/04/19/trump-administration-grudgingly-faces-reality-on-the-iran-nuclear-deal/?utm_term=1c44923e2111.

Wilkinson, Tracy, "Trump's 'America First' Policy Changes US Role on World Stage," *LA Times*, June 2, 2017. http://www.latimes.com/nation/la-fg-trump-assess-20170602-story.html.

Williams, Katie Bo, "Trump Administration Unveils New Iran Sanctions," *The Hill*, July 18, 2017. http://thehill.com/policy/national-security/342505-us-hits-iran-with-new-sanctions-over-ballistic-missiles.

Wilson, Scott, and Cohen, Jon, "Poll: More Americans Disapprove of Obama's Management of Afghanistan War," *Washington Post*, August 25, 2011. https://www.washingtonpost.com/politics/poll-more-americans-disapprove-of-obamas-management-of-afghan-war/2011/04/25/AFBjpnjEstory.html?utm_term=743486f5c42e.

Wolf, Martin, "Donald Trump and the Surrendering of US Leadership." *Financial Times*, May 30, 2017. https://www.ft.com/content/f0b9fba6-4241-11e7-9d56-25f963e998b2.

Wolfe, Richard, "How Trump's Foreign Policy Threatens to Make America Weak Again," *The Guardian*, July 2, 2017. https://www.theguardian.com/us-news/2017/jul/02/donald-trump-foreign-policy-diplomacy.

Woodward, Bob, *Fear: Trump in the White House* (New York: Simon and Schuster, 2018).

Woody, Christopher, "Here's Why the Navy is Reactivating the 2nd Fleet to Patrol the Atlantic," Taskandpurpose.com, May 7, 2018. https://Taskandpurpose.com/navy-reactiving-2nd-fleet-russia.

Woody, Christopher, "Mattis and Tillerson Are Trying to Soothe a Crisis in the Persian Gulf, But Trump Keeps Picking on a US Ally," *Business Insider*, July 1, 2017. http://www.businessinsider.com/mattis-and-tillerson-try-to-sooth-gulf-crisis-as-trump-fights-qatar-2017-6.

Wooley, James, "The Foreign Policy Views of Donald Trump," *Foreign Policy Research Institute*, August 6, 2016. http://www.fpri.org/article/2016/11/foreign-policy-views-donald-trump/.

Wynne, Mike, "The Case for Donald Trump on National Defense," Breakingdefense.com, October 31, 2016. http://breakingdefense.com/2016/10/the-case-for-donald-trump-on-national-defense/.

Yoon, Eunice, "Here's Who Wins with the New US-China Trade Deals," *CNBC.com*, May 12, 2017. http://www.cnbc.com/2017/05/12/heres-who-wins-with-the-new-us-china-trade-deals.html.

Yu, Roger, "US-China Trade Scorecard: Advantage China," *USAToday*, April 4, 2017. https://www.usatoday.com/story/money/2017/04/04/united-states-china-trade-relations/999891116/.

Zenko, Micah, "Donald Trump Is Pushing America's Special Forces Past the Breaking Point," *Foreign Policy*, August 1, 2017. http://foreignpolicy.com/2017/08/01/donald-trump-is-pushing-americas-special-forces-past-the-breaking-point-jsoc-navy-seal/.

Ziezulewicz, Geoff, "Commander of 2nd Fleet Latest to Sound Alarm Over Russia Subs," *NavyTimes.com*, November 28, 2018. https://www.navytimes.com/news/your-navy/2018/commander-of-2nd-fleet-latest-to-sound-alarm-over-russian-subs/.

Zoellick, Robert, "The Currency of Power: Economics & Security in US Foreign Policy," *FPRI*, January 2016. https://www.fpri.org/wp-content/uploads/2016/01/zoellick-dinnertranscript.pdf.

Index

Abbas, Mahmoud, 152
Abdullah, King, 58
Abrams, Elliott, 76
Abu Jaber, Kamel, 149
Afghanistan, x, 4, 10, 19, 20, 55, 70, 71, 72, 73, 74, 75, 77, 81, 85, 101, 168, 172, 218, 232, 234, 243; Trump's War, 75
Al Assad, Bashar, 63, 160, 161, 163, 184, 188, 194, 236, 242
Allyn, General Daniel, 100
Al Nusra Front, 10, 84, 160, 162. *See also* Al Qaeda in Syria
Al Qaeda Central, xi, 10, 28, 33, 58, 59, 61, 64, 83, 101, 103, 147, 154, 194, 217, 225, 226, 227, 233; US Attacks on Organizational Leadership, 64
Al Qaeda in the Arabian Peninsula (AQAP), 10, 55, 59, 65, 169, 170, 233
Al Qaeda in the Islamic Maghreb (AQIM), 65
Al Qaeda in Syria, 10, 160, 162, 194, 226, 227, 244
Al Shabab, 59, 65, 244
Ansar al Sharia, 65
Anton, Michael, 164
Arab Spring, 147
Araral, Eduaro, 209
Argentina, 193
Astore, William J., 22
Auslin, Michael, 7

Australia, 201

Bacon, Kevin, 68, 81
Bahrain, 167, 169
Baker, James, 35
Baldor, Lolita C., 67
Bannon, Steve, 7
Barno, Lieutenant General David,, 98
Belgium, 23, 63, 70
Bergsten, C. Fred, 37, 38
Biden, Joseph, 7
Bierman, Noah, 28
Bin Laden, Hamza, 225
Bin Laden, Osama, 65, 225
Bin Sultan, Mohamed, 172
Blair, Dennis, vii, viii
Boko Haram, 59
Bolling, Eric, 183
Bolton, John, 85, 194, 201
Brands, Hal, 7, 8, 41, 67
Brennan, John, 195
Bremmer, Ian, 242
Brown, Sherrod, 75
Buchanan, Patrick, 16, 39
Burns, Nicholas, 20
Burns, Robert, 67
Bush, George H. W., 44, 118, 119, 120, 128; US-Japan Relations, 44
Bush, George W., vii, 37, 38, 55, 60, 62, 84, 101, 104, 119, 121, 122, 124, 150, 152, 157, 188, 217, 221, 229;

273

Afghanistan, 37; axis of evil, 122; Doha Rounds of Trade Negotiations, 37; foreign economic policy, 37, 221; Iraq War, 37; Nuclear Posture Review, 122; removal of US nuclear weapons from South Korea, 119; Six-Party Talks, 122, 123, 126; South-North Declaration on Denuclearization, 120; US-China relations, 235, 239; US-North Korea relations, 118, 121, 128; US-Russian relations, 188, 235, 239
Bush, Jeb, 148

Calstrom, Gregg, 152
Campbell, Jon, 233
Canada, 41, 47, 48, 49, 69, 222, 241
Carter, Jimmy, 121, 234
Cassidy, John, 21
Central Intelligence Agency (CIA), 57, 75, 135, 149, 169, 170, 195, 201
Cha, Victor, 128
Chavez, Hugo, 239
Chen, Ding Ding, 205
China, viii, x, 1, 2, 4, 8, 10, 20, 24, 25, 36, 40, 110, 111, 118, 122, 126, 127, 129, 131, 132, 134, 138, 159, 160, 198–200, 201, 201–202, 202–203, 205, 207, 217, 218, 219, 222, 223, 224, 229, 230, 231, 241–242, 244
Chol, Kim Yong, 137
Chollett, Derek, 240
Clapper, James, 127
Clark, Richard, 166
Clinton, Bill, vii, 5, 36, 40, 118, 119, 120, 121, 122, 124, 125, 126, 150, 229; agreed framework, 121; foreign economic policy, 36; NAFTA, 5, 36; preparation for war with North Korea, 120; US-China relations, 36, 206, 235; US-North Korea relations, viii, 128; US-Russia relations, 235
Clinton, Hillary Rodham, vii, 4, 5, 40, 57, 58, 59, 95, 117, 240, 241
Cohn, Gary D., 26, 27, 41, 46, 219
Cold War, 16, 17, 35, 36, 44, 103, 108, 111, 118, 236
Columbia, 239
Combined Joint Task Force Horn of Africa (or CJTF-HOA), 83

Cooper, Helene, 81
Courtney, Williams, 187
Cordesman, Anthony, 67, 107
Croatia, 187
Cuba, 45, 79, 239

Dannvers, William, 191, 192
Davidson, Adam, 24
Davis, Captain Jeff, 67, 68
Defense Intelligence Agency (DIA), 132
Democrat Party, viii, 40, 55, 72, 96, 106, 107, 110, 117, 173, 194, 240
Diaz, Hugo Perezcano, 48
Dionne, E. J., 28
Dolan, Chris, 35
Dolley, Steven, 118
Doshi, Rush, 198
Dunford, General James, 66, 68, 83, 109

Eglash, Ruth, 151
Egypt, 4, 58, 165, 167, 169, 171, 244
Eisenhower, Dwight, 118; atoms for peace, 118
El-Issa, Mohammed, 171
El Sisi, Abdel Fatah, 171
Eui-yong, Chung, 136
Erdogan, Recep Tayyip, 81, 82
European Union (EU), x, 10, 36, 41, 49, 132, 169, 219, 222, 234, 241
Exum, Andrew, 67

Fanivar, Masood, 62
Feffer, John, 6
Feickert, Andrew, 102
Feierstein, Gerald, 163
Finland, 194
Fischer, Max, 1, 3
Fleitz, Fred, 199
fly-over states,, viii
foreign policy establishment,, viii
Forsby, Andrea, 205
France, 157, 161, 226
Friedman, George, 23, 24, 219

Gabriel, Sigmar, 167
Gaddaffi, Muammar, 126
Gallucci, Robert, 120
Georgia, 188
Germany, 10, 23, 157, 159, 162, 167, 194

Ghan, Ashraf, 74
Glasser, Susan, 164
Graham, David, 152
Graham, Langtree, 161
Graham, Lindsey, 74, 75
Graham, Thomas, 189, 194
Gorenburg, Dmitry, 184
Guaido, Jean, 239
Guam, 132, 133, 228
Gulf Cooperation Council, 70
G-7, 23, 35
G-20, 161, 162, 193

Haberman, Maggie, 18
Hader, Leon, 171
Haffe, Greg, 19
Haley, Nikki, 132, 161, 188, 193
Hamas, 234
Haqqani Network, 72
Harding, Warren G., 34
Haspel, Gina, 173
Hass, Lawrence, 20
Hayden, Michael, 75
Hendrickson, John, 34, 39, 43
Heydemann, Steven, 161
Hertling, Lieutenant General Mark, 102
Hezbollah, 80, 159, 162, 227, 238, 242
Hoffman, Frank, 99
Hooker, Alison, 117
Hoon, Suh, 136
Houthis, 234
Hsu, Sara, 197
Hughes, Charles Evans, 16
Hussein, Ibish, 153
Hussein, Saddam, 28
hyper partisanship and US foreign policy, vii, ix, 1, 75, 110, 135, 189

India, 75, 201
Indonesia, 10
Ing-wen, Tsai, 197
In-Ryong, Kim, 129
International Atomic Energy Agency (IAEA), 120, 121, 139
International Crisis Group (ICG), 60; recommendations for dealing with threat of ISIS, 60
International Monetary Fund (IMF), 35

Iran, viii, 8, 10, 19, 33, 97, 106, 107, 110, 111, 118, 122, 124, 132, 147, 148, 153, 155, 156, 156–157, 157, 159, 160, 161, 162–163, 163, 169, 190, 194, 217, 218, 227, 232, 234, 238
Iraq, viii, 10, 19, 55, 65, 66, 68, 77, 85, 101, 118, 122, 147, 159, 172, 225, 226, 227, 232, 234, 244
Islamic State (ISIS), viii, x, 10, 19, 20, 28, 33, 64, 65, 66, 67, 68, 70, 71, 73, 74, 78, 79, 80, 94, 95, 99, 101, 103, 147, 148, 153, 154, 160, 161, 162, 164, 166, 167, 171, 184, 217, 218, 221, 225, 226, 227
Israel, xi, 148, 149, 150, 151, 154, 159, 162, 163, 171, 231, 238, 244
Israeli-Palestinian Dispute, xi, 147, 150, 151, 231

Jabhat Fatah Al-Sham. *See* Al Nusra Front
Jae-in, Moon, 46, 134, 136, 230
Japan, x, 2, 3, 122, 129, 131, 201, 219, 221, 223, 229, 243
Jinping, Xi, 134, 135, 199, 200, 202, 204, 206, 223, 229, 230, 231
Johnson, President Lyndon, 103; Vietnam War, 103
Joint Comprehensive Plan of Action (JCPOA), 5
Jong Un, Kim, 134, 136, 137, 199, 221, 222, 228, 230, 238, 243
Jordan, 58, 162, 169

Kahl, Colin, 7, 8, 41
Karako, Thomas, 111
Kazianis, Harry J., 128
Keene, Jack, 74
Kelly, John F., 137
Kennan, George F., 210
Kennedy, John F., 101
Kerry, John, 43
Kesler, Charles, 39
Khashoggi, Jamal, xi, 10, 170, 172, 173
Kiley, Sam, 209
Kim, Andrew, 135, 136, 137
Kislyak, Sergei, 189
Kissinger, Henry, 220
Kofman, Michael, 184

Korea and United States Trade Agreement (KORUS), 45, 46, 47
Kusher, Jerod, 151
Kuwait, 28, 169

Lauter, David, 28
Lavrou, Sergei, 161, 188
League of Nations, 35
Lebanon, 10, 163, 234
Lee, Carol E., 117
Leventhal, Paul, 118
Lewis, Admiral Andrew, 109
Lewis, Jeffrey, 128
Libya, 10, 19, 20, 21, 23, 26, 57, 85, 101, 126, 148, 149, 154, 167, 232
Ligthizer, Robert, 36, 47, 202
Litwak, Robert, 128
Lohman, Walter, 118, 202
Loveluck, Louisa, 227

Macfarland, Lieutenant General Sean, 66
Maduro, Nicolas, 239
Matlock, Jack, 189
Mattis, James, xi, 19, 20, 65, 66, 68, 81, 96, 100, 107, 130, 133, 167, 194, 227, 233
May, Theresa, 23
McCain, John, 74, 99
McGarry, Brendon, 95
McGraw, Ken, 101
McIntyre, Jamie, 120
McMaster, H. R., 20, 26, 41, 100, 162, 219
media, viii, 16, 19, 21, 25, 28, 41, 68, 72, 81, 95, 96, 98, 117, 120, 126, 133, 164, 166, 170, 173, 183, 184, 199, 209, 219, 220, 226, 230, 233, 240
Merkel, Angela, 23; EU First or Europe First, 23
Mexico, 5, 43, 47, 48, 69, 148
Middle East, ix, xi, 1, 55, 58, 67, 70, 78, 106, 147, 148, 149, 150, 152, 152–153, 155, 158, 160, 161, 164, 165, 170, 171, 190, 191, 217, 225, 226, 231, 234, 242, 244
Middle East North Africa (MENA), 62, 85, 170, 172
Miller, David Aaron, 148, 149, 152, 154
Mitchell, A. Wes, 190
Mnuchin, Steve, 45, 50, 156

Mohib, Hamdullah, 74
Morocco, 167
Moyar, Mark, 102
Mueller, Robert Investigation, xi, 189, 236
Mullen, Admiral Michael, 118
Murphy, Chris, 170

Nasr, Vali, 71
National Security Agency (NSA), 75
Netanyahu, Benjamin, 149, 152, 153, 171
never-Trumpers, viii, 69, 219, 230, 239, 241
North Atlantic Treaty Organization (NATO), 3, 5, 23, 24, 49, 70, 71, 74, 75, 77, 106, 129, 167, 187, 190, 193, 220, 234, 245
North American Free Trade Agreement (NAFTA), x, 241
North Korea (Democratic Peoples Republic of Korea or DPRK), xii, 1, 2, 5, 8, 24, 47, 97, 106, 107, 110, 111, 117, 117–118, 119, 120, 121, 122, 124, 125, 126, 126–127, 127–128, 128, 130–131, 131–132, 132, 133, 134, 135, 136, 137, 139, 184, 190, 194, 199–200, 201, 202–203, 206, 207, 217, 218, 222, 228, 229, 230, 231, 234, 238, 239, 243, 245
Nuclear Proliferation Treaty (NPT), 119, 126

Obama, Barack, vii, viii, ix, 1, 2, 10, 21, 24, 37, 38, 45, 64, 65, 66, 67, 68, 69, 71, 78, 97, 98, 99, 100, 101, 117, 118, 119, 123–124, 124, 124–125, 125, 129, 148, 150, 155, 157, 160, 164, 196, 204, 206, 208, 217, 219, 221, 229, 234, 235, 239, 241, 244; Afghanistan strategy, 71, 73; AF-PAK, 71; counterterrorism-plus, 71; drone strikes, 72; Executive Order 13551, 123; foreign economic policy, 37, 221; killing of Osama Bin Laden, 72; light footprint strategy, 101, 102, 106; Nuclear Security Summit, 2; Obama-Clinton decision making, 57, 62; Statement to Trump of the importance of North Korea's threat, 117; strategic patience, 124; strategy against Islamic State, x, 5, 55, 57, 79;

US-China relations, 207–208; US-North Korea relations, 118, 124; US-Pakistani relations, 72; US-Russia relations, 149, 188; US-Yemen relations, 169, 172; TransPacific Partnership, 24, 37
Obrador, Andres Manuel Lopez, 47
O'Brien, Jason, 220
O'Reilly, Bill, 72, 241
Organization of American States (OAS), 239

Pagliarulo, Diego, 147
Pakistan, 2, 10, 71, 72, 73, 75, 102, 169
Pakistani Taliban (Terhrik-I-Taliban Pakistan or TTP), 72
Palestinian Authority (PA), 231
Panda, Ankit, 133
Panetta, Leon, 169
Patrick, Stewart, 21
Pelosi, Nancy, 75
Pence, Mike, 109, 110, 129, 201
Perry, William, 120
Philips, Noah, 173
Pindell, James, 220
Pompeo, Mike, xi, 26, 85, 135, 137, 139, 158, 173, 174, 201, 245
Popular Mobilization Forces (or PMF), 80
Porter, Geoff, 64
Porter, Rob, 46
Pottinger, Matt, 117
Pritchard, Charles, 124
Putin, Vladimir, xi, 162, 172, 184, 185, 187, 188, 190, 191, 192, 194, 195, 231, 236

Qatar, 167–168, 169, 175, 232, 233, 234
Quetta Shura, 72

Rachman, Gideon, 240
Ray, Christopher, 201
Reagan, Ronald, 35, 40, 44, 103, 104, 217, 223, 245; foreign economic policy, 35, 100, 119, 126; military build-up, 96; Uruguay Round, 35; trade war with Japan, 44
Remnick, David, 173
Republican Party, 16, 40, 55, 59, 96, 107, 110, 138, 173, 184, 218, 222, 223

resistance, 69, 75
Revere, Evans J. R., 127
Richardson, Admiral John, 108
Rhodes, Ben, 125
Roosevelt, Franklin Delano, 220
Rogin, Josh, 166
Rood, John, 233
Roosevelt, Teddy, 6, 39
Rosati, Jerel, 35
Ross, Dennis, 150, 152
Ross, Wilbur, 45, 46, 49, 50, 200
Roth, John, 107
Russia,, xi, 20, 24, 63, 110, 111, 132, 147, 156, 157, 159, 160, 161, 162, 163, 164, 172, 199, 209, 217, 218, 219, 227, 229, 231, 232, 239, 242

Salman, King, 70
Samuelson, Robert, 220
Sanders, Bernie, 40
Sanders, Paul, 190
Sanders, Sarah Huckabee, 163
Sanger, David, 4, 18
Sargent, Daniel, 34
Saudi Arabia, 10, 42, 63, 69, 163, 164–165, 166, 167, 168, 169, 171, 172, 173–174, 232, 233, 243, 244; Terrorist Financing Targeting Center, 70
San Bernadino Terrorist Attack, 56
Seib, Gerald F., 117
September 11, 2001 Terrorist Attacks, 56
Sessions, Jeff, 95, 96
Shane, Leo, 96
Sigal, Leon V., 121
Singapore, 230
Sisi, Abdel, 165, 171
Shanahan, Patrick M., 233
Sokolsky, Richard, 149, 152, 154
Somalia, 10, 19, 20, 65, 101, 102, 244
Solomon, Jay, 117
South Africa, 118
South China Sea, xii, 9, 105, 202, 203, 204, 207, 219
South Korea, x, 2, 3, 40, 45, 46, 47, 49, 118, 119, 120, 122, 129, 130, 131, 134, 136, 138, 139, 221, 222, 229, 231, 236, 241, 243
Soviet Union, 35, 118, 119, 237

Special Operations Command (SOCOM), 64, 101
Spicer, Sean, 42, 73, 161
Stephanopoulos, George, 184
Stoltenberg, Jens, 129, 186
Straub, David, 124
Sudan, xi
Sung, Kim Il, 118
Syria, xi, 4, 9, 10, 19, 55, 61, 63, 66, 67, 68, 77, 79, 80, 81, 82, 83, 101, 102, 106, 147, 148, 159, 160, 161, 162, 163, 168, 170, 171, 172, 175, 184, 186, 187, 188, 190, 191, 194, 199, 225, 225–226, 226, 227, 231, 232, 234, 236, 237, 242, 243; Kurdish fighters, 61, 77, 79, 80, 81, 82, 85
Syrian Democratic Forces (or SDF), 81, 82, 83, 84, 232, 238
Szuplat, Terrence, 21

Tae-Sung, Han, 228
Taiwan, 118, 197, 206, 208, 236
Taliban, 55, 62, 70, 74, 75
Tiezzi, Shannon, 135
Tilghman, Andrew, 96
Tillerson, Rex, xi, 25, 26, 130, 133, 152, 156, 161, 167, 168, 186, 188, 199, 204, 219, 232, 236
Thomas, General Raymond, 103
Thornberry, Mac, 99
Tomlinson, Lucas, 100
Transactionalism Terrorism, 69
Trudeau, Justin, 47, 49
Truman, Harry S, 209, 210; Containment Doctrine, 210
Trump, Donald J., viii, ix, xi, xii, 4, 8, 10, 11, 15, 16, 17, 18, 19, 20, 21, 24, 25, 26, 27, 28, 33, 38, 39, 40, 41, 43, 44, 45, 46, 47, 48, 49, 50, 55, 63, 64, 65, 66, 67, 68, 69, 70, 71, 72, 73, 74, 75, 76, 77, 78, 80, 81, 82, 83, 84, 85, 93, 94, 95, 96, 98, 99, 101, 102, 103, 104, 105, 106, 107, 108, 109, 111, 117, 119, 125, 126, 126–127, 127, 128, 129, 130, 133, 134, 135, 136, 137, 138, 139, 140, 147, 148, 148–149, 149, 150–151, 151–152, 152, 152–153, 153, 154, 155, 156–158, 159, 161, 162, 163, 163–164, 164, 166, 168, 169, 169–170, 171, 172–173, 183, 184–185, 185, 186, 187, 188, 188–189, 190, 191, 192, 193, 194, 195, 196, 197, 198, 199, 200, 202, 204, 205, 207, 208, 210, 217, 218, 219, 220–221, 221–222, 223, 224, 225, 226, 227, 228, 229, 230, 231, 232, 233, 234, 235, 237, 238–239, 240, 240–241, 241, 242, 242–244, 244–245; ad hoc counterterrorism strategy, 61, 63; administrative coup d'etat, 46; Afghanistan strategy, 72, 73; America First, ix, 8, 16, 17, 20, 21, 41, 43, 50, 105, 147, 219–221, 224, 245; American leadership, 242–245; anti-coalition, 71, 79, 83, 245; anti-ISIS strategy, 55, 63, 76, 77, 78, 84; Ballistic Missile Review, 98; chaos in the Middle East, 231–234; counterterrorism, 77, 78, 79, 84, 85, 163, 164, 166, 171; Cyber Command, 99; defeating ISIS quickly, 57, 63, 67; defeating radical Islam, 59, 93; Defense Space Command, 110; Defense Strategy Commission (DSC), 106, 111; domestic agenda, 10; economic unilateralist impulse, 15; ending Obama's counterterrorism approach, 59; failure to set defense priorities, 103; features of US foreign policy, 17, 18; foreign policy agenda, viii, ix, x, xi, xii, 77, 81, 127, 242; foreign economic policy, 12, 33, 34, 44, 47, 50, 221–224, 241–242; foreign policy campaign statements, x, xi, 5, 6, 40, 41, 43, 55, 56, 57, 58, 60, 93, 126, 148, 149; globalization, 43, 44; immigration, 56; Iraq War, 148; Jerusalem, xi; Joint Comprehensive Plan of Action (JCPOA or Iran Nuclear Deal), 155, 155–156, 157, 158, 159, 234; Khashoggi Affair, 170, 172, 173; management of rogue states, 238, 238–239; maximum pressure, 129, 131, 132, 134, 230, 243; Middle East Agenda, 149, 152; Middle East Strategy, 168, 170–171; Missile Defense Review (MDR), 111; Mother of All Bombs (MOAB) Strike Against Islamic K, 243; multilateralism, ix, 15, 21, 217, 219–221; nation-building, 62; National Counterterrorism Strategy

Index

(NCS), 83; National Defense Strategy (NDS), 105, 111, 190; National Security Strategy (NSS), 76, 77, 83, 104, 105, 164, 190; National Space Command, 109; new relationship with North Korea, 134; nightmare and new reality, 228–231; North American Free Trade Agreement, x, 7, 24; Nuclear Posture Review, 98; Obama dilemma, 217, 219, 227; Paris Accord (Climate Change Agreement), 41, 220, 242; rebuilding the military, x, 93, 95, 98, 99, 107, 108, 111, 217–218; redefining US foreign policy, 24, 25, 27; relations with Saudi Arabia, 11; renegotiation of trade agreement, 45; response to missile threat to Guam, 132, 133; rules-based diplomacy, 191–195, 205–209, 219, 237; Space Force, 109, 110; strategy and the Islamic State, x, 19, 24, 28, 56, 64, 65, 66; summits, 137, 138; temperament and unpredictability, 240–241; reckoning: Russia and China, 235; trade agenda, 12; trade war with China, 9, 10, 49, 50, 224; TransPacific Partnership (TTP), 11, 12, 21, 203, 223, 241–242; Trump Doctrine, 1, 28, 132; unpredictability, 125, 126; use of Special Operation Forces (SOFs), 101, 102, 225; US-China relations, xi, xii, 106, 107, 108, 109, 196, 196–197, 197, 198–202, 205, 236, 237; US-China trade relations, 196, 196–197, 197, 198–202, 206, 207, 209, 210, 223; US-EU Trade Agreement, 241; US-North Korea relations, 118; US-Russian relations, viii, xi, 56, 80, 105, 106, 107, 108–109, 109, 209, 210, 235–236, 237, 238–239, 240; US-Saudi relations, 172–173, 173, 174, 174–175; US-Yemen relations, 169, 169–170; vision military, 97, 111; war on terrorism, 75, 217, 225–227; worldview, ix, 6; Trump, Ivanka, 151

Turkey, 4, 63, 80, 81, 82, 83, 85, 172, 173, 232; Kurdistan Workers Party (PKK), 80

Ukraine, xi, 63, 106, 108, 183, 184, 186–187, 188, 192, 193, 195

United Arab Emirate (UAE), 19, 70, 167, 169

United Kingdom (Britain), 10, 23, 119, 157, 159, 226, 240

United Nations (UN), 27, 118, 126, 132, 139, 157, 161, 188, 221, 228, 233, 239, 243; General Assembly, 28, 228; Security Council, 132, 193, 228; Security Council Resolution (UNSCR) 2317, 132

United States, vii, ix, x, 5, 8, 12, 16, 17, 18, 19, 20, 24, 26, 27, 28, 34, 35, 36, 38, 44, 46, 47, 48, 49, 50, 63, 65, 66, 67, 71, 72, 73, 76, 77, 78, 79, 80, 81, 82, 83, 84, 85, 101, 104, 105, 106, 107, 109, 110, 111, 117, 118, 120, 121, 122, 126, 127, 128, 129, 131, 132, 133, 134, 137, 148, 149, 150, 152, 155, 156, 157, 158, 159, 160, 162, 163, 163–164, 164, 165, 166, 167–168, 169, 170, 172, 174, 199–200, 201, 202–203, 203, 207–208, 209, 217, 219, 220, 221–222, 223, 224, 225–226, 226–227, 229, 231, 232, 233, 234, 235, 236, 237, 238, 239, 240, 241, 243, 244, 245

United States Central Command (USCENTCOM), 64, 66, 70, 169

United States, Mexico, and Canada Agreement (USMCA), 11, 49, 241

Un, Kim Jung, 118, 124, 125, 126, 127, 129, 131, 134, 136, 137

Van Grasstek, Craig, 38
Venezuela, 238, 239
Vietnam, 231, 238
Votel, General Joseph, 66, 169

Wagner, Daniel, 21
Wahzhou, Meng, 49
Walt, Steven F., 171
Weisgerber, Marcus, 68
Wolfe, Martin, 43, 50
Woo, Roh Tae, 119
Woodrow, Wilson, 16, 35
Woodward, Bob, 46
Woosely, James, 149
World Trade Organization (WTO), 36, 37

Wright, Thomas, viii, 1, 8, 9
Wuttke, Joerge, 200
Wynne, Mike, 97

Yemen, xi, 10, 19, 55, 60, 65, 101, 102, 106, 167, 168, 169, 170, 233, 234, 238, 243, 244; SEAL Raid, 55, 174, 175
Yi, Wang, 197

Yong-ho, Ri, 132, 134
Youn, Lee, 209
Yun, Joseph Y., 137

Zenko, Micah, 102
Zimmerman, James, 200
Zoellick, Robert, 35

About the Author

Dr. John Davis is a recognized foreign policy and counterterrorism expert. He has published several books, most notably, *The Arab Spring and Arab Thaw: Unfinished Revolutions and the Quest for Democracy* (2013); *The Barack Obama Presidency: A Two-Year Assessment,* (ed.) (2011); *Barack Obama and US Foreign Policy: Road Map for Change or Disaster?* (2009); and *Presidential Policies and the Road to the Second War in Iraq: From 41 to 43* (ed.) (2006). Some of Davis's other areas of expertise include National Security, Counterterrorism, International Relations, and Presidential Studies. In addition, he is a blogger: editor-in-chieftheglobalwaronterrorism.com.